CIVIL WAR

LUCAN (Marcus Annaeus Lucanus) was born AD 39 into a family prominent in the Roman élite—Seneca the Elder was his grandfather and Seneca the Younger his uncle, and he was for several years a close friend of the young emperor Nero. During this period he received advancement from Nero and was a prolific poet. The friendship between poet and emperor then faded and in AD 65 Lucan joined Calpurnius Piso's conspiracy to overthrow Nero. When the plot was discovered Lucan chose to commit suicide and died reciting lines on suicide from his *Civil War*. His unfinished epic poem on the civil war between Caesar and Pompey is his only work to survive. This powerful poem has its fans and its critics—but no reader can fail to be impressed by the stark power of Lucan's condemnation of civil war. He presents the horror of civil war in grimly realistic terms—as brothers killing brothers and, ultimately, as the suicide of a powerful nation. The poem's impact is further enhanced by Lucan's rhetorical energy and his interest in the sensational. So it is not surprising that Dante ranked Lucan with Homer, Virgil, and Ovid.

SUSAN BRAUND is a graduate of King's College Cambridge and since 1981 has been a lecturer in Classics at the University of Exeter, where she is also now Head of the Department. She has published *Beyond Anger: A Study of Juvenal's Third Book of Satires* (1988), *Satire and Society in Ancient Rome* (1989) and the *Greece & Rome New Survey in the Classics* on 'Roman Verse Satire' (Oxford, 1992).

OXFORD WORLD'S CLASSICS

——

LUCAN

Civil War

——

Translated with an Introduction and Notes by
SUSAN H. BRAUND

OXFORD
UNIVERSITY PRESS

OXFORD
UNIVERSITY PRESS

Great Clarendon Street, Oxford OX2 6DP

Oxford University Press is a department of the University of Oxford.
It furthers the University's objective of excellence in research, scholarship,
and education by publishing worldwide in

Oxford New York

Athens Auckland Bangkok Bogotá Buenos Aires Calcutta
Cape Town Chennai Dar es Salaam Delhi Florence Hong Kong Istanbul
Karachi Kuala Lumpur Madrid Melbourne Mexico City Mumbai
Nairobi Paris São Paulo Singapore Taipei Tokyo Toronto Warsaw

with associated companies in Berlin Ibadan

Oxford is a registered trade mark of Oxford University Press
in the UK and in certain other countries

Published in the United States
by Oxford University Press Inc., New York

Translation, Introduction, and Notes © Susan H. Braund 1992

The moral rights of the author have been asserted

Database right Oxford University Press (maker)

First published as a Clarendon Press hardback 1992
First published as a World's Classics paperback 1992
Reissued as an Oxford World's Classics paperback 1999

British Library Cataloguing in Publication Data

Data available

Library of Congress Cataloging in Publication Data

Lucan, 39-65.
[Pharsalia. English]
Lucan Civil War translated with introduction and notes by S. H. Braund.
Originally in Latin.
Includes bibliographical references.
1. Rome—History—Civil War, 49-18 B.C.—Poetry. I. Braund, S. H.
PA6479.E5B73 1991 873'.01—dc20

ISBN 0-19-283949-7

5

Printed in Great Britain by
Clays Ltd, St Ives plc

This Book is Dedicated
to Georgia

ACKNOWLEDGEMENTS

MUCH of this translation was done during a period of Study Leave from the University of Exeter spent in Transcaucasian Georgia. My thanks are due to the Georgian Academy of Sciences for the warm hospitality which I received while there and to the friends in Georgia and England who have encouraged and supported me throughout this project.

I am glad to acknowledge my debt to the following friends and colleagues who read parts of the translation, notes, and introduction: David Braund, Duncan Cloud, John Henderson, Ted Kenney, Gareth Roberts, and Peter Wiseman. Their comments and criticisms have been immensely helpful and I have adopted most of their suggestions. I am grateful too to Rodney Fry for preparing the maps.

I have also been so fortunate as to have the benefit of the learning and acuity of Leofranc Holford-Strevens at the Oxford University Press: there is no part of this volume which has not been improved by his suggestions and I take full responsibility for the few places where my stubbornness has prevailed.

CONTENTS

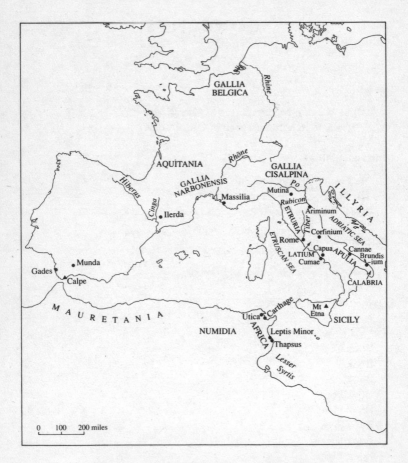

Map 1. The Western Mediterranean in Caesar's day

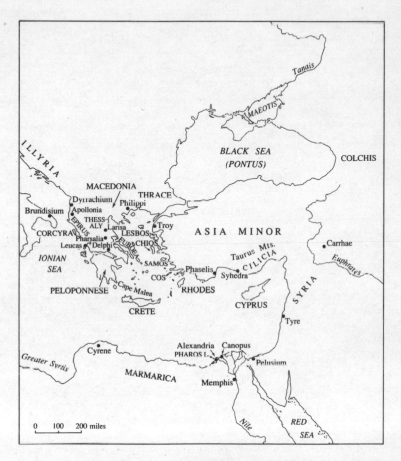

Map 2. The Eastern Mediterranean in Caesar's day

INTRODUCTION

I. LUCAN: HIS LIFE AND TIMES

1. *The life and death of Lucan*

We can glimpse the major events of Lucan's life from several ancient sources: from two ancient biographies written by Suetonius and by Vacca, from a poem by Statius to Lucan's widow (*Silvae* 2. 7), and from incidental details mentioned by Tacitus and Dio in their histories of the period.

Lucan—Marcus Annaeus Lucanus—was born at Corduba (modern Córdoba) in Spain in AD 39, into a family prominent not only in the local aristocracy but also at Rome. His father, Marcus Annaeus Mela, was a member of the élite (a knight, *eques*) and his family wealthy and eminent: Seneca the Elder, the rhetorician and historian, was his grandfather; Seneca the Younger, the philosopher, dramatist, and tutor to the emperor Nero, was his uncle; and Gallio, consul and proconsul of Achaea (Acts 18: 12), was another uncle. Before Lucan had reached the age of 1, his father moved to Rome. Consequently, Lucan received an education typical of the sons of the élite in the capital city. This consisted of a training in literature and rhetoric (public speaking). It is also very probable that Lucan studied Stoic philosophy under Cornutus, a freedman of Seneca; Cornutus was also the mentor of Persius, a satiric poet only five years older than Lucan. Lucan went to Athens to complete his education, as was usual for members of the élite, but he was recalled by the young emperor Nero to join his circle of close friends. Nero then honoured Lucan, just two years his junior, with the positions of quaestor and augur, a particular distinction because Lucan was at or younger than the usual minimum age of 25 for the quaestorship. Possibly this reflects a boyhood friendship or association between Nero and Lucan; the fact that Lucan's uncle, Seneca, was appointed Nero's tutor in AD 49 and exercised considerable influence over him for the next thirteen years may have brought the two young men together during that period.

But subsequently the friendship of emperor and poet faded. This may well be connected with Seneca's enforced retirement from public life in 62, although our sources tend to personalize and dramatize the situation by suggesting that Nero was jealous of Lucan's literary ability. Whether for personal or for broader political reasons, it seems that in 64 Nero banned Lucan from public recitation of his poetry and from advocacy in the law-courts, both of which would have been among Lucan's chief pursuits. It is hardly surprising that early in 65 Lucan joined Calpurnius Piso's 'conspiracy' to overthrow Nero and is described by one source (Suetonius) as its 'standard-bearer'. On the discovery of the plot, the conspirators were forced by Nero to commit suicide or be put to death. Lucan chose the course of suicide, in April 65, aged 25. By the end of 66, his father and both his uncles, who were also involved or implicated in the plot, had also committed suicide. Tacitus portrays Lucan as narcissistic in his suicide:

Next he ordered the death of Annaeus Lucanus. As the blood flowed freely from him and he felt a chill creeping through his feet and hands and the life gradually ebbing from his extremities, while his heart was still warm and he retained his mental power, Lucanus recalled some poetry he had composed in which he had told the story of a wounded soldier dying a similar kind of death, and he recited the very lines. These were his last words. (*Annals* 15. 70.)

Whether reliable or not, this account suggests an attitude of defiance towards Nero together with a self-confidence in his own poetry which seem highly appropriate.

2. *Lucan's attitude to Nero*

Clearly, at the end of his short life, Lucan had taken up a position of opposition to Nero: hence his involvement in the 'Pisonian conspiracy'. On this basis, some scholars regard the praise of Nero at the opening of book 1 as flattery which is heavily ironic. But there is no necessity to view Lucan as an enemy of Nero all his life. It is important to understand the political situation of the period and the framework within which poets like Lucan were working: Lucan was living in an autocratic regime, quite different from our modern democratic perspective, which created different expectations and imposed different constraints upon the poet.

It seems that Lucan did participate in an attempted political coup to remove Nero. Yet the aim of the 'conspirators' was not to restore the Republic, but to replace Nero with another emperor, one who would treat the Senate with more dignity and respect. That is, this opposition to Nero was based not on the fact of his absolute power but on the

way he chose to use it—badly, instead of well. This perhaps helps to
explain the emphasis Lucan places upon Caesar's destructiveness and megalomania: he views Caesar as the epitome of the bad autocrat run riot.
But, although he presents Cato as the epitome of the virtuous wise man,
the Stoic sage, Lucan offers no alternative picture of the good autocrat
wielding power in a way the Roman élite might approve. His poem
is too stark and too grim for that.

But it is a safe assumption that, in his early years, Nero's exercise of
power aroused no complaint from the likes of Lucan. In fact, we can
go further than that. It is evident from the outburst of literature at the
time of Nero's accession that there were high hopes for Nero's reign:
that it would be a long and prosperous era of peace in which the emperor
would uphold the rule of law, would show himself humane and merciful,
and would offer his patronage to the arts. In this light, the praise of
Nero at the beginning of book I is not to be seen as ironic, even if
it is generous. Such expressions of praise were simply part of what was
expected of poets working within imperial or autocratic regimes. Numerous parallels exist, from the Principate and from other similar regimes
in different periods and different places.

Nor is Lucan's condemnation of Caesar for his ruthless ambition to
be read as a direct criticism of Nero, although it may be thought to
offer a warning in the form of a model of behaviour to be avoided.
There is no reason to suppose that Nero would have identified closely
with Julius Caesar. On the contrary, it is possible that Nero identified
with the Pompeian party through his ancestor Lucius Domitius Ahenobarbus, who is given a favourable presentation by Lucan—probably more
favourable than the facts warranted. Domitius, Nero's great-great-grand-
father, first appears in the poem at Corfinium (2. 478–525) where, on
being surrendered to Caesar, his bearing is described in noble terms: 'with
threatening face and neck unbowed, his high nobility demanded death
by the sword' (2. 509–10). This is a striking contrast with Caesar's own
account, according to which Domitius betrayed his garrison. We might
have expected Domitius to appear next in book 3, as commander-in-chief
of the Pompeians at Massilia; but Lucan keeps him out of a second ignomi-
nious episode and saves him for the spotlight in book 7. Domitius'
death during the battle of Pharsalus is presented almost heroically—he
responds defiantly to Caesar's taunt—and rather differently from other
versions (see my note on 7. 597–616). It seems evident that Lucan wished
to present Nero's ancestor in as favourable a light as possible. In any
event, those who argue that Lucan sought to denigrate Nero through

a hostile portrayal of Julius Caesar must explain his decidedly positive treatment of Domitius.

Other features later in the poem suggest Lucan's continued accord with Nero, for example Acoreus' disquisition on the source of the Nile (10. 193–331). This reflects a contemporary interest which was shared by Nero: he planned to send an expedition to find the source of the Nile (Seneca, *Nat. Qu.* 6. 8. 3). In sum, as Bramble says, 'there is nothing in the poem to warrant the hypothesis of a growing discontent with Caesarism' (pp. 534–5). It seems that Lucan lived contentedly and wrote prodigiously under Nero until, late in 64 or early in 65, something impelled him into the 'Pisonian conspiracy'. Whether this was simply Nero's ban or broader political issues will always remain unclear.

3. The literary climate

Lucan flourished in the stimulating literary climate promoted by Nero. Not only did Nero himself have aspirations towards poetic excellence (fragments of poems attributed to him survive) but he set out to inaugurate a new golden age of literature which would match or surpass the 'Golden Age' under Augustus (emperor 27 BC–AD 14), not least by acting as a patron of poets (e.g. of Lucillius: see *Palatine Anthology* 9. 572). Poets in the time of Nero looked to the poets associated with Augustus to provide models for them to imitate, develop, and surpass. It is therefore no surprise to find, early in Nero's reign (probably), Calpurnius Siculus taking up the genre of pastoral and producing a book of *Eclogues* heavily indebted to Virgil's *Eclogues*. At the same time, the young poet Persius turned to Horace as his model when he wrote a short but well-received book of *Satires*. Lucan too joined this literary outburst. In fact, he was exceedingly prolific, according to the evidence of our sources. Apart from his epic poem, *Civil War*, fragments survive of a *Journey to the Underworld* (*Catacthonia*), *Tale of Troy* (*Iliaca*), *Orpheus*, and epigrams. Other works are known to us only by title: his *Eulogy of Nero* (*Laudes Neronis*), read by the poet at the Neronia, the quinquennial games established by Nero in 60; his *Address to Polla*, his wife (*Adlocutio ad Pollam*), ten books of *Silvae*, *Saturnalia*, *Medea* (a tragedy), fourteen books of *Dancing Plays* (*Salticae fabulae*), a poem *On the Burning of Rome* (*De incendio Vrbis*), *Letters from Campania* (*Epistulae ex Campania*, probably in verse, perhaps modelled on Horace's *Epistles* or Ovid's *Epistulae ex Ponto*), and prose orations for and against Octavius Sagitta. This list would constitute an impressive catalogue for any 25-year-old, even without his major work, *Civil War*. All this seems to be proof of the revitalization of literature encouraged by Nero.

4. *The impact of the Roman education in rhetoric*

Lucan responded to the conditions of his time and situation in his pre-cocious and prolific production of literary works. In his writings he also reflects the intensive literary and rhetorical nature of Roman education. The study of classic works of Greek and Latin literature was standard. This was followed by tuition in rhetoric: at the age of about 16, members of the élite went on to study in the schools of declamation. This training was designed to prepare young men for participation in politics and for advocacy in the courts of law. As time went on, the emphasis in declamatory exercises was increasingly placed upon the novel and original handling of traditional or standard themes. If we are to believe Petronius, Lucan's contemporary, this trend sometimes reached bizarre extremes. In his *Satyrica*, he presents his protagonist criticizing the teachers of rhetoric for

> making complete fools of our young men, because they see and hear nothing of everyday life in the schools. All they get is pirates standing on the beach dangling manacles, tyrants writing orders for sons to cut off their fathers' heads, oracles in times of plague demanding the blood of three or more virgins, honey-balls of phrases, every word and act besprinkled with poppy-seed and sesame. (*Satyrica* 1, cf. Tacitus, *Dialogus* 35.)

This kind of charge is often levelled against the poets of this era too, against Persius in his *Satires*, Seneca in his *Tragedies*, and, perhaps above all, Lucan in his *Civil War*. Quintilian, writing some thirty years later, most famously expresses this view in his verdict on Lucan as 'fiery and passionate and remarkable for his pointed thoughts (*sententiae*) and, to say what I think, suitable for imitation more by orators than by poets' (*The Training of an Orator* (*Institutio oratoria*) 10. 1. 90).

But for the modern reader to endorse such a verdict would imply a failure to appreciate inventiveness in the face of the overwhelming weight of tradition. We should not forget that Virgil's acknowledged supremacy in the realm of epic presented a huge problem to his successors in that genre. Ovid in his *Metamorphoses* responds in one way to that challenge; Lucan in his *Civil War* in another. Lucan chooses to import into his epic poem the discourse of contemporary rhetoric. In so doing, he both reflects his education and culture and responds to the need for innovation. If we understand this, we may refrain from using the word 'rhetorical' as a derogatory term to apply to Lucan's poem and try instead to judge him by the standards his contemporaries would have used.

Although we should be unwilling simply to dismiss Lucan as 'rhetorical', such charges do highlight one crucial feature of ancient poetry which it shares with oratory: it was written for oral delivery, either on private occasions such as dinner-parties or at public recitations or celebratory festivals. This is especially true of poetry from the time of Augustus onwards, when public *recitatio* came fully into vogue. We should never forget that Lucan was not composing for the *reader* reading privately (who in any case read aloud, it seems) so much as for the audience listening collectively.

II. THE POEM: CONTENT

1. *The events of the civil war, 49–45 BC*

The civil war began in January 49 BC when Caesar crossed the Rubicon and entered Italy. As he advanced swiftly down the east coast, Pompey and the Senate withdrew from Rome to Brundisium. In March Pompey sailed over to Epirus, leaving Italy in Caesar's control. Caesar went first to Rome, then to Massilia, where he began a siege of the city, and proceeded to Spain, where he conducted a victorious campaign against Pompey's generals. In Africa his lieutenant Curio was defeated and killed by King Juba, an ally of Pompey. In December Caesar returned to Rome, where he was elected consul for the following year; in January he crossed to Epirus and faced Pompey at Dyrrachium. The battle of Pharsalus ensued on 9 August 48. After his defeat there, Pompey fled to Egypt and was killed on 29 September. Three days later Caesar arrived in Egypt; there followed the difficult war against Ptolemy XIII and the Alexandrians, which ended in the spring of 47 with the establishment of Cleopatra as ruler. Caesar returned to Italy in the summer, after overcoming King Pharnaces at Zela in Asia Minor, the occasion of his famous boast, 'ueni, uidi, uici'. Meanwhile the Pompeian forces were mustering in Africa in huge numbers under Pompey's father-in-law Scipio. Caesar crossed to Africa in December 47 and after four months' siege took Thapsus with a bloody victory. Shortly afterwards, Cato committed suicide at nearby Utica. News of Caesar's victory resulted in his being voted dictator for ten years in the spring of 46 and he returned to Rome to celebrate a magnificent fourfold triumph. The war seemed to be over. But before the end of 46 he had to go to Spain to face the troops which Pompey's sons had assembled there. The campaign was brief. The decisive battle was fought at Munda on 17 March 45, again with heavy slaughter of the Pompeians. Caesar returned to Rome and celebrated another triumph and remained there until his assassination in March 44.

Our sources for the civil war of 49–45, apart from Lucan on events of 49–48, are Caesar's *On the Civil War* (*De bello ciuili*); the *Alexandrian War* (*Bellum Alexandrinum*), possibly written by Hirtius, one of Caesar's officers and covering events down to Zela; the *African War* (*Bellum Africum*) on the events of 47–46; and the *Spanish War* (*Bellum Hispaniense*) on the Munda campaign. Other narratives are provided by Appian (writing in the second century AD) in book 2 of his *Civil Wars* and by Dio Cassius (second–third centuries) in books 41–3 of his *Roman History*.

2. *The civil war as subject*

Lucan's poem is an epic poem in hexameters, of which nine complete books and an incomplete tenth survive (on the scope of the poem see below, ii. 12). It has as its subject the civil war fought between Pompey and Caesar, starting with Caesar's crossing of the Rubicon and invasion of Italy in 49 BC, including the battle of Pharsalus in the summer of 48 BC and Pompey's death in Egypt less than two months later. The poem breaks off incomplete in the tenth book, but probably continued or was planned to end with the suicide of Cato at Utica after the battle of Thapsus in 46 BC.

Lucan was by no means the only or the first poet to take the civil war as his theme, a theme which was far from confined to epic but featured in history, declamation, and iambus too. Augustan writers of epic, including Cornelius Severus, Albinovanus Pedo, Sextilius Ena, and Rabirius seem to have chosen the civil war or parts of it as their material; it is hard to deduce anything securely from the fragments which survive, but it looks as if a sparse, unelevated, prosaic style was favoured for this topic. Similarly, the portion of a *War at Actium* (*Bellum Actiacum*) written early in the first century AD and preserved on a Herculaneum papyrus shows that both this topic and this style continued to remain viable. It appears that in his choice of theme and style Lucan was working within a tradition, a tradition significantly different from that of the mythological epic exemplified by Homer and Virgil. Fragments of Augustan historical epics suggest that his poem is not on those grounds as controversial as has sometimes been supposed. Moreover, the topic of civil war was one of permanent relevance under the Principate. A portrayal of the horrors of civil war might convey a message, implicit or explicit, urging loyalty to the emperor, for fear that failure to offer loyalty might provoke civil war. There might also be a message for the emperor, that he should conduct himself in such a way as to ensure the loyalty of his subjects.

3. *Lucan's sources*

Lucan's historical sources included Livy, whose account of this period unfortunately does not survive, Pollio (probably), and Caesar's own account, *On the Civil War*. Although it is probably nothing more than coincidental that Lucan's poem breaks off at virtually the same point as Caesar's *On the Civil War*, it seems highly likely that Lucan intended his poem 'as a counterpoise' (Ahl 307; cf. Henderson, §2. 17) to Caesar's own narrative of the events that gave him supremacy.

But while following the broad outline of events as presented by Livy and others, Lucan did not feel inhibited from omitting or minimizing some incidents and amplifying or inventing others. Notable among his inventions is the appearance of Cicero in Pompey's camp on the eve of the battle of Pharsalus; in fact, we know that Cicero was not present at Pharsalus because of illness (e.g. Plutarch, *Cicero* 39). It seems that Lucan presents Cicero as the spokesman of the Senate in a deviation from historical fact which dramatizes the essence of the situation (see Ahl 162–3). Equally readily, he invents minor characters where appropriate. At all times, it is most illuminating of Lucan's interests and techniques to compare his presentation of the events and characters of the civil war with those of Caesar in his *On the Civil War* and Plutarch in his biographies of Pompey, Caesar, and Cato the Younger (written in the late first and early second centuries AD and apparently following a diverse, primarily Greek, tradition). In contrast with those sources, Lucan tends to simplify, cut down or entirely eschew straightforward narrative in favour of speeches and set pieces.

4. *The protagonists*

There are three main protagonists in the poem, although whether or not any of them can be called 'the hero' in any meaningful sense is another matter (see below, iii. 3); in ancient epic there was no necessity for a central heroic figure. Caesar is the most prominent character, but also the least sympathetic. Until his death in book 8 Pompey is pitted against

Caesar and receives a favourable treatment from Lucan; yet he has few standard 'heroic' qualities. Cato is prominent after Pompey's death, when he takes over the leadership of the 'Republican' cause, but he is a rather limited character and to some readers seems less than appealing with his austere strict Stoicism. A brief consideration of each of these protagonists will bring out their chief characteristics and show how they relate to the heroes of previous epic poems, especially Aeneas.

Caesar and Pompey are introduced near the start of book I in description and in simile. Caesar is portrayed as an active and energetic military leader who is clear-sighted, decisive, and ambitious and who revels in war. The simile of the thunderbolt (151–7) confirms this picture:

> Just so flashes out the thunderbolt shot forth by the winds through clouds,
> accompanied by the crashing of the heavens and sound of shattered ether;
> it splits the sky and terrifies the panicked
> people, searing eyes with slanting flame;
> against its own precincts it rages, and, with nothing solid stopping
> its course, both as it falls and then returns great is the devastation
> dealt far and wide before it gathers again its scattered fires.

It implies that Caesar inspires fear and is a destructive and irresistible force with quasi-divine power. In many respects, Lucan's Caesar resembles the traditional heroic warrior who possesses great military prowess and some superhuman qualities, such as Achilles in the *Iliad* and Aeneas in the second half of the *Aeneid*.

Pompey is introduced in book I as a former warrior past his prime, resting on his laurels, soft with peace-time living, and verging on old age. Lucan uses a simile of an oak-tree to portray him (136–43):

> like in a fruitful field a lofty oak,
> bearing the people's spoils of old and generals'
> hallowed dedications; clinging with roots no longer strong,
> by its own weight it stands firm, and spreading naked branches
> through the air, it makes shade with trunk, not foliage;
> and though it totters, ready to fall beneath the first Eurus,
> though all around so many trees upraise themselves with sturdy trunks,
> yet it alone is venerated.

The oak-tree in the simile is old and virtually dead, still standing but doomed to fall soon, yet adorned with emblems of past successful campaigns and the sole object of veneration, despite the younger trees growing up around it. The juxtaposition of the two similes suggests that the thunderbolt (Caesar) will strike and annihilate the oak-tree (Pompey). This unflattering portrayal of Pompey continues through the poem; he is depicted as indecisive, hesitant, and insecure. It seems that Lucan has taken the weaker, essentially *human*, elements of Aeneas' character— Aeneas doubting his mission, Aeneas as husband and lover—and bestowed them upon Pompey. Consequently, Pompey is the only one of the three protagonists to be shown to have an emotional life, primarily in his close, empathetic relationship with Cornelia his wife (see below, ii. 8), but also in the warm devotion and loyalty he inspires in his followers, even after his defeat at the battle of Pharsalus. What is more, Lucan as narrator even enters the poem himself on occasion, to express his emotional devotion to Pompey.

Cato is introduced in book 2 but does not actually enter the action until book 9, after Pompey's death. From the start, Cato is presented as concerned not for himself but for the welfare of the state. He is the epitome of virtue and moral rectitude, endowed with superhuman wisdom and endurance. He is, perhaps, the Stoic wise man. This is confirmed by his conduct throughout book 9; similarly, his remarriage to his wife, Marcia, in book 2 is done not for any personal motivation. It appears that Lucan has assigned to Cato the patriotic, self-denying elements of the character of Aeneas—the Aeneas who suppresses his personal wishes out of devotion to the cause of the founding of Rome. But, unlike Aeneas, Cato is endowed with none of the softer, human qualities that make a rounded character. Cato is a stark, austere, one-dimensional character.

So none of the three protagonists can qualify for the description 'hero' in the conventional (modern) sense of the word. Caesar and Cato are both superhuman and impersonal in different ways, but neither is attractive. Pompey is all too human—and attractive—but his flaws along with his defeat and death make it impossible to regard him as the hero. In creating an epic poem with three powerfully-presented protagonists but with no hero, Lucan is making a comment about his subject-matter: in civil war, there can be no heroes.

5. *The divine machinery*

Just as Lucan abandons the traditional epic device of the hero, so he abandons the traditional divine machinery of epic. Lucan's poem contains no anthropomorphic deities, no Olympian gods debating and intervening in human affairs out of favouritism, malice, and revenge, such as feature in Homer's *Iliad* and *Odyssey* and in Virgil's *Aeneid*. This is not because of lack of divine candidates for inclusion: the 'excerpt' of a poem on the civil war put into Eumolpus' mouth by Petronius (*Satyrica* 119–24) has a lavish divine machinery. Caesar's champion among the Olympian gods was, most obviously, Venus, from whom (through Aeneas) he claimed descent. Similarly, Hercules, a hero and exemplar in Stoic thought, might have been shown as acting for the Republican cause of Pompey and Cato. But all that we find in Lucan's poem are vague references to 'god' and 'the gods', both 'the gods above' and the gods of the Underworld, particularly in prayers and reproaches to the gods, but generally these only serve to underline the fact that the gods exercise no influence over and take no interest in human life (thus 7. 454–5).

Lucan replaces the traditional divine machinery with the Stoic concepts of Fate and Fortuna. Fate, *fatum* or *fata*, is, essentially, destiny: the fixed, immutable order of the world. Fortune, *fortuna* and, personified, *Fortuna* (the closest approximation to an anthropomorphic deity in the poem), is chance: a fickle and capricious power who can bestow success and failure on any individual. Thus it is a fact of Fate that Caesar is victor and Nero is, consequently, emperor (1. 33); but it is Fortune who presides over Caesar's rise (that is why he swears allegiance to her as he crosses the Rubicon at 1. 225–7 and commits himself into her hands as he ventures the dangerous sea-crossing at 5. 510 and 696–7) and over Pompey's fall, hence the frequent references to Fortune during books 7 and 8 (7. 23–4, 665–6, 8. 21–2, 701–8, 713).

Lucan may have abandoned the traditional machinery from a feeling that it was inappropriate for the historical subject-matter of the civil war. Yet it is more likely that he considered that the presence of anthropomorphic deities would have distracted attention from his three protagonists and would have subtracted from the human responsibility for civil war. The impersonal concept of Fate and relatively impersonal concept of Fortune seem instead to underline the horror of civil war, with its inevitable conclusion and its chance victims along the path to that conclusion.

6. *Stoicism in the poem*

Lucan's replacement of the traditional divine machinery of epic with the concepts of Fate and Fortune is a reflection of the philosophy which pervaded and shaped his thoughts. Stoicism is Lucan's idiom. This is no surprise, as he was associated with men like Seneca who espoused Stoicism (see above, i. 1). Another manifestation of Stoicism is the several descriptions of or allusions to the final cataclysm, for example in the storm and floods in book 4 (48–120), in which some of the details are derived from Seneca's *Natural Questions*. The character of Cato presents another strand of Stoicism in the poem. Cato in any case was often used by moralists as a model, *exemplum*, of moral rectitude; Lucan develops this to present him as the Stoic wise man, stern, strict, and austere, as found in the prose treatise by Lucan's uncle Seneca, *On the Firmness of the Wise Man* (*De constantia sapientis*). This is especially true of book 9, where the difficulties which Cato experiences in crossing the desert present in allegorical form the trials of the Stoic sage.

Another episode which presents a classic example of the Stoic sage overcoming evil is Lucan's description of the fight between Hercules and Antaeus in book 4 (593–660). Hercules was one of the central mythological figures of the Stoic litany and was used to symbolize the victory of courage (*uirtus*) and civilization over frenzy (*furor*) and barbarism. The Labours of Hercules in particular fitted him for presentation as the Stoic wise man who successfully endures impossible-seeming trials and tests. It is no surprise, then, to find that Lucan has incorporated one of the stories about Hercules' struggles into his poem; and we may note that the North African setting of the story anticipates the setting of Cato's trials, described in book 9.

Cato's function in the poem is primarily symbolic, to represent Freedom (*Libertas*) in its struggle against Tyranny, personified by Caesar. It is significant that, after his introduction in book 2 in saint-like or even oracular terms, Cato is kept separate from the sordid conflict between the two rivals until after Pompey's death. At this point, Cato is reintroduced. He raises the moral tone of the poem by delivering an impressive funeral speech for Pompey and is then established by the hardships he endures so resolutely in the deserts of Africa as the epitome of the Stoic wise man. In the missing conclusion of the poem (see below, ii. 12), it is probable that Lucan consolidated this picture of Cato to present the civil war even more starkly as the conflict between Freedom and Slavery. It is likely that the climax to the poem would have been Caesar's victory at Thapsus immediately followed by Cato's suicide at Utica. This would have reconciled fact (the ultimate victory of Caesar and subsequent establishment of the Principate) with a moral victory for the cause of Stoic Republicanism.

Suicide was regarded with particular favour by the Stoics, for it offered freedom from slavery by one's own act. Cato's suicide at Utica would have linked with a scene of heroic mutual killing earlier in the poem. In book 4 Lucan presents an episode of strange suicide, when the raft of the Caesarian Vulteius is caught while trying to escape from the Republican forces. Vulteius persuades his men to perform mutual slaughter—in effect, mass mutual suicide—rather than undergo the indignity of defeat and capture by the vastly superior numbers of the Republicans, and thereby attain freedom by their own action. (That even Caesarians could achieve freedom through suicide would not have been problematic to Lucan's Roman audience.) His speech (4. 476–520), which is rich in Stoic terminology, achieves its aim and the slaughter ensues, with Vulteius gratefully falling first. Lucan finishes the episode with a few lines praising suicide as the means of escaping slavery. Clearly, Vulteius' action is extreme, but its motivation is shown to bear a marked resemblance to Stoic thought.

7. *The supernatural*

Although Lucan has dispensed with the traditional divine apparatus of mythological epic, this by no means prevents him from incorporating the supernatural into the poem. 'The supernatural' in Lucan's poem falls into two categories: first, dreams and visions (it is worth remembering that dreams were a regular feature of history as well as mythological and historical epic); secondly, portents, prophecies, and consultations of supernatural powers through divination, oracles, and necromancy.

There are four dreams and visions in the poem as it stands, although it seems certain that Lucan planned at least one further vision in the remaining books. These four are placed at significant points to provide balance and contrast. The first is Caesar's vision of his country as he is about to cross the Rubicon (1. 185–203). The sight of Rome, personified as a woman in deep mourning who challenges the Caesarians' right to proceed, is profoundly shocking and causes even Caesar to hesitate. But he soon recovers and delivers a lengthy prayer to the gods of Troy and Rome in which he reminds Rome of his past victories and declares allegiance to her. This vision, then, marks Caesar's knowing transgression into illegality and his reaction to it confirms his characterization as ruthless, forward-looking, and confident; for him, the end justifies the means.

The corresponding vision occurs at the very opening of book 3. Pompey has just been expelled from the harbour of Brundisium and has been gazing back at Italy, which he will never see again. After this moment of retrospection, a ghost from the past comes to haunt his sleep. His former wife, Julia, the daughter of Caesar, appears like a Fury standing on a blazing funeral pyre, speaks bitterly of Pompey's marriage to Cornelia,

and declares that Pompey cannot sever his bonds with her (3. 8–35). Julia
draws a contrast between the victories enjoyed by Pompey when he
was married to her and the defeats which Cornelia (formerly married
to the younger Crassus, who died at Carrhae) brings upon her husbands.
Particularly powerful is Julia's designation of Cornelia as a 'paramour'
(*paelex*) and her final statement, which has prophetic status, that Pompey
cannot escape from Julia—or, by implication, from her father, Caesar.
This vision confirms the image of Pompey as a man obsessed with the
past, as a man easily affected by emotion and as a doomed man: it in
effect objectifies his pessimism, indicating that he is bound to lose.

No further visions occur until book 7, which features two contrasting
dreams, one at the opening and one at the close of the book, flanking
the battle of Pharsalus. On the night before the battle, Pompey has a
happy dream of the past in which he recalls the public acclamation and
adulation he received for his great successes and achievements (7–19).
Lucan offers several interpretations of the dream (19–24) before lamenting
the fact that Pompey and Rome are never to see one another again,
in terms which suggest the separation of a pair of lovers and which recall
his description of the parting of Pompey and Cornelia at the end of
book 5. This dream reinforces the characterization of Pompey as a man
rooted in his past and portrays the relationship of Pompey and Rome
in intimate terms—a telling contrast with the portrayal of Caesar and
his country in book 1.

A stark antithesis to Pompey's happy dream is provided by the dreams
of Caesar and his troops on the night after the battle as they sleep in
the camp which they have captured from the Republicans (760–86). They
are tormented by images of the battle and of the fellow-citizens they
have killed. Lucan introduces a simile, comparing their dreams with
Orestes' visions of the Furies, a detail which echoes Pompey's dream
of Julia in book 3. In both passages, Lucan emphasizes the sheer horror
of civil war, a horror from which not even Caesar is exempt.

The other type of manifestation of the supernatural in the epic tends
to be more public and not confined to the individual experience. In
the latter part of book 1, Lucan describes the portents in the sky and
temples and city of Rome which herald disaster (522–83); particularly
significant among these are the flame split in two (550–2), symbolizing
civil war, and the Fury circling Rome (572–7). The people's response
to these portents is to seek their meaning. This is first attempted by summoning the prophet Arruns from Etruria (584–638). He commands that
rites of purification be performed. But the celestial portents are confirmed

by the inauspicious sacrifice of the bull. Arruns examines its entrails and there too discovers portents of civil discord. Then Figulus, a Roman expert in astrology, adds his interpretation of the portents in the sky and comes to a similar conclusion—that civil war followed by tyranny is foretold (639–72). The climax to the book is provided by the Roman matron overtaken by a prophetic frenzy (673–95): she is said to resemble a Bacchante as Apollo takes possession of her. She is granted the clearest vision yet of the civil conflict to come.

This entire episode serves a number of purposes for Lucan. It conveys his revulsion towards civil warfare by reflecting Rome's turmoil on the supernatural plane. It emphasizes the terrifying character of Caesar by dwelling on the fear he inspires; it is significant that the episode is placed after his entry into Italy and his capture of Ariminum but before his arrival at Rome, thereby creating or heightening suspense. Further, the passage allows Lucan to incorporate a prophecy embracing later events of the civil war, both those he treats in subsequent books and (probably) those outside the scope of his epic. Moreover, the descriptions of portents, ill-omened sacrifice, and sinister haruspicy (examination of the entrails) closely reflect contemporary taste: similar descriptions are found in Seneca's tragedies, for example.

Another form of communication with the divine is the consultation of an oracle. Lucan includes in his poem two episodes set at oracles: his treatment of this standard theme is typically unorthodox. The first is Appius Claudius Pulcher's visit to Apollo's oracle at Delphi (5. 64–236). Lucan suggests that the oracle had been silent and defunct for a long time. The consequence of this is that Appius has to fight a battle, so to speak, to obtain a prophecy from the oracle. The priestess, Phemonoe, knowing that to utter Apollo's prophecy will cause her death, is unwilling to enter the temple. She has to be thrust forcibly into the temple and even then attempts to avoid the prophetic frenzy by feigning inspiration. Appius sees through this and compels her to undergo full possession. She finally delivers an ambiguous oracle about Appius' fate and dies. This could be said to be a disappointing climax to such a lengthy episode—but that would be to miss the point. The incident offers Lucan an opportunity to include a graphic description of the oracular frenzy of the priestess, again reflecting contemporary literary taste; and more generally to contribute to the atmosphere of sinister foreboding, without offering any general prophecy of the events of the civil war. In Lucan's handling of the standard incident of consultation of an oracle, it is the consultation itself and not the oracle which results which is important.

Appius' visit to Delphi is matched by an episode in book 9 in which Cato finds himself at the oracle of Jupiter Ammon in North Africa (511–86). In contrast with Apollo's shrine at Delphi, the oracle of Ammon was active and functioning. A further contrast lies in Cato's chance arrival at the oracle, as opposed to Appius' trip to Delphi for the set purpose of consulting the deity. On his arrival, Cato's officers, represented by Labienus, attempt to persuade him to consult the oracle. Cato's response to this confirms the characterization of him as the Stoic sage. He regards the notion that he should need to consult an oracle as absurd, because he already knows everything he needs to know. In this way Lucan invites us to compare Cato with the oracle—and to regard Cato's self-reliance as superior. In fact, the episodes at oracles in books 5 and 9 reinforce Lucan's portrayal of the role of the gods in human affairs as relatively insignificant.

The supernatural pinnacle in Lucan's poem is undoubtedly the necromancy in book 6. Soon after his arrival in Thessaly, Pompey's son Sextus goes to the witch Erichtho to seek a prophecy of the outcome of the war. To fulfil this request, Erichtho performs a necromancy: that is, she resuscitates a corpse and compels it to utter a prophecy. Lucan's description of the witch and her ritual occupies half of book 6 (413–830). Once again, Lucan seems in tune with contemporary taste: of particular note is his uncle Seneca's play *Oedipus*, which includes a consultation of the Delphic oracle (225–39), a sinister sacrifice and haruspicy (297–402), and finally a necromancy (530–68), in which the ghost of Laius reveals his murderer. And as with the prophecy given to Appius in book 5, the interest lies not so much in the prophecy as in the elaborate, chilling ritual which leads up to it. When the corpse eventually speaks, his prophecy is relatively brief (777–820: just over forty lines long) and exceedingly generalized. Most of the speech, in fact, is given over to a description of how civil war has invaded the Underworld. The sole element of prophecy in the speech is the promise of a further prophecy to Sextus and the implication that he will not die at Pharsalia. This entire passage, then, shows again how Lucan adapts standard elements of epic to his audience's taste for the gruesome and the macabre.

The necromancy in book 6 was evidently not planned to be the final prophecy in the poem. The corpse compelled to speak by Erichtho tells Sextus: 'a surer prophet will foretell all to you in the fields of Sicily, your father Pompey, himself' (813–14). It seems that Lucan intended to include in a later book an episode in which Sextus had a vision of the ghost of Pompey, who revealed his fate to him. Lucan may have taken the same opportunity to provide a prophecy of broader scope anticipating the outcome of the civil war; alternatively, he may have planned for Brutus or Cato to experience a vision foreseeing the assassination of Caesar. This must remain speculation. But it seems evident that the supernatural in all its manifestations played a highly significant part in the structuring of the epic.

8. *The role of women in the poem*

Several of the female characters in the poem are linked with the supernatural, in a stereotype, ancient and modern, which is standard but none the less powerful for that. First is the ranting matron who provides the terrifying, prophetic finale to book 1. The Pythian priestess Phemonoe in book 5 is, like the raving matron, taken over by Phoebus Apollo, but in her case with fatal consequences. Erichtho the Thessalian witch in book 6 is surely Queen of Witches in ancient literature. None other is portrayed in such a black, sinister, and gruesome way nor with such attention to detail.

Whereas the women connected with the supernatural are used by Lucan to enhance the horror of events, other female characters complement and supplement the characterization of the three protagonists. Marcia, the wife of Cato, is portrayed in book 2 as returning to him after the death of Hortensius, whom she had married at Cato's bidding. She seeks remarriage to Cato simply so that she can die as Cato's wife. We are told that this union will be sexless and ascetic. Marcia's role in the poem, then, is to emphasize Cato's suppression of personal pleasures and desires and his selfless devotion to the state. She echoes this aspect of his character in offering him support and companionship to face the horrors of civil war. There is an added significance to the reunion of Cato and Marcia when we compare it with the parting of Aeneas and Creusa in book 2 of the *Aeneid*. There, the impossibility of reunion of husband and wife symbolizes that Aeneas' task is to leave Troy, represented by Creusa, behind him and to go on to a new existence. In contrast, by the remarriage of husband and wife, Lucan symbolizes that both Cato and Marcia are living in the past, in their devotion to the dying Republic.

The only woman with whom Caesar is associated in the poem is Cleopatra. The rich, beautiful, and powerful *femme fatale* is introduced in book 10, immediately after we are told that her seduction of Caesar will be successful (68–81). Lucan portrays her as directly calculating the effect her looks will have on Caesar. She emerges from book 10 as a shrewd politician who uses all the resources available to her to achieve her ends: a fine match for the dazzling, energetic, determined Caesar.

The scenario of a Roman general seduced by the queen of a city on the coast of Africa could not fail to evoke Virgil's Aeneas and Dido. The superficial analogy serves to highlight the profound differences, of course. In contrast with the naïve Dido, victim of the gods, and the travel-weary Aeneas, Caesar and Cleopatra are both resourceful, enterprising characters who are prepared to use any opportunity presented them to further their personal objectives, chiefly of gaining power.

The third protagonist, Pompey, is associated with two female characters, his former wife, Julia, Julius Caesar's daughter, and his present wife, Cornelia. Julia plays a small but highly significant part in the poem; she is mentioned several times but appears only once, as a ghost haunting Pompey's sleep at the beginning of book 3. In this respect, she may be seen as a further manifestation of the link between the supernatural and the female in the poem. There, she symbolizes Pompey's rootedness in the past and confirms the picture of him as a man doomed to lose, doomed never to shake off his connection with Caesar (see above, ii. 7).

But the most prominent and most sympathetic female character in the poem is undoubtedly Cornelia. Her deep distress at Pompey's decision to send her away to a place of safety (5. 722–815) is touching and moving; so is the reunion of husband and wife on the beach of Lesbos (8. 40–108). Lucan links the two episodes with several repeated motifs: in both, the relationship is portrayed in warm, physical terms: in book 5 they are lying in each others' arms; in book 8 Pompey embraces Cornelia; in book 5 Cornelia foresees that she will haunt the cliffs of Lesbos awaiting the ship that brings news, and in book 8 she is described doing precisely this; in both passages Pompey weeps and in both passages Cornelia faints. Particularly touching is Lucan's description of Cornelia's first night alone after Pompey has sent her away, when she reaches out for him in the night and leaves his part of her bed empty (5. 805–15). Lucan thus portrays the relationship between husband and wife as deeply devoted and loyal.

This continues in Cornelia's conduct in the face of Pompey's imminent death, later in book 8. As he enters the Egyptian boat, she attempts to accompany him, desperately pleading with him to allow her to remain with him (577–92). Then, on witnessing his murder, her reaction is one of frantic emotion and bravery. Not for the first time she blames herself for Pompey's death (639–50, cf. 88–105, reiterating Julia's allegation that Cornelia brought bad luck). She goes on to demand that her companions help her die or commit suicide (651–61). At this emotional climax she collapses in a faint (661–2).

We next meet her (for the last time in the poem as it survives) at the beginning of book 9 (51–116) where she reproaches Fortune for depriving her of Magnus' body and the opportunity for her to perform the proper funeral ritual. She goes on to deliver to her son a rousing message from Pompey, instructing him to continue the war. She finishes by seeking the darkness of the ship's hold, as a fitting place for one who desires death and 'enjoys her tears and loves her grief in her husband's stead' (112).

The deep love of Cornelia and Pompey, a stark contrast with the arid relationship of Cato and Marcia and the lust of Caesar and Cleopatra, serves to emphasize once more the human side of Pompey. It also epitomizes the unquestioning devotion which he is capable of inspiring, even in defeat. Lucan uses Cornelia to highlight his greatness, at the very moment of his fall and death.

9. *The minor characters of the poem*

The role of minor characters in Lucan's poem, whether they are historical or not, provides a further illustration of the influence of the Roman rhetorical training as well as the episodic manner of his writing. Many minor characters appear in only one episode or one context, to illustrate a single point. They are often a means for Lucan to simplify a potentially complex narrative and to convey forcefully the moral and emotional thrust which he wishes to emerge from a particular scene or incident.

A good illustration of this is Caesar's centurion Scaeva, a historical figure it seems (see note on 6. 144), who appears in Lucan's poem only for his *aristeia* (narration of an episode of an individual's heroic exploits) in book 6 and again, fleetingly, just as the poem breaks off in book 10. His role in the poem is very limited: to illustrate how heroism (*uirtus*) can be perverted into a sinister superhuman force by totally selfless devotion towards an ambitious master like Caesar. Thus the minor character is a reflection, or a microcosm even, of one of the main protagonists. This is true both in Scaeva's own episode, in book 6, and in his recurrence in book 10, where he serves as a kind of exemplar for Caesar himself of Caesar's kind of heroism (10. 542–6; see Henderson, §§2. 6–10).

Pothinus, the Egyptian eunuch who wields power in Ptolemy's court, another historical figure, similarly has a single function in the poem. Both in book 8 (484–535) and in book 10 (353–98) his role is to advocate the assassination of a Roman general—of Pompey, successfully, in book 8; of Caesar, without success, in book 10. In both episodes, Lucan puts a speech into his mouth and presents him as an immensely powerful orator, prepared to use any argument from expediency and appeals to self-interest and to emotion to achieve his end.

An apparently unhistorical character is the young Roman, Cordus, whom Lucan produces after Pompey's murder to give a makeshift burial to the headless corpse. Comparison with Plutarch's much more complex and cluttered account of events after Pompey's murder illuminates Lucan's use of minor characters. Plutarch has two characters, Philip, an ex-slave of Pompey, and an old man who had in his youth served under Pompey, who collaborate in the burial. By contrast, in Lucan there is only Cordus, a young man devoted to Pompey as son to father (and, appropriately, specified as quaestor, since the relationship of the quaestor and his senior officer was supposed to resemble the son–father relationship), acting on his own and extremely nervously. He emerges from his hiding-place to perform the rites, has to filch charred wood from another pyre, nearly loses the corpse to the sea, and breaks off the rites half-way because of his terror (8. 712–93). The character excellently illustrates both the depth of devotion which Pompey continues to inspire in his followers even after death and the unglamorous, unheroic, undignified end to which Pompey has come.

Just as Cordus is a devoted follower of Pompey, so Brutus' devotion is to Cato alone (2. 247: 'for Brutus Cato will be the only leader'). Brutus' role in the poem, as it survives, is to elicit from Cato a justification for taking sides in the civil war. This is achieved through mutually respectful, philosophical argument, in which Brutus advocates non-involvement in political affairs. This cleverly allows Lucan to deal early in the poem with the issue of why Cato adopts the Republican cause. Particularly remarkable is Brutus' reverential attitude to Cato: he treats him almost as an oracular source of wisdom and authority. For this reason, this episode is crucial to the establishment of Cato's characterization in the poem. It is possible that Lucan planned a more developed role for Brutus in the later books, after Pompey's death, not least because Brutus, like Cato, was an object of interest among Lucan's contemporaries. Especially appropriate would be a premonition or prediction of Brutus' assassination of Caesar. How Lucan would have handled this it is hard to tell. However, it is almost certain that Brutus would have continued to be closely linked with Cato in the remaining books and portrayed as the Stoic pupil of the Stoic sage.

One further historical figure in the poem is Curio, tribune of the plebs and Caesar's legate. He appears twice, in book 1 and book 4, on each occasion enhancing themes important to Lucan. In book 1 he is introduced as 'reckless' with a 'mercenary tongue' (269). He uses his tongue, purchased by the liquidation of his debts (4. 820), to deliver a speech (273–91) in which he urges Caesar to prosecute the civil war by offering justifications for this course of action. For Lucan, Curio symbolizes the corruption of the Roman state, a state in which anything can be bought, including the tongue of a tribune of the plebs. Curio features again, more prominently, in 4. 581–824, where he travels to Africa, defeats the Republican Varus, but is then defeated by Pompey's ally King Juba. Inserted into this narrative is the tale of Hercules and Antaeus. Throughout this part of book 4 runs a strand of imagery drawn from gladiatorial combat, which, as Ahl (ch. 3) powerfully argues, suggests that the civil war is presented as a spectacle on the African sands/arena (the word 'arena' is from Latin *harena*, 'sand'), virtually as an appeasement of the ghosts of Africa seeking revenge for the defeat of Hannibal. Lucan links these two aspects of his treatment of Curio in the closing lines of book 4 (788–824), deploring this 'sacrifice' to the Carthaginians and deploring Curio's role in promoting the conflict between Caesar and Pompey. In this way a minor character is the vehicle of some central themes of the poem.

10. *Lucan's use of historical exemplars*

The same principle can be seen in Lucan's use of historical exemplars of behaviour, *exempla*. Where appropriate, he incorporates or adapts standard illustrations of particular qualities, good or bad, attaching them to characters either named or not but usually one-dimensional. Such *exempla* serve a similar purpose to the minor characters: their existence is forgotten once the point has been made. In this respect, as in many others, Lucan reflects the Roman rhetorical training familiar to him and his audience. In fact, familiarity with such *exempla* was so central to educated Romans that handbooks like Valerius Maximus' *Deeds and Sayings Worthy of Record* (*Facta et dicta memorabilia*) had been compiled, to provide a ready quarry for declaimers and historians alike. Valerius Maximus organized his material according to topic; thus anyone requiring an example of, say, poverty or justice, of cruelty or greed, of parents' generosity or strictness towards their children, had only to turn to that section. In a number of places Lucan presents *exempla* which may have been drawn from Valerius Maximus or a similar handbook and which in any case satisfy the need for

concrete illustration of an abstract moral or political principle. Two examples feature the love of money: 3. 118–21, where the tribune Metellus
attempts to stop Caesar breaking into the treasury in Rome, and 4. 93–7,
where greed for money has the power to make a starving soldier sell
his bread to another; other passages evoke the stereotypes found in Valerius
Maximus and other authors, for example at 10. 151–4, where early Roman
leaders such as Fabricius and Curius and Cincinnatus are mentioned as
epitomes of the simple, modest life-style. Another passage again occurs
in both Valerius Maximus and Lucan, namely Appius' consultation of
the Delphic oracle (5. 64–236 and Valerius Maximus 1. 8. 10): comparison
of the two reveals clearly Lucan's interest in the supernatural (see above,
ii. 7).

Lucan also introduces historical material relating to famous and infamous
individuals to point comparisons and emphasize certain characteristics of
his protagonists and his theme. Thus early in book 2, as Rome is in
a state of deepest fear at Caesar's approach, an old man recalls the civil
wars between Marius and Sulla in a lengthy description of the dreadful
outrages perpetrated then (2. 68–232). This reminiscence allows Lucan
to set up a 'norm' for civil war which *his* civil war will proceed to breach
and surpass (see Henderson, §2. 15). We are invited to see Caesar as
the successor of Marius and Sulla (4. 821–3); Pompey is portrayed by
his opponents as the pupil of Sulla who surpasses his teacher (1. 326–31).
In short, Lucan utilizes the horror evoked in earlier literary and declamatory contexts by the names of Marius and Sulla to provide a scale for
his own work.

Another historical figure used symbolically by Lucan is Hannibal. The
character linked with Hannibal is Caesar: Lucan draws this analogy to
suggest that Caesar is not only terrifying but an enemy of Rome. He
establishes the analogy early on in the epic, comparing Caesar to an angry
Libyan lion (1. 205–12), then making the people of Ariminum complain
of being the first victims when enemies, among whom Hannibal is listed,
march on Rome (248–57), and finally, explicitly, when Caesar remarks
that Rome is reacting to his advance as if he were Hannibal (303–5).
Later, after the battle of Pharsalus, Lucan condemns Caesar for treating
the dead Republicans less humanely than Hannibal the dead Romans after
the battle of Cannae (7. 799–803). Again, Lucan adapts historical *exempla*
to his theme: he sets Caesar and Hannibal in a relationship designed to
imply that Caesar's behaviour towards Rome and her citizens is worse
than that of Rome's archetypal foreign enemy. Moreover, it is highly
likely that Lucan would have pursued this analogy—to Caesar's further

detriment—in the missing climax to the poem: Caesar's victory at the battle of Thapsus, in North Africa, invited the comparison.

Lucan's use of Alexander, another historical figure who featured frequently as an *exemplum*, is the same. On Caesar's arrival at Alexandria in book 10, he heads directly for the tomb of Alexander. This suggests his admiration for the man whom Lucan unflatteringly styles as 'the crazy offspring of Pellaean Philip . . . the lucky bandit' (20–1). Lucan soon makes explicit the analogy between Caesar and Alexander when he describes Alexander's thirst for power and his unflinching shedding of blood (28–33) and then calls him 'a thunderbolt which struck all the peoples equally, a star baneful to humankind' (34–6). All this recalls the simile which introduces Caesar in book 1 and gives Caesar a horrific precedent of blood thirsty power-crazed maniacs.

A highly significant figure who appears in the poem for his symbolic value is Hercules. In Stoic thought, Hercules was the bringer of civilization, overcoming the monsters and barbarians of the world. Accordingly, in Lucan's epic, Hercules is shown struggling with Antaeus and finally winning (4. 593–660). His fight and victory over Antaeus, the native who derives strength from his mother Earth, symbolizes the Stoic sage's struggle with and conquest of the impediments to wisdom. Moreover, Hercules' fight and victory also prefigure Cato's determination to survive whatever North Africa can afflict him with—sand-storm, thirst, or poisonous snakes (9. 368–949). The presence of Hercules is designed to knit with other Stoic material in the poem and, in view of its North African setting in particular, to encourage a view of Cato as superhuman, as a hero or almost a deity.

II. *Lucan's learning*

Lucan reflects his literary, moral, and rhetorical training, not only in his use of historical material and *exempla* but also in his incorporation of mythological episodes and what can be styled scientific discussions of geography, astrology, astronomy, and natural phenomena. A typical mythological episode is the uneducated African's narration to Curio on his arrival in Libya of the fight in that region between Hercules and Antaeus. Typical scientific material includes Lucan's list of the rivers that run from the Apennine range into the two seas, the Etruscan and the Adriatic (2. 399–427)—which is followed by an explanation of the formation of Sicily as an island (2. 428–38)—and the disquisition about the cause of the tides in the Atlantic (1. 412–16).

Often several items of learning are combined. One brief example is Lucan's description of the site of Brundisium (2. 610–27), in which he includes a reference to the city's foundation legend. Similarly, into his lengthy geographical description of the land of Thessaly (6. 333–412), which includes a catalogue of its rivers, peoples, and claims to fame, he incorporates a brief summary of the myth telling the formation of the valley of Tempe.

Book 9 is particularly rich in this kind of material. Cato's decision to attempt the journey from Cyrene to Juba's kingdom further west gives Lucan the opportunity to incorporate a variety of learned material relating to North Africa. He starts with a discussion of the origin and nature of the Syrtes, a treacherous area of sandbanks notoriously dangerous to shipping (303–18). Lucan narrates the passage of Cato's fleet past the Syrtes and brings them to land near Lake Triton. This enables him to tell the story of the goddess Pallas' affection for the lake and another story associated with this region, Hercules' capture of the apples from the Garden of the Hesperides (348–67). After Cato's speech, firing his men for the difficult crossing of the desert, Lucan provides a full geographical description of the land of Libya: its extent, climate, people, and natural resources (411–62). Eventually, Cato and his men arrive at the shrine of Jupiter Ammon. Lucan here incorporates a description of the oasis (511–27), which he locates on the equator, which in turn leads him into speculation about the astronomical differences experienced by peoples living there (528–37 incorporating 538–43). Lines 533–7 present an admirable *tour de force*: into these five lines Lucan incorporates all twelve signs of the zodiac, arranged in opposing pairs.

Probably the most memorable scientific 'digression' in Lucan's poem is his catalogue of the snakes of Libya which assail Cato and his men. The catalogue is introduced by a mythological (as opposed to scientific: 9. 619–23) explanation of the origin and abundance of African snakes. Lucan tells at some length the story of Perseus' killing of the Gorgon Medusa, whose blood, falling from her severed head as Perseus flew over Africa, generated snakes (619–99). There follows first the catalogue of numerous types of snake (700–33) and then chilling descriptions of the various types of death they inflicted (734–836). Eventually, the sufferings of Cato's troops are ended by the intervention of a local tribe, the Psylli, who are themselves immune to the snakes. They have the knowledge to drive the snakes away and to cure any bites inflicted (890–937). This entire episode illustrates that Lucan's interests embraced natural history and ethnography.

All this material is designed to show off Lucan's versatility and ingenuity—his is a very different 'narrative' of the civil war from, say, Caesar's own. It is also a sure inference that this material appealed to contemporary taste. The finale to book 9, which describes Caesar's sight-seeing tour of the ruins of Troy, must have satisfied the taste for antiquarianism and the travelogue alike (as well as showing Caesar in a strongly negative light). But nowhere is this more so than in the differing stories about the source of the Nile which Lucan puts into the mouth of Acoreus, an elderly member of Ptolemy's court (10. 194–331). This passage combines astrology, geography, and scientific speculation. What is more, the search for the source of the Nile was highly topical for Lucan and his contemporaries: Nero, following the precedent of Alexander and the others mentioned by Lucan (10. 268–82), planned an expedition to find the source of the Nile (see above, i. 2).

To regard such episodes as digressions is to fail to understand Lucan. His narrative of the civil war is pared down to a bare minimum; this is overlaid with a rich and varied virtuoso display of learning which reflects contemporary interests.

12. *Structure, scope, and title of the work*

The poem breaks off incomplete at l. 546 of book 10. Whether it was unfinished at the time of Lucan's suicide in 65 (as is usually assumed) or whether part of the original codex was lost at an early stage must remain a matter for speculation. The scope and structure of the poem as planned by Lucan are also difficult to judge in its incomplete state and a number of different hypotheses have been advanced. (Many of the arguments are presented in Ahl 306–26.) Some believe that Lucan intended to continue his poem as far as the battle of Philippi in 42 BC, or even down to the battle of Actium in 31 BC. Both of these are intrinsically improbable, unless we also accept the possibility of a massive poem, because in the ten existing books Lucan has covered the events of some twenty months only. To continue at the same rate for a further six (let alone seventeen) years would seem to require a poem on an enormous scale.

More attractive is the argument advanced by Marti that the poem would have consisted of sixteen books and ended with the assassination of Caesar in 44 BC. A sixteen-book epic, though unparalleled, is by no means implausible, especially given Ovid's *Metamorphoses* in fifteen books a little earlier and Silius Italicus' *Punica* in seventeen books a few years later. But there are problems in supposing that the poem ended with Caesar's death: Lucan would need to introduce and develop characters to replace Pompey and Cato on the Republican side after their deaths; and though Brutus appears in the poem fleetingly there is not enough to suggest that he or any other Republicans will serve the function of protagonists. Moreover, Caesar's assassination might seem to present almost a happy ending, which would be entirely inappropriate to this poem so full of gloom and horror and terror.

It seems most likely that Lucan planned a twelve-book epic, on the model of Virgil's *Aeneid* (cf. Statius' *Thebaid*, an epic in twelve books, written a little later, under the emperor Domitian), although lacking the highly complex structural organization of the *Aeneid*. One of the prime internal arguments for a twelve-book work is that Sextus Pompey's consultation of the witch Erichtho in the second half of book 6 appears to be a reworking and inversion of motifs which feature in Aeneas' consultation of the Sibyl in *Aeneid* 6. If Lucan's poem was planned in twelve books, the most likely climax and conclusion to the epic is the suicide of Cato at Utica after the battle of Thapsus in 46 BC. Not only is this chronological point attainable in a further two and a half books (for suggested summaries see Due, Marti (1968)) but Cato's death—and probably his apotheosis as a Stoic hero too—would have drawn together many themes of the poem (see Ahl 319–26).

Our view of the intended scope of the poem affects our view of the title. Many scholars have thought that it was called *Pharsalia*, on the basis of lines 9. 980–6:

> O how sacred and immense the task of bards! You snatch everything
> from death and to mortal people you give immortality.
> Caesar, do not be touched by envy of their sacred fame;
> since, if for Latian Muses it is right to promise anything,
> as long as honours of the Smyrnaean bard endure,
> the future ages will read me and you; our Pharsalia
> shall live and we shall be condemned to darkness by no era,

together with Statius' reference to the poem in the words 'the Pharsalian wars'. Yet no manuscript gives *Pharsalia* as the title, while the majority of manuscripts give the title *De bello ciuili*, 'On the Civil War'. Ahl (326–32) provides a detailed discussion of the arguments before coming down in favour of *Pharsalia*. But this seems to privilege excessively an episode which occupies only one book and occurs in the centre of the poem rather than as its climax. Far preferable is the title *De bello ciuili*, for Lucan is concerned with the many horrors and catastrophes inflicted on itself by the Roman state not solely in the battle of Pharsalus but in all the preceding and following incidents which he includes. For similar reasons, Henderson refers to the poem as *Bellum Ciuile*, *(The) Civil War* (§2. 3). It is even possible that the opening line of the epic might be regarded as its title: *bella per Emathios plus quam ciuilia campos*, 'Of wars across Emathian plains, worse than civil wars', since many poems in antiquity were known by their opening words. This would emphasize the extremes and paradoxes which Lucan continually presents to us in his poem: for him, this civil war exceeds anything previously experienced.

The original scope and title of the poem can only be surmised; about its structure we can make a firmer judgement. Some have perceived a tetradic structure, with the first four books focusing on Caesar, the second four on Pompey, and the final four on Cato. But in fact the focus shifts variously between the two sides and from character to character. More plausible is the view that Lucan conceived the poem as two hexads; the lists of omens in books 1 and 7 along with the climactic finale to book 6 support this view. Ultimately, perhaps, it seems that Lucan's epic (at least, as it survives) does not lend itself to structural analysis in the same way as Virgil's *Aeneid*. Rather, it has an episodic structure more akin to that of Ovid's *Metamorphoses*. Possibly both Ovid and Lucan were reacting against the literary tyranny of the *Aeneid*; at any rate, concentration on the small episode rather than the whole gives Lucan the opportunity to shine, again and again.

It is easy to imagine the performance of self-contained excerpts to an enthusiastic audience in Nero's court as virtuoso masterpieces in their own right: for example, the portents from book 1; the reminiscences of the days of Marius and Sulla in book 2; from book 3 the sea-battle at Massilia; from book 4 the fable of the fight between Hercules and Antaeus or the mass suicide initiated by Vulteius; the mutiny or the storm in book 5; Scaeva's *aristeia* or the necromancy in book 6; Lucan's apostrophe of Thessaly with which book 7 ends; the speeches of Pompey and Lentulus from book 8; the snakes episode or Caesar's visit to Troy from book 9; or from book 10 Acoreus' speech on the sources of the Nile; the list could continue.

III. THE POEM: CHARACTERISTICS AND STYLE

1. *Lucan's treatment of warfare and violent death*

Given that Lucan's theme is civil war, it is particularly interesting and rewarding to consider Lucan's treatment of warfare. Of course, he was working within an epic tradition stretching back to the *Iliad* which prescribed certain episodes as standard. Thus any epic on a martial theme, whether mythological or historical, might be expected to include some or all of the following: narration of the cause and outbreak of hostilities, catalogues of the opposing forces, preparations for battle, speeches of the leaders, accounts of battle on land, including tactics and various forms of death, the *aristeia* of one or more eminent individuals, the treatment of the defeated and the dead. Both epic poetry and other literary traditions, most obviously the historians, supplied further possible set-pieces, for example the sea-battle, the siege, fire, plague, mutiny. Lucan chooses to incorporate many of these standard scenes but alters and even inverts their conventional presentation where possible to accord with his condemnation of civil warfare.

For example, the conduct of the war in Spain, described in the first half of book 4, is adapted by Lucan to provide a series of shocks and surprises. He compresses more than forty chapters of Caesar's own narrative of the campaign into a couple of hundred lines but devotes nearly a hundred lines to an incident of fraternization between the opposing armies (169–253). This he uses to emphasize the horror of civil war: when the troops see one another's faces, 'they grasped the crime of civil war' (172). But worse is to come. When the commander of the Pompeian army discovers Caesarian troops in his camp, he has them massacred. If the soldiers' recognition of their crime was bad, how much more horrific is their slaughter of the men they were recently embracing! This gruesome scene seems to epitomize Lucan's horror of civil war.

Immediately preceding and following this episode are two contrasting incidents involving water: the flooding of Caesar's camp (48–120) and the thirst in Pompey's (254–336). Both incidents are standard in the repertoire of potential military disasters, but, typically, Lucan uses them to present paradoxes. Firstly, when Caesar's camp is flooded, Lucan describes the army in an adaptation of a commonplace of declamation as 'shipwrecked' (88). Then, as famine ensues, he presents a paradox: 'the soldier starves while besieged by no enemy' (94–5). Later, when Caesar cuts off the Pompeian troops from the rivers, Lucan presents the paradox of men dying within sight of water: 'caught between the pools of Sicoris and rapid Hiberus, the thirsting army gazes at the nearby rivers' (334–6).

Later in book 4, Lucan adapts the standard situation of the siege to present an extreme example of heroism in adversity. The Pompeians are besieging some of Caesar's troops off the coast of Illyria. The Caesarian soldiers attempt to escape on three rafts, the last of which is captured by the Pompeians. The captain of this raft, Vulteius, urges his men to kill one another rather than fall into the enemies' hands (474–581). Although this amounts to mass suicide (see above, ii. 6), Lucan presents it as an extreme or perverted version of military resolve and duty. He points to this by presenting a paradox: they 'fight, and on one side performed the entire crime of wars' (548–9). Rather like the massacre which follows the incident of fraternization, this mass, mutual slaughter epitomizes the horror of the civil war for Lucan.

Another set piece is the mutiny of troops, incorporated by Lucan into book 5 (237–373). He uses this episode to enhance his characterization of Caesar—to illustrate his ruthlessness and determination and his power over his men. Caesar's speech engineers a surprising reversal in the situation: that not only are his soldiers ready to perform the execution of the ringleaders of the mutiny, but the ringleaders actually volunteer themselves as victims.

At the start of book 6, Lucan presents two classic situations which beset encampments of troops—plague (in Pompey's camp) and famine (in Caesar's). But he introduces surprise by locating the famine in the camp of the besiegers rather than the besieged: 'just as if surrounded in a tight blockade, he suffers brutal famine' (108–9) and 'they besiege a well-fed enemy' (117).

Another extraordinary battle-episode is that of Scaeva's *aristeia*, also in book 6. This centurion of Caesar makes an incredible single-handed stand against Pompey's troops and, on his own, prevents them from breaking out of the blockade (118–262). This unbelievable scene of fighting includes the paradoxical idea that 'nothing now protects his naked vitals except the spears sticking fast in the surface of his bones' (194–5) and the graphic image of Scaeva carrying in his breast a forest of spears (205). Lucan introduces this warrior with a comment that perhaps puts him in the same category as Vulteius: 'eager for every wrong, he did not know how great a crime is valour in a civil war' (147–8). Scaeva acts out of the same perverted concept of heroism (*uirtus*) and devotion (*pietas*) towards Caesar.

Caesar's siege of Massilia in book 3, one of the first scenes of sustained fighting in the poem, allows Lucan plenty of scope for his paradoxical treatment of civil war. First, he points out that the people of Massilia, though Greeks, exhibit a quality rarely associated with Greeks in Latin literature, namely loyalty (*fides*), and follow their principles rather than luck (301–3). That is, the Greek population of Massilia is portrayed as fighting for the ideals which ought to be espoused by the Romans, a piquant and telling reversal of roles.

Then, after describing the unsuccessful attempts to take the city by land, Lucan devotes the finale of the book to the sea–battle (509–762). Paradoxically, this soon resembles a battle on land, once the Greek ships have rammed Caesar's ships and become fixed to them ('the sea is hidden and war stands still', 566). This then gives Lucan ample opportunity to describe many extreme and bizarre forms of death. Of these perhaps the most memorable is the Greek warrior, one of twins, who when his right hand is cut off, continues fighting only to have his left hand cut off too. He then offers his bare chest to protect his brother's shield (another paradoxical inversion) and finally jumps with all the force he can muster on to the Roman ship and sinks it (603–33). This description of death is typical of Lucan. Most of the deaths in the poem are striking for their strangeness, suddenness, and lack of dignity and heroism. Lucan is not concerned to glamorize death; on the contrary, his descriptions convey the full force of horror through their graphic detail, especially when the weapons which deal death are personified (see Henderson, §3. 9 on Lucan's treatment of weapons and bodies).

In his treatment of warfare, Lucan seldom misses an opportunity to portray the horror of civil war—of Roman fighting Roman, of brother fighting brother, father fighting son—and to present it in a stark light stripped of glamour and heroism. Blood flows abundantly, not to the glory but to the shame of Rome. The total wrongness of civil war is reflected in the strangeness of its course, so that death comes by unexpected means and the battles are full of paradoxes. All this exemplifies the opening theme of the poem, that the wars which Lucan is describing are 'worse than civil wars'.

2. *Corpses and burial in the poem*

The same is true of Lucan's portrayal of the outrageous treatment of dead bodies, in terms of their mutilation and their burial or lack of burial.

This is an important theme in the poem, chiefly for artistic reasons—to provide a context for the decapitation and 'burial' of Pompey in book 8 (see Mayer's note on 712)—but also more generally to maintain the emphasis on the wickedness of civil war. The raving matron at the end of book 1 foresees Pompey's headless corpse lying on the sands of Egypt (685–6) and the old man who at the beginning of book 2 recalls the massacres perpetrated under Marius and Sulla talks of examining the unburied corpses to find a body to match the severed head of his brother (169–73). Book 3 ends with the scene on the shore after the naval battle off Massilia. Lucan paints a gruesome picture of women embracing disfigured faces and men fighting over headless bodies, in the mistaken belief that they are those of their husbands and sons (756–61). Similarly, book 4 closes with a picture of the carrion crows of Libya feeding on the unburied body of Caesar's lieutenant Curio (809–10).

In the mutiny of book 5, one motivation given by Caesar's troops for their revolt is their desire for a proper burial conducted by their loved ones, as opposed to the mass grave that may await them in the battlefield (278–82). Book 6 portrays with graphic horror the indignities and terrors to which an unburied corpse may be liable: at the hands of the witch Erichtho, a corpse is chosen to be revived and is made to deliver a prophecy (624–825). The final scene of action in book 7 is Caesar's breakfast on the battlefield of Pharsalia, when he refuses the corpses of the Republicans burial and leaves them to be torn apart by the beasts and birds of Thessaly (786–846).

The narrative of Pompey's murder in book 8 is followed by a description and condemnation of his decapitation (8. 663–91). The remainder of book 8 is devoted to the makeshift burial of Pompey's headless corpse by his follower Cordus. It includes a contrast between the magnificent tombs of Alexander the Great, the Pharaohs, and the Ptolemies, and Pompey's as yet unburied corpse on the shore; then the fearful, furtive performance of burial rites of a sort by Cordus; and finally Lucan's wish to convey the remains to Rome for proper burial, which is superseded by a wish for the destruction of the Egyptian grave—so that Pompey can be thought immortal.

Similar ideas recur in the reaction of Pompey's son to the news of his father's murder—he wishes to give proper burial to the unburied corpse and to remove the bodies of Alexander the Great and the kings buried in the pyramids to atone for Pompey's lack of a tomb (9. 148–60). Finally, even Caesar is portrayed as shocked at what the Egyptians have done in embalming Pompey's severed head, abandoning his corpse, and denying him a fitting burial (9. 1089–93). It is evident that Lucan uses the mutilation of corpses and denial of proper burial as a potent symbol of the breakdown in morality marked by and brought by civil warfare.

3. *Lucan and earlier epic*

Lucan's handling of the staples of martial epic epitomizes his relation with earlier epic generally. He readily embraces the conventional elements of the epic tradition, but almost invariably alters or inverts them (thus Henderson, §4. 13). Thus his poem has no hero in the conventional sense (see above, ii. 4), unlike an *Aeneid* or *Theseid*, but instead, in Caesar, a dynamic protagonist who can only be described adequately as an anti-hero.

Lucan accepts the role of prophecy and prediction in the epic poem but invests all such episodes with profound horror, for example, in his portrayal of the Roman matron-become-Bacchante at the end of book I (see above, ii. 7). In particular, he transfers the emphasis from the content of the prophecy to the terrifying process of gaining it, as we see in Appius' consultation of the Delphic oracle in book 5 and in Sextus' visit to the witch Erichtho in book 6. Similarly, such conventional elements of epic as dreams and visions, omens and prodigies, present further opportunities for grisly horror which Lucan seizes wholeheartedly.

Another feature which he adapts from mythological epic is the *topos* of felling trees to provide wood for a funeral pyre. This occurs in *Iliad* 23 when wood is gathered for the funeral pyre of Patroclus; one of the surviving fragments of the early Latin epic writer Ennius is evidently part of a tree-felling *topos*; and Virgil incorporates two such episodes into the *Aeneid*, one in book 6, which leads to Aeneas' discovery of the Golden Bough and subsequent visit to the Underworld, the other in book II (see my note on 3. 399–452). Lucan, in contrast with his predecessors, uses the *topos* not in connection with burials and funerals, despite ample opportunity, but to enhance his characterization of Caesar as a ruthless and vengeful megalomaniac who will stop at nothing, not even the profanation of a sacred grove, to achieve his ambition. Lucan's tree-felling *topos* occurs in book 3, during the siege of Massilia (399–445). Caesar gives orders that the grove sacred to the local gods is to be torn down, partly to supply material for his immense siege-works but also partly because it is the only wood in the vicinity still standing. When none of his men dare wield the axe, Caesar steps forward and strikes the first blow, declaring 'mine is the guilt!'

Lucan's technique becomes especially clear when we consider his handling of the epic storm, a standard component of epic from the *Odyssey* onwards, and particularly prominent in the *Aeneid*, of course, which commences with the storm which drives Aeneas to Carthage. Lucan works into his poem no less than four storms (4. 48–120, 5. 504–677, 9. 319–47, 9. 445–92). Of these, the storm and flood in book 4 evoke the Stoic conception of the final cataclysm. The other storms all contribute to characterization. The two in book 9 enhance that of Cato: to survive the storm in the dangerous waters of the Syrtes and the Libyan dust-storm are to be interpreted as marks of the Stoic sage. Probably the ultimate treatment of the epic storm is that in book 5. All the possible traditional features are present, present in abundance and taken to the extremes of imagination. This storm does not contribute to the narrative as such, since Caesar's attempt to cross the sea is a failure, but it does serve the purpose of epitomizing Caesar's confidence in himself and in Fortune and of arousing a reluctant admiration of his mad fearlessness.

On the basis of Lucan's novel treatment of many of the conventional features of epic poetry, it has been suggested that Lucan's poem should be viewed as an anti-Virgilian poem. This seems to be the case, although not in the sense of a wholesale antipathy towards Virgil, since it is clear that Lucan was steeped in Virgil's language and ideas. But the evidence suggests that, for poets who chose the civil war as their theme, the elevated style and glorification of martial exploits found in mythological epic were deemed inappropriate (see above, ii. 2). Lucan appears to embrace this principle and to go further, to the extent of omitting conventional elements (e.g. the gods) and inverting some of the conventional *topoi* to gain the maximum horror quotient. This often involves him in a direct relationship with the *Aeneid*. On a number of occasions he presents a shocking, black, pessimistic version of a stirring, patriotic episode in the *Aeneid*, perhaps most obviously in the reworking of Aeneas and Sibyl in the Underworld in the scene of Sextus' and Erichtho's necromancy in book 6. But this need not imply a hostility towards Virgil. Rather, as with many instances of imitation in Roman poetry and literature, it is a tribute and an acknowledgement of a deep debt.

To describe Lucan as an anti-Virgilian poet may also seem to make an adverse value-judgement on him. Yet the works of the two poets are so very different that such verdicts do not compare like with like. Virgil's is a nationalistic and essentially optimistic poem, celebrating the elevation of Augustus and the principles of Roman-ness which Augustus promoted. Lucan's is an essentially pessimistic poem which paints a black and despairing picture of a megalomaniacal ego on the loose, a picture relieved only by a few austere visions of Stoic virtue in the face of adversity. Both poets select and shape content and style to suit their needs; to prefer one or the other is therefore ultimately a matter of the reader's personal choice and temperament.

4. *Lucan's style*

In style, too, Lucan rejects the Virgilian precedent as inappropriate to his subject-matter. Gone is Virgil's versatile, musical treatment of the hexameter. In its place is a more repetitive, even monotonous, use of rhythm (for details see Heitland, pp. xciv–ci), more suited to the grim portrayal of the horrors perpetrated by citizens against their fellow-citizens. Matching this, his diction is prosaic. He uses straightforward, everyday words rather than romantic or heroic poeticisms, and includes technical terms which other epic poets tended to avoid. (Some illustrations of these points are found in Bramble 541.) On occasions, Lucan displays a virtuoso's ingenuity in language (as in the storm-episode, where every conceivable word and idea concerning the sea occurs); but in general his range of vocabulary is limited and he avoids ornamental embellishment. This is especially true of words relating to colour: from an analysis of Lucan's use of colour terms, Bramble (542) styles the poem a 'predominantly monochrome epic', one in which black, grey, and white figure most often, followed by red (here decorative and sensuous words like *purpureus* and *roseus* are absent, replaced by *ruber* etc.); other colours are rare. In Lucan, colour does not decorate and seduce but emphasizes the stark, dark horror of civil war.

Throughout the poem, certain key words recur, again underlining the destructiveness of civil war. They include nouns and verbs indicating disintegration and destruction, on the individual level and on the level of the state and the cosmos, for example, *ruina* ('collapse'), *spargere* ('to scatter, disperse'), *calcare* ('to trample'), *uiscera* ('guts'), *tabes* ('decay, putre-faction'), *sanguis* ('blood, gore'), *cadauera* ('corpses'), *truncus* ('torso, headless corpse'). The setting of the events of the civil war is typically portrayed by Lucan in extremes, either with an excess of water (mountainous seas, floods, rivers of blood) or as oppressively dry; here words like *puluis* ('dust'), *harena* ('sand'), *cinis* ('ash(es)'), and especially the adjective *siccus* ('dry, arid') recur. Another word—*praeceps* ('headlong')—symbolizes the surprise and panic which features in the poem. The frequent recurrence of words which denote fleeing—*fuga* and *fugio*—helps convey the anti-heroic mood

of the poem. Another key word is *mora*, 'delay' or 'obstacle': throughout
the poem, Lucan portrays the obstacles to civil war, the reluctance to
bring about the destruction of Rome (cf. Henderson, §2. 19). Even apparently favourable words become tinged with irony or pathos as Lucan
turns them into key words, for example, *felix* ('blessed, lucky'), *laetus*
('happy'), *fides* ('loyalty'), and the words denoting 'greatness' (*magnus, tan-
tus*). And the poem is emphatically guilt-laden, with the words *nefas*,
scelus, and *crimen* repeated frequently. Cumulatively, these words din into
the audience's head an insistent message of Rome's self-inflicted collapse.

Lucan's use of imagery accords with the same pattern. His similes (for
a list see Heitland, pp. lxxxiv–lxxxviii: 79 in all) and metaphors tend
to be memorable and often link with and express key words and themes
in the poem. For example, a prominent strand of imagery in the poem
is that drawn from gladiatorial combat. At the opening of book 6 Lucan
depicts Caesar and Pompey facing one another for the first time as a
pair of gladiators (*par*, 3). A little later in the same book he describes
the combat between Pompey's army on one side and Scaeva on the other
as 'a novel pair of adversaries, an army and a man' (*par nouum*, 191–2);
and a few lines further on, Scaeva is compared to a bear attacked by
a Libyan fighter, a scene from the amphitheatre (220–3). But this is by
no means the first occurrence of gladiatorial imagery in the poem. Earlier,
in book 4, Lucan introduces a developed simile about a wounded gladiator
(285–91). He proceeds to present the struggle between Hercules and
Antaeus as if it were a fight in the gladiatorial arena (Ahl, ch. 3). Finally,
he shows Curio rousing himself to fight Varus with a gladiator's professional
attitude (4. 708–10): 'just as those brought out at the shows of the deadly
arena are not compelled to fight by ancient rage: they hate each other
as opponents.' This strand of imagery presents a reversal of roles: instead
of Romans watching barbarians and wild beasts killing and being killed
for entertainment, it is Romans who now take their place on the sand
of the arena, to provide a grim entertainment for the world with futile,
self-inflicted slaughter.

Other types of imagery complement other important themes in the
poem. The opening pair of similes, of the oak tree and the thunderbolt,
in book 1 have already been considered (see above, ii. 4) in terms of
their contribution to Lucan's portrayal of Caesar as energetic, ruthless,
and destructive and Pompey as past his prime and on the point of collapse.
The simile in which Caesar is compared to a Libyan lion, gathering his
rage (1. 205–12), provides a link with the emphasis on Africa and in particular with Hannibal, whose presence is often evoked. The raving matron

compared with a Bacchante at the close of book 1 (674–5) not only pre-
figures the loss of control experienced by the priestess Phemonoe in book
5 but also symbolizes Rome's hurtling course towards destruction.

Similar again is Lucan's technique within passages of reiterating the
same central idea in a number of different expressions. Typical is the
opening of the poem (1. 1–7):

> Of wars across Emathian plains, worse than civil wars,
> and of legality conferred on crime we sing, and of a mighty people
> attacking its own guts with victorious sword-hand,
> of kin facing kin, and, once the pact of tyranny was broken,
> of conflict waged with all the forces of the shaken world
> for universal guilt, and of standards ranged in enmity against
> standards, of eagles matched and javelins threatening javelins.

About a hundred years after his death, Lucan was criticized for precisely
this reiteration by Fronto:

In the first seven verses at the beginning of the poem he has done nothing but
paraphrase the words 'wars ... worse than civil'. Count up the phrases in which
he rings the changes on this ... Annaeus, what end will there be? (*De orationibus*
6 (van den Hout²), transl. Haines ii. 105–7.)

But this criticism seems to miss the point. Lucan uses this technique to
make the audience stop and confront the issue. He has no interest in
wafting us swiftly, mellifluously, unthinkingly along.

The same principle accounts for the arresting maxims (*sententiae*) and
paradoxes which Lucan inserts into the poem. Typical of his maxims,
or generalizations (listed by Heitland, pp. lxvif.), are: 'Mighty structures
collapse on to themselves' (*in se magna ruunt*, 1. 81), 'where the Fates
lead, confident will Virtue follow' (2. 287), 'a starving people knows
not terror' (3. 58), 7. 104–7, 'In life prosperity is changed: death does
not make a man unhappy' (8. 631–2), 'To know how to die is the warrior's
best lot, the next to be compelled to die' (9. 211), 'No loyalty, no duty
have the men who follow camp' (10. 407). Lucan's antitheses include
'Caesar knows he wants the final penalty and fears a pardon' (2. 511),
'they besiege a well-fed enemy' (6. 117) and, probably the most memorable,
'they abandon Rome and flee towards war' (*in bellum fugitur*, 1. 503–4).
There are many more (see Heitland's list, pp. lxxixf.). They represent
the same phenomenon as Lucan's inversion of the standard features of
epic poetry, but on a verbal level.

A similar explanation can be offered for Lucan's liking for 'negative enumeration'(cf. Bramble 548, Henderson, §3. 5)—lists of the things which do not happen but which might, in normal circumstances, be expected to happen. A good example of this is his description of the renewed marriage of Cato and Marcia in book 2. The ceremony is depicted in ll. 354–73 as lacking all the usual features of a Roman wedding with an abundance of negative words. Another, briefer, example, is Lucan's description of the sham of a mock-election at 5. 392–6; a third is his portrayal of Pompey's 'funeral' in book 8: Cordus' speech delivered over the body evokes the aspects of the Roman funeral procession which Pompey deserves and so evidently lacks on the Egyptian shore (729–35). This technique seems designed to deliver a startling reminder of the gap between 'normality' and the perverted world which Lucan is portraying.

Another feature of Lucan's poem which can be explained by his wish to stop the reader in his or her tracks is the marked disproportion between narrative and speeches in the poem. Mythological epic was concerned with presenting a narrative of the exploits of gods and heroes, a narrative punctuated by occasional speeches which were the causes or explanations of subsequent actions or were themselves narratives of events. But Lucan has no need of conventional narrative patterns like these. As Bramble well expresses it (p. 540), Lucan 'refuses to narrate'. In any case, the 'story' of the civil war was already familiar to his audience. And his purpose is to arrest the flow of expectations, to make us stop and dwell upon the actual horror of civil war—a further explanation of why *mora* ('delay, obstacle') is a key word in the poem. Consequently, the sections of narrative of the *events* of war in the poem are brief and sparse and often punctuated by exclamations or condemnatory outbursts from the poet. In place of narrative of events such as battles, tactical manœuvres, and troop movements, Lucan supplies narrative of emotive scenes which have no actual impact upon the events of the civil war—in book 5 Appius' visit to the Delphic oracle and Caesar's battle with the storm, in book 6 the necromancy, and so on—together with many long speeches. Speeches by the protagonists, by minor characters, and by characters introduced solely to deliver a single speech feature before, during, and after every event. One particular type of speech deserves emphasis—that delivered by the poet when he enters the poem as an unnamed character in order to address one of the actors or the land in which the action is set or even the gods. This technique is called by the Greek name of apostrophe, which denotes a 'turning away' from the narrative. Lucan's favouring of this device—there are 144 instances in the poem, an average of one every fifty-six lines—epitomizes his approach to his theme. He continually invites us to pause and to comprehend the horror of the events of civil warfare.

In all aspects of his style, then—metre, range and variety of diction, imagery, balance of narrative and speeches—Lucan seeks to convey the horror of civil war. He presents it in grimly realistic terms—as brothers killing brothers and, ultimately, as the suicide of a powerful nation. If this is not to our taste—and there are many who do not find Lucan's poem to their taste—this could be because it raises issues and asks questions which we should prefer remained silent; because it is too uncomfortable and too disconcerting.

It may, in that case, be salutary to remember that many poets and scholars of medieval, Renaissance, and modern times had a high regard for Lucan. In Dante's view, Lucan ranked with Homer, Horace, Ovid, and Virgil as an exponent of elevated poetry; for him, these five poets made up *la bella scuola / di quel signor de l'altissimo canto* (*Inferno* 4. 94–5).

BIBLIOGRAPHY

AHL, F. M. *Lucan: An Introduction* (Ithaca, NY, 1976).

BRAMBLE, J. C., 'Lucan', in E. J. Kenney and W. V. Clausen (eds.), *The Cambridge History of Classical Literature,* ii: *Latin Literature* (Cambridge, 1982), 533–57.

DICK, B., '*Fatum* and *Fortuna* in Lucan's *Bellum Ciuile*', *Classical Philology*, 62 (1967), 235–42.

DUE, O. S., 'An Essay on Lucan', *Classica et Mediaevalia*, 23 (1962), 68–132.

GETTY, R. J., *De bello civili liber I* (Cambridge, 1940).

HEITLAND, W. E., introduction to *M. Annaei Lucani Pharsalia*, ed. C. E. Haskins (London, 1887).

HENDERSON, J. G. W., 'Lucan/ The Word at War', in A. J. Boyle (ed.), *The Imperial Muse: Ramus Essays on Roman Literature of the Empire* (Berwick, 1988), 122–64.

HOUSMAN, A. E., *M. Annaei Lucani Belli Ciuilis libri decem* (Oxford, 1927).

LAPIDGE, M., 'Lucan's Imagery of Cosmic Dissolution', *Hermes* 107 (1979), 344–70.

MARTI, B., 'The Meaning of the *Pharsalia*', *American Journal of Philology*, 66 (1945), 352–76.

——'La structure de la *Pharsale*', in *Lucain* (Entretiens Hardt, 15; Vandœuvres-Geneva, 1968), 1–50.

MARTINDALE, C. A., 'Paradox, Hyperbole and Literary Novelty in Lucan's *De Bello Civili*', *Bulletin of the Institute of Classical Studies*, 23 (1976), 45–54.

MAYER, R., *Lucan Civil War VIII* (Warminster, 1981).

MORFORD, M. P. O., *The Poet Lucan* (Oxford, 1967).

NEWMYER, S., 'Imagery as a Means of Character Portrayal in Lucan', in C. Deroux (ed.), *Studies in Latin Literature and Roman History*, iii (Collection Latomus, 180; Brussels, 1983), 226–52.

POSTGATE, J. P., *M. Annaei Lucani liber VII* (Cambridge, 1917).

RAWSON, E., 'Sallust on the Eighties?', *The Classical Quarterly*, NS 37 (1987), 163–80 = *Roman Culture and Society* (Oxford, 1991), 546–69.

RUTZ, W., 'Lucan 1964–1983', *Lustrum*, 26 (1984), 103–203.

——— 'Lucans *Pharsalia* im Lichte der neuesten Forschung', *ANRW* II 32. 3 (1985), 1457–537.

SHACKLETON BAILEY, S. R., *Lucanus: De bello civili* (Stuttgart, 1988).

NOTE ON THE TRANSLATION, NOTES, AND GLOSSARY

I resolved from the outset that my translation of Lucan's epic poem should be in verse with the same number of lines as the Latin. Prose translations tend to obscure the vigour, excitement, and horror of the original; verse translations which use a greater number of lines than the original profoundly alter the pace and balance, as well as making cross-reference to the Latin difficult. I found no English metre suitable for the length of line required and therefore decided to use free verse, with lines of varying lengths, and an underlying iambic rhythm which is designed to convey something of Lucan's insistent use of the hexameter. I have tried to reproduce Lucan's enjambments and some of his emphatic word-order where this is possible without making the English incomprehensible. How to convey the subtleties of an inflected language in English translation is, of course, one of the central problems.

My translation is not intended to be evaluated as an original artistic creation, nor as an interpretation only loosely based on the Latin. Rather, I have attempted to reproduce as accurately as possible both the content and the 'feel' of Lucan's poem. In terms of style, I belong to the literalist school of translation. That is, I believe that where the language of the original is difficult or obscure or compressed, it is the translator's duty to convey that. Lucan's Latin is often one or all of those things. A particularly striking feature of his style which is alien to the modern English reader is his use of such devices as rhetorical questions and exclamations and, above all, apostrophe (discussed in the Introduction, iii. 4). There are many instances of apostrophe in Lucan's poem with a wide variety of addressees. Apostrophe tends to sound unnatural in English, but I have faithfully reproduced every case, believing that to do otherwise would be a betrayal.

Proper names are explained in the Notes or, if they occur several times, in the Glossary. The names of the winds, Zephyr, Boreas, Eurus, Notus, and so on, are retained in the translation, because they are virtually personifications, and explained in the Glossary.

The Notes serve two functions. They provide a brief introduction to each new paragraph in the translation, summarizing its content. Notes on particular words and phrases explain references or allusions to Roman life, literature, and history, and attempt to clarify especially difficult, compressed, or elliptical passages in the text.

NOTE ON THE LATIN TEXT USED

I have used the traditional line-numbers throughout; hence there occur a few breaks and changes in the numerical sequence where I omit spurious lines or accept the editors' reordering of lines.

I have adopted Housman's text, except in the following places, where I follow Shackleton Bailey, unless otherwise stated:

1. 16 oris   304 transcenderet   397 rupem
426 rostrati; *Housman and Shackleton Bailey* monstrati   461 rapaces
464 bellis *MSS; Housman and Shackleton Bailey adopt Bentley's* Belgis
481 tunc   615 nigrum   622–3 iacet . . . latet
623 prauus   636 aut

2. 26 natantes   292 compressas   295 pudorem
387 maximus   426 tecta; *Housman and Shackleton Bailey adopt*
Heinsius' tesca   480 pullato

3. 77–8 et . . . ut   101 fausta   112 excict   286 Xerses
348 frangere   416–17 timeant . . . metuunt   435 telo
638–9 emicuit;   752 rem

4. 112 intendas   158 cauae   294 nutris   483 spernere
553 immissa   595 genetricis   652 medius
684 Arzux   719 metuens incauto   816 nunc

5. 305 urbem   325 ac   474 partem
535 tuis saeuamue quereris / pauperiem deflens   548 *delete*
549 nota Ω   650–1 non litora . . . pauent
651 Leucadiae

6. 18 rupibus   25 collo   61 capitur   127 hac
157 Magno   158 steterit   200 torta   236 Aunus
237 tecto   244 putastis   346 unus   637 pectore
638 ducitur   715 exhauriat *Braund (CQ² 39 (1989), 275–6)*

7. 43 texere   180 dementibus   264–5 sed uos . . . turba
precor, gentes   387–8 non expleat   388 *retain*
415 possint   431 seras   462–4 quae . . . manus, penitus,
parentes   477 tundit   504 uergens   505 distulit
616 pressere s   652 sua   658 fouit *Braund*
768 nocentes

8. 41 tu   75 cura   90 duxit   157 nulla …
turba   195 Oenusae   294 pugnandi   335 quid?
341–2 qui … qui   345 extollet   562 longe
563 appellat   665 placatam   716 idalio   761 nudo
860 es   861 iaces

9. 153 caries   241 quem   299 Catonem
427 quorum   568 nostra   568 breuis, nil, longane
674A *I omit Housman's extra line, adopted by Shackleton Bailey*
722 spumantia ZG   737 Aulem   833A putaret
898 illa   954 natatum   956 adtulit

10. 117 Meroitica   122A *I omit Housman's extra line, adopted by*
Shackleton Bailey   166 cui   167 terra   492 bella
518 retain

CIVIL WAR

BOOK ONE

Of wars across Emathian plains, worse than civil wars,
and of legality conferred on crime we sing, and of a mighty people
attacking its own guts with victorious sword-hand,
of kin facing kin, and, once the pact of tyranny was broken,
of conflict waged with all the forces of the shaken world
for universal guilt, and of standards ranged in enmity against
standards, of eagles matched and javelins threatening javelins.

What madness was this, O citizens? What this excessive freedom
with the sword—to offer Latian blood to hated nations?
And when proud Babylon was there to be stripped of Ausonian   10
trophies and when Crassus wandered with his ghost unavenged,
did you choose to wage wars which would bring no triumphs?
A bitter thought—how much of earth and sea might have been won
with this blood shed by the hands of fellow-citizens:
where Titan rises, where Night conceals the star,
where midday blazes with its scorching regions,
where winter, stiff and never eased by spring,
binds with Scythian chill the icy Pontus!
Beneath our yoke already the Seres and barbarian Araxes could
have come and the race, if it exists, which knows Nile's birth.   20
If your love of an abominable war is so great, Rome,
only when you have brought the entire world beneath the laws of
      Latium,
turn your hand against yourself; not yet are you without an enemy.
But now the walls are tumbling in the towns of Italy,
the houses half-destroyed, and, the defences collapsed,
the huge stones lie; no guardian occupies the homes
and in the ancient cities wanders only an occasional inhabitant;
Hesperia bristles now with thorns, unploughed
through many a year, lacking the hands for fields which demand
      them—
the author of such a great calamity will prove to be not you,   30
fierce Pyrrhus, nor the Carthaginian; no foreign sword has ever
      penetrated

so: it is wounds inflicted by the hand of fellow-citizen that have sunk
    deep.

But if the Fates could find no other way
for Nero's coming, if eternal kingdoms are purchased
by the gods at great cost, if heaven could serve its Thunderer
only after wars with the ferocious Giants,
then we have no complaint, O gods; for this reward we accept
even these crimes and guilt; though Pharsalia fill its dreadful
plains, though the Carthaginian's shade with blood be sated;
though the final battle be joined at fatal Munda;   40
though added to these horrors, Caesar, be the famine of Perusia
and the struggles of Mutina, the fleets overwhelmed
near rugged Leucas, and the slave wars under burning Etna;
yet Rome owes much to citizens' weapons, because it was
for you that all was done.

                                You, when your duty is fulfilled
and finally you seek the stars, will be received in your chosen palace
of heaven, with the sky rejoicing. Whether you choose to wield
the sceptre or to mount the flaming chariot of Phoebus
and to circle with moving fire the earth entirely unperturbed
by the transference of the sun, every deity   50
will yield to you, to your decision nature will leave
which god you wish to be, where to set your kingdom of the universe.
But choose your seat neither in the northern sphere
nor where the torrid sky of opposing south sinks down:
from these positions you would view your Rome with star aslant.
If you press on either side of the boundless ether,
the sky will feel the weight: maintain the mass of heaven poised
in the sphere's mid-point; let that part of the clear ether
be wholly empty, let no clouds bar our view of Caesar.
Then may humankind lay down its weapons and care for itself   60
and every nation love one another; may Peace be sent throughout
the world and close the iron temple-gates of warring Janus.
But already to me you are deity, and if I as bard receive you
in my breast, no wish have I to trouble the god who has control
of Cirrha's secrets or to distract Bacchus from Nysa:
you are enough to give me strength for Roman song.

My spirit leads me to reveal the causes of such great events,

and an immense task is opened up—to tell what drove
a maddened people to war, to tell what cast out peace from the world.
It was the envious chain of destiny, impossibility of the very high   70
standing long, huge collapses under too much weight,
Rome's inability to bear herself. So, when the final hour
brings to an end the long ages of the universe, its structure dissolved,
reverting to primeval chaos, then fiery stars will plunge
into the sea, the earth will be unwilling to stretch flat her shores
and will shake the water off, Phoebe will confront
her brother and for herself demand the day, resentful
of driving her chariot along its slanting orbit, and the whole
discordant mechanism of universe torn apart will disrupt its own laws.   80
Mighty structures collapse on to themselves: for prosperity the powers
have set this limit to growth. And not to any outside race
does Fortune lend her spite against a people powerful
by land and sea. You were the cause of ruin,
Rome, made common property of masters three, and tyranny's
ill-omened pact, never shared among a crowd.
O you men, so evilly in unison and blinded by excessive desire,
why do you choose to combine your forces and rule the world
in common? As long as earth supports the sea
and air the earth, as long as Titan revolves in his lengthy toils   90
and in the sky night follows day through all the constellations,
there will be no loyalty between associates in tyranny
and no power will tolerate a partner. Do not rely
on any foreign races or seek examples of destiny afar:
Rome's first walls were drenched with a brother's blood;
nor were land and sea the prize of such great madness
then: the small Asylum set at variance its masters.

    For a narrow time discordant concord remained
and there was peace, though not by the leaders' wish: the only check
to future war was Crassus in between. Just as the slender   100
Isthmus, which cuts the waves and separates twin seas
and stops the waters meeting, if its land receded,
would smash Ionian Sea against Aegean: such was Crassus—
he kept apart the leaders' savage weapons. But when in lamentable
death he stained Assyrian Carrhae with Latian blood,
the Parthian disaster unleashed Roman madness.
More by that battle you achieved than you suppose,
sons of Arsaces: to the conquered you gave civil war.

Power was divided by the sword, and a mighty people's
prosperity, holding land and sea, the entire world,   110
was not big enough for two. For Julia, cut off
by the cruel hand of the Parcae, took to the shades below
the bond of joined blood, the wedding-torches
doomed by grim omen. But if destiny had granted you
a longer stay in the light, alone you could have
here restrained your frenzied husband, here your frenzied father,
thrown away their swords and joined their armed hands,
as Sabine women in between joined fathers—with their sons-in-law.
By your death the alliance was shattered and the leaders felt free
to commence the war.

                    Rivalry in excellence spurs them on.   120
That fresh exploits will overshadow former triumphs
and victory over pirates give place to Gallic conquests,
this, Magnus, is your fear; Caesar, you are roused by your long chain
of tasks, experience of toil and your fortune not enduring second place;
Caesar cannot now bear anyone ahead
nor Pompey any equal. Who more justly took up weapons
is forbidden knowledge; each has on his side a great authority:
the conquering cause the gods, the conquered Cato.
   They met not equally matched. One with years declining
towards old age and grown milder through long experience of civil
     life   130
had now in peace unlearnt the general's part, and, seeking fame,
was generous to the crowd, wholly driven by the popular
winds, rejoicing in applause in the theatre he had built,
and without restoring his strength afresh, he relied chiefly
on his former fortune. He stands, the shadow of a great name;
like in a fruitful field a lofty oak,
bearing the people's spoils of old and generals'
hallowed dedications; clinging with roots no longer strong,
by its own weight it stands firm, and spreading naked branches
through the air, it makes shade with trunk, not foliage;   140
and though it totters, ready to fall beneath the first Eurus,
though all around so many trees upraise themselves with sturdy trunks,
yet it alone is venerated. Contrast Caesar: he had not only
a general's name and reputation, but never-resting
energy; his only shame was conquering without war;

fierce, indomitable, wherever hope and indignation called
he moved to action, never shrank from defiling his sword,
he followed up his own successes, pressed hard upon the deity's
favour, driving back all obstacles to his high
ambitions and rejoicing to create his path by destruction.   150
Just so flashes out the thunderbolt shot forth by the winds through
    clouds,
accompanied by the crashing of the heavens and sound of shattered
    ether;
it splits the sky and terrifies the panicked
people, searing eyes with slanting flame;
against its own precincts it rages, and, with nothing solid stopping
its course, both as it falls and then returns great is the devastation
dealt far and wide before it gathers again its scattered fires.

These were the leaders' motives; but in the state there also lay
the seeds of war, which always have engulfed powerful peoples.
For when Rome had subdued the world and Fortune introduced   160
excessive wealth, when morals gave way before prosperity,
when booty and the plunder from the enemy urged luxurious life,
then there was no limit to gold and houses, and hunger spurned
the tables of former times; clothes hardly decent
for young wives to wear were seized upon by men; warrior-bearing
poverty they shun, and from all the world import
the bane of every nation; next their fields' boundaries
they prolonged and joined, and under unknown tenant-farmers
they stretched out far the lands once ploughed by the hard share
of Camillus and worked by ancient spades of the Curii.   170
This people could not take pleasure in tranquil peace
or be satisfied by liberty with weapons untouched.
That was the cause of passions quickly roused, of crime despicable
urged by want; it was an honour great and to be sought by sword,
to have more power than the state; the yardstick of legality was
violence—hence the forcing through of laws and rulings of the plebs;
tribunes, consuls all alike disrupting justice;
hence the Rods of office seized by bribery, the people
selling its own votes, corruption bringing death to Rome,
repeating annual contests on the mercenary Campus;   180
hence ravenous money-lending, interest greedy for its appointed time,
and credit shaken and war advantageous to many.

Now swiftly Caesar had surmounted the icy Alps
and in his mind conceived immense upheavals,
coming war. When he reached the water of the little Rubicon,
clearly to the leader through the murky night appeared
a mighty image of his country in distress, grief in her face,
her white hair streaming from her tower-crowned head;
with tresses torn and shoulders bare she stood before him
and sighing said: 'Where further do you march?   190
Where do you take my standards, warriors? If lawfully you come,
if as citizens, this far only is allowed.' Then trembling struck
the leader's limbs, his hair grew stiff, and weakness checked
his progress, holding his feet at the river's edge.
At last he speaks: 'O Thunderer, surveying great Rome's
walls from the Tarpeian Rock; O Phrygian house-gods of Iulus' clan
and mysteries of Quirinus, who was carried off to heaven;
O Jupiter of Latium, seated in lofty Alba,
and hearths of Vesta; O Rome, the equal of the highest
deity, favour my plans. Not with impious weapons   200
do I pursue you—here am I, Caesar, conqueror by land and sea,
your own soldier everywhere, now too if I am permitted.
The man who makes me your enemy, it is he will be the guilty one.'
Then he broke the barriers of war and through the swollen river
quickly took his standards. Just so in torrid Libya's
barren fields the lion, on seeing his enemy at hand,
crouches in hesitation till he has concentrated all his anger;
next he goads himself with fiercely lashing tail,
his mane is bristling, from his massive jaws
deep he roars—then if a lance, hurled by a swift Moor,   210
or hunting-spears pierce and stick in his broad chest, ignoring
such a terrible wound he rushes onward, driving the weapon deeper.

 The ruddy Rubicon flows forth from a tiny spring
and in summer's burning heat moves with meagre waters;
through the valley's depths it snakes and separates the Gallic
fields from the farmers of Ausonia, a fixed boundary.
But at that time winter was strengthening it, its waters had been
      swollen
by rainy Cynthia with laden crescent for three nights running
and by the Alpine snows melted in the moist blasts of Eurus.
First the cavalry is drawn up aslant the stream   220
to take the waters' force, then the remaining throng passes through

the unresisting waters of the river broken now—an easy ford.
When Caesar had crossed the flood and reached the opposite
bank, on Hesperia's forbidden fields he took his stand
and said: 'Here I abandon peace and desecrated law;
Fortune, it is you I follow. Farewell to treaties from now on;
I have relied on them for long enough; now war must be our referee.'

With these words, the leader pushed his army through night's darkness
tirelessly, swifter than the whirled thong of Balearic sling
or the Parthian's arrow shot over his shoulder: 230
with menace he invaded Ariminum when the stars
were fleeing the fires of the sun and only Lucifer was left.
And now arose the day which would witness war's first
turmoil, but clouds confined the mournful light,
perhaps by wish of the gods, perhaps driven by the stormy Auster.
In the captured forum the soldiers halted at the order
to set down the standards, and strident clarion
and shrill trumpet with raucous bugle sounded the impious alarm.
The people's rest was broken, and summoned from their beds
the menfolk tore down weapons hanging by the holy house-gods   240
—such as they are after lengthy peace: the shields they grab
are rotting now with frame exposed, the javelins' points
are crooked and the swords are rough with bite of dark rust.
When they recognized the gleam of Roman eagles, Roman standards
and caught a sight of Caesar towering among his troops,
they stiffened in fear, their icy limbs were seized by terror,
and in their breasts they silently turned over unuttered complaints:
'O how unlucky are these city-walls, established next to Gauls,
doomed by bitter position! Throughout all peoples
deep peace reigns, tranquillity, but we are madmen's victims,   250
their first halt. Fortune, better you had granted us
a home beneath the eastern sky or icy Arctos
or wandering abodes than to guard the gate of Latium.
We were the first to witness movements of Senones, the Cimbrian
attack, the Libyan war-god, and the charge of frenzied
Teuton: whenever Fortune challenges Rome,
this is the path of war.' Thus each with stifled sigh,
not daring to expose his fear; no utterance was entrusted
to their grief, but deep the silence—so when winter checks
the birds, the fields are hushed, and so mid-sea is mute,   260

unmurmuring.

     Day had dissipated night's chill shadows
and now the Fates put to his undecided mind the torch of war
and goads which urge to battle, so breaking
all the barriers of restraint; Fortune works to justify
the leader's moves and finds pretexts for fighting.
The Senate-house had threatened and expelled the turbulent tribunes
from a Rome divided, violating their rights and bragging of the
   Gracchi's doom.
As they headed for their leader's standards, now brought close to Rome,
with them came the reckless Curio and his mercenary tongue
—once the people's voice, he dared to champion   270
liberty, to level with the people armed grandees.
And when he noticed Caesar turning in his breast conflicting
worries, he says: 'While with my voice I could assist
your party, Caesar—when I had the right to hold
the Rostrum and bring over wavering citizens to your side,
I extended your command, against the Senate's wish.
But now that laws are silent under war's constraint,
we are driven from our ancestral homes and suffer exile,
willingly—your victory will make us citizens again.
While the other side in panic has not fortified its strength, 280
end delay! Procrastination always harms the men prepared for action. 281
For twice five years Gaul kept you fighting   283
—such a tiny part of the world! If you wage a few battles
with favourable outcome, yours will be the world subdued by Rome.
But as it is, when you return, no long triumphal march awaits you,
the consecrated laurel crown is not required by the Capitol:
devouring spite denies you everything, and for subduing foreign races
you will scarcely escape punishment. To thrust from power his
   father-in-law
is the son-in-law's decision; share the world with him you cannot, 290
rule alone you can.' By these words he much inflamed
his general and increased his indignation, though Caesar anyway
was keen for war—as much as the Elean race-horse
is aroused by the shouting, and though enclosed in starting-gate
he already reaches for the door and pressing forward loosens the bars.

Immediately he summons his armed companies to the standards

and, once the agitated uproar of assembling throng was quelled
sufficiently by his look and silence ordered by his hand, he said:
   'O comrades in battle, veterans with me of warfare's
thousand perils, for ten years now victorious,   300
is this your prize for blood poured out in northern fields
and wounds and death and winters spent beneath the Alps?
By warfare's vast commotion Rome is shaken
just as though the Carthaginian were crossing the Alps,
Hannibal: the cohorts are filled to strength with recruits,
every wood is felled for the fleet, the order has gone out:
"By land and sea go after Caesar." What would they do if my standards
lay subdued in defeat and the fierce Gallic peoples
were charging at our backs? It is now I am assailed, now
when Fortune grants prosperity to me and gods are summoning me   310
to the heights. Let them come to war—their leader, weakened
by long peace, with makeshift troops, his civilian partisans,
verbose Marcellus and those empty names, the Catos.
I ask you—shall Pompey's lowest minions, bought,
bestow on him his fill of power unbroken through so many years?
Shall Pompey guide triumphal chariots although his age does not
    allow it?
Shall Pompey never yield the privileges he once usurped?
Why need I now bemoan his limitation of grain through all the world
and famine made his slave? Who does not know how soldiers
infiltrated the trembling Forum, when the dreadful glitter of swords   320
ringed the frightened court, not the usual audience,
when soldiers dared break through the rule of law,
when Pompey's standards hemmed in Milo the accused?
Now too, afraid that obscure old age will confine him in his weariness,
impious battles he plans, accustomed to civil war,
—Sulla's pupil, he surpasses his instructor in crime.
And as the wild tigers in the Hyrcanian forest
traversing their mothers' haunts, fed deep on blood
of cattle slain, never cease from slaughter,
so too, Magnus, grown accustomed to licking Sulla's sword,   330
your thirst endures. Blood, once tasted,
never lets the defiled throat return to gentle ways.
What end will such long tyranny yet find?
What limit is there to his crimes? Presumptuous man, now let
your Sulla at least teach you to step down from this reign.

After wandering Cilicians and Pontic battles with the war-worn
king with difficulty finished off by barbaric poison,
shall Caesar be the ultimate task of Pompey,
because I did not obey his order to lay down
my victorious eagles? If I am robbed of my reward for toil,   340
then let my men at least be granted recompense of lengthy warfare,
    without
their leader; under whatever general let these troops have their
    triumph.
And after war what refuge will they have in feeble age?
What home for their retirement? What fields will be given
for my veterans to plough? What city-walls for men worn out?
Or will your pirates, Magnus, make better farmers?
Men, raise your standards long victorious, raise them;
the strength we have created we must now deploy. The person
    who denies
the warrior his due surrenders everything. Nor will the gods
    abandon us,
since with my weapons I seek neither plunder nor power: 350
we are ridding of its masters a Rome prepared for slavery.'

He ceased; but the wavering mass with inarticulate murmur
mutters indistinctly. Their swelling minds and spirits
made fierce in slaughter are crushed by love of country and ancestral
gods, but they are recalled by their hideous love of the sword
and by their terror of their leader. Then Laelius—he held the post
of first centurion and wore the decoration of the merited prize,
the oak-leaves which declare the reward for a Roman life preserved—
exclaimed: 'Greatest helmsman of the Roman race,
if I may and if it is right to utter words of truth,   360
our complaint is that your forbearance so prolonged has checked
your strength. Was it confidence in us you lacked?
Will you endure dishonourable peace and the Senate's tyranny,
while still these bodies breathe and move with hot blood
and arms are sturdy still to hurl the javelin?
Is victory in civil war so very terrible?
Come, lead us through the Scythian peoples, through Syrtis'
inhospitable shores, through parched Libya's burning sands:
to leave a conquered world behind as it marched on, this army
subdued with oar the Ocean's swollen waves   370

and curbed the northern whirlpools of the foaming Rhine:
to carry out your orders the necessary power and will I have.
For no fellow-citizen of mine is the man against whom your trumpets,
Caesar, sound. By your standards prosperous in ten campaigns,
by your triumphs over all your enemies, I swear
that, if you bid me plunge my sword in brother's breast
or parent's throat or womb of wife great
with child, I will do it all, though with unwilling hand;
that if you bid me rob the gods and fire their temples,
the flame of our military mint will melt the deities down;　　　380
that if you bid me pitch my camp by the waters of Etruscan Tiber,
boldly will I enter the fields of Hesperia to mark the lines;
that if you want any walls levelled to the ground,
these arms of mine will drive the ram to scatter stones,
even though the city whose annihilation you command
be Rome.' With these words all the cohorts agreed together,
and they pledged their hands, lifted high, to fight wherever
he summoned them. Their mighty shout travels to the ether,
as loud as the noise of forest bowed down with its trunks bent low
or springing back towards the sky, when Thracian　　　390
Boreas pounces on the pine-clad rocks of Ossa.

When Caesar sees his soldiers welcome war so eagerly
and destiny proceeding onward, to avoid impeding Fortune
by any apathy, he summons cohorts scattered through the Gallic fields
and advancing standards from every region he heads for Rome.
His men abandoned tents which they had pitched by deep Leman
and encampments high above Vosegus' curving rock
controlling the aggressive Lingones with their painted weapons.
Others left Isara's fords, a river that through many shallows
runs with his own stream and flows into a river of greater fame　　　400
and does not convey his own name to the waters of the sea.
The blond Ruteni are released from lengthy occupation;
placid Atax rejoices that he does not carry Latian ships;
likewise Varus, now Hesperia's boundary, the frontier advanced,
and the harbour sacred under the name of Hercules
which with its hollowed cliff encroaches on the sea: over it
neither Corus has control nor Zephyr; its master, Circius, alone
disturbs its shores and bars the ships from Monoecus' safe anchorage;
the stretch of changing shore rejoices too,

claimed by land and sea alternately when the mighty Ocean   410
floods in or with receding waves withdraws.
Does the wind from furthest zone thus forward roll the sea
and while bearing it abandon it? Or are restless Tethys' waters
set in motion by the lesser star and do they ebb and flow with
          lunar hours?
Or does flaming Titan lift the Ocean and draw his billows
towards the stars, to drink the waves which feed him?
Inquire, you students of the workings of the universe; but for me,
stay for ever hidden, as the gods have wished, whatever you are
that causes movements so regular. Then the troops who hold the
          fields
of the Nemetes and banks of the Atyrus, where with curving shore   420
the Tarbelli enclose the sea as it approaches gently,
shift their standards, and at the enemy's withdrawal the Santoni,
Bituriges, and Suessones nimble with their lengthy weapons rejoice;
the Leuci and the Remi who excel in throwing,
the Sequani who excel in wheeling horses with the rein;
the Belgae, skilled drivers of the chariot with scythes;
the Arverni venturing to claim brotherhood with Rome
as a people come from Trojan blood; the Nervii, excessively
rebellious, polluted by the treachery of Cotta's murder;
the Vangiones copying your loose-worn breeches,   430
Sarmatians; the fierce Batavi, incited by the shriek of war-trumpets
of curving bronze. They too rejoice where Cirta's stream
wanders, where the Rhône with rapid waters sweeps
the Arar to the sea, where high on mountain-peaks
there lives a nation on Cebennae's snowy and precipitous crag.   435
Transferral of the warfare pleased you too, Treviri,   441
and you, Ligures, now shorn of hair but once in all of Long-Haired
Gaul unrivalled for your tresses flowing gracefully over your necks;
and the people who with grim blood-offering placate
Teutates the merciless and Esus dread with savage altars
and the slab of Taranis, no kinder than Diana of the Scythians.
The Bards too—you poets who with praise send forth
into eternity the valiant spirits cut off in war—
then free from worry you poured out a multitude of songs.
And Druids, you laid down your weapons and returned   450
to your barbaric rites and weird manner of ceremonial.
To you alone is granted total knowledge of the gods and heaven's

powers—or total ignorance. Inhabiting deep groves
in remote woods, you teach that ghosts do not head
for Erebus' silent home or for the colourless realm
of Dis below, but that the self-same spirit rules the limbs
in another sphere. If what you sing is known for fact, then death
is the mid-point in prolonged life. Without a doubt the people
    overlooked
by Arctos are fortunate in their mistake, not to be oppressed
by that greatest terror, fear of death. This explains their warriors'   460
willingness to rush upon the sword, their spirits keen for death,
and their belief that it is cowardly to spare a life which will return.
And you, the soldiers posted to keep the curly-haired Cauci
from war, you head for Rome, leaving the savage
banks of Rhine, leaving the world exposed to foreign nations.

Caesar's massive forces with their gathered might
made him confident to venture higher: he extends
through all of Italy; he occupies the nearest towns.
And empty rumour, speedy messenger of quickening
war, augmented genuine fears; it invaded   470
people's minds with pictures of calamity to come
and unlocked countless tongues to utter false assertions.
One man there is who tells that brazen squadrons
charge to combat where Mevania spreads into the plains
which breed the bulls, that brutal Caesar's barbaric troops
are ranging where the Nar flows into Tiber River;
that he advances all his eagles and his standards in a mass
and marches on with many a column and dense-packed camp.
They picture him not as they remember him: in their thoughts
he seems greater, wilder, more pitiless from the conquest of the
    enemy.   480
Then follow close behind, they say, the peoples
from between the Rhine and Elbe, uprooted from ancestral home
in northern lands; fierce foreign races are ordered to sack Rome—
with a Roman looking on. So by his panic each
gives strength to rumour, and they fear ungrounded evils
of their own invention.

                   The multitude is not alone in panicking,
struck by empty terror, but the Senate, too, yes even

the Fathers leapt up from their seats, and as they flee assign
to the consuls the dreaded declaration of war.
Then, uncertain where to go for safety, where to run from danger,   490
wherever impulse of flight sweeps them on, they drive
the people rushing headlong, breaking out in hordes who stick
       together
in a long chain. You might suppose that impious fire-brands
had ignited houses, that homes were swaying, tottering,
shaken by imminent collapse: so the throng rushed
through the city heedlessly, frantic with headlong pace,
as if the sole salvation for their battered fortunes
were to leave the ancestral walls. When stormy Auster
has driven back the mighty sea from Libyan Syrtes
and when the broken weight of the mast has crashed down with its
       sails,   500
the captain and the crew abandon ship and leap
into the waves, and each, before the vessel's frame is smashed,
creates his own shipwreck—just so, they abandon Rome and
flee towards war. Now none could be detained
by his father weak with age, nor a husband by his wife's
laments, nor by ancestral Gods for long enough to utter prayers
for preservation so uncertain; none lingered on the threshold
and then left, after looking his fill maybe for the last time
on beloved Rome: the multitude raced on, unstoppable.
       O gods, you are so ready to bestow supremacy, but to preserve it   510
so reluctant! Rome, a city teeming with peoples and with conquered
nations, large enough (should the masses gather)
for all of humankind, was abandoned at Caesar's coming
by cowardly throngs, easy prey. In furthest lands
the Roman soldier, when hemmed in hard by his enemy,
escapes the dangers of the night with a flimsy stockade;
a turf-made rampart torn up quickly for defence
gives him untroubled sleep inside his tent:
but, Rome, as soon as the word 'war' is heard,
you are deserted, your walls not trusted for a single night.   520
Yet such great panic we must pardon, we must pardon:
they fear since Pompey flees.

                                  Then preventing any hope
even for the future lifting up their frightened minds, came

proof manifest of fate still worse to come, and menacing gods
filled earth and sky and sea with prodigies.
Dark nights witnessed unfamiliar stars,
the sky ablaze with flames, meteors flying aslant
through heaven's empty space, the tail of fear-inspiring
star, the comet, herald of a shift in power on earth.
Lightning flashed repeatedly in the deceptive cloudless sky,   530
its fire presenting different shapes in the dense air,
now, with lengthened light, a spear, now, with light spread out, a
    torch.
A silent thunderbolt flashed out in the cloudless
heaven and, gathering fire from northern parts,
it struck the head of Latium. Lesser stars which usually
proceed on course through the empty hours of the night
appeared at noon. Phoebe, her crescent full
and now with all her orb reflecting her brother Sun,
was struck by the sudden shadow of the earth, and dimmed.
Titan himself, while lifting up his head in mid-Olympus,   540
hid his blazing chariot in a black cloud,
enveloping his sphere in darkness, making mortals
despair of day: just such a night came on
at Mycenae of Thyestes when the sun fled eastwards.
Fierce Mulciber unclosed Sicilian Etna's mouths
—not skywards shot the fire's flames but eddying sideways
they fell on to Hesperia's flank. Black Charybdis
wrenched from the depths a blood-red sea and the savage dogs
howled dolefully. From Vesta's altar fire was stolen.
The flame which marks the Latin Festival's completion   550
is split in two and rises with twin tongues,
resembling the Theban funeral-pyre. Then the earth sank
down its pivot, shaking ancient snows from
swaying Alpine ridges; with waves increased,
Tethys covered western Calpe and Atlas' heights.
They say the Native Gods shed tears, the hearth-gods
by their sweat confirmed Rome's hardship, offerings
tumbled in their temples, ill-omened birds
darkened the day, and wild beasts boldly left their woods
at night's approach and made their dens in the midst of Rome.   560
Then tongues of animals took readily to human sounds,

and people's offspring were unnatural in shape of limbs
and number—the mother was terrified by her own baby—
grim verses of Cumae's prophetess are spread abroad
among the people. Then those inspired by fierce Bellona
slash their arms and chant the gods' intent; the Galli whirl
their bloodied locks and howl dread omens to the people.
Urns full of bones laid to rest emitted groans.
Then through pathless forests was heard the crash of weapons,
loud cries, and the clash of ghosts in battle.   570
And inhabitants of fields near the outmost city-walls
disperse in flight: a huge Erinys was circling Rome,
shaking hissing locks and a pine-tree with its blazing
top turned downwards—like the Eumenis who drove
Agave of Thebes and hurled the weapons
of fierce Lycurgus; like Megaera, who on resentful Juno's order
caused Alcides to shudder, though he already had seen Dis.
Trumpets of war resounded; black night gave a shout
as loud as cohorts clashing, though the breeze
was still. From the Campus the shade of Sulla   580
was seen to rise and uttered dreadful oracles,
and the farmers fled as Marius burst his tomb
and raised his head by Anio's chill waters.

Hence their decision in accord with ancient custom,
to send for prophets from Etruria. Of these, the eldest,
Arruns, lived in empty Luca's city-walls,
expert in the movement of the thunderbolt, in the warm pulse
of entrails, and in warning of the wing which flits in air.
First he orders the destruction of the freaks produced
by riotous nature from no seed, incineration in accursed   590
flames of the abominable progeny of barren womb.
Next he orders a procession of the frightened citizens
all round Rome: the chief priests, who are permitted to perform
the rite, purify the city-walls with solemn ceremony,
and move around the furthest limit of Rome's long Pomerium.
Behind them comes the lesser throng, clothes hitched up in Gabine
        manner,
and the priestess wearing chaplets leads the Vestal band
—she alone may rightly look on Troy's Minerva.
Next come the keepers of the gods' decrees and mystic verses,

the priests who reinstate Cybele when she has bathed in little Almo,   600
the augur skilled at spotting lucky birds,
the Seven festive at the banquets, the Titian brethren,
and the Salians rejoicing to bear the sacred shields on their shoulders
and the Flamens who raise aloft the pointed cap on noble head.
And while with long and wheeling path they circle Rome's
great spread, Arruns collects the scattered fires
of the thunderbolt, with gloomy mutter buries them in the earth,
and declares them holy places. Then he guides towards the sacred
    altars
the bull with chosen neck, had now begun to pour
Bacchus and sprinkle with the slanting knife the salted grains.   610
The victim long resisted the ritual displeasing to the gods,
and only when the belted attendants pushed down its fierce horns
did it sink upon its knee and offer its defeated neck.
And no blood as usual spurted out, but black slime
instead of red gore spread from the gaping wound.
Arruns blanched, appalled by the ill-omened rites,
and seized the entrails to seek the cause of divine wrath.
Their very colour terrifies the prophet; the pale guts
were tinged with foul blotches, darkened with congealed gore,
and chequered with grey stains and bloodspots.   620
He sees the liver dripping with decay and, in its hostile half,
defiant veins. The lobe of gasping lung
lies still and a crooked line divides the organs.
The heart is invisible, through yawning cracks the guts exude
corrupted blood and the caul betrays its hidden things.
And look, he sees a portent which never occurs in entrails
unthreateningly. On the liver's head there grows the lump
of a second head: one part droops, weak and flabby,
the other throbs, and boisterously it moves the pulse with rapid beat.
When from these signs he understood the prophecy of great disaster,   630
he exclaims: 'It is hardly right for me, gods, to reveal to the peoples
all the turmoil which you plan; and, greatest Jupiter, I have not
    appeased
you with this offering, but infernal gods have come into
the slain bull's breast. Unutterable are the things we fear, but soon
our fears will be exceeded. May the gods make these sights prosperous,
or may the entrails prove unreliable, a mere invention of Tages,
founder of the art.' So the Etruscan prophesied, and wrapped

and veiled the omens in obscure ambiguity.

Then spoke Figulus, keen student of the gods
and secrets of the sky, unequalled by Egyptian Memphis   640
in stellar observation and in calculations following the stars:
    'It may be that this universe for ever drifts
ungoverned and the stars range at random.
But if the Fates are in control, imminent destruction is planned
for Rome and humankind. Will the earth yawn wide
and cities downwards sink? Or will the scorching air destroy
the mild climate? Will faithless soil withhold the crops?
Or will all water be infected by streams of poison?
What kind of disaster do you plan, O gods? With what instrument
of doom for your cruelty? At a single time the final days   650
of many have converged. If at the height of heaven Saturn's
cold and harmful star were lighting his black fires,
then Aquarius would have poured down rains rivalling Deucalion's
and all the earth would lie hidden beneath the flood's wide spread.
If with your rays you, Phoebus, now were overwhelming
the fierce Nemean Lion, then through all the world
would conflagration flow and ether blaze, ignited by your chariot.
Such fires are nowhere to be found. But what are your dread plans,
Gradivus, as you set fire to Scorpio, so menacing with blazing tail,
and scorch his claws? For kindly Jupiter is sunk   660
deep in the west and Venus' beneficial
star is dim and swift Cyllenius is retarded on his course
and Mars is sole lord of the sky. Why have the constellations left
their paths to move obscurely through the universe?
And why does sword-girt Orion's side so intensely shine?
Because war's frenzy is upon us: the power of the sword
shall overthrow legality by might, and impious crime
shall bear the name of heroism, and this madness shall extend
for many a year. And what use is it to ask the gods to end it?
The peace we long for brings a master. Rome, prolong your chain   670
of disaster without a break and protract calamity
for lengthy ages: only now in civil war are you free.'

These portents greatly terrified the people into panic,
but they are overwhelmed by worse. As the Bacchante races down
from Pindus' summit, filled with Lyaeus of Ogygia,

so a matron sweeps through stunned Rome, revealing
with these words that Phoebus is harrying her breast:
　'O Paean, where are you taking me? You whisk me over the ether;
where do you set me down? I see Pangaea white
with snow-clad ridges and broad Philippi under Haemus' crag.　　680
What madness this, O Phoebus, tell: why do Roman battle-lines
contend with hands and weapons? Why war without an enemy?
Where else now are you taking me? You lead me eastwards,
where sea is dyed by Egyptian Nile's flood:
him I recognize, lying on the river sands,
an unsightly headless corpse. I am taken over seas to shifting
Syrtes and to parched Libya: this is where grim Enyo
has shifted Emathia's battle-lines. Now I am hurried
over mountains of the cloud-capped Alps and soaring
Pyrenees. Back I come to the abodes of my native Rome,　　690
to impious war waged in the Senate's midst.
The factions rise again, again I travel through
all the world. Let me gaze on different sea-shores,
different land: already have I seen Philippi, Phoebus.'
So she spoke and then collapsed, abandoned by exhausted frenzy.

BOOK TWO

And now the anger of the gods was patent, the universe
gave open signs of war, foreknowing nature
overturned her laws and bonds with turmoil full of portents
and proclaimed civil war. Ruler of Olympus, why did you
decide to impose this anxiety on troubled mortals—
to learn of coming calamity by hideous omens?
Perhaps when the Creator first took up his shapeless realm
of raw matter after the conflagration had died down,
he fixed causes for eternity, binding himself too by his
all-controlling law, and with the immovable boundary of destiny   10
arranged the universe to introduce prescribed ages.
Or perhaps nothing is ordained, but Chance at random wanders
bringing change after change, and accident is master of mortal affairs.
Whatever you intend, let it be sudden; let men's minds
be blind to future disaster; let the fearful have hope!

So realization that the world would pay with great calamities
for the gods' truthfulness put a dismal end to business
throughout Rome; every magistrate lay low, clad in
ordinary dress, no purple robe accompanying the Rods of office.
Then their complaining they suppressed, and deep and voiceless   20
grief pervaded all. Just so at the moment of death
the stunned house falls silent—not yet is the body
laid out and bewailed, not yet does the mother with loosened hair
impel the slave-girls' arms to savage breast-beating—
the moment when she hugs limbs stiffening as life flees,
the inanimate features, eyes swimming in death.
Fear is past and grief not yet arrived: distraught, she bends over him,
stunned by her loss. Their former finery the Roman matrons
laid aside and in grieving bands they fill the temples:
some sprinkled the gods with tears, some hurled themselves   30
breast-first on to the hard floor, on the sacred threshold, stunned,
they loosed and tore their locks, and with their constant howling
struck ears more used to hearing prayerful invocation.

And they lay in supplication, not all in temple of the Thunderer
    supreme:
they divided up the gods so that every altar had a mother
who would bring reproach. One of them spoke, with torn
and dripping cheeks, her arms black and blue from her blows:
   'Now bruise your breasts, O miserable mothers,
now tear your locks; do not defer your grief
or save it for the last disaster. Now, while the leaders' destiny   40
is undecided, you may weep; once one of them has conquered,
you must rejoice.' With these goads grief provokes itself.
The men, too, as they head for war and the opposing camps,
pour out just complaints against the cruel deities:
   'O how unfortunate that we were not born in the time
of the Punic war, to fight at Cannae and at Trebia!
It is not peace we ask for, gods: inspire with rage the foreign nations,
now rouse the fierce cities; let the world league together
for war: let lines of Medes swoop down from Achaemenid
Susa, let Scythian Danube not confine the Massagetae,   50
let the Elbe and Rhine's unconquered head let loose
from furthest north the blond Suebi; make us again
the enemies of all the peoples, only ward off civil war.
From here let the Dacian strike, from there the Getan; let one
    leader face
Iberians, the other turn his standards to confront the eastern quivers;
let no hand of yours, Rome, be swordless. Or if it is your decision,
gods, to devastate the Hesperian name, then let the mighty ether
gather into fires and fall to earth in thunderbolts.
Cruel creator, strike both parties and both leaders together,
while they are still innocent. Must they contest   60
the rule of Rome with this great crop of crimes unprecedented?
It was hardly worth the cost of waging civil war
to stop them both.' Such the complaints expressed by patriotism,
soon to perish. But miserable parents are tormented by a special
    sorrow:
they detest their long-enduring lot of oppressive age,
their years preserved for civil war a second time.
And one spoke, seeking a precedent for his mighty fear:
   'The commotions caused by Fate were just the same
when Marius, victorious after his Teutonic and his Libyan
triumphs, in exile, hid his head in muddy sedge.   70

Lagoons of greedy earth and spongy swamps concealed
your treasure, Fortune; then the old man was corroded
by iron chains and lengthy squalor in a prison.
Destined to die in happiness as consul in the Rome he ruined,
first he paid the penalty for his crimes. Often death itself
ran from the warrior: uselessly power to take his hated blood
was granted to an enemy who in the first act of slaughter
stiffened and let fall his sword from paralysed hand.
In the dark prison he had seen an enormous light,
the frightening gods of crime and Marius of the future;   80
in terror he had heard: "It is not right for you to touch
this neck; to the laws of time this man owes many deaths
before his own; drop your useless frenzy."
If you wish to take revenge for the extermination of your people,
Cimbrians, preserve this old man. Not by favour of a deity
is he protected, but by the gods' huge wrath
—a warrior fierce, enough for destiny's desire
to destroy Rome. That very man was carried by a stormy sea
to enemy land and driven through the plundered kingdom
of Jugurtha, whom he had paraded in a triumph, and lay down   90
in deserted huts and trod on Punic ashes. Marius and Carthage
had consolation for their fate: both equally prostrate,
they forgave the gods. Here he gathered his Libyan wrath.
As soon as Fortune returned, he set free bands
of slaves and in gangs they wielded their hands fierce-armed
with iron melted down. To bear the leader's standards
was granted only to those experienced in crime, who brought
their guilt to camp. In the name of Fate! What a day,
what a day that was when Marius in victory seized
the city-walls! How huge the strides of savage, racing death!   100
Noble and plebeian together died, and the sword ranged
far and wide, with blade called back from no one's breast.
Deep stands the gore in the temples: the stones are slippery,
drenched and reddened by much slaughter. Age was no protection:
there was no remorse in anticipating the old man's final day
in his declining years nor in breaking the rising fate
of helpless babe on life's first threshold.
For what crime could these little ones deserve to die?
But now it is sufficient to be able to die. The very impetus of frenzy
carries them away: it seems a mark of sloth to seek a guilty victim.   110

Many die to round the number up; the blood-stained victor
grabs a head cut off from neck unknown, ashamed
of empty hands. The only hope of preservation
was to kiss with trembling lips his polluted hand.
How degenerate a people: though a thousand swords obey
these novel signals of death, hardly is it decent for warriors
to gain long centuries like this, let alone life's brief disgrace
of time till Sulla returns. Who has the leisure to lament
the deaths of a multitude?—hardly you, Baebius: you disappeared,
torn to guts between the countless hands of the encircling mob   120
ripping your limbs; hardly you, Antonius,
foreknowing troubles: your head the soldier carried,
hanging, by its torn white hair and placed it dripping
on the festive table. The decapitated Crassi were by Fimbria
    mutilated;
the cruel prison oak-post was sodden with a tribune's blood.
You, too, Scaevola, they sacrificed, unheeded, before
the very inner shrine and ever-burning hearths
of desecrated Vesta: your weary old age poured from your throat
a trickle of blood and allowed the flames to live.
After this the seventh year restored the Rods of office.   130
That for Marius was life's end: all of worse Fortune's works
he had suffered, all of better Fortune's works
enjoyed, and measured the extremes of human destiny.
How many corpses now fell at Sacriportus?
How many squadrons overthrown did the Colline Gate endure,
on that day when the capital and power of the world
was nearly changed to another place, when the Samnites hoped
to inflict wounds on Rome exceeding the Caudine Forks.
Sulla too increased the countless slaughter as avenger.
What little blood remained to Rome he drained;   140
and while he cut back limbs now grown too rotten,
his remedy exceeded limit and his hand pursued
too far where disease led it. The guilty died,
but at a time when the only survivors must be guilty.
Then freedom was granted to vendettas and anger raced away,
    released
from the bridle of the laws. Not to one man was everything
    attributed,
but each committed crime for himself: the victor, by his single order,

had endorsed everything. Through his master's guts the slave drove
sword unspeakable; sons were drenched with father's
blood, competed for possession of the parent's   150
severed head; brothers fell as brothers' prizes.
Tombs were full of fugitives and living bodies mingled
with the buried, and wild beast's lairs could not contain the people.
One man broke his windpipe with a noose and choked his throat,
another headlong hurled himself and split apart
when he smashed on hard ground, and so deprived the blood-stained
victor of their deaths; another personally piles up
the wood of his own funeral-pyre and leaps into the flames
before all his blood has poured away and takes the fires while he can.
Leaders' heads are carried on javelins through terrified Rome   160
and heaped up in the middle of the Forum: there is seen whatever
anywhere lies low in death. Such quantity of crime was not
by Thrace witnessed hanging in the Bistonian tyrant's stables
nor by Libya on Antaeus' doorposts, nor did Greece in mourning
weep for so many mangled limbs in Pisa's palace.
Already the corpses, melting with decay and blurred with time's
long passage, have lost their features; only now do miserable parents
gather and steal in fearful theft the parts they recognize.
I recall how I myself, keen to place my slain brother's
disfigured face on the pyre's forbidden flames,   170
examined all the corpses of Sulla's peace
and searched through all the headless bodies for a neck
to match the severed head. Why tell of the ghost
of Catulus appeased with blood?—when as victim Marius,
with the shades perhaps not liking the bitter offerings,
made a sacrifice unspeakable to a tomb never satisfied,
when we saw mangled limbs, each with a wound,
and no death-blow dealt although the entire body
was gashed; we saw the dreadful practice
of unutterable cruelty—to keep alive the dying man.   180
Down fell the hands, torn off; the cut-out tongue
quivered, beating empty air with noiseless movement.
One cut off his ears, another the hooked nose's nostrils;
a third tears out the eyeballs from their hollow sockets
and, compelling him to view his body, finally gouges out his eyes.
Hardly will a crime so savage be believed, that one man
can incur so many tortures. Limbs look like this when crushed

and smashed by falling building's mass beneath the mighty weight;
no worse disfigured do headless corpses come to shore,
perished in mid-sea. What made them want to spoil their reward   190
by mangling Marius' face, as if it were worthless?
For this crime to please Sulla with proven murder,
it had to be recognizable. Praeneste's Fortune saw
all her inhabitants together met with the sword,
a people perishing in the time it takes for a single death.
Then fell Hesperia's bloom, now Latium's only
soldiers, staining with their blood forlorn Rome's Sheepfold.
Often have so many men together fallen in savage death
by famine, by the frenzy of the sea, by sudden fall of building,
by plague of earth or sky, or by calamity of war,   200
but never by execution. Hardly could the victors move
their heads amid the packed crowd's ranks and squadrons
pale at the launch of death; the slaughter over, hardly can the bodies
tumble forward, but totter with rolling neck; the massive
carnage crushes the survivors and corpses carry out some of
the slaughter: living bodies are smothered by heavy headless trunks.
Unperturbed, indifferent, from a lofty seat he watched
the terrible crime, not dismayed that he had consigned to death
so many thousands of the lowly masses. The Tyrrhenian flood
received in a heap all the Sullan corpses.   210
The first fell down into the river, the last on top of bodies.
Ships travelling downstream were halted, and the river's
front part, cut off by bloody debris, flowed into the sea
while the water behind stood still at the dam. Now the deep flow
of blood forces a way for itself, and flooding all the plain
and racing on with headlong stream into the Tiber's flow
it swelled the sluggish waters; now the river, not contained
by bed or banks, returned the corpses to the plain.
At last with difficulty struggling into the Tyrrhenian waves,
it streaked the blue sea with its torrent of blood.   220
For *this* did Sulla earn the name of "Saviour of the State",
of "Fortunate", the right to raise his tomb in the middle of the
        Campus?
These sufferings await, again to be endured, this will be the sequence
of the warfare, this will be the outcome fixed for civil strife.
Yet graver threats arouse our fears, the rush
to battle brings much greater loss to humankind.

For the Marian exiles, war's greatest prize
was Rome regained; for Sulla, victory provided
no more than complete destruction of enemy factions:
these rivals, Fortune, you summon for another purpose   230
—they go to war long powerful. Neither would rouse civil war,
if content with what contented Sulla.' Like this, melancholy elders
lamented, remembering the past and fearful of the future.

But great-hearted Brutus' breast was not struck
by terror nor was he among the people mourning in great alarm
at frightening commotions; but in drowsy night,
as Parrhasian Helice turned her chariot aslant,
he knocked at the modest house of his kinsman Cato.
He found the hero in sleepless worry pondering
the nation's fate, the plight of Rome, alarmed for all   240
without thought of himself, and with these words began to speak:
   'Of Virtue long ago expelled and banished from all lands
you are now the sole support, and Fortune will not with any
      whirlwind
strike her from you: I call on you, as I hesitate and waver,
to guide and reinforce me with your resolute strength.
Let others follow Magnus or Caesar's weapons:
for Brutus Cato will be the only leader. Say: are you the guardian
of peace, keeping your steps unshaken in this tottering world?
Or have you decided by involvement with the leaders of crime
and disasters of the frenzied people to make civil war innocent?   250
Each is drawn to criminal battle by his own motive:
some a house polluted and a fear of peacetime laws,
some to repel famine by the sword and in the ruins of the world
to liquidate their debts. None is driven to weapons by blood-lust;
they head for camp overcome by the massive wages: are you the
      one man
who loves war for itself? What good was it through so many years
to stay immune from the morals of this corrupt age?
This will be your sole reward for lengthy virtue:
wars which others will enter already guilty will make you guilty.
O gods, do not give so much power to ill-omened weapons,   260
to rouse even these hands to war. And javelins thrown
by your arm will not travel in the blinding cloud of weapons:
that such great virtue should not pass without effect,

all the fortune of war will fling itself at you. Who will not wish
to die upon your sword, though sinking from another's wound,
and be your crime? You will better live alone
in tranquil peace without weapons, just as heaven's
stars glide on their course unshaken ever.
By thunderbolts the air nearer the earth is ignited,
and winds and flashing trails of flame visit   270
the lower parts of the world: Olympus overtops the clouds.
By the law of the gods, discord disturbs the least of things
but the great have peace. How happily will Caesar's ears
hear that such a mighty citizen has deigned to enter battle!
And your preference of the opposing camp, under Magnus'
        leadership,
to his own will never rankle; if civil war is acceptable to Cato,
then so is he, excessively. A large section of the Senate
and the consul soon to wage war under an unofficial leader
and the other chiefs are incitements; but if Cato too
goes under Pompey's yoke, then in all the world, Caesar will be   280
the sole free man. But if as champion of freedom
and your country's laws you please to take up weapons,
you have a Brutus enemy now not of Pompey nor of Caesar,
but of the victor when the war is over.' So he speaks; but in reply
Cato utters sacred words from his inmost breast:
    'That civil warfare is the greatest crime, I admit, Brutus,
but where the Fates lead, confident will Virtue follow.
To make guilty even me will be the gods' reproach.
Who would wish to watch the stars and universe collapsing,
free from fear himself? to fold his arms and keep them still   290
when ether rushes from on high and earth shudders
beneath the weight of the condensing universe? Shall I alone live
in peace if unknown races and kings beneath another sky,
separated by the sea, comply with the frenzy
of Hesperia and with Roman wars? Keep far away this shame,
O gods, that Rome should fall and by her fall rouse up
the Dahae and the Getae—and I remain unmoved. As grief itself
bids the father robbed of his son by death conduct the long
funeral procession to the grave, he wants to thrust
his hands into the black fires, and on the pyre's piled-high mound 300
himself to hold the torches black, so I will not be torn away
before embracing your lifeless body, Rome; and, Liberty,

your name, even an empty shade, I shall follow all the way.
So be it: let the pitiless gods have in full Rome's
sacrifice of expiation, let us defraud the fighting of no blood.
O if only this head, condemned by heaven's gods
and Erebus', could be exposed to every punishment!
When Decius offered his life, enemy squadrons overwhelmed him:
let me be pierced by twin battle-lines, let Rhine's barbarous
horde aim its weapons at me, let me, exposed to all the spears,   310
standing in the midst, receive the wounds of all the war.
Let this my blood preserve the people, let this my death
atone for all the penalties deserved by Roman morals.
Why should peoples ready for the yoke and willing to endure
cruel tyranny perish? With your sword attack me, me
alone, in vain the guardian of laws and empty rights.
This slaughter, this, will give the people of Hesperia peace
and an end of troubles: when I am dead, the would-be tyrant
has no need of war. Why do I not then follow the nation's standards
and Pompey as my leader? Of course, I know for sure   320
that he too promises himself, if Fortune favours,
control of the entire world: with me his soldier let him conquer then,
to stop him thinking that he conquers for himself.' So speaking,
he applies fierce goads of wrath and rouses the young man's
ardour to excessive desire for civil war.

Meanwhile, as Phoebus banished chilly darkness,
a beating on the doors rang out and in burst hallowed
Marcia in mourning, straight from the pyre of Hortensius.
Once, as a virgin, she was joined in marriage to a better husband;
soon the prize and the reward of marriage, a third   330
child now, was paid and, pregnant, she is given
to fill another home with offspring, to ally the two houses
with her mother's blood. But, after placing his last
ashes in the funeral urn, she rushed with pitiable face,
her loosened tresses torn, her breast bruised
by repeated blows, and covered in the ashes of the tomb
—not otherwise likely to please her husband—spoke thus in grief:
    'While the blood and while maternal strength was in me, I did
your bidding, Cato, and fruitfully received two husbands;
with womb exhausted, tired from child-bearing, I return   340
to be given to no other husband now. Renew the ties unimpaired

of our former marriage, grant me only the empty name
of spouse and let my tomb read "Marcia, wife
of Cato" and let there be no dispute in the future
whether by divorce or by transferral I changed my first marriage.
As no partner in prosperity or joy do you receive me:
into anxieties I come, to share your struggles.
Allow me to accompany the camp. Why should I be left in peace
    and safety?
Why should Cornelia be closer to civil war?'

    These words influenced her husband and although the time   350
was inappropriate for marriage with Fate already calling him to war,
yet he takes pleasure in the ties and simple oaths,
free of empty show: the gods alone are witnesses to the rites.
On the threshold hang no festal crowns and garlands;
no white woollen band zigzags along the twin door-posts.
Missing are the customary torches, the couch which stands on ivory
steps with coverlets embellished by embroidery of gold,
the matron weighing down her head with towered crown,
preventing her from touching the threshold as her foot is lifted over;
no flame-yellow veil lightly to screen the timid   360
shyness of the bride covered her lowered gaze,
no belt with gems bound tight her flowing dress,
no graceful necklace was on her neck, no narrow scarf clinging
to shoulders' edge encircles her bared arms.
Just as she was, keeping on the mourning clothes of grief's attire,
she embraced her husband as she did her sons.
The purple was concealed, covered up by funeral wool.
The usual jokes did not make merry, nor was the grim-faced husband
greeted in Sabine fashion with festival abuse.
No relations of the house, no kinsmen gathered: 370
in silence they are joined, content with Brutus as the witness.
And from his sacred face the husband did not remove
the bristling hair, did not admit rejoicing to his hard expression,
when first he saw ill-omened weapons raised:
he let his white hair descend unshorn on to his stern brow
and let the beard of grief grow upon his cheeks,
as he alone, without favour or antipathy, took the time
to mourn for humankind. Nor were the ties of the former
marriage-bed attempted: his firm resolve resisted
even lawful love. This was the character and this the unswerving

     creed
of austere Cato: to observe moderation, to hold to the goal,
to follow nature, to devote his life to his country,
to believe that he was born not for himself but for all the world.
In his eyes to conquer hunger was a feast, to ward off winter
with a roof was a mighty palace, and to draw across
his limbs the rough toga in the manner of the Roman citizen of old
was a precious robe, and the greatest value of Venus
was offspring: for Rome he is father and for Rome he is husband,
keeper of justice and guardian of strict morality,
his goodness was for the state; into none of Cato's acts   390
did self-centred pleasure creep in and take a share.

Meanwhile Magnus left with his fearful throng
and occupied the Campanian walls of the Dardanian settler.
This he chose as his seat of war, from here his chief objective
was to stretch out his scattered party to meet the enemy,
where Appennine lifts central Italy
with shady hills; with no other peak does the earth
swell higher or approach Olympus nearer.
Midway between twin waters of the Lower and Upper Seas
the mountain-range extends, on this side bounded   400
by Pisa's hills which in the shallows break Tyrrhenian seas,
on that side by Ancona exposed to Dalmatian waves.
From vast springs it produces mighty rivers
and scatters streams on to the slopes of the twin seas.
On to the left flank fall the swift Metaurus
and rapid Crustumium and Sapis joined with Isaurus
and Sena and Aufidus, who lashes the Adriatic waves;
and Eridanus, who rolls shattered forests into the seas
and drains Hesperia of waters; into no other river
is earth dissolved more. This river was the first,   410
the story says, to shade its banks with a ring of poplars;
and when Phaethon drove the day downwards on a crossways
path and with blazing reins ignited the ether
and the streams were torn completely from the scorched earth,
this river had waters equal to the fires of Phoebus.
No less he than Nile, did Nile not flood
the Libyan sands across the levels of low-lying Egypt;
no less than Danube he, did Danube not, while wandering

the world, receive streams which could fall into any seas
and pass into Scythian waves, accompanied by them.   120
Heading for the mountain's right-hand slopes the waters
form Tiber and deep Rutuba; from there glides down
swift Vulturnus too and Sarnus, the emitter of night-time
vapour, and Liris pushed by Vestine waters
through shady Marica's realms and Siler skirting
Salernum's houses and Macra, who with his channel delays
no ships and runs on into seas of nearby Luna.
Where the mountain rises further on with ridge raised up
into the air, it sees Gallic lands and intercepts declining Alps.
Then, fertile for the Umbrians and Marsians and tamed by Sabine   430
ploughshare, it embraces with its pine-clad crags
all Latium's native peoples, not abandoning
Hesperia until cut short by Scylla's waves
and stretching its crags to Lacinium's temple,
longer once than Italy, until the sea's attack
destroyed the junction and the water drove back the land;
but after earth was smothered by twin depths,
its furthest hills became the property of Sicilian Pelorus.

Caesar, mad for war, rejoices to proceed only by shedding
blood, rejoices that Hesperia's lands he tramples   440
are not empty of the enemy, that the fields he invades are not
        deserted,
that his march itself is not for nothing, that non-stop he wages
war after war. He would rather smash the city-gates
than enter them wide open, with sword and fire devastate
the fields than tread them with the farmer unresisting.
He is ashamed to go by paths permitted, like a citizen.
At that time Latium's cities, faltering and poised with wavering
allegiance, though ready to submit at the initial panic
of war's approach, yet fortify their walls with thick
ramparts and on all sides surround them with a sheer palisade   450
and equip the walls' high towers with round stones
and with weapons to shoot the enemy from far above.
The people favour Magnus more, and loyalty contends
with threatening terror; as, when the Auster controls the sea
with dread-sounding blasts, all the waters follow it:
if the earth again struck open by Aeolus' trident

launches Eurus on the swollen waves, the waters
hold to the first wind though smitten by the second,
and while the sky submits to cloud-bringing Eurus,
the waves claim Notus. But terror turned their minds   460
with ease, and Fortune carried off their wavering loyalty.
The Etruscan race is exposed by frightened Libo's flight
and Umbria loses independence now with Thermus' rout.
Sulla too wages civil war not with his father's luck
but turns tail at the mention of Caesar's name.
When the units neared Auximum and assailed it, Varus
raced through the walls opposite where the back was undefended
and fled through rocks and forests. From Asculum's citadel
was Lentulus expelled: the victor harried his retreat
and drew off his army, and out of such a mighty force   470
the general escaped alone and the standards heading no cohorts.
You too, Scipio, abandon unprotected Nuceria's
citadel entrusted to you, though in this camp is stationed
a most stalwart company, withdrawn from Caesar's army long ago
in terror of the Parthians, the company with which Magnus replaced
the Gallic losses, granting his father-in-law the loan
of Roman blood until he summoned them to war himself.

But you, warrior Domitius, are stationed in Corfinium's abodes,
surrounded by strong walls, and your trumpet-call is obeyed
by the recruits arrayed against dark-clothed Milo once.   480
When he saw far off an enormous cloud rising
from the plain and battle-lines aflame with weapons struck
by glittering sun, he said: 'Comrades, race down
to the river's banks and sink the bridge in the waters,
and you, stream, come out now from your mountain springs
in full force and muster all your waters to break its structure
and carry off timbers in your foaming flood. At this line let the war
come to a halt, on this bank let the enemy waste time in delay.
Stop the general's gallop: Caesar halted for the first time here
will be our victory.' And speaking no more,   490
rapidly he moved his troops down from the walls—in vain,
since Caesar from the plain saw first his passage being barred
by unbridged river, and in hot anger he exclaims:
    'Are hiding-places behind walls not enough for your terror?
Are you blocking the plains and trying to keep me off with rivers,

cowards? After the waters of the Rubicon, Caesar
will now halt at no river, not if Ganges prohibit me
with his swollen flood. Make haste, squadrons of the cavalry,
forward, infantry, too: ascend the bridge before it falls.'
At these words, the light-armed cavalry were given   500
full rein on to the field and across the bank
strong arms hurled weapons like showers of rain.
Caesar repels the guard and takes possession of the undefended
river, forcing the enemy to the citadel's protection.
And now he erects towers which will move their mighty
stones, the siege-shed creeps beneath the centre of the walls:
look—O crime of war!—the gates unbarred, the troops
dragged out their general, a captive. He halted at the feet
of his proud fellow citizen, and yet, with threatening face
and neck unbowed, his high nobility demanded death by the sword.   510
Caesar knows he wants the final penalty and fears a pardon.
He said: 'Live, against your will, and by my generosity
look upon the light of day. Be now a bright hope to the
          conquered side,
a proof of my behaviour. Even take up weapons again, if you wish:
I myself seek nothing in return for this pardon, if you win.'
He speaks and bids the fetters be unfastened from his hands
bound tight. What dishonour! How much more could Fortune
have spared his Roman sense of shame, by even carrying out the murder!
The citizen's worst punishment for joining the army
of his fatherland, his leader Magnus, all the Senate is—   520
to be forgiven. Domitius fearlessly suppresses his fierce indignation
and to himself: 'After this disgrace, will you head for Rome
and the retreats of peace? Do you not now make ready to plunge
into warfare's frenzy, long doomed to die? Race directly to the target,
break all ties of life, and escape the generosity of Caesar.'

Magnus meanwhile, ignorant of his general's capture,
was raising troops to reinforce his side with added manpower.
And now, about to sound the war-trumpets, with Phoebus soon to
          rise,
he thought to test the indignation of the soldiers soon to fight
and he addressed with awe-inspiring voice the silent cohorts: 530
    'O you avengers of crimes and followers of the better standards,
O truly Roman army, given weapons by the Senate

on the State's behalf, pray for battle.
The Hesperian fields are ablaze with savage devastation,
the rabid frenzy of Gaul is pouring over icy Alps,
already there is blood on the defiled swords of Caesar.
It was better that the gods made us the first to bear the injuries of war:
from his side let the guilt begin; now, now, with me as leader,
let Rome seek punishment and penalty. And in fact those battles
        ahead are not
called rightly real battles, but the wrath of your avenging country;   540
this is war no more than when Catiline made ready
to attack our homes with burning torches with Lentulus his partner
in madness and Cethegus' frenzied arm stripped bare for action.
O the pitiable frenzy of Caesar! When destiny is willing
to match you, Caesar, with the Camilli and with the great Metelli,
you deign to join the ranks of Cinna and of Marius. You will
        undoubtedly
be overthrown, as Lepidus by Catulus was brought low, as Carbo,
buried now in a Sicilian tomb, submitted to my Axes
and Sertorius, who in exile roused the fierce Iberians.
And yet upon my word I am loath to link you, Caesar, too,   550
with these, I dislike the fact that Rome has set my hand against you
in your madness. I wish that Crassus had returned victorious
and safe from Scythian regions after Parthian battles,
that with your cause alike, you might fall to the enemy who felled
        Spartacus.
If you too are to augment my fame by the order of the gods,
look at my right hand: it has the strength to hurl the javelin,
the seething blood around this heart of mine has warmed
again; you will learn that men who can submit to peace
are no runaways in war. Though he call me listless and worn out,
do not be alarmed about my age: let the general in this camp   560
be the older, provided the soldiers are so in that one.
I have reached the highest point to which a people can raise a citizen
while remaining free; nothing higher have I left but tyranny.
You, whoever, who try to outstrip Pompey in the Roman state,
you have ambitions more than ordinary. On this side both consuls,
on this side an army made of generals, will take their stand. Will Caesar
be the Senate's conqueror? No: Fortune, you do not lead on events
in so blind a course, you have a sense of shame. What gives him spirit?
Gaul rebellious now for many a year and a lifetime devoted

to the task? Because he fled from the chill waters of the Rhine 570
and showed a frightened back to the Britons he had sought
and gave the name of Ocean to the shallows of shifting sea?
Or have his empty threats swollen up because the rumour of his
blood-lust
has driven Rome in weapons from her ancestral abodes?
What delusion! It is not you they flee but I they follow.
When I took my standards gleaming over all the deep,
before Cynthia had filled and hidden twice her orb,
the pirates then in fear abandoned every channel of the sea
and asked for a home on land in a narrow niche.
More successful than Sulla, I chased to his death 580
the king till then unconquered and delaying Roman destiny,
fleeing through the parting of the Scythian Euxine.
No region of the world is without me, but the entire earth,
whatever sun it lies beneath, is filled by my trophies:
on one side the north has seen my victories on the icy waters
of Phasis, the southern clime is known to me in torrid
Egypt and Syene, which does not slant its shadows to either side,
the west fears my control, Hesperian Baetis too,
which, furthest of rivers, strikes retreating Tethys,
I am known to the conquered Arab, to the Heniochi 590
fierce in war and Colchians famous for the stolen fleece,
my standards terrify the Cappadocians and Judaea, devoted
to rites of unknown god, and soft Sophene;
Armenians and fierce Cilicians and Taurus I subdued:
what war have I left for my father-in law but civil war?'

His faction met their leader's words with no acclaim
nor do they demand the speedy trumpet-signal of the promised
battle.
Even Magnus sensed their fear himself, and decided to recall the
standards
rather than to send into the crisis of a battle so immense
a force already overcome by rumour about Caesar as yet unseen. 600
When a bull is banished from the herd after his first fight
he heads for the forests' recesses and through empty fields
in exile he tests his horns on tree-trunks as opponents
and does not return to pastures until satisfied with vigorous muscles,
his neck's strength recovered: soon victorious, he leads

his regained multitude, accompanied by bulls, to whichever groves
he likes, against the herdsman's will: like this Magnus, in strength
unequal, surrendered Hesperia and fleeing through Apulia's
lands withdrew into Brundisium's safe citadel.

    This city once was occupied by Dictaean settlers,   610
fugitives from Crete who were carried over the seas by Cecropian
ships with sails that lied of Theseus' defeat.
From here Hesperia's flank now contracts itself
into a narrow leg and into the seas extends a thin tongue,
which encloses Adriatic waves within curving horns.
Yet the sea admitted by the narrow jaws here would not be
a harbour if an island did not with its rocks receive the force
of the violent Cori and repel the tired waves.
From here, from there, has nature set mountains of projecting
rock to face the open sea and kept away the blasts,   620
enabling ships to lie at anchor, held by a swaying rope.
Far and wide from here the entire sea is open to view, whether
sails travel to your harbours, Corcyra, or on the left
they head for Illyrian Epidamnus, sloping into the Ionian waves.
Here is the sailors' refuge, when the Adriatic mobilizes
all its strength and Ceraunia has vanished into cloud
and when Calabrian Sason is drenched with foaming sea.

He has no confidence now in matters left behind
nor can he shift the war to the tough Iberians' land
since in between lie the vast regions of the Alps.   630
So he addresses his son, the elder of his noble
offspring: 'I command you, probe the world's remotest parts:
stir up Euphrates and Nile, as far as my name's
fame has reached, through cities in which Rome
became renowned since my command. Restore to the sea the
    Cilician
settlers, now dispersed across the fields; next rouse up the Pharian
    kings
and my Tigranes; and do not omit Pharnaces' weapons,
I advise, or the nomad people of both Armenias
or the wild races along the shores of Pontus
or Riphaean hordes and those whose home is the marsh of Maeotis,   640
sluggish with frozen water, which bears Scythian wagons,
or—but why delay further? Through all the east, son,

you will bear my war and rouse the cities I have subjugated
in all the world; let all my triumphs return to my camp.
But you, who mark the Latian calendar with your names,
the first Boreas must drive you to Epirus; from there
through lands of Greece and Macedon acquire new forces
while winter grants a time for peace.' So he speaks, and all
carry out his commands and cast off from the shore the hollow ships.

But Caesar follows, never tolerant of peace   650
and long respite from fighting, and dogs the steps
of his son-in-law, to prevent the Fates from making any change.
Others might be satisfied with capture of so many city-walls at first
assault, with sudden conquest of so many citadels, the enemy
    dislodged,
and with the easy seizure of Rome itself, the capital of the world
and war's greatest prize; but Caesar fiercely presses on,
impetuous in everything and thinking nothing done when there
    remains
still something more to do: although he occupies all Italy,
yet because Magnus remains on the seashore's edge it rankles
that the country is shared between them still; nor on the other hand   660
does he wish the enemy to wander over open sea, but barricades
the waves and wide ocean with barriers and with rocks hurled down.
The futile toil on an endless task proceeds: the ravenous sea
swallows all the stones and mingles mountains with its sands,
just as no rocks would stand clear of the water
even if lofty Eryx were thrown down amidst the waves
of the Aeolian Sea or if Gaurus with its summit uprooted
dropped deep into the depths of stagnant Avernus.
So when no barrier maintained its weight upon the sea-bed,
next he resolved to fell the woods and with them weave together   670
links and fasten trunks with enormous chains.
Rumour sings that such were the roads constructed over water
by the arrogant Persian when with his bridges bold
he brought together Europe and Asia, Sestos and Abydos,
and marched across the strait of rapid Hellespont,
fearless of Eurus and of Zephyr, since his sails and ships
he brought to the middle of Mount Athos. In this way the
    mouth of the sea
is narrowed by the fall of forests; then the structure rises

with many a mound and tall towers sway above the waters.

At the sight of the mouth of sea constricted   680
by the new-made land, Pompey's mind was pained by biting worry
how to unlock the open sea and spread warfare over the waters.
Often his ships, their sails filled with Noti, driven through the very
barricade of the sea with their ropes pulled tight, shattered
the barrier's topmost sections in the salty sea, giving space to the vessels,
and often the ballista, wound up by sturdy arms, hurled
splintered firebrands through the shadows of the night. At last
the moment came for furtive flight. His orders to his comrades:
no sailors' shout to stir the shore, no signal of the horn
to mark the hours, no trumpet-call to summon to sea   690
the mariners, forewarned. Now the extremities of Virgo had begun
to come ahead of Claws which with their rise would bring Phoebus,
when they unmoored their ships in silence. The anchor stirs
no voices as its hook is dragged up from the stubborn sands;
while the mast's yard-arm is bent and while the lofty pine-mast
is erected, the fearful masters of the fleet were silent,
and sailors hanging from the ropes pull down the sails furled
and do not shake the stout rigging in case the breeze should whistle.
The leader in his prayers asks even this of you, Fortune,
that you let him at least abandon the Italy which you forbid him   700
to keep. The Fates hardly permit it: with roar immense
the sea resounded as it was struck by prows, the water seethes,
stirred up by criss-crossing wakes of so many ships.

Then all the gates are opened by the city's loyalty reversed
along with destiny, and the enemy, admitted within the walls,
turning with a headlong rush along the harbour's spits, head for
the mouth and are annoyed that the fleet enjoys the open sea.
What shame, that Magnus fleeing is a victory too small!
A narrow passage sent the ships on to the seas,
tighter than the Euboean wave which batters Chalcis.   710
Here two ships halted, caught by detachments
ready for the fleet, and with warfare dragged towards the shore
here first did Nereus grow red with citizens' blood.
The remaining fleet departs, robbed of its last vessels:
just as when the Pagasaean ship was heading for the waters
of Phasis, the earth launched on to the seas the Cyanean Rocks;

from the mountains was the Argo rescued smaller than before,
with stern torn off, and in vain Symplegas struck the empty sea
and then recoiled, to remain for ever fixed. Now the changing
    colour
of the eastern ether warned that Phoebus was imminent, and the
    light   720
is white and not yet red, and steals their flames from the nearer stars,
and now the Pleiads grow dim, now revolving Boötes' wagon
grows faint and merges into clear heaven's face
and the greater stars disappear and Lucifer himself recoils
from hot day. Already, Magnus, you held the open sea,
but not with the luck you had when chasing the pirates over water
through all the sea: exhausted by your triumphs,
Fortune has deserted you. You go, driven out
with wife and sons and taking all your household-gods
to war, accompanied by nations, an exile but still great.   730
A far-off place is needed for your undeserved fall.
Not because the gods preferred to rob you of a tomb in this
your fatherland are the sands of Pharos cursed with your grave:
it is Hesperia that is spared· far away in sphere remote
let Fortune hide this crime; let Roman soil
be kept unstained by the blood of her own Magnus.

BOOK THREE

As Auster drove along the fleet with sails yielding
before the pressure and the ships ploughed the middle of the deep,
every sailor was watching the Ionian waves:
Magnus alone did not turn his gaze from the land
of Hesperia until he sees disappear his country's harbours,
the shores never again to return to his sight,
the peak veiled in clouds and indistinct mountains.
 Then the leader's weary limbs give way
to drowsy sleep; then he dreamt that Julia, a phantom
full of dreadful horror, raised her mourning head through gaping   10
earth and stood upon the flaming pyre like a Fury.
She said: 'Since civil war began, I have been driven
from the Elysian abodes and Field of the Good and drawn
to Stygian darkness and the guilty shades. I myself have seen
the Eumenides holding torches to brandish at your weapons;
the ferryman of scorched Acheron prepares countless
ships; Tartarus is widened for many a punishment;
all three Sisters are hardly equal to the work
though their hands make haste; breaking threads tires the Parcae.
While I was your wife, Magnus, you led happy triumphs home: 20
your fortune changed with your marriage-bed, and that paramour,
Cornelia, condemned by Fate to drag her mighty husbands down
always to disaster, married into a warm tomb.
Let her cling to your standards through warfare and through
        waters,
provided that I may disturb and break in upon your slumbers,
provided that no time is free for love between you,
but that Caesar occupies your days and Julia your nights.
The oblivion of Lethe's bank has not made me
forget you, husband; the kings of the dead have permitted
me to chase you. When you are waging wars I shall come   30
into the middle of the ranks. Never, Magnus, by the ghosts
and by my shade, will you stop being his son-in-law;
in vain you sever with the sword your pledges: civil

war will make you mine.' So spoke the ghost and fled
away, melting through her trembling husband's embrace.

He, though gods and shades threaten calamity,
more resolutely races to war, his mind certain of disaster,
and says: 'Why am I alarmed by the apparition of an empty vision?
Either no feeling is left to the mind by death
or death itself is nothing.' Titan now was sinking   40
in the waves, and of his fiery orb had dipped as much
as is always missing from the moon when she is soon to be full
or shortly afterwards: then hospitable land provided
easy access to the ships; they haul in the ropes,
lay down the mast, and row towards the shore.

As the winds carried off the vessels in escape and the strait
concealed the fleet and Caesar stood, the sole commander
on the Hesperian shore, the glory of Magnus' rout
does not delight him: he resents the enemy's retreat
in safety over the sea, because no fortune is enough now   50
for the impetuous warrior, and victory was not for him
worth postponement of the war. Then from his heart
he drove anxieties of warfare and concentrated on peace
and on how to rouse the people's fickle affections:
he knew that causes of wrath and the greatest swings
of favour are both influenced by the price of corn. Only famine
sets cities free: and when the mighty feed the lethargic mob,
its abject fear is bought: a starving people knows not terror.
Curio was ordered to cross over to Sicilian cities,
where the sea either with sudden wave overwhelmed the land   60
or severed it and made mid-land its shores:
mighty is the sea's force there and the waters ever toil
to stop the interrupted mountains restoring their proximity.
And into the Sardinian regions too the warfare spreads.
Each island is renowned for corn-rich fields;
no lands filled Hesperia and Roman granaries
with harvests from afar earlier or more lavishly than these.
For richness of soil Libya hardly surpasses them, when her Austri
are still and Boreas drives the clouds beneath the southern sky
and rains pour down and she produces an enormous harvest.   70

When the leader had made these provisions, he then in victory
headed for the houses of his fatherland, leading companies not armed
but with the face of peace. Oh! if he had returned to Rome
only with the peoples of Gaul and the north subdued,
what a chain of exploits, what scenes of war he could have paraded
ahead of him in the long procession!—how he fettered
the Rhine and Ocean, how the noble Gaul together
with blond Britons followed his high chariot.
What a triumph he lost by conquering more!
As he marched, the cities saw him not with happy gatherings   80
but silent with fear, and nowhere did a crowd
assemble to meet the leader. Yet he rejoices to be so dreaded
by the people and would not prefer to have their love.
And now he had surmounted the sheer citadels of Anxur
and where Pomptine marshes are divided by a watery road,
where the lofty grove is, Scythian Diana's realm,
and the path for Latian Rods to Alba's height;
now from high-up cliff far off he catches sight of Rome,
not seen by him in all the time of the northern war,
and marvelling at his city's walls, he spoke like this: 90
    'Were you, abode of gods, abandoned by men who were compelled
by no warfare? For what city, then, will people fight?
Thank the gods that eastern frenzy did not now swoop down
upon the Latian borders, nor the swift Sarmatians, joined
with the Pannonians, nor the Getae mixed with Dacians;
when your leader is so fearful, Rome, it is merciful that Fortune
made this war a civil war.' So he speaks and enters a Rome
thunderstruck by terror, because they believe that he will sack
the walls with black fires and scatter the gods,
as if he had captured Rome. This was the extent of their fear: 100
they equate his wishes with his power. No favourable greetings,
no feigned cries of happy uproar do they pretend;
hardly have they room for hatred. The Palatine halls of Phoebus
are filled by a crowd of Fathers brought out from their lairs,
though no one has the right to summon the Senate; the sacred chairs
were not resplendent with the consul, no praetor—by law the
        next in rank—
is present, and the empty curule chairs are missing from their place.
Caesar was everything: the Senate-House listened to one
man's voice. The Fathers sat, prepared to vote in favour

if he asks for tyranny, for temples for himself, for the slaughter   110
and the exile of the Senate. Thank the gods his sense of shame
exceeded Rome's self-degradation.

                        Yet Freedom rouses
wrath, through one warrior testing if right
can resist force: and when aggressive Metellus
sees Saturn's temple being torn apart by huge
exertion, with rapid step he breaks through Caesar's lines
and stands before the doors of the temple, not yet opened.
—To this extent the love of gold alone knows
no fear of sword or death: the laws are lost and perish
with no crisis, but you, wealth, the lowest part of life,   120
you provoked a fight.—Keeping the victor
from the booty, the tribune declares with ringing voice:
  'Only over my body will you smash the temple open;
no wealth will you carry off unless stained
by my sacred blood, you robber. Without a doubt, this rank of mine
finds gods to avenge its violation; the tribune's curses
followed Crassus to war, promising cruel battles.
Now unsheathe your sword: nor need you fear a crowd
to witness your crimes: we stand in an abandoned Rome.
No wicked soldier will take his pay for his crimes from our treasury: 130
there are other people for you to overthrow, other city-walls
    for you to give your men.
Poverty does not compel you to despoil the peace which you have
    thrown aside:
Caesar, you have your war.' By these words the conqueror was inflamed
to mighty wrath and said: 'Empty are the hopes of honourable death
which you conceive: my hand will not pollute itself
with your slaughter, Metellus; no office you hold will make you
deserving of Caesar's wrath. Are you the champion to whose safe-
    keeping
Freedom has been left? The length of time has not confused the highest
and the lowest to this extent, that, if by Metellus' voice
the laws are saved, they would not rather be destroyed by Caesar.'   140
    He ceased, and when the tribune does not yet move from the doors
a fiercer wrath comes on him; he looks around for his savage swords,
forgetting to feign the toga of peace: then Cotta forced
Metellus to renounce his scheme too daring.

He says: 'The freedom of a people coerced by tyranny
perishes by freedom; its semblance you will preserve
if willingly you do whatever ordered. In defeat we have submitted
to so many wrongs; for our dishonour and degenerate fear
this is the only excuse—that nothing now could be refused him.
Quickly let him steal away the evil seeds of hideous war.   150
Loss affects any peoples protected by their own laws:
the poverty of slaves is dangerous not to themselves but to their
    master.'
At once Metellus was led away and the temple lay open.
Then the Tarpeian rock resounds and with loud rumbling
witnesses the doors unclosed; then hidden deep
inside the temple and untouched for many a year,
the wealth of the Roman people is unearthed—wealth
from Punic wars, from Perseus, from conquered Philip's booty,
gold left to you, Rome, by the Gaul in hasty flight,
gold for which Fabricius did not sell you to the king,   160
all the savings of you ancestors of frugal habits,
the tribute sent by Asia's wealthy peoples
and paid by Minoan Crete to conquering Metellus
and brought by Cato over seas from far-off Cyprus.
Then the riches of the east and the remotest treasure
of captured kings, carried before Pompey in his triumphs,
is brought out. With dreadful plunder the temple is robbed
and then for the first time Rome was poorer than a Caesar.

Meanwhile through all the world Magnus' fortune
had roused to battle cities doomed to fall with him.   170
Nearest Greece sends forces for the neighbouring war.
Phocaean troops were sent by Amphissa and rocky
Cirrha and Parnassus, both his peaks deserted.
Boeotian leaders gathered, surrounded by swift Cephisus
with his fate-declaring water and Cadmean Dirce;
troops came from Pisa and from Alpheos who sends his waters
through the seas to Sicily's peoples. Then Arcadians left
Maenalus and Trachinian soldiers left Oeta of Hercules.
Thesprotians and Dryopes hurry and the ancient Selloi
left the oaks now silent on the Chaonian hill.   180
Although recruitment drained Athens totally,
a few ships reach Phoebus' dockyards

and three vessels ask us to believe that Salamis is true.
Now ancient Crete of a hundred peoples and dear to Jupiter
comes to war, and Cnossos, expert at wielding
the quiver, and Gortyna, equal of the eastern arrows.
Then come the inhabitants of Dardanian Oricos, the wandering
Athamanians scattered through high forests, and Enchelians
with ancient name testifying the death of Cadmus metamorphosed,
and Colchian Apsyrtos foaming in the Adriatic wave;   190
men who farm Peneus' fields and with Thessalian
ploughshare work to till Haemonian Iolcos.
—From there the sea was challenged first, when untaught Argo
violated the shore and mingled unknown races
and first matched mortal-kind against the winds and frenzied
waves of the sea: through that ship men's fates
increased by one new form of death.—Then Thracian Haemus
is abandoned and Pholoë pretending a people of double form.
Strymon is deserted, regularly entrusting
to warm Nile the birds of Bistonia, and barbarous Cone,   200
where one mouth of much-divided Danube loses
its Sarmatian waters and washes Peuce, sprinkled by the deep;
and Mysia too and land of Ida, flooded by the chill
Caicus, and Arisbe, in soil too poor;
and inhabitants of Pitane and Celaenae, which was doomed
by Phoebus' victory and so laments your gifts, Pallas,
where swiftly Marsyas descends with his sheer banks,
joins wandering Maeander and is borne backwards mingling,
where the earth lets Pactolus emerge from gold-rich
mines, where Hermus, no less rich, divides the fields.   210
Trojan bands too, with their usual bad omens, head for the standards
and the camp, doomed to perish, not restrained by the story
of Troy or by Caesar's claim of descent from Phrygian Iulus.
The peoples of Syria come: Orontes was deserted
and Ninos once prosperous (so rumour says), windy Damascus
and Gaza and Idume, rich in palm-groves,
and unstable Tyre and Sidon, precious for its purple.
These ships were steered to war on an unswerving track
across the sea by Cynosura, a surer guide to no other vessels.
—Phoenicians were the first, if rumour is believed, who dared   220
to mark speech to last for ever with crude symbols:
not yet had Memphis learnt to weave its rivers'

reeds; only animals carved on stones,
both birds and beasts, preserved magic utterances.—
Taurus' forest is deserted and Persean Tarsus
and the Corycian cave, gaping with its hollowed rocks;
Mallos and furthest Aegae resound with their dockyards
and Cilicians, not now pirates, come in lawful vessels.
Eastern retreats too were roused by rumour of war,
where Ganges is worshipped, the only river on earth   230
who dares unleash his mouths facing Phoebus as he rises
and who pushes his waters towards the opposing Eurus,
here where the Pellaean commander halted after reaching Tethys'
waters and confessed that he was beaten by the world's great size;
roused too was the place where Indus rushes his rapid stream
with divided flood, unaware of the Hydaspes joining his vast waters;
roused too are the men who drink sweet juices from the soft cane,
who tint their hair with yellow dye
and bind their flowing linen robes with coloured gems
and build their own pyres and climb the hot   240
piles while still alive. O! how glorious!—for a people
to take the fates into its hands and when sated with life
to give what remains to the gods! The fierce Cappadocians came,
the people of Amanus, too hard to plough,
the Armenians who dwell where Niphates rolls down his rocks.
The Choatrae left their forests which touch the sky.
Arabs, you entered a world unknown to you,
amazed that the forests' shadows do not fall towards the left.
Then the Roman madness roused the furthest Orestae
and the Carmanian leaders—whose sky, already turning   250
southwards, sees Arctos sink below the horizon but not entirely,
where Boötes, swift to set, shines in the tiny night—
and the Ethiopians' land, which no part
of the Zodiac would cover if curving Taurus
on sinking knee did not project his furthest hoof;
and where great Euphrates and rapid Tigris raise
their heads, rivers sent forth by Persia from springs
not far apart: if the earth mixed them, it is uncertain
which name the waters would bear. But fertile Euphrates
floods over fields like the Egyptian waters,   260
while the earth with a sudden chasm swallows up Tigris
and covers his secret course, but does not withhold

from sea's waves the river, which is born again from a new source.
Between Caesar's battle-line and the opposing standards
the warlike Parthians held a neutral position,
content to have made the rivals two in number. The nomad people
of Scythia, enclosed by chill flood of Bactros
and vast Hyrcanian forests, dipped their arrows in poison.
From here came the Spartan Heniochi, a nation fierce in handling
the rein, and Sarmatians, neighbours of the savage Moschi;   270
where Phasis cuts the Colchians' wealthy lands,
where flows Halys, fatal to Croesus, where Tanais falls
from Riphaean heights and confers upon his banks the names
of different worlds, and as the common boundary of Asia
and of Europe, divides the neighbouring parts of the middle of the
     earth
and where he curves enlarges now this world, now that;
and where Pontus drains off the waters of Maeotis, the torrential
strait, and steals glory from the Pillars of Hercules,
and so men say that Ocean does not enter only at Gades.
From here the Essedonian peoples come and you, Arimaspians,   280
tying up your locks bound with gold; from here come the strong Arii
and Massagetans, who break the long fast of war against the Sarmatians
with the horses on which they escape, and the swift Geloni.
Not when Cyrus led down his host from Memnonian kingdoms
or when Xerxes descended with his soldiery counted
by thrown weapons or when the avenger of his brother's love
struck the waters with such mighty fleets
did so many kings have a single leader, there never came together
races so varied in their dress, voices of a mass
so different-sounding. So many peoples Fortune roused to send   290
as companions in his immense downfall, as a procession
fit for Magnus' burial. Horned Ammon was not
slow to send to war Marmaric squadrons,
from as far as parched Libya reaches—from western Moors
to Paraetonian Syrtes on its eastern shores.
To ensure that lucky Caesar received everything at one stroke,
Pharsalia offered him the world to be conquered all at once.

Caesar left the walls of trembling Rome
and, hurrying his troops, races over cloud-capped Alps
and, though other peoples cowered in terror at his name,   300

the Phocaean warriors, with no Greek fickleness, ventured
in dangerous times to preserve loyalty and sealed pacts
and to follow principles, not Fate. Yet first they try
with pacifying words to deflect the unbridled fury
and pitiless mind of the warrior: they beseech the enemy
when he is near, holding out Cecropian Minerva's bough:
      'That Massilia has always shared your people's
fates in foreign wars is attested
by every age included in the Latian annals.
And now, if you seek triumphs from an unknown sphere,   310
our hands are ready, pledged to foreign battles.
But if in discord you plan deadly battle-lines
and ill-omened conflicts, to your civil war we give
our tears and our withdrawal. Let sacred wounds be handled
by no alien hand. If frenzy had armed the immortals
or if earth-born Giants attacked the stars,
human reverence would still not venture to help
Jupiter with weapons or with prayers, and mortal-kind,
ignorant of the gods' affairs, only by his thunderbolts
would know the Thunderer still ruled alone in heaven.   320
What is more, countless races on every side are rallying to the fight
and the world does not so shrink in dread from the infection of crime
that civil wars require conscripted swords.
Let everyone indeed share this intent, to refuse a part in your
fate and let no foreign soldier wage these battles:
who will not drop his arm when he sees his father facing him?
      who will not
be stopped from throwing weapons by brothers on the other side?
The end of the crime is here if you refuse to fight
your lawful enemy. This is the sum of our prayer:
that you leave your terrifying eagles and threatening standards   330
far from the city and willingly entrust yourself to our walls
and permit war to be kept out, but Caesar allowed in.
Let there be a place exempt from crime, safe for Magnus and for you,
a place where you can meet unarmed if Fate keeps
Rome unconquered and you decide on peace-treaties.
Why do you divert your rapid march to us when such great crises
of Iberian warfare summon you? Not weighty in the world are we
nor do we swing the balance; never have we used weapons
prosperously, exiles from our country's first abodes;

and since burnt-out Phocis' citadels were transferred,   340
we are protected on a foreign shore by tiny city-walls,
with loyalty our only glory. If you are ready to blockade
our walls and to shatter the gates by force, we are ready
to receive your firebrands and your weapons on our houses,
ready to seek gulps of water stolen from us by your diversion
of the springs and in thirst to lick the earth when we have dug it up;
and if generous Ceres fails, we are ready then to grind
with polluted bite things horrible to look at and repulsive to touch.
And this people is not afraid to endure for the sake of freedom
the ordeal of Saguntum besieged by Punic warfare.   350
Babes torn from mothers' embrace, in vain pulling
on breasts dry from famine, will be thrown into the fires;
wives shall ask for death at their dear husbands' hands,
brothers will exchange death-wounds and, if compelled, this kind
of civil war will they prefer to wage.'

                    So ended the Greek
warriors. The leader's wrath, already betrayed by his agitated
face, at last attested his indignation in words:
   'In vain are these Greeks inspired by confidence in my speed.
Although we are hurrying to the western region of the world,
there is time to destroy Massilia. Rejoice, soldiers!   360
By a gift of Fate, war is presented to you as you proceed.
As the wind loses strength and is dissipated in empty space
unless the forests thick with timber block its path,
and as a great fire dies without fuel,
so lack of enemies hurts me and we think it a loss
of warfare if those who could be defeated do not fight back.
But if I disband my army and go alone, dishonourably,
then their houses are open to me. Now not so much to shut me out
but to shut me in is their wish. Why? to drive away the dreadful
infection of war. You will suffer for your bid for peace   370
and learn that in my day nothing is safer than war
waged under my leadership.' After saying this, he directed
his march towards the fearless city; then sees the city-walls
barred and fenced by a thick ring of soldiers.
Not far from the walls a hill of earth rises up
and on its widened top opens out a little plain
—this rock seemed to the general fit for ringing

with a long defence-work, precisely right for a safe camp.
The city's closest part rises to an elevated citadel
level with the hill, the land sinking with deep valleys in between.   380
Then he decided on a project which would cost immense toil,
to join the opposing heights with an enormous ramp.
But first, to blockade the entire city on its landward
side, Caesar carried a long siege-work from his camp's
heights to the sea, encircling springs and pastures
on the plain with a trench, building up the ramparts with turf
and raw earth and topping them with frequent battlements.
Now the Greek city gained this eternal glory,
well deserving mention, that, not compelled or prostrated
by sheer terror, it checked the headlong rush of war   390
raging through the world and when Caesar seized all else at once
it alone took time to be defeated. What an achievement, to
        detain the Fates,
to make Fortune waste these days in her haste to set
her warrior in command of the entire world! Then far and wide
all the forests are felled, the woods are robbed of timber
to bind and to compress the earth by constructing a vertical frame
at the sides, since the light earth and twigs provide no sound support
to the middle of the structure, to prevent it giving way beneath
        the towers' weight.

A grove there was, never profaned since time remote,
enclosing with its intertwining branches the dingy air   400
and chilly shadows, banishing sunlight far above.
In this grove there are no rustic Pans or Silvani,
masters of the forests, or Nymphs, but ceremonies of the gods
barbarous in ritual, altars furnished with hideous offerings,
and every tree is sanctified with human blood.
If antiquity at all deserves credence for its awe of the gods,
the birds fear to sit upon those branches,
the beasts fear to lie in those thickets; on those woods
no wind has borne down or thunderbolts shot from black
clouds; though the trees present their leaves to no breeze,   410
they have a trembling of their own. Water pours
from black springs and the grim and artless
images of gods stand as shapeless fallen tree-trunks.
The decay itself and pallor of the timber now rotting

is astonishing; not so do people fear deities worshipped
in ordinary forms: so much does ignorance of the gods
they dread increase their terror. Now it was rumoured
that often the hollow caves below rumbled with earthquakes,
that yew-trees fell and rose again,
that flames shone from trees which were not on fire, 420
that snakes embraced and flowed around the trunks.
That place the people do not visit with worship near at hand
but leave it to the gods: when Phoebus is in mid-sky
or black night commands the heavens, even the priest dreads
to approach and fears to surprise the master of the grove.

This wood he orders to fall beneath the axe's blow,
because, near his siege-work and untouched by earlier warfare,
it stood thick among the hills stripped of trees.
But courageous hands faltered: and affected by the place's
awesome majesty, they believed the axes would rebound 430
on their own limbs if they struck the sacred trunks.
When Caesar saw his cohorts were entangled
by a great reluctance, he was the first to dare to grab
an axe, to balance it and gash with iron the towering oak.
When he had sunk the blade into the desecrated trunk, he says:
'Now none of you need hesitate to cut down the wood:
mine is the guilt—believe it!' Then all the throng
obeyed his orders, not free from fear with dread removed,
but weighing in the scales the wrath of gods and Caesar.
Down fall the ash-trees, the knotty holm-oak is overthrown; 440
and Dodona's wood and alder, more fit for the waves,
and cypress, witness to no plebeian grief,
then for the first time shed their tresses and, robbed of foliage,
let in the daylight: and thrown down on its packed timber
the falling grove supports itself. The Gallic people
groaned at the sight, but the soldiers blockaded inside the walls
are jubilant—for who would think that gods are injured
without revenge? Often their good fortune guards the guilty
and the deities can only be enraged with the unlucky.
And when enough of the grove is felled, it is carried on wagons 450
seized throughout their territory and, their oxen stolen, the farmers
weep for the harvest of the soil untouched by curving plough.

But, impatient of protracted warfare at the walls, the general

turned to Spanish battle-lines and the limits of the world,
ordering continuation of the siege. The ramp is erected
with criss-cross planks and on it placed twin towers, level with
the city-walls, which spiked the earth with no timber beam
but crept on their long path with unseen cause.
When this huge mass swayed, the soldiery believed
a wind had struck the hollow caverns of the earth in its quest   460
to burst out and they marvelled that their walls were standing.
From the towers weapons fall on to the city's lofty citadels.
But greater was the force of Greek weapons against Roman
bodies, because the lance was thrown not by arms
alone but shot by the taut whirl of the ballista;
it comes to rest only after passing through more than one body;
it opens up a path through armour and through bones and speeds
      away,
leaving death behind: after dealing wounds the weapon still
      moves onwards.
But whenever a stone is shot by the thong's
enormous force, like the rock severed   470
from the mountain-top by age assisted by the winds' blast,
it crushes everything in its path, not merely killing
the pounded bodies but pulverizing entire limbs and blood alike.
But when courage approaches the enemy walls, shielded
by the dense-packed tortoise—the front line carrying
overlapping shields, with shield-boss held out to protect the helmet—
then missiles which, when shot from distant point, had damaged them
      before
now fall behind them. And for the Greeks it is no easy task
to steer the throw or alter the range of the machine
made to hurl its weapons far; but with their bare hands   480
they roll down rocks, relying on their weight alone.
While the chain of shields lasts, it repels
all weapons, just as roofs rattle when struck
by harmless hail; but after the warriors' valour wavered
and the continuous lattice was broken by exhausted soldiers,
one by one beneath incessant blows the shields gave way.
Then the mantlet advances, lightly covered with earth,
concealed by its screens and covered front:
now they try to undermine and knock down the walls' lowest parts
with crowbars; now the ram, stronger with its suspended blow,   490

attempts to loosen the thick wall's framework
by its impact and to remove one stone from those placed on it.
But struck from above by flames and massive jagged rocks,
by numerous stakes and the blow of fire-hardened oak,
the lattices give way and the weary soldiers
return to their tents, their toil sapped in vain.

The Greeks' greatest prayer had been that their walls should stand;
but now they prepare to initiate attack: concealing glittering
torches in their shields at night, their warriors boldly
broke out. Their weapon was not the spear, not deadly bow,   500
but flame; and the wind whirled the conflagration
and carried it swiftly through the Roman fortifications.
And though it struggles with green wood, not slowly
does the fire drive its forces onwards, but from every torch
it chases massive coils of black smoke,
and it destroys not only timbers but enormous stones,
and solid rocks were melted into crumbling dust.
Down fell the ramp and seemed still greater on the ground.

Hope of victory by land now left the defeated and they resolved
to try the fortune of the sea's deep. No painted wood   510
graced their vessels, no gleaming figurehead adorned them,
but wood is joined together, rough and as it falls
on the hills, to make a steady site for war at sea.
And now the fleet accompanying Brutus' towered
vessel had sailed on the Rhône's flood and reached the waves,
anchoring off the fields of the Stoechades. The Greek soldiers were
just as willing to entrust their whole strength to destiny
and armed aged men and lads together.
They manned not only the fleet riding tall
upon the waves; also they recalled retired boats from dockyards.   520
  Phoebus scattered his morning rays above the seas
and splintered them upon the waters; the ether was free of clouds;
Boreas was still and the Austri held their peace and the sea
lay calm, reserved for warfare: then from every station
each advances his ship, and with equal strength of arm
from this side Caesar's boats leap up, from that the fleet
with Greek rowers; the vessels vibrate, driven on by oars;
frequent strokes tug along the lofty ships.

The wings of the Roman fleet were surrounded by sturdy
triremes and ships powered by rising tiers of rowers   530
built up fourfold and those which dip still more blades
into the sea; by boats of many kinds. This force barricades
the open sea, while Liburnian galleys, content to rise
with twin tiers, are further back in crescent formation.
But, loftier than all, the praetorian ship of Brutus
is propelled by sixfold strokes and advances its bulk across
the deep, with its highest oars reaching for waters far away.
     When in between there is as much sea as each fleet
can race across by one stroke of the oars,
innumerable voices are mingled in the mighty ether,   540
and shouting drowns the sound of oars and no
trumpets can be heard. Then they sweep the blue,
falling on to the bench and striking breasts with oars.
When first beak met with beak and gave a crash,
the ships ran astern, and the volley of weapons
veiled the air and empty sea as it fell.
And now they separate the prows and widen the wings
and by spreading out the fleet receive the enemy ships.
As whenever the tide battles against the Zephyrs or the Euri,
the waves go this way, but the sea that way, so when the ships   550
traced different tracks in the furrowed flood, one thrust back
the sea which was thrust forward by another ship's oars.
Whereas the Greeks' vessels were ready to provoke battle
and resort to flight, to break off their course with no long
circle and to respond to the guiding helm with no delay,
yet the Roman ship was more sure to offer a steady
vessel, valuable for warriors like dry land.
Then Brutus says to his helmsman sitting in the ensign-bearing
stern: 'Why do you let the battle-lines range across the deep
and compete with them in manœuvres on the sea? Now join battle   560
and present our vessels' sides to the Phocaean prows.'
He obeyed and offered his boats sidelong to the enemy.
Then every ship which attacked Brutus' timbers
stuck captive to the one it hit, defeated by its own impact,
while others are held fast by grappling-irons and smooth chains
or tangled by their oars: the sea is hidden and war stands still.
     Now no missiles are hurled or shot by arms,
no wounds from weapon thrown fall from afar,

but hand meets hand: in the naval battle the sword
achieves the most. Each stands leaning from his own boat's   570
stronghold to meet the enemy's blows and none when killed
fell in his own ship. Deep blood foams
in the water, the waves are choked by clotted gore
and the ships, when hauled by iron chains thrown on board,
are kept apart by crowds of corpses.
Some sank, half-dead, into the vast deep
and drank the sea mixed with their own blood;
others, while still drawing breath in a struggle with death
prolonged, perished in a sudden collapse of wrecked ships.
Weapons, ineffectual at first, perform a slaughter of their own   580
in the flood and every steel that falls with disappointed weight
finds a wound to inflict in the middle of the waves.
    A Roman ship hemmed in by Phocaean vessels
defends right and left side with strength divided
and equal fighting. While from its high stern
Catus fights, boldly holding on to Greek post,
at one moment he is pierced in his back and chest alike
by weapons shot together: the steel meets in the middle of his body
and the blood stood still, unsure from which wound to flow,
until at one moment a flood of gore drove out both spears,   590
split his life, and dispersed death into the wounds.
Here unlucky Telo also steered his ship:
vessels on the turbulent sea obeyed no hand more readily
than his and, whether he observes Phoebus or the moon's horns,
to no one was tomorrow's light better known,
skilled to set the sails to the coming winds.
He had shattered a Latian boat's framework with his beak,
but quivering javelins entered the middle of his breast
and the dying steersman's hand turned his ship away.
While Gyareus tries to clamber on to the allied stern,   600
a weapon is launched and strikes him through the groin as he there
        hangs;
he swings, nailed to the ship with the steel pinning him back.
    There stand twin brothers, glory of a fruitful mother,
born from the same womb for differing fates.
Cruel death distinguished the warriors and removed confusion:
the unhappy parents now recognize the one survivor—
a cause of everlasting tears; he maintains their anguish

for always and presents his lost brother to them as they mourn.
One of the twins dared grab a Roman vessel
from his Greek stern when oars were interlocked   610
in slanting comb; but a heavy blow from above cut off
his hand, which clung there still, such was the pressure of its grasp
and, holding on with tightened muscles, it grew stiff in death.
In adversity his courage grew: mutilated, his noble wrath
increases and with strong left hand he renews the battle
and leans across the waters to seize his own right hand:
but this hand too with all the arm is severed.
Now without his shield and weapons, he is not hidden deep
inside the ship but exposed, and as he protects with naked breast
his brother's shield, he stands firm, though pierced by many a spear,   620
and in a death already well earned he receives the weapons which
in their fall would have killed many of his own people. Then he
          gathered
into his tired frame the life that was departing by many wounds
and braced his limbs with all the blood remaining
and, though his muscles were failing in their strength, he leaped
on to the enemy ship, to damage it by his weight alone.
Piled high with slaughter of its men and running with blood,
the ship took blow on blow along its sidelong flank
and, when it drank the sea through broken structure,
it filled up to the topmost gangways and sank into the waves,   630
whirling round the sea nearby with a coiling eddy.
The waters parted, separated by the sunken vessel,
and the sea closed up into the place of the ship. And on that day
many amazing sights of varied death were presented to the sea.

    As a grappling-iron was fastening its grasping hooks on to a ship,
it pierced Lycidas. He would have been submerged in the deep
but for his comrades, who held on to his legs as he swung.
He was torn and split apart and blood did not spurt out as from a
          wound;
slowly from his broken veins it falls everywhere,
and as the stream of life passed into his separated limbs   640
it was intercepted by the waters. From none in death has life
departed by so wide a path. The lowest part of his torso
handed over to death limbs empty of vitals;
but where the swelling lung lies, where the organs are warm,
the Fates stuck for a long time and, after a long struggle

with this portion of the man, took all his parts with difficulty.
    While one vessel's throng, too aggressive,
leans over the tilting side and leaves unmanned the section
free from enemy, by their massed weight the ship
was overturned and covered sea and sailors with its hollow keel: 650
they could not strike the vast deep with their arms
but perished in their ocean prison. That day a unique form
of hideous death was seen, when a young man in the water
by chance was transfixed by the beaks of converging vessels.
The middle of his chest was split apart by such tremendous blows,
the bones were ground away, his limbs could not prevent
the bronze of the beaks resounding: from his crushed belly the blood
mixed with entrails spouted gore through his mouth.
When the ships back water and withdraw their beaks,
the body with its breast stabbed through dropped into the sea   660
and took in water in its wounds. Most of a shipwrecked
crew struggled with death by tossing their arms
and resorted to an allied ship for help; but as they
tried to grab the timbers higher up with arms forbidden so to do
and as the ship rocked, doomed to sink if she took the crowd on
        board,
the wicked crew above with swords cut off their arms.
Leaving their limbs hanging on the Greek ship
they fell away from their own hands: no more did the waves
support the heavy mutilated bodies on the surface of the water.
    And now, though all the soldiers were weaponless, their steel   670
cast, frenzy finds them weapons: one whirled an oar
at his enemy, these with their strong arms an entire stern-post,
and they drive away the rowers to swing their torn-up benches.
For the fight they broke the ships. They catch slain bodies
as they sink to the bottom and rob the corpses of their weapons.
Many who lacked a weapon pulled and tore out the fatal
javelin from their own wounds and with their left hand
pressed their entrails until the blood could deal a sturdy
thrust and flow again only after hurling the enemy's spear.
    Yet no scourge caused more destruction on this water   680
than the enemy of the sea: for fire is spread,
attached to oily torches and kept alive in covered
sulphur; and the vessels easily provided fuel
and spread the conflagration, now with pitch and now with melting

wax.
The waves do not overcome the flames but, with ships already
    scattered
over the water, the wild fire claims the wreckage for itself.
One man lets in waves to extinguish the flames with the sea,
others cling to blazing planks for fear of drowning.
Among a thousand ways of death the only one men fear is the way
they have begun to die. And in shipwreck, courage does not cease: 690
weapons which have dropped into the sea they collect and hand
to the ships or move their unsteady hands through the waves
with enfeebled blow; now if the supply of steel is scarce,
they use the sea instead: fierce enemy grapples
with enemy and they rejoice to sink with limbs entangled,
to die while drowning the opponent.
                        In that fight was Phoceus,
a man remarkable at holding his breath beneath the waves,
at searching the sea for anything buried in the sands,
and at tearing out the bite of hook too firmly fixed
when the anchor does not feel the tug of the rope.   700
He had seized an enemy and pulled him deep down
and was returning to the surface, safe and victorious;
but believing that he rises through empty waves he strikes
the ships and finally stayed for ever beneath the sea.
Some flung their arms over enemy's oars
and checked the vessels' flight. Not to die in vain
was their greatest concern: many a dying man fixed
his wounds to the stern to ward off blows from the beaks.

    As Tyrrhenus stood in his prow's lofty height,
Lygdamus, whirler of the Balearic thong, aimed and shot   710
a bullet and smashed his hollow temples with the solid lead.
After blood has burst every ligament, his eyes fall down,
forced from their sockets: he stands there stunned
by loss of sight, thinking this to be the darkness of death.
But when he sensed that strength remained in his limbs
he said: 'O comrades, just as you do with the engines,
me too you must position straight to shoot my weapons.
Tyrrhenus, spend what remains of life in all
the hazards of war. This your corpse already
largely dead has the heroic value of a soldier: 720
it will be struck in place of a living man.' So he spoke and throws

weapons at the enemy with blind hand, yet not in vain.
Argus, a youth of noble blood, received the blow
where the lower belly now slopes towards the groin,
and falling forward drove home the point with his own weight.
At the opposite end of the conquered vessel stood
Argus' unhappy father, who in his youth
would have been second to none of the Phocaean army;
overcome by time, his strength had faded and, worn out by age,
he was no soldier but an example. When he saw his son's death,　730
he made his way to the stern over the long vessel's benches,
often stumbling, an old man, and found the body breathing still.
No tears fell from his cheeks, he did not beat his breast,
but all his body stiffened and his hands spread wide.
Night came over him and mighty darkness covered his eyes
and his gaze could no more recognize unhappy Argus.
He, on seeing his father, lifts his drooping head and neck
already weakening; he unlocked his throat, but no voice
follows, only with a silent look he asks for kisses
and invites his father's hand to close his eyes.　740
When the old man was recovered from his faintness and his savage
anguish began to wield its strength, he said: 'I will not waste
the time allowed by the cruel gods: I will pierce
my aged throat. Grant pardon to your unhappy parent,
Argus, for running away from your embrace, from your last kisses.
Not yet has the hot blood left your wounds
and only half-dead do you lie: you can still outlive me.'
So he spoke and, though he had driven a sword through his entrails
until the hilt was stained, still with headlong leap he passed
beneath the deep waters: in the hurry to precede his son's　750
demise, he trusted his life to no single form of death.

　　Now the leaders' fates swing the matter and now no more was
the outcome of battle in doubt. Of the Greek fleet most
are sunk, while other ships conveyed their conquerors
with changed crews; a few reached the dockyards
in headlong flight. What weeping of parents there was
in the city! What loud lamentation of mothers along the shore!
Often a wife embraced a Roman corpse, its features mangled
by the wave, believing it her own husband's face;

and by blazing pyres unhappy fathers fought　　　　　　　　760
over a headless body. But Brutus was victorious on the water
and first conferred on Caesar's warfare glory at sea.

BOOK FOUR

But far off on the furthest borders of the earth, Caesar
fiercely wages warfare not stained with much bloodshed
but destined to give the greatest swings of fate to the leaders.
In Pompey's camp Afranius and Petreius ruled
with equal authority; harmony divided their shared
command into even parts and the vigilant watch,
defenders of the rampart, obeyed the password of each in turn.
Besides Latian lines they had energetic Asturians,
light-armed Vettones, and the Celts who, fugitives
from an ancient race of Gauls, joined name with the Iberians.   10
    The rich land swells with a moderate hill and increases
on high in a gentle knoll; on this Ilerda rises,
founded by an ancient hand; Sicoris flows by
with placid waters, not last among the western rivers,
embraced by a stone bridge with an enormous arch,
able to withstand the winter's waters. But the nearest crag
is the position of Magnus' standards, and Caesar raises his camp
on no lesser hill: in between the flood divides the tents.
From here the spacious land unfolds spreading plains
whose limit the eye can hardly grasp, and you, greedy Cinga,   20
enclose the plains, forbidden to strike the Ocean's waves
and shores on your course, because Hiberus who gives his name
to the region joins his flood with yours and takes away your name.
The first day of warfare was free of bloody fighting
and displayed to view the forces and numerous standards
of the leaders. Their crime revolted them and shame restrained
the weapons of frenzy: one day they granted to their fatherland
and broken laws. When Olympus was sinking into night,
Caesar surrounded his troops with a rough-and-ready trench
while his front line stayed in position, and deceived   30
the enemy by screening the camp with serried companies.
At new light he gave the order to climb with speed
the hill which in between divided and defended Ilerda
from the camp. Both fear and shame alike impelled the enemy

to this point and reaching it first with hurried troops he took the hill.
This side hope to gain the place by their courage and their weapons,
but that side have the place itself. The burdened soldiers struggle up
the high rocks and the lines cling to the hill in front
with upturned faces and when about to tumble backwards are righted
by the shield of the line behind. None was free to hurl his weapon   40
while slipping and then steadying his steps by javelin planted in the
      ground,
while grabbing rocks and stumps and cutting a path with the sword,
the enemy forgotten. Their general saw that his troops
would fall down with a crash and bids the cavalry take over the warfare
and place their protected side in front with a circle to the left.
In this way the infantry were rescued easily and without pursuit,
and the disappointed victor perched on high in vain with warfare
      withdrawn.

So far only were the tests those of weapons: the rest of the battle's
fates came from the air, unreliable with shifting changes.
Clogged by sluggish frost and dry Aquilones, winter   50
had congealed the ether and confined the rains in cloud.
Snows scorched the mountains and frosts the low-lying
plains, not destined to last once the sun is seen,
and all the earth near star-dipping heaven
was dry and hard beneath the clear winter sky.
But soon warm Titan was brought back by the spring-time carrier
of fallen Helle, looking back towards the constellations,
soon the hours had again been balanced according to
true Libra's weights and day had won; then Cynthia, leaving
the sun, gleaming hesitantly at first, with her crescent   60
shut out Boreas and took flames in Eurus.
And he with Nabataean blasts hurled into the western world
whatever clouds he found in his own region,
all the mists which the Arab feels, which Ganges'
land exhales, vapours allowed to collect
by first sun, vapours driven by Corus, darkener
of the eastern sky, vapours which had been protecting the Indians.
The clouds taken from the orient set the day on fire
and could not settle laden on the middle of the world
but swept along the rain-clouds in their flight. North and south   70
were free from rains; the moist air flowed to Calpe alone.

Here where are the bounds of Zephyr, where Olympus' furthest point
restrains Tethys, the clouds, forbidden to pass beyond,
coil up in thick round masses and the space which separates
the earth from ether can hardly hold the accumulation of black air.
And now, they are squeezed and thickened by the sky into
    abundant rains
and pour down condensed; thunderbolts cannot preserve their flames;
although they flash incessantly, the rain-clouds quench the
    lightning-flashes.
Then the rainbow embraces the air with its hoop
incomplete, its colour hardly varied by light,   80
and drank the Ocean and swiftly carried up the waves
to the clouds and restored the water which had flooded from the sky.
And now the Pyrenaean snows, which Titan never could melt,
have poured down, the ice is fractured, and the rocks are drenched.
Then the stream emerging from its usual source
cannot find its path, such abundant waters flooded
into every river-bed from the banks. Now Caesar's army
is floating shipwrecked on the plain and the camp collapses, struck
by many a deluge; the rivers form pools within the high rampart.
No seizure of cattle is easy, the submerged furrows   90
produce no fodder; the foragers scattered over
hidden fields are deceived, mistaking the concealed roads.
And next came savage famine, always the first companion
of great disasters, and the soldier starves while besieged
by no enemy; though no lavish spender, he gives his entire fortune
to buy a little bread. How terrible is the pallid corruption of greed!
When gold is offered there is no shortage of hungry sellers.
    Now mounds and hills lie hidden, now a single lagoon
concealed all the rivers and in its vast gulf swallowed them:
it devoured rocks entire and carried off the wild beasts'   100
shelters and engulfed the beasts themselves, and with sudden eddies
it whirled its roaring waters and drove back the tides
of Ocean, stronger than they. And night woven underneath the sky
does not feel Phoebus rise: the sky's disfigured face
and continuous darkness confound the distinctions of the world.
Like this lies the world's lowest part—under
a girdle of snow and never-ending winters: it sees no stars
in the sky, in its barren cold it produces nothing,
but by ice it moderates the fires of the southern constellations.

So be it, O supreme father of the universe, so be it, Neptune,   110
ruler of the watery trident with second jurisdiction—
may you devote the air to never-ending rains;
may you forbid the return of all the tides that you have sent out.
Let rivers not find a downward course to the shores
but be carried back by the waters of the sea! Let the earth shake
and open up channels for the streams! Let Rhine, let Rhône
flood these plains! Let the rivers divert their mighty flows!
To this place release Riphaean snows, to this place pour out
the pools and lakes and sluggish marshes wherever they lie
and rescue these unhappy lands from civil war!   120

But Fortune returns in full force, content with her warrior's
little fright, and more than usual do the propitious gods
favour him and earn forgiveness. Now the air is clearer,
and Phoebus, a match for the waters, had scattered the thick clouds
into fleeces and nights grew red as light approached,
and with the elements in their proper place moisture departed
from the stars and all the waters poised above sought the depths.
Woods began to lift their foliage, hills to rise
from pools and valleys to harden at the sight of day.
And as soon as Sicoris has found his banks and left the plains,   130
white willow twigs are soaked in water and woven
into little boats, and, covered in the slaughtered ox's hide,
able to bear a passenger, dart across the swollen river.
In this way the Venetan sails upon Po's lagoons and Briton
on the wide Ocean; in this way when Nile covers everything,
Memphis' boat is constructed from thirsty papyrus.
In these boats troops are ferried across and hurriedly cut down
a wood to form an arch from both sides, and fearing an increase
of the violent river they did not place the timbers on the edges
of the banks but stretched the bridge into the middle of the fields.   140
And to prevent Sicoris acting boldly with his flood renewed,
he is divided into trenches and, with his flood split into channels,
pays the penalty for his swollen water. When Petreius sees
everything give way to Caesar's fates, he abandons
high Ilerda and, in distrust of the known world's forces,
he seeks for battle people indomitable and always wild
through their love of death: he heads for the world's furthest parts.

On seeing the hills undefended and the camp deserted,
Caesar bids his men take up their weapons and, without seeking
a bridge or ford, to go across the river with their sturdy arms.   150
He is obeyed—and as the soldiers race to battle they eagerly
seized on a path which they would have feared in retreat. Soon
  they retrieve
their weapons, they warm wet limbs and by running revive
their frames chill from the flood, until the shadow shrinks
as the day rises towards noon; and now the cavalry harasses
the enemy's last ranks and they are held between flight and fight.

  Two crags raise rocky ridges on the plain, hollow
with a valley in between; from here the high earth joins together
lofty hills which hid between them routes safe with a shadowed,
winding course; Caesar sees that if the enemy   160
gain this gorge, war is unleashed upon the earth's
remote parts and upon wild races, and says: 'Go on, break ranks
and head back the warfare stolen by their flight,
advance with face of battle and with threatening looks;
and let them not in terror lie low in a coward's death:
as they run away let them receive the weapon full in the breast.'
He spoke and arrived ahead of the enemy making for the hills.
There with a tiny rampart, they pitch their camps
a little way apart: after their eyes, undimmed
by distance, had each others' faces in full view,   170
they grasped the crime of civil war. For a moment they restrained   172
their voices out of fear; only with a nod or movement of the sword
they greet their friends; soon, when burning love with its more powerful
spurs broke the rules, the soldiers dare to climb across
the rampart, to stretch their hands wide for embraces.
One calls out the name of his host, another shouts to his kinsman;
youth shared on boys' pursuits stirs this man's memory;
and he who had not recognized an enemy was not a Roman.
They drench with tears their weapons, with sobs they break their
  kisses,   180
and though stained by no blood the soldiers dread
what they could have done. Why beat your breast?
Why groan, you madman? Why pour out empty laments
and not admit that willingly you follow crime's commands?
So much do you fear the man whom you yourselves make fear-
  inspiring?

Let him sound the trumpets for war, ignore the brutal blast;
let him advance his standards—do nothing: soon, soon will civil
      war's Erinys
cease and Caesar, as a private citizen, will love his son-in-law.
   Now come, O Harmony, embracing all with eternal bond,
the salvation of nature and the muddled universe   190
and the sacred love of the world: now our age controls
the great decision of what is to come. Gone are the refuges
of all those crimes; excuse is torn away from a guilty people:
they have recognized their friends. A curse upon the Fates of hostile
divinity who swell disasters already so great with a brief respite!
There was peace and the soldiers mingled and in both camps
freely wandered: on the hard ground they set up tables
of concord and made libations with mingled Bacchus;
the turf-built altars glowed and on couches side by side
talk of the wars prolongs the sleepless nights: 200
on which field first they stood, from which strong hand the lance
flew. While they boast about their bravery
and deny many deeds, their trust is renewed,
poor men—the sole aim of the Fates—and all their guilt
to come increases with their love. For when Petreius learnt
about the pact of peace and sees that he and his camp
have been betrayed, he calls to wicked battle the sword-hands
of his slaves and, screened by the throng, he hurls from the camp
the unarmed enemy, with the sword parts men joined
in embrace and shatters the peace with abundant blood.   210
His fierce wrath added words sure to provoke battle:
   'O soldiers, unmindful of your fatherland, forgetful
of your standards, can you not do this for your cause,
conquer Caesar and return, the Senate's champion? At the least,
you can be defeated. While you have swords, while the Fates hang
in the balance and there is blood enough to flow from many a wound,
will you go over to a master, will you bear his standards you once
      condemned,
will you have to plead with Caesar to treat his slaves
with no discrimination? And for your generals too has life been
      begged?
Never shall our safety be the price and the reward   220
of abominable betrayal: that we should live is not the aim
of civil war. We are dragged off into slavery in the name of peace.

If it were ever right to surrender Liberty for peace,
iron would not by men be dug up from the mine
running deep, no walls would fortify the towns,
the spirited steed would not race to war, the fleet
would not be launched to spread its towered vessels over the sea.
My enemies, it seems, are bound by sworn oaths
to abominable crime; but in your eyes is your loyalty
worth less because you fight for a just cause   230
and can even hope for pardon? How dreadful is the death
of honour! Now through all the world, ignorant of your fates,
Magnus, you are raising forces and rousing kings who dwell
at the world's end, when perhaps by our pact
you are already promised safety.' So he speaks and shook
every mind and brought back their love of wickedness.
Just so the wild beasts unlearn the ways of the woods
and grow tame in the locked prison, dropping their threatening looks
and learning to submit to man, but if their parched mouths
find a little gore, their rabid frenzy returns   240
and their throats swell at the memory of the taste of blood;
their anger seethes, hardly sparing the trembling keeper.
They proceed to every guilt and their loyalty commits horrors
which if Fortune had inflicted them in battle's blind night
would have been to the gods' discredit. Among the tables, among beds
they slay the breasts which they had warmly hugged just now;
and though at first they unsheathed their weapons with a groan,
when the sword, discourages from justice, clings to their hands,
they hate their friends as they strike them and every blow reassures
their faltering spirits. Now the camp is seething in turmoil,   250
and as if a hidden crime would be wasted, all their horrors   252
they set before their leaders: they delight in their guilt.

You, Caesar, recognize the favour of the gods, though robbed
of many a soldier; since your fortune was not greater
on Emathian fields or the waves of Phocian
Massilia, nor was the exploit in the Pharian sea so great,
seeing that thanks to this crime of civil war alone
you will be the leader of the better cause. The generals
do not dare entrust their troops stained with wicked slaughter   260
to a nearby camp but to high Ilerda's walls again
directed their escape. Caesar's cavalry met them, kept them

from all the plains, and hemmed in the enemy in the dry hills.
Next Caesar is eager to surround with a sheer trench
the men without water, to prevent the camp reaching the river banks
or its outworks curving round abundant springs.
When they saw the course of death, their fear was changed
to headlong rage. The soldiers killed the horses—
no use or help to men blockaded—and, finally compelled
to give up hope and reject flight, they rush towards the enemy,   270
suicidally. When Caesar saw them racing down
with impetuous pace and proceeding purposely to certain death,
he says: 'My soldiers, now withhold your weapons and draw back
your sword from the enemy's approach: let the battle cost me no
          blood.
He who challenges the enemy with his throat is not conquered
          without cost.
Look! here comes an army, in their own eyes worthless, hating life,
destined to die with cost to me; they will not feel the blows,
they will fall upon the swords, they will rejoice to shed their blood.
Let this fervour leave their minds, let the mad impulse fade;
let their wish to die be wasted.' So by refusing battle   280
he let their threats burn out in vain and lose their edge,
until Phoebus went down and night substituted its lights.
Then, with no opportunity of mutual death,
gradually their violent rage recedes and their spirits cool,
as the gladiator's wounded breast shows greater courage
while the pain and wound are fresh, while the hot blood
gives free movement to the muscles, while the skin has not yet shrunk
upon the bone: if his conqueror stands still and restrains the blow,
aware that his sword has been driven home, then a cold numbness
binds the limbs and mind and steals his strength,   290
after congealed blood has closed the dried-up wounds.
And now the men without water first seek
concealed rivers and hidden streams by digging open the earth;
not only with the shovel and the sturdy mattock did they dig
the soil, but with their own swords, and a well is sunk
in the tunnelled mountain to the level of the watered plain.
Not so deep, with daylight left so far behind,
would the pallid searcher for Asturian gold bury himself.
But no rivers sounded with hidden course,
no new springs gushed out when the volcanic rock was struck,   300

no sweating caves drip with scanty dew,
nor is the gravel moved or disturbed by a meagre flow.
Then, drained by much exertion, the young men are hauled
to the surface, wearied by mining the flinty rocks.
Their search for you, waters, made them less able
to endure the dry heat. And in their weakness they do not support
their feeble bodies with feasts but, loathing food,
they make their hunger help them. If softer soil
showed signs of moisture, with both hands they squeeze
the sticky clods above their mouths; if muddy filth lies   310
stagnant on black slime, every soldier dropped down
in competition to drink foul draughts, and in death took
waters he would refuse if destined to live; and like wild beasts
they suck dry the swollen cattle and, when milk failed
from the drained udder, the dirty blood is sucked.
Then they crush grasses and leaves and strip off branches
wet with dew and squeezed any juices they could
from a tree's green shoot or tender pith.
O how blessed are those laid low through the fields
by the barbarian enemy who in flight mixed poison in the springs!   320
Caesar, though openly you pour into these rivers
pus and carrion of wild beasts and pallid aconite
which grows on the Dictaean rocks, the Roman troops
will drink without delusion. By flame their guts are burnt,
dry mouths stiff and rough with scaly tongues;
now veins are withered and the lung, wetted
by no moisture, chokes the air's journeys in and out,
and rasping gasps hurt the cracked palate; still they open
their mouths, gulping at the air which will injure them.
They hope for the rains which recently attacked   330
and inundated everything and fix their faces on the dry clouds.
And to weaken the unhappy soldiers still more with lack of water,
they were camped not beyond scorching Meroë or beneath the Crab's
region, where the naked Garamantes plough, but, caught
between the pools of Sicoris and rapid Hiberus,
the thirsting army gazes at the nearby rivers.

Now overcome, the generals yielded and Afranius, advocate
of seeking peace, a suppliant with weapons renounced,
dragged his squadrons half-dead into the enemy camp

and stood before the conqueror. As he asked he kept   340
his dignity unbroken by disaster, and between his former
fortune and his fresh misfortunes he behaves entirely as a man defeated
but a general yet, and with a breast free from fear he asks for pardon:
    'Had the Fates laid me low beneath a degenerate enemy,
my strong right hand would not have failed to snatch death.
But as it is, my only reason for requesting safety
is my belief that you are worthy to grant life, Caesar.
We are not driven by party enthusiasm; we did not go to war
to oppose your plans. In fact, civil war found us
already generals and we preserved our loyalty to our former cause,   350
as long as we were able. We do not obstruct the Fates at all:
we hand to you the western races, we open up those of the east,
and we allow you freedom from fear about the sphere left behind your
        back.
Neither blood poured out upon the fields nor sword
nor wearied hands finished off your battle: pardon your enemies
for this alone—that you are victorious. And our request is not large:
that you give rest to the weary and allow us to spend unarmed
the life you grant. Think of our troops as lying
defeated in the fields, because it is not right to mingle
doomed with prosperous armies or for your captives to share   360
in your triumph: this throng has fulfilled its destiny.
This we seek—that you do not compel the conquered to conquer
        with you.'
    He ceased; but Caesar favourable and with unclouded face
relents, exempting them from punishment and war-service.
As soon as the pact of proper peace was settled,
the soldiers race towards the waters now unguarded,
lie down on the banks, and muddy the rivers granted them.
For many the continuous drawing of sudden waters
stopped the passage of the air through empty veins,
constricted and shut off the breath; and not yet does the burning   370
plague recede, but the craving disease demands water for itself
though the guts are already filled with liquid. Soon strength
returned to muscles and might to the men. O luxury
extravagant of resources, never content with what costs little,
and ostentatious hunger for foods sought
by land and sea, and pride in a lavish table:
learn how life can be prolonged at tiny cost

and how little nature asks. The ailing men are revived
not by noble Bacchus bottled under long-forgotten consul,
they do not drink from gold or agate, but life returns   380
from the simple liquid. The river and Ceres are enough for the people.
　　How unlucky are the men who continue fighting! Next, the troops
　　　　abandon
weapons to the victor and safe, though with breast disarmed,
free from guilt and without worries, they disperse to their own
cities. O how much they regret, now that they possess the gift
of peace, that they ever brandished weapon with effort
of arm and suffered thirst and asked the gods
for successful wars in vain! Certainly, for those lucky in the battle
many doubtful fights remain, so many struggles through the world;
though Fortune never falter or waver in successes   390
so often must they conquer, must blood be shed across all
lands, and Caesar must be followed through his entire destiny.
Happy is the man who has already learned the place where he
　　　　must lie
when the world's collapse is tottering. No battles summon them
when weary, no trumpet-signals break their slumbers safe.
Now wives and children not yet grown and lowly homes
and their own land welcome them, not settled elsewhere as colonists.
From this burden too Fortune relieved them, made them free
　　　　from worry—
their minds are without uneasy bias: one is the giver
of their safety, one had been their leader. So they alone   400
are happy, watching civil battles with no prayer.

The Fortune of the war did not remain the same through
all the world but dared one blow against Caesar's party.
Where the water of the Adriatic Sea beats straggling Salonae
and warm Iader runs out towards the gentle Zephyrs,
there Antonius, confident in the Curictae's warlike race,
who live on land surrounded by the Adriatic Sea,
is blockaded, camped upon on the shore's edge,
secure from war's attack if only famine would recede,
famine which storms the safest places. The earth sends up   410
no fodder to feed his horses, blonde Ceres produces
no corn; the soldiers had stripped the plain of grass,
and when their unhappy teeth had already cropped close the field

they tore the withered blades from the turf of the camp.
   As soon as they saw their comrades and general Basilus
on the shore of land opposite, they sought a new trick
for escape across the sea: they do not follow custom and build
long keels or lofty sterns, but in a strange line
link together timbers strong to carry great bulk.
And the craft is supported on every side by empty barrels   420
tied together in a continuous double line by chains
stretched out, upon which planks are sidelong laid;
and it does not carry its crew of rowers exposed to weapons
with an open front, but they beat the sea which is enclosed
by beams: so it presents a marvel of silent movement,
neither bearing sails nor lashing water visibly.
Then they watch the straits until the tide moves
with falling waves and sands are exposed by the ebbing sea.
And now the water was receding and shore growing:
the craft is launched and carried down, gliding over   430
the sloping deep with its two comrades. Above all three rise
lofty towers and storeys, threatening with shaking parapets.
Octavius, guardian of Illyrian waters, did not wish
at once to attack the craft and withheld his rapid vessels
until his prey grew larger after a successful passage,
and now that they have rashly started, he entices them to take
         to the water
again by peace at sea. So the hunter: until he surrounds the stags,
alarmed by the scare and fearing the waft of scented feather,
or until he lifts the nets set out on props,
he checks the noisy mouth of the swift Molossian dog   440
and ties his Spartan and his Cretan hounds, entrusting the forest
only to the dog which picks up traces with its muzzle
on the ground and when the prey is found knows not to bark,
content to show the lair with quivering leash.
And no delay: the hulks are manned, the island is deserted
as eagerly they board the rafts, towards night
at the time when the last light even now hinders the first darkness.

But Pompey's Cilicians with their skill of old prepare
to weave stratagems in the sea: leaving the water's surface
empty, in the sea's mid-depth they hang chains   450
and let them drift loosely, and attach them

to the rocks of the Illyrian cliff. Neither the first raft
nor the next was checked, but the third hulk
stuck and was drawn by rope towards the cliffs.
Hollow rocks hang over the sea and —strange!—their mass stands
ever likely to fall and with its forests overshadows the water.
To this place the sea often brought ships wrecked by Aquilo
and drowned bodies and hides them in blind caves;
the hidden sea restored its plunder and when the caverns
spewed out the water, the twisted whirlpool's waves   460
surpass in agitation Tauromenian Charybdis.
Here the hulk halted, laden with men of Opitergium;
it is surrounded by ships unmoored from every station,
and other enemy mass together on the rocks and shore.
Vulteius—he was captain of the craft—realized
the silent stratagems beneath the sea; in vain he tried with sword
to burst the chains, then calls for battle without hope,
unsure where he was presenting his rear and where his front to war.
Yet in this calamity, valour did all that valour could
when caught surprised: there was a battle between   470
the many thousands spread around the captured raft and on board
hardly a full cohort, not a lengthy battle, it is true, since night hid
with shadow the faltering light and darkness brought on peace.

Then Vulteius with his noble voice guided like this
his cohort stunned and dreading their approaching destiny:
'Soldiers, free for no longer than one short night,
in this narrow time give thought to your final state.
Life which remains is short for no one who finds in it the time
to seek death for himself; and the glory of death is not
diminished, men, by advancing to meet a fate close at hand.   480
Since the period of life to come is uncertain for everyone,
praise of courage is equal whether you reject years
you hoped for or cut short a moment of life's end,
so long as by your own hand you invite the Fates: no one is forced
to wish to die. No escape lies open, all around us
stand citizens intent upon our slaughter: decide on death,
then all fear is gone. Desire what is inevitable.
Yet we need not fall in warfare's blind cloud,
when battle-lines are covered by their own weapons mixed
with darkness, when bodies lie in crowds upon the plain,   490

every death is merged in a common account, valour is crushed and
        vanishes:
but we have been set by the gods in a vessel visible
to friends and to the enemy. The sea, the land, the island's
highest rocks will provide and give us witnesses,
both sides will watch from opposite shores.
In our fate, Fortune, you intend some great
and memorable example. All the records
that loyalty and the soldier's duty observed by the sword
have shown throughout the ages, our army could have surpassed.
And of course we know that it is not enough for your men to fall   500
on their own swords for you, Caesar; but as men besieged we have
no greater pledge to give of our deep love.
Grudging chance has cut off much from our praise
because we are not held captive with our elders and our children.
Let the enemy know that we are unconquerable warriors, let him fear
our courage, frenzied and ready for death, let him rejoice
that no more rafts were stuck. They will try to tempt us
with pacts and will want to seduce us with dishonourable life.
O I wish that they would promise pardon, bid us hope for safety,
so that our unique death would grow in fame,   510
to prevent them thinking we have given up hope when we pierce
our guts with the warm sword. By our great valour we must deserve
that Caesar calls it a loss and a disaster, to lose
a few among so many thousands. Though the Fates bestow
retreat and let me go, I would refuse to avoid what is imminent.
I have discarded life, my comrades, I am wholly driven
by the spurs of coming death: this is an obsession. Only those
already touched by fate's nearness may know—the gods conceal
it from those destined to live on, to steel them to live—
that death is a blessing.' So passion changed and lifted   520
all the minds of the young men. Before their captain's words,
all watched with moist eyes the stars
in the sky and dreaded the Bear's turning pole;
the same men now, when his advice had entered their courageous
        minds,
longed for daylight. And at that time of year the sky was not slow
to tilt the stars into the sea, for the sun was in the sign
of Leda, when his light is highest and Cancer near;
then a brief night only followed on the heels of the Thessalian arrows.

The rise of day revealed Histrians posted on the rocks
and warlike Liburnians on the sea with the Greek fleet.   530
They first suspended war and tried to conquer
with pacts, in case the mere delay of death might make life
sweeter to the captured men. Determined to die, the soldiers stood
with life already renounced, fierce, indifferent to the battle's outcome
because the end was promised them by their own hand, and no uproar
shook the warriors' resolve, prepared for the worst;
and, few in number, they resisted countless hands at once
on land and sea; so great is the confidence of death.
And when they thought that blood enough had flowed in battle,
they turned their frenzy from the enemy. The vessel's captain,   540
Vulteius himself, was first now to demand death with throat laid bare:
'Is there any of my soldiers', he says, 'whose hand is worthy
of my blood, who can prove his wish to die by sure proof
through my wounds?' And before saying any more
his guts are pierced already by more than one sword.
He commends them all but as he dies he kills
with grateful blow the man to whom he owed his first wound.
The others fight, and on one side performed
the entire crime of wars. So from Cadmus' seed
sprang up the Dircaean cohort and fell by one another's   550
wounds, a dreadful omen for the Theban brothers;
so in Phasis' plains the Sons of Earth, created
from the unsleeping tooth, filled furrows so vast
with kindred blood in a wrath inspired by magic spells,
and Medea herself took fright at the first crime committed
by her untried herbs. So the soldiers fall, agreed
upon a mutual destiny, and in the warriors' deaths death
involves the smallest amount of valour. Equally they kill and fall
with fatal wound and though they strike with dying hand
it never fails them, nor is the wound produced   560
by the sword's deep thrust but the weapon is struck by the breast
and the hand attacked by throat. When with bloody destiny,
brothers charge at brothers and son at father,
they thrust their swords not with shaking hand
but with all their weight. The single duty of those who strike
was not to strike a second blow. Now half-dead, they dragged
their tumbling guts to the wide gangways and poured much gore
into the sea. They delight to see the light

they have despised, with disdainful face to watch
their conquerors, to feel death. Now the raft is visibly   570
heaped with bloody slaughter and the conquerors release the bodies
to be burnt and their leaders are amazed that to any man
a leader can be worth so much. Fame running through all
the world spoke of no craft with a louder voice.
Yet even after the example of these warriors, cowardly
races will not grasp that to escape slavery by one's own hand
is not an arduous act of valour, but tyranny is feared
thanks to the sword and liberty is chafed by cruel weapons
and they do not know that swords are given to prevent slavery.
Death, I wish that you would not remove the fearful from life   580
but that you could be bestowed by valour alone!

                                                 Just as fierce
as this warfare was that which then blazed up in Libya's fields.
For daring Curio unmoors his vessels from the Lilybaean
shore, and with Aquilo gently filling the sails
he reached the shores of the famous anchorage between
Clipea and great Carthage's citadels, half in ruins,
and he places his first camp far from the whitened sea,
where leisurely Bagrada proceeds, the furrower of the dry sand.
From there he seeks the hills and crags hollowed out all around
which antiquity not falsely calls the kingdom of Antaeus.   590
In his wish to learn the origins of the ancient name, a primitive
inhabitant taught what he had learned through many forefathers:
    'After the Giants' birth, Earth not yet exhausted
mothered a dreadful offspring in Libyan caves.
And not so justly was Typhon his mother's pride
or Tityos or fierce Briareus; she was merciful to heaven
in not raising Antaeus on the Phlegran fields.
With this gift too did Earth enhance her offspring's
mighty strength—that his now tired limbs
thrive with strength renewed when they touch their mother.   600
This cave was his home: beneath the tall crag
he lay hid, they say, and feasted on the lions he had caught;
no wild beast's skins used to offer him a bed
for sleep, no forest a couch, but lying on the naked earth
he regained his strength. The farmers of Libya's
fields perished; men brought to land by the sea perish;

and for long his valour spurns the Earth's help, not aiding
himself by falling: he was utterly invincible in strength,
even when he stayed standing. At last the rumour
of the blood-stained evil spread and summoned to the shores of Libya 610
great-hearted Alcides, who was ridding land and sea of monsters.
He threw down the skin of the lion of Cleonae,
Antaeus that of the lion of Libya; the stranger drenched his limbs
with liquid, following the custom of the Olympic wrestling-place;
the other, not confident enough in touching his mother with his
    feet,
poured burning sand on his limbs to help him.
They linked hands and arms in many a clasp,
long tested the other's neck in vain with massive biceps,
and each head is held unmoved with forehead rigid;
and they are amazed to meet their match. Alcides, not wishing 620
to use all his strength at the contest's start,
wore out his opponent, as the frequent gasps
and cold sweat from his tired body revealed to him.
Then his neck grows weak and trembles, then breast by breast
is shoved, then legs totter, struck by hand
aslant. Now the victor encircles his opponent's
yielding back and crushes his sides and squeezes his waist
and by thrusting with his feet spreads wide the thighs and laid
his man flat out from head to toe. The dry earth drinks
his sweat; his veins are filled with warm blood, 630
his muscles bulged, his entire frame grew tough,
and with body restored he loosened Hercules' hold.
Alcides stood dazed by such great strength.
not in the waters of Inachus, though then inexperienced,
did he fear so the Hydra with her snakes renewed where severed.
They clashed as equals, one with the strength of Earth,
the other with his own. Never could his savage stepmother
have higher hopes: she sees the hero's limbs and neck drained
by exertion, the neck which stayed dry when he supported Olympus.
And when again he grappled with the tired limbs, 640
without waiting for his enemy's force, Antaeus fell
voluntarily and rose more mighty with added strength.
All the power of the land pours into his tired
frame and Earth labours as her warrior wrestles.
When at last Alcides realized the help he gained

from his mother's touch, he said: "You must stand, no more are
    you trusted
to the soil, you will be forbidden to lie prostrate upon the earth.
You will stick with limbs crushed within my embrace:
so far only, Antaeus, shall you fall." So speaking he raised aloft
the youth as he struggled for the Earth. She could not convey   650
her strength into her dying son's frame:
Alcides was in between them, holding his breast already tight
in torpid chill and for a long time did not trust his enemy to the earth.
That is how antiquity—the giver of renown, the guardian of
    ancient time
and admirer of herself—marked the land with his name.
But a greater name was given these hills
by Scipio, who recalled the Carthaginian enemy from the citadels
of Latium; for this was his position when he reached
the Libyan land. Look, you can see traces of the ancient rampart.
These are the fields first held by Roman victory.'   660

Curio was delighted, as if the fortune of the place would wage
his wars and maintain for him the destiny of former leaders,
and pitching his unlucky tents on lucky ground
he spread wide his camp and robbed the hills of their good omen
and with unequal strength provokes a fierce enemy.
    All of Africa which had yielded to Roman standards
was then under Varus' rule; though relying
on Roman might, still he summoned from everywhere the forces
of the king—the Libyan races and the world's furthest
troops accompanying their Juba. No master had   670
a broader land: where his realm is longest
it is bounded at the western point by Atlas, near to Gades,
on the middle line by Ammon, next to the Syrtes;
but where its breadth extends, the burning tract of his vast kingdom
keeps apart the Ocean and the parched hot zone.
The great area is matched by its peoples, so many follow his camp:
the Autololes, wandering Numidians, Gaetulians always
ready for action on undecorated horse; next Moors as dark
as Indians, poor Nasamonians, swift Marmaridae
with sun-scorched Garamantes, the Mazaces rivalling the Medes'   680
arrows when they shoot their quivering missiles,
and the Massylian race who ride bare-back

and with light stick guide mouths unacquainted with the bit,
and the Arzucian hunter who often roams through empty
huts and covers furious lions with his flowing clothes
as soon as confidence in his weapon is gone.
Juba was preparing his forces, not only from political cause
but, roused, he granted war to his personal indignation.
Curio had tried by tribune's law, in his year
of defiling gods and mortals, to expel him too   690
from his ancestral throne and to steal Libya from its tyrant
while he makes you, Rome, into a tyranny! Not forgetting his
      resentment,
Juba considers this war the harvest of retaining his sceptre.
So Curio now trembles at this rumour of the king,
and because his army had never been greatly devoted
to Caesar's camp or his soldiers tested on the waters
of the Rhine, captured in Corfinium's citadel,
because not trusted by their new leaders and treacherous to the old,
they consider both sides right. But when he sees that everything
is weak and paralysed with fear and the rampart's night-time duties 700
are deserted by flight, with anxious mind so he speaks:
   'Great terror is masked by boldness: I myself will be the first
to take up weapons. Let my soldiers—while they are mine—descend
to the level plain; leisure always breeds fickleness.
Remove their plots with fighting: when dreadful pleasure
comes on with the sword gripped tight, when helmets cover shame,
who thinks of comparing leaders? of weighing causes?
Where he stands, there he sides: just as those brought out at the shows
of the deadly arena are not compelled to fight by ancient
rage: they hate each other as opponents.' So speaking, he drew up   710
his lines on the open plains; and fortune of war met him
with smiles, soon to cheat him with disasters in the future:
he drove Varus from the plain and cut down his rear
exposed in shameful flight until stopped by his camp.

But when Juba heard about the dreadful battles
of defeated Varus, he was happy that warfare's glory
was kept for his efforts, and he hurries his forces secretly
and veils report of his approach by imposing silence,
fearing this alone from the incautious enemy—to be dreaded.

Sabbura, to the Numidians second after the king, is sent   720
with a tiny band to provoke first battle
and to lure them out, feigning that the war is to him entrusted;
while Juba himself keeps back his kingdom's forces in a hollow valley.
Just so are Pharian asps deceived by their cleverer enemy
with his tail; he angers and provokes them with the shifting shadow
and when the serpent stretches out into empty air,
his head aslant he grabs its throat with bite safely
short of the deadly venom; then the bane without effect
is squeezed out and its jaws run with wasted poison.
Fortune made the stratagem successful and, without   730
surveying his hidden enemy's strength, fierce
Curio makes his cavalry sally forth from camp
at night and range far and wide over unknown fields.
At dawn's first stir, himself he bids the troops
leave the camp, though often and in vain they begged him
to be in fear of Libyan tricks and Punic warfare
always tainted by deceit. The fortune of imminent death
had handed over the young man to the Fates, and civil war
was dragging down its cause. He leads his troops
on a sheer path over precipitous rocks and over crags.   740
When from the hill-tops the enemy were sighted far away,
in their stratagem they withdrew a little, waiting for him to leave
the hill and entrust his stretched-out line to the spreading fields.
Ignorant of the treacherous ruse and thinking they were fleeing,
as if victorious, he forced his line down into the plains below.
At once the trickery was evident: swift Numidians
massed upon the hills and enclosed the troops on every side.
At that moment the leader and doomed host alike were stupefied.
The fearful did not seek escape, the brave did not seek battle,
for there the steed, unmoved by trumpets' blare, does not shake   750
the rocks with beating hooves or rub his mouth by chafing
on the hard bit, does not let his mane stream out or prick his ears
or fight not to stand still with restless shifting feet.
His weary neck hangs down, his limbs steam with sweat,
his mouth is dry and rough, with tongue protruding,
his hoarse chest moans, driven by repeated panting,
and the laboured throbbing far contracts his worn-out flanks,
and foam dries and hardens on the blood-stained bit.
And now they quicken their pace, not compelled by whips

and goads or commanded by the spurs however frequent: 760
the horses are driven on by wounds. And no one gained
by ending his steed's delay, as neither charge nor attack
was possible: he is only carried towards the enemy
and shortens the space for the javelins by presenting a target.
But as soon as the roaming Africans launched their cavalry against
the troops, then the fields shook with the noise, the earth was
  broken up
and dust as vast as spiralled by a Bistonian whirlwind
veiled the air with its clouds and drew on darkness.
Truly, when the lamentable fate of war bore down upon
the foot-soldiers, fortunes hung in the balance on no decision   770
of uncertain warfare, but death ruled the duration
of the fight. And in fact there was no chance of running to attack
and joining battle. So, totally surrounded, the soldiers
are crushed by spears sent slanting from nearby and straight
from a distance, doomed to die not by wounds
and blood alone but by the rain of weapons and the weight of iron.
So the mighty forces are packed into a little cluster
and if anyone in panic crept into the middle of the troops,
hardly without injury can he turn among his comrades' swords;
the knot grows denser whenever the front line reduced   780
the circle by stepping back. The crowded men now have no space
for wielding weapons and their compressed limbs are ground together:
armed breast is struck on breast and smashed.
The victorious Moors did not enjoy to the full the sight
which Fortune gave: they do not see the streams
of gore, collapsing limbs, and bodies hitting
the earth: every corpse stood erect, crushed in a mass.
Let Fortune call up grim Carthage's hated ghosts
with these new offerings, let blood-stained Hannibal
and the Punic shades accept this grim expiation.   790
It is a crime, gods, that Roman ruin on the earth
of Libya helps Pompey and the Senate's prayers!
Better that Africa should conquer us for herself. When Curio
saw his troops routed on the plains and dust, smothered
by blood, permitted him discern how great the slaughter was,
in his shattered state he could not bear to prolong his life
or hope for escape, but fell amid the wreckage of his own men,
vigorous for death and brave with necessary valour.

What help to you now is the Forum and the Rostrum disturbed,
the tribune's citadel from which you, the standard-bearer of the
    plebs,   800
gave weapons to the people? What help the Senate's rights betrayed
and father- and son-in-law bidden join in battle?
You lie low before grim Pharsalia pits the leaders together
and the spectacle of civil warfare is denied you.
This, doubtless, is the penalty, mighty men, you pay to unhappy Rome
with your own blood, like this you make atonement with your slaughter.
How happy Rome would be, how blessed her future citizens,
if Liberty's preservation was as important
to the gods as its avenging. Look!—Curio, a noble corpse,
covered by no tomb, feeds the birds of Libya.   810
But it is no use to keep quiet about deeds whose own fame
fends off all decay of time—so to you,
young man, we give worthy commendation to the life which
    earned it.
No other citizen of such great talent did Rome produce,
to no other did the laws owe more had he followed what was right.
As it was, depraved ages damaged Rome, once
ambition, luxury, and the dreaded power of wealth
had carried off his wavering mind with sideways current;
and won over by Gallic booty and Caesar's gold,
the altered Curio turned the balance of events.   820
True, mighty Sulla and fierce Marius and bloody Cinna
and the chain of Caesar's house created for themselves
the power of the sword over our throats. But who was ever granted
such great power as he? They all bought, but he sold Rome.

BOOK FIVE

So Fortune mingled failure with success, and kept the leaders
for the Macedonians' land, well-matched after suffering wounds
of war in turn. Already winter had sprinkled
snows on Haemus, Atlas' daughter was sinking in chill Olympus,
and the day was near which gives new names to the Calendar,
which is first to worship Janus who ushers in the months.
But while the final part of their expiring authority remained,
both consuls summon to Epirus the Senators dispersed
on duties of the war. A foreign and a lowly place
received the Roman chieftains, and, as a guest   10
in an alien house, the Senate heard the secrets of state.
For who can give the name of 'camp' to so many Rods, so many Axes
bared legally? The venerable Order taught the nations
that they were not Magnus' party but that Magnus was in theirs.
     As soon as silence held the grim assembly,
aloft from his high seat speaks Lentulus:
'If in your minds you have the strength worthy of the Latian
character and of ancient blood, do not see the land in which
we are convened or how far from the homes of captured
Rome we sit, but recognize the appearance of your own company   20
and, Fathers, empowered to issue any order, first make this decree,
a fact clear to kingdoms and to peoples—that we are the Senate.
For whether Fortune carries us beneath the icy wagon
of Hyperborean Bear or where the burning zone
and clime enclosed by heat lets neither nights nor days
grow unequal, rule of the state will attend us,
and power will be our companion. When the Tarpeian sanctuary
was burnt by Gallic torches and Camillus lived at Veii—
there, was Rome. Not ever has our Order lost
authority by change of soil. The mourning houses,   30
empty homes, the silent laws, and Forum closed
in grim suspension—those are Caesar's; that Senate-House
sees only those Senators whom it expelled when Rome was full:
from such a mighty Order whoever is not an exile is here.

War's first frenzy scattered us, ignorant of wickedness,
reposing in long peace: now all the limbs return
to their place again. See! with all the forces of the world
the gods make up for Hesperia: the enemy lies overwhelmed
in Illyrian waves, on Libya's barren fields
Curio has fallen—a large part of Caesar's Senate.   40
Raise the standards, generals, forward the course of Fate,
render to the gods your hopes and let Fortune give you
courage as great as your cause gave you when fleeing
from the enemy. *Our* authority is ended when the year
runs out; but *your* power will experience no limit,
so, Fathers, look to the common good and bid Magnus
be your leader.'

                        With joyful shout the Senate greets
his name and imposed on Magnus his country's fate
and his own. Then to deserving kings and peoples
honours were distributed: Phoebean Rhodes, the mistress of the sea,   50
and uncouth soldiers of chill Taÿgetus were glorified
with gifts; Athens, ancient in renown, is praised
and Phocis freed as a compliment to her own Massilia;
then they commend Sadalas and valiant Cotys
and Deiotarus, loyal in warfare, and Rhascypolis, the master
of an icy region, and on authority of the Senate they tell Libya
to obey sceptred Juba. And—O what bitter fate!—
to you, Ptolemy, shame of Fortune, a reproach against the gods,
well deserving power over a race not trustworthy,
leave is given to encircle your piled hair with the Pellaean   60
diadem. You, a boy, receive a sword so cruel towards your people
—and I wish towards your people only! When Lagus' palace was given,
Magnus' slaughter was included, and when the sister was robbed
of her kingdom, so was the father-in-law of his crime.

                        Now once the assembly is dispersed
the company heads for war. While the peoples and the generals
prepared to fight, their fortunes unsure and destiny hidden,
Appius alone fears to descend into the hazardous events
of Mars and stirs the gods to disclose
the outcome and he unbars prophetic Phoebus'
Delphic shrine, closed through many a year.   70
As far removed from western as from eastern

point, Parnassus seeks the ether with twin hill, a mountain
sacred to Phoebus and to Bromius, whom Theban Bacchants
honour in triennial rites, merging the two gods.
When flood engulfed the earth, this peak alone
protruded and was the dividing-line of sea and stars.
Even you, Parnassus, split by the water, hardly raised
your topmost rock, with one ridge lying invisible.
There Paean, the avenger of his mother driven out when offspring
burdened her womb, stretched out the Python with his arrows   80
as yet untried, when Themis held the power and the tripods.
When the victor saw the earth's vast chasms
breathe out divine certainty and the soil exhale
talking winds, he hid himself in the sacred caves
and there, become a prophet, Apollo settled on the shrine.

    Which of the gods lies concealed here? Which power sinking
from the ether condescends to live enclosed in these blind caves?
Which god of heaven endures the earth, holding all
the secrets of the sequence of eternity and knowing
the future of the universe, ready to show himself to the peoples,   90
undergoing human contact, both great and powerful,
whether he prophesies Fate or Fate becomes what he commands
in prophecy? Perhaps a large part of all Divinity,
inserted in the earth to rule it and holding up
the sphere poised in the empty air, through the caves of Cirrha
issues forth and is inhaled, linked to the Thunderer in the ether.
When this power is received in virgin's breast
and strikes her human spirit, it sounds out and unlocks
the prophetess' mouth, as the Sicilian peak gushes when Etna
is pressured by the flames, as Typhoeus, buried underneath   100
the everlasting mass of Inarime, roars and heats Campania's rocks.

    This power, though available to all and denied to none,
yet alone keeps itself free from stain of human
madness. No wicked prayers are uttered there in silent whisper,
because by prophesying what is fixed and changeable
by none, the power forbids mortals to pray; and generous to the just,
he often gave abode to people leaving entire cities, such as
the Tyrians; he often gave ability to drive back threats of war,
as the sea of Salamis remembers; he removed the wrath
of barren earth by revealing the remedy, he released   110
the poisonous air. Our generation lacks

no greater gift of gods than that the Delphic sanctuary
has fallen silent, ever since kings feared the future
and forbade the gods to speak. And Cirrha's prophetesses
do not grieve that voice is denied, but enjoy the temple's
idleness. Because, if the god enters any breast,
an early death is the penalty of taking in the deity,
or the reward; because the human framework falls apart
under frenzy's goad and surge, and the beatings of the gods
shake their brittle lives.

     So the tripods   120
long unmoved and the vast rock's silence are disturbed
by Appius, inquiring deeply into the destiny of Hesperia
to the final detail. Told to open up the dreaded shrine
and send the frightened prophetess in to the gods,
the priest seized Phemonoe as she was wandering at will
around Castalian waters and retreats in the forests,
free from worries, and forces her to rush inside the temple-doors.
Afraid to stand upon the terrifying threshold, by a hollow trick
Apollo's prophetess tries to deter the general from his desire
to know the future. She says: 'Why does presumptuous hope   130
of learning truth attract you, Roman? Its chasm dumb, Parnassus
has fallen silent and suppressed its god—either because the Spirit
has deserted those jaws and has turned its path to the world's
remotenesses; or because, after Python burnt with barbarian
torches, the ashes fell into the enormous caves
and obstructed Phoebus' path; or because by the gods' will
Cirrha is silent and it is enough that future secrets are told
in the ancient Sibyl's prophecies, entrusted to your race;
or because Paean, who always keeps the guilty from his temple,
does not in our age find people to unlock his mouth for.'   140
The virgin's trick was obvious and her fear itself induced
belief in the powers she denied. Then the coiled headband
binds her hair in front and her tresses, let loose down her back,
are encircled by white woollen band with Phocis' laurel.
As she lingered, hesitant, the priest thrust her forcibly
inside the temple. Dreading the remote prophetic
inner shrine, she halts in the first part of the temple
and, feigning the god, she speaks fictitious words
from a tranquil breast, proving her mind inspired

by sacred frenzy by no mutter of indistinct voice;   150
not so likely to harm the general to whom she gave false prophecy
as the tripods and good name of Phoebus. Because her words did not
erupt with trembling sound, her voice was not enough to fill
the vast cave's space, the laurels were not shaken off
by stiffening of her hair, the temple's threshold was unmoved
and the grove untroubled: everything betrayed her fear to trust
herself to Phoebus. Appius realized that the tripods were not
      functioning
and, in a rage, he says: 'Wicked woman, to me and to the gods
      you feign,
you will pay the penalty which you deserve unless you plunge into
      the cave
and cease to speak in your own words when consulted about the
      turmoil   160
so immense of the anxious world.' At last the virgin, terrified,
takes refuge at the tripods and, drawn towards the vast chasms,
there she stayed, receiving in her unaccustomed breast the power
which the Spirit of the rock, still not exhausted after
all those centuries, poured into the prophetess; and at last Paean
mastered her Cirrhaean breast and never more completely
invaded his priestess' frame, drove out her former mind,
and told the mortal part to leave her breast to him
entirely. Mad, she runs wild through the cave with frenzied neck,
and dislodging with her bristling hair the headbands of the god   170
and Phoebus' garlands, she whirls them with her tossing head
through the temple's empty spaces, scatters the tripods
in her wandering way, and boils with a mighty fire,
suffering your anger, Phoebus. And you use not the whip alone
and goads, but plunge flames into her guts:
the prophetess submits to the bridle too, and she is not allowed to tell
as much as she is allowed to know. All time converges into
a single heap and all the centuries oppress her unhappy breast,
the chain of happenings so lengthy is revealed and all the future
struggles to the light and the Fates grapple   180
as they seek a voice; everything is there: the first day, the end
of the world, the Ocean's size, the number of the sand.
As the prophetess of Cumae in her Euboean retreat,
resentful that her frenzy was the slave of many
peoples, with disdainful hand selected from the mass

of destinies so great the destiny of Rome; just so Phemonoe,
full of Phoebus, toils until with difficulty she finds you,
Appius, consulter of the god concealed in Castalian land,
long seeking you unseen among such mighty destinies.
Then at first through her foaming lips the rabid frenzy   190
flowed out with groans and with loud mutters from the panting
channel; next a mournful howling in the vast cave;
and finally, the virgin now subdued, the sound of speech:
'Roman, you escape the mighty threats of warfare, taking no part
in the crisis so enormous; you alone will gain
repose in a mighty valley of the Euboean coast.'
The rest Apollo stifled and he blocked her throat.

O tripods, guardians of destiny, O secrets of the universe,
and you, Paean, master of the truth, kept by the gods
in ignorance of no future day, why do you fear to reveal   200
the final moments of a tumbling empire, slaughtered generals,
the deaths of kings, and so many nations falling down
in the blood of Hesperia? Is it because the powers not yet have decreed
a crime so great and, with the stars still hesitating
to doom Pompey's head, so many destinies are withheld?
Or are you silent on the deed of the avenging sword, the punishments
of madness and tyranny again returning to vengeance of the Bruti,
to enable Fortune to perform them? Then the doors gave way,
struck by the prophetess' breast, and, driven from the temple,
out she sprang; her frenzy persists and the god she has not sent
        away   210
remains in her, as she has not spoken everything. She still
rolls fierce eyes and roaming glances over all
the sky, now with frightened look, now grim with menace;
her face is never still; a fiery redness dyes
her face and livid cheeks; she has the pallor
not of one afraid, but terrifying; her weary heart
is not at rest but, as the swollen sea moans hoarsely
after Boreas' blasts, so silent sighs relieve the prophetess.
And while she is returned to common daylight from the sacred light
by which she saw the Fates, darkness intervened.   220
Paean admitted Stygian Lethe into her guts
to snatch away the secrets of the gods. Then truth flies
from her breast and the future returns to Phoebus' tripods,

and, hardly recovered, down she falls. And death's proximity
does not terrify you, Appius, deceived by the ambiguous oracle;
but, seized by groundless hope, you prepared to lie in wait for the
    realm
of Euboean Chalcis, while rule of the world was undecided.
What a madman! which of the gods can ensure
that you feel no battle uproar, that you escape
the world's so many evils—except Death? Buried in a memorable   230
tomb, you will occupy seclusion of Euboean shore,
where the throat of sea is narrowed by rocky Carystos
and Rhamnus, worshipper of powers hostile to the haughty,
where the restricted sea boils with rapid flood
and Euripus with waves shifting course draws
the ships of Chalcis towards Aulis, treacherous to fleets.

Meanwhile Caesar was returning, the Iberians subdued,
soon to carry his victorious Eagles into another world,
when the gods nearly turned aside his mighty course
through destiny's successes. For the commander, not subdued   240
by warfare, feared to lose the advantage of his crimes
inside his camp's tents, when the soldiers, loyal
through so many wars, at last now sated with blood, almost
deserted their leader. Perhaps the trumpet ceasing for a while
from its gloomy sound and the sword, shut away and cold,
had banished mania for war; perhaps in search of greater prizes
the troops reject both cause and leader and even now
offer up for sale their swords stained with crime.
In no crisis did Caesar learn more clearly
how he looked down on everything from a height which was   250
not firm but shaking and how he stood supported on a rocking
    platform.
Maimed by the loss of so many hands and almost left
to his own sword, the man who drew to war so many nations
knows that unsheathed swords are not the general's but the soldier's.
Now there was no fearful muttering, no anger lying hidden
in breast concealed, because they are not checked by the factor
which generally inhibits wavering minds: each man's fear of those
he himself alarms, each man's belief that he alone feels oppressed
by tyranny's injustice. Why? The daring multitude itself

put an end to its fears: the offence of many goes unavenged.   260
They hurled their threats: 'Let us depart, Caesar,
from crime's madness. You seek by land and sea
a sword for these our throats, you are ready to shed our lives
so cheap by any enemy: some of us were snatched from you
by Gaul, some by Spain in harsh warfare,
some lie low in Italy—in all the world your army
dies when you conquer. What use is it to have shed
our blood in northern lands while taming Rhône and Rhine?
In return for so many wars, you have given me civil war.
When we drove out the Senate and took our country's homes,   270
which mortals and which gods were we allowed to rob?
We proceed to every crime, guilty in hand and sword,
guiltless in our poverty. What limit is sought for warfare?
What is enough, if Rome is too little? Now notice
our white hair and feeble hands and see our wasted arms.
The time for enjoying life has gone, we have spent our lives in
        fighting:
we are old—disband us to die. See how outrageous is our prayer:
not to place our dying limbs on the hard
turf, not to beat the helmet with our fleeing breath
and seek in vain a hand to close our eyes in death;   280
but to fall amid our wives' tears and to know the pyre
is ready for one body only; to end old age in sickness;
that under Caesar's rule there be some other death besides the sword.
Why do you lure us on with hope as if ignorant of the horrors
we are to face? Are we then the only ones in civil warfare
not to know which crime awards the greatest pay?
Nothing have the wars achieved if he has not yet learnt
that our hands can do anything. Neither duty nor the bonds of law
prevent this daring deed: on the waters of the Rhine Caesar was
my leader, here he is my comrade; crime levels those it stains.   290
And anyway our valour is wasted with a judge ungrateful
of our services: all our achievements are called "Fortune".
He must know that we are his destiny: Caesar, though you hope
for absolute compliance of the gods, if your troops are angered,
there will be peace.' This said, they began to rush throughout
the camp and with hostile face demand their leader.
So be it, O gods: since duty and since loyalty
fail and the only hope remaining is in wicked ways,

let discord bring an end to civil war.

What leader could that uproar fail to terrify? 300
But Caesar comes, accustomed to commit his destiny
headlong and rejoicing to wield his own fortune
in the highest risks: without waiting for their anger
to abate, he hurries to test their frenzy at its peak.
He would not have refused them Rome and temples to be plundered
and Jupiter's Tarpeian seat and the Senate's mothers and daughters
to suffer the unspeakable. He wants them to demand from him
all atrocities, without a doubt, to love the prizes of war;
only the sanity of his unbridled troops makes him afraid.
Oh, does it not shame you, Caesar, that you alone enjoy the wars 310
now rejected by your men? Will they be revolted by blood
before you are? Will they be troubled by rule of the sword, while
     you race
through every right and wrong? Grow weary, learn that without
     fighting
you can endure; may you impose upon yourself a limit to crime.
Brutal man—why press on? Why threaten men now unwilling?
Civil war is deserting you.—On a mound of piled turf
he stood with face undaunted, and his fearlessness
deserved to be feared; he speaks these words at anger's prompt:
'Soldiers, you were raging recently in face and hand against
an absent man: you now have his breast bare and ready for your
     wounds. 320
Here leave your sword and flee, if you want an end of war.
Your unwarlike spirits are revealed by your rebellion without bold
     deed
of bravery and by your soldiers contemplating flight alone,
wearied by success of an undefeated leader.
Go, leave me and warfare to my destiny.
These weapons will find hands to hold them, and after discarding you,
Fortune will give back as many warriors as vacant swords.
If the peoples of Hesperia with a fleet so great attend
the retreat of Magnus, will not victory give me
a multitude to carry off just the prizes of the war 330
which you urged onwards, to seize the reward of your toil,
to escort unwounded my laurelled chariot?
You old men, a crowd despised and drained of blood,

now Roman citizens, will watch our triumphs.
Do you think that Caesar's career can feel
the loss of your flight? It is as if all rivers
threatened to withdraw the streams they mingle with the sea:
with those waters gone, the sea-level would fall
no more than it now rises. Do you think that you have turned
the scales for me? Never will the gods' concern   340
so lower itself that Fate has time for *your* death
and *your* safety: all such events ensue from actions of the chieftains;
for a few does humankind live. As soldiers under my name,
you were the terror of the Iberian and the northern world;
with Pompey as your leader, doubtless you would have fled. Labienus
was brave in Caesar's armour; now a contemptible deserter,
he traverses lands and seas with his preferred leader.
And I will not rate your loyalty more highly if you wage wars
neither under nor against me. Whoever leaves my standards
without delivering his weapons to Pompey's side   350
wishes never more to be mine. This my camp is certainly
looked after by the gods—they did not wish me to engage
in wars so great without a change of troops.
Alas! What a mighty burden Fortune removes from my shoulders
already tired by the load! I am permitted to disarm right hands
with hopes unbounded, for whom this world is not enough:
now for myself, assuredly, I will wage war. Leave the camp,
hand over my standards to warriors, you cowardly civilians.
But the few responsible for this blaze of frenzy are detained
not by Caesar but by punishment. Lie down upon the ground   360
and stretch your treacherous heads and necks for the blow.
And you raw recruits—on your strength alone my camp
will stand now—watch the punishments and learn how to strike,
learn how to die.' Under his fierce and threatening voice
the spiritless crowd quaked, and an army so enormous fears a single
man—a man they could depose—as if he commanded their very
swords and could move the blade against the soldier's will.
Caesar himself dreads that hands and weapons will be
refused him for this crime: but their obedience surpassed their cruel
leader's hope and offered him throats, not swords alone.   370
Nothing more binds minds which are familiar with crime
than to destroy and be destroyed. By the stroke of pact so grim
was order gained—the troops return to duty, calmed by the

punishment.

These soldiers he commands to reach Brundisium in ten encampments
and to summon back all the ships sheltered in distant Hydrus
and ancient Taras and the secluded shores of Leuca,
in the Salapian swamp and Sipus situated underneath
the mountains, where fruitful Apulian Garganus
bends Ausonia's coast and extends into the Adriatic waves,
exposed to Boreas from Dalmatia and to Auster from Calabria.   380
Safe without his troops, himself he heads for trembling Rome,
which now had learnt to serve the garb of peace. Giving in, of course,
to the people's prayer, he honoured the highest office as dictator,
and by his consulship made the calendar rejoice.
And indeed all those expressions with which for so long now
we have lied to our masters were invented by that age,
when Caesar, to preserve every right to wield the sword,
wanted to combine Ausonian Axes with his blades
and added Rods to Eagles: grabbing the empty
name of authority he stamped the gloomy times   390
with fitting mark; for by what consul will Pharsalia's year
be better known? The Campus feigns the ceremony,
sorts the votes of the excluded plebs,
recites the Tribes, and stirs the lots in useless urn.
Nor is it allowed to watch the sky; the augur is deaf to thunder
and the omens are declared auspicious despite an unfavourable owl.
From that time first perished the once venerable power,
stripped of its authority; except, to prevent time lacking a name,
consuls for a month mark out the ages in the calendar.
And the deity presiding over Trojan Alba   400
saw the Latin Festival performed in flame-lit night,
though, with Latium quelled, he did not deserve the sacred rites.

Hurrying his course from Rome, he races on through fields
deserted by the Apulian, inactive with his hoes, and surrendered
to the useless grass, swifter than the flames of heaven,
than a tigress with her young. Reaching the Minoan homes of curving
Brundisium, he finds the waves hemmed in by winter winds
and his fleets afraid of wintry constellation.
To the leader it seemed disgraceful that the moment for hastening
      war

had extended into slow delays, disgraceful to be kept in harbour   410
while the sea is safely open to others, even the unlucky.
Like this he fills with strength minds inexperienced in the sea:
   'When winter's blasts seize sky and strait
their hold is firmer than those which the treacherous fickleness
of cloud-bearing spring prevents from settling certain.
Nor must we trace the shores and windings of the sea,
but cut the waves straight and with Aquilo's help alone.
I hope it bends the high mast-heads and in a rage
bears down on us and blows us to the Greek walls;
otherwise Pompey's men from all Phaeacia's shore   420
may catch our drooping canvas by wielding their oars.
Break the bonds which check our successful prows;
long have we been wasting the clouds and savage waves.'
As Phoebus sank beneath the waves the first stars of the sky
came out, and now the moon made shadows of her own
when together they unmoored the ships; the ropes untied
the sails' entire fullness, and the sailors slant the canvas
on curved yard-arm with sheets to port and, by spreading
highest topsails, gather breezes easily lost.
At first with difficulty, a slight wind begins to distend   430
the sails and they swell a little, droop against
the mast, and fall down upon the ship, and once land was left behind,
the breeze which had carried the vessels had not power itself to
       follow them.
Inert lies the sea; the waves stood still, bound
by deep paralysis, more sluggishly than unmoved swamps.
So stands motionless the Bosporus binding Scythian waves
when Danube does not strike against the deep, prevented by the ice,
and the huge sea is covered by frost; the water hems in
every ship it catches and the horseman smashes the expanse
untraversable by sail, and the wheel-track of migrating Bessi   440
cleaves Maeotis, resounding with concealed surge.
Savage is the sea's calm and inactive the pools of water
lying on the dismal deep; as if deserted by nature's
ruling force the waters are still and the sea, forgetting to maintain
its ancient alternations, does not move to and fro with tide
or quiver with a ruffled surface or shimmer with the sun's reflection.
To countless perils the stationary ships were exposed.
On one side hostile fleets, about to stir with oars

the sluggish waters, on the other painful famine, ready to approach
    them,
blockaded by the stillness of the deep. New prayers were found   450
in terror new—prayers for waves and for excessive
force of winds, provided that the water would shake itself
from torpid pools and be a real sea. Nowhere are there clouds
or signs of waves; with sky and sea unmoving,
gone is every hope of shipwreck. But, with night dispelled,
the day displayed its light, disfigured by cloud, and gradually stirred
the sea's depths and brought Ceraunia towards the sailors.
Then the ships began to race, and curving waters
followed the fleet, and now, gliding on with help of wind and wave,
it pierced Palaeste's sands with its anchor-hooks.   460

First land to see the leaders halt with camps
adjoining was that encircled by the banks of swift Genusus
and the gentler Apsus. That Apsus carries vessels is explained
by a swamp, which it drains deceptively with placid water;
but Genusus is torrential with the snows dissolved now by sun,
now by rain; neither wearies itself by lengthy stream
but with shore nearby they little know of land.
This was the place where Fortune matched two names of fame
so great, and futile was the miserable world's hope
that the leaders might, when parted by the plain's tiny area,   470
renounce the crime now brought so close; for they can see their faces,
hear their voices, and your father-in-law, beloved by you
through many a year, Magnus, never saw you closer
after such great bonds —the offspring of unlucky blood,
the sharing of grandchildren —except on Nile's sand.

    His party, left behind, compelled Caesar's mind, frantic
for joining battle, to endure delay of wickedness.
Commander of all these troops was bold Antony,
even then rehearsing Leucas in civil war.
As he delays, Caesar often summons him with threats   480
and prayers: 'O cause of such huge labours for the world,
why do you check the gods and destiny? The rest has been achieved
by my speed, and Fortune asks of you the final touch
to a war sped onwards through successes. Libya broken
by the shallow Syrtes does not part us with its restless tide.
Am I entrusting your army to the untried deep?

Are you drawn into unknown perils? No. Coward, Caesar
        commands
you come, not go. Ahead of you myself, through the midst
of enemies, I struck the sands in another's power:
do you fear a camp that is mine? I bewail the loss of hours   490
of destiny, on winds and sea I waste my prayers.
Do not hold back men who are eager to go across the fickle water:
if I know them right, the troops will want to join
Caesar's army at the cost of shipwreck. Even a word of resentment
I must utter: not equally have we divided up the world:
Caesar and the whole Senate has Epirus but you alone
have Ausonia.' With these words he summoned him
three times, four times, but when he saw him motionless,
in the belief that he was failing the gods and not the deities him,
he ventures through the unsafe darkness to attempt the sea   500
willingly, a thing which others, though commanded, feared, in his
        knowledge
that recklessness succeeds when god is well-disposed, and he hopes
in a tiny vessel to surmount the waves which terrify the fleets.

Drowsy night had relaxed the weary cares of war,
a brief repose for the miserable men into whose breasts
their lesser fortune gives strength in sleep; now the camp was silent,
now the third hour had woken up the second watch:
Caesar with troubled step through desolate silence
tries a venture too bold even for a slave and, leaving all else behind,
chooses Fortune as his sole companion. After passing by   510
the tents he jumped over the sentries' limbs, which were yielding
to sleep, silently complaining that he could elude them,
picks his way along the curving shore and at the water's edge
finds a boat attached by a rope to the hollowed rocks.
Not far from there the vessel's captain and master
had his home from troubles free, not supported by any timber
but woven from barren rush and marsh reed
and protected on its exposed side by an upturned hull.
Twice and three times with his hand Caesar struck this threshold,
shaking the roof. From his soft bed provided by seaweed   520
Amyclas rises. He says: 'Say, what shipwrecked man
seeks my home? Who is driven by Fortune to hope
for help from my hut?' So speaking, he lifted

the rope from the deep mound of ash still warm
and fed the tiny spark till he had roused the fire,
not thinking of the war: well he knows that in civil warfare
huts are not the loot. O safe the lot of a poor man's
life and humble home! O gods' gifts not yet
understood! Which temples or which walls
could enjoy this blessing, not to shake in panic   530
when Caesar's hand is knocking? Then, when the door was opened,
the leader says: 'Expect more than your modest wishes
and expand your hopes, young man: if following my orders
to Hesperia you carry me, no longer will you owe everything
to your vessel and your hands or, lamenting cruel poverty,   535
complain of living an impoverished old age.
Do not delay to present your destiny to the god who wants   536
to fill your humble home with sudden riches.'
So he speaks, though dressed in plebeian garb,
untrained to speak as an ordinary man. Then poor Amyclas:

    'Very many signs prevent me trusting the sea tonight: 540
the sun did not draw down into the waters ruddy clouds
or bear its rays in harmony: with light divided,
one part of Phoebus summoned Notus, the other Boreas.
And he vanished, hollowed out and faint in the middle of his orb,
with feeble light allowing eyes to gaze.
And the moon arose not bright with slender crescent,
or hollowed in mid-orb into clear recess,   547
but she reddened with the sign of winds; then, pale, she had   549
a yellow look, gloomy as her face began to pass behind a cloud.   550
But I do not like the tossing of the forests or the blows
upon the shore or the restless dolphin who rouses up the seas,
or the gull's love of dry land, or the heron's venture
to fly aloft, trusting her floating wing,
or the crow's pacing of the shores with unsteady step,
sprinkling her head with water, as if anticipating rain.
Yet if the crisis of immense events demands, I cannot
hesitate to offer my hands: either I shall touch the shores
which you command or this will be refused by sea and squalls, not me.'

He speaks these words, unmoors his boat, and spreads his sails   560
to the winds; at their blast not only did the falling stars
which glide through lofty air trace scattered

trails, but even the stars which remain fixed
in highest skies seemed to tremble. A black shudder stains
the surface of the sea, the wave seethes, threatening and uncertain
of the coming squall through many a roll on its lengthy track,
the waters' turbulence attests the winds conceived.
Then says the helmsman of the quivering boat: 'Look at what
the cruel sea has in store: whether it threatens with Zephyr or with
     Auster
is not clear; the shifting deep strikes the boat from every side.   570
Notus is in clouds and sky; if we consult the murmurs
of the deep, Corus' sea will come. In such a mighty flood,
neither ship nor shipwrecked man will touch Hesperian shores:
our only safety is to despair of our journey and reverse
our forbidden course. Permit me to reach the shore with ravaged
ship, or else the nearest land may be too far.'
     Confident that for him all dangers will give way, Caesar
says: 'Despise the sea's threats, entrust your sail
to the raging wind. If you refuse Italy at heaven's command,
seek it at mine. The sole legitimate cause of fear for you is this: 580
ignorance of who your passenger is, someone never deserted
by the gods, someone who is treated ill by Fortune
when she comes only after his prayers. Secure in my protection,
break through the gales' midst. That toil belongs
to sky and sea, not to this our ship: weighed down by Caesar,
its load will defend it from the surge. And no long duration
will be granted to the winds' fierce frenzy: this boat
will help the waves. Do not turn your hand, with sails flee the nearest
shores; believe that you have reached the harbour of Calabria then
when no other land can be granted to the ship   590
and to our safety. You do not know what is made ready
in such vast destruction: by turmoil of the sea and sky,
Fortune seeks to favour me.'

                         No more had he said
when a greedy whirlwind struck the boat, ripped away
the tattered ropes, and bore the flapping sails
over the flimsy mast; the vessel groaned as its joints gave way.
Then come rushing dangers, roused from all the world.
Corus, you are first to raise your head from Atlas'
ocean, stirring the tides. Now the sea, reared up by you,

was raging and had lifted all its waves on to the rocks: 600
chill Boreas meets it and quells the sea,
and the water hangs undecided which wind to succumb to.
But Scythian Aquilo's rage prevailed: it whirled
the waves, made shallows of the sands hidden deep below.
And Boreas does not bear the deep right to the rocks but shatters
his sea against Corus' waves, and even with the winds
removed, the waters roused can clash together.
I could believe that Eurus' threats were not inactive,
that Notus black with rains did not lie idle in the prison
of Aeolus' rock, that all winds racing from their usual parts   610
defended their own lands with violent whirlwind
and so the sea remained in place. For separate waters,
seized by the gales, they carry off: the Tyrrhenian Sea passes
into Aegean waves, the Adriatic moves and sounds in the Ionian Sea.
That day submerged mountains battered in vain, ah how often,
by the sea. What lofty peaks the conquered
earth sent to the depths! From no shore arise
such powerful waves but from the mighty sea they came,
rolled from another region, and the water which encircles
the world drives on the freakish billows. So Olympus' ruler,   620
when his thunderbolt was tired from punishing the generations,
      helped it
with his brother's trident, and earth was added to the Second Realm
when the sea swept away the peoples, when Tethys would endure
no shores, happy to be bound by sky alone.
Now too would the sea's vast mass have risen to the stars
had the ruler of the gods not subdued the waves with clouds.
That night was not a night of heaven: the air lies hid, enveloped
in the pallor of the infernal abode and heavily weighed down
by rain-clouds, and so the wave receives the rain directly.
Even this terrifying light dies, and no lightnings brightly   630
race, but the rain-clouded air dimly bursts apart.
Then the gods' dome quakes, the lofty sky thunders,
and the heavens suffer with their structure strained.
Nature dreaded chaos; it seems the elements
have burst their harmonious checks and night again
returns to mix the dead with gods. Their one hope of safety
is that not yet have they perished in the world's collapse so great.
As far below as tranquil sea is seen from the Leucadian

peak, quaking sailors from the wave-top
saw the sea's sheer drop; and when again the swollen waves   640
gape wide, hardly does the mast project above the water.
The sails touch the clouds, the keel touches earth.
For where it sinks, the sea does not conceal the sands;
it is used up in the billows, and all the water is in the waves.
Terror conquered skill's resources and the helmsman does not know
which stream to break and which to yield to. The discord of the sea
helps them in their trouble: wave against wave cannot
overturn the ship: the surge drives back and rights
the vessel's beaten flank and it rises erect amid all the winds.
Not Sason low with shallows, not the rocky shores   650
of winding Leucadia and the mean harbours
of Ambracian coast, but Ceraunia's craggy peaks
do the sailors fear.

                    Now Caesar thinks the perils
worthy of his destiny. He said: 'How mighty is the gods'
toil to throw me down, attacking me with sea so great
as I sit in a tiny boat! If the glory of my death
has been granted to the sea, if I am denied to warfare,
fearlessly will I accept whatever death you give me,
gods. Although the day hurried on by destiny
cuts short my mighty exploits, great enough I have done.   660
I have tamed the northern peoples, by fear subdued
hostile soldiers, Rome has seen Magnus second to me,
by ordering the people I have won the Rods denied to me by warfare;
no Roman office will my inscription lack,
and none but you will know this, Fortune,
the only sharer of my prayers, that though I go to Stygian shades
heaped with honours, consul and dictator both,
as an ordinary man I die. No need have I
of burial, O gods: keep my mangled corpse
in the billows' midst: let me be without a tomb and pyre,   670
provided I am always feared, by every land awaited.'
As this he said, the tenth wave—remarkable to tell—
lifts him with his flimsy boat, and did not cast him
down again from the sea's high heap but carried him on
and, where the narrow shore is free from jagged rocks,
set him on the land. When he touched earth, in one moment

he regained so many realms, so many cities, and his own fortune.

But now with daylight near, Caesar on his return did not elude
his camp and his companions as he had in silent flight.
A multitude of men surrounded their leader, wept, assailed   680
him with groans and with complaints which did not displease him:
    'Pitiless Caesar, where has your reckless valour taken you?
To what fate did you abandon us, worthless souls,
when you gave your limbs to be scattered by unwilling gales?
When the life and safety of so many peoples hinge
on this your soul, when the world so great has made you its head,
willingness to die is cruelty. Is there none of your
companions who did not deserve the chance not to survive
your death? When the sea was sweeping you along, dull sleep
held our bodies. O the shame! This was your reason   690
for seeking Hesperia yourself, that it seemed cruel
to send anyone on sea so fierce. Crisis
often plunges men into risky perils and dangers
which incline to death: but how could you allow the sea so much
when you now hold the mastery of the world? Why tire the deities?
The goodwill and the toil of Fortune drove you on to our sands;
but is that enough to show the outcome of the war?
Are you content to use the favour of the gods to be not ruler
of the world nor master of the state but survivor of a shipwreck?'
As they hurled such remarks, with night dispelled, the day   700
came on them cloudless with the sun, and the weary sea
with winds permitting calmed the swollen waves.

And the generals in Italy, on seeing the water
tired by the waves and pure Boreas rising in the sky,
soon to check the sea, unmoored their vessels.
These long were kept together by the wind and by hands
skilled with equal guidance, and across the wide water
the force moves in a group, as if on land, with ships close-packed.
But cruel night robbed the sailors of the mildness of the wind
and of sail's even course, and threw the ships out of line.   710
So when winter drives the cranes to leave the icy
Strymon, soon to drink your water, Nile, they form
in their first flight various shapes taught by chance;
then, when Notus, higher up, has struck their outstretched wings,

they mingle at random and mass into muddled clusters
and, disrupted by the scattered wings, the letter vanishes.
As soon as day returned and a stronger breeze,
stirred by Phoebus' rising, settled on the ships,
they attempt in vain the shores of Lissus, pass them by,
and reach Nymphaeum, where Auster, coming after Boreas,   720
had now made a harbour of the waves exposed to Aquilones.

With Caesar's troops combined from everywhere into full strength,
Magnus saw the supreme crisis of pitiless war
now looming over his camp, and he decided to deposit
safe the burden of his marriage and to hide you,
Cornelia, in Lesbos far removed from savage warfare's
din. O, how much power has lawful Venus
over tranquil minds! Love made even you, Magnus, hesitant
and afraid of battle; the only thing you wished not to expose
to the blow of Fortune which was waiting for the world and
      Roman destiny   730
was your wife. His mind, made up already, is deserted
by words, and, postponing things to come, he prefers to indulge
in sweet delay and steal time from destiny.
Just before night's end, with the heaviness of sleep banished,
while Cornelia hugs in her embrace his breast weighed down
with troubles and seeks her husband's pleasing kiss, he turns away:
amazed at his wet cheeks and struck by unseen
wound, she does not dare discover Magnus weeping.
With a groan he says: 'Wife, dearer to me than life,
life not now when I am tired of it but in the happy times,   740
the gloomy day has come which I have put off both too long
and not long enough; now Caesar in all his might is here for battle.
To warfare we must yield; Lesbos will be a safe refuge
for you from warfare. Stop attempts at prayers: already I have
refused myself. You will not suffer a long separation from me;
sudden will events be on us: with hurrying collapse
the highest fall. It is enough for you to hear of Magnus' dangers;
and your love has deceived me, if you can witness
civil war. And as for me, now that battle is near
I am ashamed to have taken carefree slumbers with my wife,   750
to have risen from your embrace when the trumpets shake
the troubled world. I fear to entrust Pompey

to civil warfare saddened by no loss.
Lie hid, meanwhile, safer than the peoples, safer
than every king, and may your husband's fortune not destroy you,
far removed, with all its weight. If the gods drive back
my troops, let the best part of Magnus survive;
and if destiny and blood-stained victor chase me, let me have
a welcome refuge.' Hardly in her weakness could she bear a grief
so great, and her senses left her stunned breast.   760
At last her voice was able to express her mournful protests:
   'No complaint is left to me about the gods, about the destiny
of marriage, Magnus: our love is not broken by death
or by the final torch of hideous pyre, but I lose my husband,
divorced in a fate frequent and too common.
At the enemy's approach let us break the pact of marriage-torch,
let us placate your father-in-law! Is that how well you know my
      loyalty,
Magnus? Do you believe my safety is different
from yours? Have we not long depended on one and the same
      chance?
Do you bid me, cruel man, present my head to thunderbolts   770
and to destruction so immense apart from you? Does it seem to you
a carefree fate, to have been destroyed while still making prayers?
Though I refuse to be a slave to hardships but with ready death
follow you down to the shades, until the gloomy news strikes
lands far removed, I shall of course live on as your survivor.
What is more, you accustom me to my destiny and teach me, cruel
      man,
to bear such mighty anguish. Forgive my confession—
I fear I can endure it. But if my wishes count for anything and the
      gods
hear me, the last to know of favourable outcome will be your wife:
while you are already victorious, anxiously shall I frequent   780
the cliffs and dread the ship which brings such a happy end.
And report of war's successes will not relieve my fears
since, abandoned in an unprotected place, I can be captured
by Caesar even as he flees. Well known will the shores become
by the exile of a famous name: and who can fail to know
of Mytilene's refuge, if Magnus' wife is lodged there?
This is my final prayer: if your conquered forces leave you
nothing more secure than flight, when you entrust yourself to waves,

steer your ill-starred ship to any land but there:
on my shores they will search for you.' This said, demented,   790
up she jumped, abandoning the bed and wishing to postpone
her agony by no delay. She cannot bear to hold
in sweet embrace unhappy Magnus' breast or neck,
and the last enjoyment of a love so long is lost,
and they accelerate their own sorrow, and neither in departing
could bear to say 'Farewell', and through all their lives
no day was so sad, because the losses which remained
they bore with mind already strong and steeled by hardships.
She collapses, the unfortunate, and caught by her attendants' hands
is carried to the sea's sands, prostrates herself   800
and grabs the shore itself and finally is taken on board ship.
Not so unfortunate did she depart from her fatherland and harbours
of Hesperia when cruel Caesar's forces were pursuing hard,
Magnus' loyal comrade. She goes alone, leaving the general,
and runs from Pompey. The next night which came to you
was sleepless; for the first time then her rest was cold and unfamiliar
to her alone in widowed bed, then first her side was unprotected
with husband not clinging close. How often, overpowered by sleep,
did she embrace the empty couch with disappointed hands
and seek her husband in the night, forgetful of her flight!   810
For though the flame was burning in her silent depths,
she does not like to fling her body over all the couch:
that part of the bed is reserved. She feared that she had lost
Pompey; but the gods were not planning such joy: the hour
was near for the unhappy woman when Magnus would be given back.

BOOK SIX

The leaders, now intent on battle, stationed camps
on neighbouring ridges and brought their armies face to face,
and then the gods saw their paired adversaries; Caesar, scorning
    capture
of all the cities of the Greeks, now refuses to be in debt
to Fate for victory in war except against his son-in-law.
In all his prayers he presses for the hour fatal to the world,
which stakes everything on the dice; he chooses the gamble of Fate
bound to plunge in ruin one or other head. Three times on the hills
he deployed all his squadrons and his standards threatening battle,
bearing witness he left nothing undone in Latium's fall.   10
When he sees his son-in-law can be roused to battle
by no commotion but trusts his closed earthwork,
he moves his standards; hidden, through the brambly fields
he marches headlong to seize the citadels of Dyrrachium.
This journey Magnus anticipated on a seaside track,
and set his camp upon the hill called Petra
by the native Taulantian, and he guards the Ephyracan walls,
defending a city made safe by its cliffs alone.
This city is protected by no work of ancients nor by built-up
masonry nor by human toil which, though raising lofty structures,   20
is ready to yield to wars or all-destroying years;
instead it has defence in the nature and position of the place
which can be shaken by no weapon: enclosed on every side
by plunging deep sea and by rocks which spew out water,
it is not an island thanks to a tiny neck.
Crags inspiring dread in ships support the walls
and when the angry Ionian Sea is raised by rapid Auster it shakes
the temples and the homes and tosses foam as far as rooftops.

Here Caesar's mind, greedy for the fight, was drawn by hope
extravagant to encircle his unwitting enemy, though he was spread
    across   30
the vast hills, with an earthwork's ramp traced far away.

He measures out the land by eye and, not content
to raise up hasty walls of crumbling turf alone,
he brings huge boulders, blocks torn from quarries,
and the homes of Greeks and dismantled city-walls.
No savage battering-ram, no other machine
of violent war can overthrow his construction.
Caesar shatters mountains and he draws his work
level through the heights: he opens trenches, places
towered forts on highest ridges, envelops   40
in a great embrace domains and glades and forested wilds
and woods, and with a mighty ring surrounds the wild beasts.
Not lacking fields, not lacking fodder is Magnus
and, though encircled by Caesar's rampart, he can shift his camp,
so many rivers rising there and plunging to the sea
run all their course; and to visit the most distant of his works
Caesar stays, exhausted, in the fields halfway.
Now let ancient legend praise the walls of Ilium
and ascribe them to the gods, let Parthians in retreat
be amazed at the walls of Babylon built of brittle brick.   50
Look: as much land as Tigris and swift Orontes encircle,
as much of eastern earth as satisfies Assyrian peoples
for their realm, is enclosed by hasty building-work,
hurried on by turmoil of war. Yet all that toil was wasted.
All those hands could have joined Sestos to Abydos
and ejected Phrixus' sea by heaping in the soil;
or could have broken off Ephyra from the wide realms
of Pelops, sparing ships long Malea's curve;
or could have altered for the better any place on earth,
though Nature said no. The field of war contracts: 60
here is held the blood which soon will flow over every land,
here the casualties of both Thessaly and Libya are confined;
civil warfare's madness seethes within a narrow arena.

     As first it rose, the construction of the works was not observed
by Pompey: as someone safe in the middle fields
of Sicily does not know that mad Pelorus barks,
as Caledonian Britons do not notice the wave disturbed
when shifting Tethys and Rutupian shores boil.
When first he sees the land enclosed by a mighty rampart,
himself he leads his army down from Petra's safety   70
and disperses it on different knolls, to spread out Caesar's

troops and put a strain on the blockade by scattering his soldiers.
For himself he claims some land, surrounded by a rampart,
as much as separates small Aricia of the grove,
sacred to Diana of Mycenae, from lofty Rome;
with this same length of land Tiber, flowing past the walls,
falls into the sea, if his stream nowhere meandered.
No trumpets sound and, without orders, weapons stray,
and often a crime is committed when the javelin is tested.
The leaders are distracted from joining battle by greater anxiety: 80
Pompey by the land which now was too exhausted for supplying
    fodder,
land trampled by his running horsemen, when with quickened steps
the horny hoof broke up the greening plain.
In fields cropped close the war-horse wearies,
and though full mangers bring imported hay,
while neighing for fresh grass he sinks down dying
and with trembling ham breaks off, mid-circle.
While decay wastes their bodies and loosens frames,
the stagnant air drew up the infection of the rotting plague
into a murky cloud. With such an exhalation   90
Nesis emits the Stygian air from foggy rocks
and her caverns breathe out deadly Typhon's madness.
Then the people totter: the water, which more readily than air
bears every poison, hardened their guts with slime.
Now the skin grows tight and stiff and bursts the bulging eyes;
into the features the plague goes on, fiery and inflamed
by the Sacred Disease, and the weary head refuses to support itself.
Ever more and more abruptly everything is driven on by Fate,
and life and death are separated by no intervening sickness,
but weakness comes with death; the plague is worsened   100
by the crowd of dying people, while bodies lie unburied, mingled
with the living: to cast the wretched citizens beyond the tents
was burial for them. Yet these hardships were diminished
by the sea behind their backs, the air stirred by Aquilones,
the shores and vessels full of foreign corn.
But the enemy, ranging free on spacious hills,
is not choked by sluggish air or stagnant waters
but, just as if surrounded in a tight blockade, he suffers
brutal famine. As the grass is not yet swelling
into high crop, he sees his pitiable multitude   110

grazing for animals' food prostrate, plucking brambles,
stripping leaves from the woods, pulling up doubtful herbs
which threaten death from unfamiliar roots.
Whatever they can soften with flame or grind with teeth
or send down to the belly through throats scraped sore—
many things before unknown to human table—
the soldiers grab while they besiege a well-fed enemy.

Once Pompey had resolved to break the barriers
and escape and get access to all lands,
he does not seek the dusky times of stealthy night   120
but scorns a march stolen while the army
of his father-in-law is resting: by wide destruction he seeks
to pass out—to knock the rampart down and smash the towers—
through all the enemy's swords and on a path made by slaughter.
Yet a section of the nearby rampart seemed suitable,
where Minicius' fort lies open and where thickets rough and dense
with trees give concealment. To this place he brings his troops,
betrayed by no dust, and, unexpected, comes upon the walls.
Then together from the plains so many Latian Birds glittered,
so many trumpets sounded. So his victory should owe nothing   130
to the sword, the enemy were stunned and overwhelmed by terror.
All their valour could achieve was that they lay in death
where they should be standing. Now there were not enough
to suffer wounds: the shower of so many weapons was wasted.
Then torches that they hurl roll pitchy fires,
then battered towers sway and threaten to collapse,
the rampart groans at blow on blow of timber battering it.

    Already Pompey's Eagles had emerged above the heights
of the lofty rampart, already world rule lay in front:
the place which Fortune could not win with a thousand squadrons   140
or with Caesar's entire strength, a single man snatched
from the victors, stopped its capture, said that Magnus
had not won while *he* still wielded weapons and was not yet laid low.
Scaeva was the hero's name: he was serving in the rank and file
before the war with Rhône's fierce races; there promoted
from the lengthy ranks by shedding copious blood, he bears
the Latian vine-staff; eager for every wrong, he did not know
how great a crime is valour in a civil war.
He when he sees his comrades fleeing, seeking safety,

war now abandoned, says: 'Where is panic driving you, 150
disloyal panic totally unknown in Caesar's troops? 151
Do you turn your backs on death? Are you not ashamed to be missing 153
from the pyres and heap of warriors, to be sought in vain among
    the corpses?
Put loyalty on one side; will you not stand firm, young men,
at least because of indignation? We have been selected from all
through whom the enemy could break out. This day shall pass
with great cost of blood to Magnus. More happy would I seek
the shades with Caesar watching: this witness Fortune has denied;
to Pompey's praises I shall fall. Break their weapons 160
with the impact of your breasts, blunt their swords with your throats.
Now the dust and sound of our destruction reaches distant parts;
the din has struck on Caesar's carefree ears.
We are the victors, comrades: he will come to claim his stronghold
while we die.' Those words aroused a frenzy greater
than the trumpet-calls ignite at their first blast;
astonished at the warrior and keen to watch, the soldiers
follow to discover whether valour caught by numbers and position
could achieve something more than death. On the tumbling ramp
he takes his stand and first rolled out the corpses from the towers 170
full of them and, as the enemy approached, he buried them
with bodies; and all the ruined mass provides the warrior with
    weapons:
with timbers, boulders, with himself, he menaces the enemy.
Now with stakes and now with hardened poles he thrusts back
from the walls opposing breasts; with his sword he chops off hands
which grab the rampart's top; with a rock he crushes head
and bones and scatters brains protected ill by flimsy
skull; another's hair and cheeks he sets
aflame; the fires hiss as the eyes burn.
As soon as the growing heap of corpses made the soil 180
level with the wall, a leap raised and propelled him
over their weapons into the squadrons' midst, a leap no slower
than carries the swift leopard above the points of hunting-spears.
Then squeezed among the packed formations, fenced in
by all the war, he overcomes an enemy he turns around to see.
And now his sword-point, blunt and dulled by clotted blood, 186
has lost the function of a sword and smashes limbs without a wound. 188
He is attacked by the entire throng, by all the weapons:

every hand was surely aimed, every lance successful,   190
and Fortune sees clash a novel pair of adversaries, an army
and a man. His stout shield-boss resounds with frequent blows
and crumpled fragments of his hollow helmet chafe
his temples and nothing now protects his naked vitals
except the spears sticking fast in the surface of his bones.
Madmen, why now with your javelins and light arrows
do you waste blows doomed never to fasten in his vitals?
He must be crushed by the falarica propelled
by twisted cords or by wall-breaching weight of a mighty stone;
he must be pushed back by iron ram and by ballista whirled   200
on the threshold. Firm he stands, no frail wall in front of Caesar,
and keeps Pompey back. He no longer protects his breast with
          weapons,
in fear that men will think his shield and left hand idle
or blame him for surviving, and all the many wounds of war
he meets alone and, bearing in his breast a dense forest,
with steps now weary, he selects an enemy on whom to fall.   206
So the elephant of Libya, overwhelmed by dense weapons,   208
repels every missile from his scaly back and breaks them
and by twitching his skin shakes off the spears which stick;   210
his guts lie hidden, safe beneath the weapons, and, not drawing blood,
the weapons pierce and stick fast in the beast; wounds inflicted
by so many arrows, so many javelins, do not achieve a single death.
From far away—look!—a Gortynian shaft is aimed
by Dictaean hand at Scaeva: sent more surely than any prayer
could hope, it falls upon his head and enters his left eyeball.
He breaks the weapon's obstacle and muscles' ligaments,
boldly tearing out the arrow clinging with the eyeball
dangling, and tramples on the weapon together with his own eye.
Just so the Pannonian bear, more savage following a blow,   220
when a Libyan has launched his javelin with a little thong,
wheels round towards the wound, and in a rage attacks the weapon
which has struck her and chases in a circle the spear which with
          her flies.
His frenzy had destroyed his features, his disfigured face was stiff
with a bloody stream. The victors' happy clamour strikes
the skies: the warriors would not have more rejoiced
at a little blood had they seen a wound on Caesar.
He, concealing deep in his mind his stifled blood-lust,

mildly, with heroism banished far from his face, says:
'Spare me, fellow-citizens; divert your weapons far from here.   230
Wounds will now not help at all towards my death:
that requires weapons not heaped on but pulled out from my breast.
Pick me up and put me down in Magnus' camp, still living;
do this for your general; let Scaeva be a model
of desertion from Caesar rather than of honourable death.'
Unlucky Aunus believed these feigned words
and did not see him holding his sword with hidden point:
and when about to lift the captive's limbs and weapons together
he received the lightning-fast sword fully in the throat.
His energy grew hot and, refreshed by a single killing,   240
he says: 'Whoever hoped that Scaeva was subdued must pay
the penalty; if it is peace that Magnus seeks from this
my sword, he must bow to Caesar, he must dip his standards.
Did you think me like yourselves and slow to meet my fate?
Your love of Pompey, of the Senate's cause, is less
than mine of death.' As he speaks the dust
aloft attests the approach of Caesar's cohorts:
this saved Magnus from disgrace in war and the reproach
that you alone, Scaeva, routed all his squadrons.
You collapse when battle is removed, because, although your blood   250
was shed, fighting gave you strength. As he falls, a crowd of comrades
catch him and, rejoicing, set him fainting on their shoulders;
and they worship the deity, so to speak, confined inside
his stabbed breast and the living semblance of mighty Heroism.
They vie to pluck the weapons from his transfixed limbs,
and they adorn the gods and naked-breasted Mars
with your armour, Scaeva, happy in this claim to fame
had robust Iberians or Cantabrians with tiny weapons
or Teutones with lengthy weapons fled from you.
But you cannot adorn the Thunderer's temple   260
with spoils of war, you cannot yell in happy triumphs.
Unhappy man! with such enormous valour you bought a master!

Though driven back in this part of the camp, Magnus
did not put off the war or idly rest inside the barrier
any more than the sea grows weary when, with the Euri rising,
it strikes the billow-shattering rock, or when the wave eats into
the lofty mountain's flank, preparing collapse on to itself in time to

come.
From here he heads for forts placed near the tranquil deep
and seizes them by attack of twofold warfare, then scattering his
    army
far and wide he spreads his tents across the spacious plain,   270
delighted with the freedom granted him to change his ground.
Just so the swollen Po with brimming mouth rushes over banks
protected by mounds and damages all the fields;
if the earth anywhere sinks down collapsing, unable to resist
the river raging with his mass of waters, then with all his stream
he passes through and covers with his flood unfamiliar plains:
land deserts some owners, other farmers gain fields
by the gift of Po.
                Scarcely had Caesar been aware
of the battle which a fire on high in a look-out post revealed:
he found the walls knocked down, the dust already settled   280
and discovered signs of ruin cold, as if of long ago.
The place's very peace inflamed him and his madness was aroused
by the Pompeians' rest and slumber after conquering Caesar.
He presses on, even to disaster, provided he can spoil their joy.
He then swooped with menace on Torquatus, but he as quick
saw Caesar's troops as when a sailor furls
all his sails on the shaking mast before Circaean gale;
and drew his forces inwards with a narrower wall,
more tightly to arrange his troops in a tiny ring.
Caesar had passed through the defences of the outer rampart   290
when, from all the hills above, Magnus launched
his army and poured down his lines against the hemmed-in enemy.
Not so does the dweller in Henna's valleys shudder
at Enceladus when Notus blows and Etna empties
all its caverns and flows molten down on to the plains
as Caesar's soldiers then: defeated by the rolling dust,
quaking under a cloud of blind terror before the battle,
fleeing they met the enemy and in their panic rush
towards their own destruction. All the blood of civil war
they could have shed, even to peace; their general himself   300
restrained their frenzied swords. Fortunate you could have been,
and free of tyrants, Rome, and your own mistress, had a Sulla
conquered for you there. How bitter now, for ever bitter,
that the greatest of your crimes is your advantage, Caesar:

to fight a righteous son-in-law. O cruel Fates!
Then Libya would not have wept for her calamity at Utica
nor Spain for Munda; nor would Nile polluted by blood unspeakable
have borne a corpse more noble than the Pharian king,
and Juba on Marmaric sands would not have lain exposed,
nor Scipio appeased the Carthaginian ghosts with blood   310
poured out nor life been gone from sacred Cato.
Rome, that could have been your final day of misery:
Pharsalia could have disappeared from destiny.

Caesar left the place he had occupied against the deity's
will and with his mangled forces headed for Emathian lands.
As Magnus was about to chase the army of his father-in-law
wherever he had routed it, his comrades tried to turn him back
by urging him to head for ancestral abodes and for Ausonia
now free of enemy. He says: 'Never shall I return
to my fatherland following Caesar's model, never shall Rome   320
see me come back unless I first disband my soldiers.
I could have held Hesperia, when turmoil started,
had I been willing to join battle in ancestral temples
and to fight in the middle of the Forum. To banish war,
I would go beyond the furthest zone of Scythian cold,
beyond the burning tracts. Rome, shall I as victor despoil you
of tranquillity when I retreated to prevent battles afflicting you?
Rather, to spare you suffering in this war,
let Caesar think you all his own.' So he spoke and fixed
a march towards Phoebus' rise and by traversing parts   330
of earth remote, where Candavia opens up its vast woods,
he reached Emathia, which the Fates were preparing for war.

Thessaly is bounded by the crag of Ossa in the part
where Titan raises up the day in hours of winter;
and when approaching summer draws Phoebus through the zenith
of the sky, Pelion puts his shadows to face the rising rays;
but the southern fires of heaven and scorching Leo's
midsummer head are warded off by wooded Othrys.
Pindus meets the full force of the Zephyrs and of Iapyx
and cuts the daylight short by hastening evening on;   340
and the dweller at Olympus' foot does not fear Boreas,
does not know Arctos, though it shines all through the night.

Between these mountains which sink down in a valley,
the fields once lay hid beneath continuous swamps
while plains held back the rivers, and no access to the sea
was given yet by Tempe's passage and, as they fill a pool,
their only course was to rise. And after the weight of Ossa
was split from Olympus by Hercules' hand and Nereus felt
a rush of sudden water, then Emathian Pharsalus, sea-born
Achilles' realm—better had it stayed beneath the waves—   350
protrudes; and Phylace, whose ship was first to touch
Rhoetean shores, and Pteleos, and Dorion lamenting
thanks to anger of the Pierides; Trachis, and Meliboea strong
with Hercules' quiver, the reward of the abominable torch,
and Larisa, once mighty; and there where now they plough
over Argos once renowned, where legend points out
ancient Thebes of Echion, where once Agave, exiled,
bearing Pentheus' neck and head committed them to the final fire,
complaining that she had seized this only of her son.
So the swamp was burst apart and split into many rivers.   360
Aeas, clear but of tiny stream, flows from there
westward to the Ionian Sea; with no stronger waters,
kidnapped Isis' father glides, and, almost your son-in-law,
Oeneus, who with muddy waters silts up the Echinades;
and stained with Nessus' blood Evenus who cleaves
the Calydon of Meleager. Spercheus with hurried stream
strikes Malian waters, and with his clear river
Amphrysus waters fields where Phoebus was a slave.   368
Asopus takes his course, Phoenix and Melas too   374
and Anaurus breathing out no moistening mists   369
nor dew-drenched air nor breezes faint;
and any river which not known by the sea in its own right
presents its waters to Peneus: Apidanus goes
robbed of his flood and Enipeus never swift till mingled;   373
only Titaresus, when entering the other stream's name,   375
defends his waters and, gliding above,
treats the flood of Peneus like dry fields.
The rumour is, this river flows from the Stygian swamps
and, remembering its source, shuns contact with
a humble stream, keeps to itself its terror for the gods.   380

    As soon as the rivers had drained off and fields appeared,
the rich furrow was split by the Bebrycian ploughshare; then

sank the plough, pressed by the Leleges' right hands;
Aeolian and Dolopian farmers broke the soil,
and Magnetes well known for their horses, Minyans for their oars.
There the pregnant cloud brought forth in Pelethronian
caves the half-beast Centaurs, sons of Ixion:
you, Monychus, shattering the jagged rocks of Pholoë,
and you, fierce Rhoecus, under Oeta's summit
hurling torn-up ash-trees which Boreas could hardly topple,   390
and Pholus, host of great Alcides, and you, the presumptuous
ferryman across the river, soon to suffer the Lernaean arrows,
and you, old Chiron, gleaming with your chilly constellation
and attacking greater Scorpio with your Haemonian bow.
    In this land did seeds of savage warfare spring to life.
First from the rocks struck by the trident of the sea
leapt forth the Thessalian steed, the portent
of fatal wars; first he champed the steel bit
and foamed at the unfamiliar reins of his Lapith tamer.
First cleaving sea from Pagasaean shore did a ship fling   400
human beings, creatures of the land, on to the unknown waves.
Ionos, ruler of the Thessalian land, was the first
to beat the lumps of heated ore in shape,
melt silver in the flames and strike gold
with a stamp and in vast furnaces to smelt copper.
There to count one's wealth became possible, and this drove
the people into wicked warfare. From here the Python, the
        enormous
snake, came down and glided into the lands of Cirrha,
—and that is why Thessalian laurels come to the Pythian games.
From here the wicked Aloeus launched his sons against the gods,   410
when Pelion nearly thrust himself among the lofty stars
and Ossa, by encroaching on the constellations, stopped their course.

When the leaders had pitched their camps in this land
doomed by the Fates, each mind is troubled by a sense
of future war, and it is clear that the hideous hour of greatest
crisis is approaching, that now the Fates draw ever nearer.
Base spirits tremble, pondering the worst;
a few fortify themselves ahead and rehearse both hope and fear
to face uncertainty. But mingled with the timid multitude
was Sextus, a son unworthy of his parent Magnus,   420

who later, prowling as an exile in Scylla's waves,
as a Sicilian pirate stained his father's triumphs at sea.
Fear goaded him to know ahead of time Fate's course:
impatient of delay and sick at heart at all to come,
he consults not Delos' tripods, not Pythian caves
nor does he wish to ask what sound Dodona, nurse of humankind
with earliest fruits, makes from the bronze of Jupiter; nor did he ask
who knows the Fates from entrails, who explains the birds, who
    watches
lightning-flashes in the sky and with Assyrian zeal examines stars,
or anything secret yet permitted. He knew about   430
the mysteries of savage magicians, detested
by the gods above, and altars grim with dreadful rites,
proof of the truth that Dis and ghosts exist; it was clear to the
    unfortunate
that the gods above know too little. His foolish, cruel frenzy
is fostered by the place itself with cities of Thessalian witches
near the camp: they can be surpassed by no invented horror
of a free imagination; their art is the unbelievable.
And on its crags the land of Thessaly produced
both harmful herbs and stones which hear magicians
chanting dreadful secrets. There arises many a substance   440
which puts constraint upon the gods: and in Haemonian lands
the Colchian stranger gathered herbs she had not brought with her.
That hideous race's wicked spells affect the ears
of heaven-dwellers deaf to all the peoples, all the races.
Alone that utterance passes through the ether's far-off parts
and delivers words which can compel the reluctant deity
who can never be distracted by care of sky and spinning
heaven. When her monstrous muttering has touched the stars,
then the Thessalian witch will force the gods from
others' altars, though Babylon of Perseus and secret Memphis   450
open up every shrine of their magicians of old.
By the witches' spells love not brought by Fate
glides into hardened hearts: austere old men
blaze with illicit flames. And there is power not only
in their harmful cups or when they steal the promise,
swelling with the forehead's juice, of mother's love:
minds polluted by no decay of drawn-off poison
are destroyed, charmed out by spells. Those not bound by union

of marriage-bed or by alluring beauty's power
are drawn by magic whirling of the twisted thread.   460
Natural changes cease; postponed by lengthened night
the day comes to a halt; the ether does not obey the law;
the racing universe is paralysed once the spell is heard;
and as Jupiter drives on the sky on its speedy axles,
he is amazed that it does not move. Sometimes they drench
everywhere with rains and muffle burning Phoebus with clouds,
and heaven thunders without Jupiter knowing; with these same
        words
they shake out mists damping far and wide and rain-clouds
with their strands undone. Though winds are still, the sea
swells up; again, forbidden to feel the gales,   470
it falls silent though Notus runs amuck and ship-speeding
sails swell out against the wind. The rigid torrent
hangs from precipitous cliff and the river runs,
but not downhill. Nile does not rise in summer,
Maeander straightens his course, and Rhône as he delays
is swept along by Arar. Mountains dip their peaks,
smooth their ridges out; from below Olympus looks up
at clouds, and snows of Scythia melt away without the sun
while winter freezes. When Tethys by the moon is driven forward,
a Haemonian spell thrusts her back, defending the shore.   480
Earth too shakes the axis of her unmoved weight,
the thrust which tends towards the centre of the world falters.
The weight of such a mighty mass is shattered by the voice
and it recedes to give a view of Olympus gliding round.
Every deadly beast and creature born to injure
fears Haemonian experts and gives them means of killing.
Hungry tigers and the high-born wrath of lions
fawn on them with gentle mouth; for them the snake unfolds
his chilly circles and stretches out on frosty field,
and vipers' knots are wrenched apart and joined again,   490
and serpent dies when breathed upon by human poison.
Why do the gods take trouble to obey the spells and drugs,
not daring to despise them? What kind of link
holds the gods bound fast? Is their obedience necessary
or by choice? Do the witches win so much merit by loyalty
        unknown
or do they prevail by secret threats? Do they have this power

over all the gods, or have these spells authority
over one particular deity, who can force the universe to do
whatever he himself is forced to do? By them the stars
were first drawn down from the racing sky and Phoebe clear,   500
assailed by dreadful poisonous words, grew dim
and burnt with black and earthy fires, just as if
the Earth kept her from her brother's image
and intruded its shadows between the flames of heaven,
and, forced down by incantation, she suffers these great hardships
till she discharges foam on to the grasses close below.

These rites of wickedness, these crimes of savage race
beastly Erichtho had condemned for their excessive holiness
and had applied her filthy skill to unknown rites.
For her it is wrong to rest her deathly head   510
beneath a city's roof or home, so in abandoned tombs she lives
and, driving out the ghosts, is mistress of the graves, the darling
of the gods of Erebus. To hear the meetings of the silent dead,
to know the Stygian homes and mysteries of hidden Dis
is not prevented by the gods or life. The blasphemer's face
is gaunt and loathsome with decay: unknown to cloudless sky
and terrifying, by Stygian pallor it is tainted,
matted with uncombed hair: if rain and black
clouds obscure the stars, then out comes the Thessalian woman
from bare tombs and catches at night's thunderbolts.   520
She tramples and she scorches up the seeds of fertile corn
and with her breath corrupts the breezes not fatal before.
She does not pray to gods above nor with suppliant chant
ask help of heaven nor does she know of propitiating
entrails: it is her joy to place on altars
funeral flames with incense she has stolen from the kindled pyre.
The gods above grant every wickedness to her at her first
utterance of prayer: they dread to hear a second spell.
Souls living, still in charge of their own limbs,
she has buried in the tomb and, while the Fates yet owe them years,   530
unwillingly death steals on; funerals she has brought back from the
        grave,
reversing the procession; corpses have escaped from death.
Smoking ashes of the young and blazing bones
she grabs from the middle of the pyre and even the torch

held by the parents; she gathers fragments of the funeral
bier which fly about in black smoke, and clothes
crumbling into cinders, and ashes with the smell of limbs.
But when dead bodies are preserved in stone, which draws the inmost
moisture off, and once the marrow's fluid is absorbed and they
    grow hard,
then greedily she vents her rage on the entire corpse: 540
she sinks her hands into the eyes, she gleefully digs out
the cold eyeballs and gnaws the pallid nails
on withered hand. With her own mouth has she burst
the noose and knots of the criminal, mangled bodies as they hung,
scraped clean the crosses, torn at guts beaten
by the rains, at marrows exposed and baked by the sun.
She has stolen the iron driven into hands, the black and putrid
liquid trickling through the limbs and the congealed slime
and, if muscle resisted her bite, she has tugged with all her weight.
And if any corpse lies on the naked earth, she camps   550
before the beasts and birds come; she does not want to tear
the limbs with knife or her own hands, but awaits
the bites of wolves, to grab the bodies from their dry throats.
Nor do her hands refrain from murder, if she needs
some living blood which first bursts out when throat is slit   555
and if her funeral feast demands still-quivering organs.   557
So through a wound in the belly, not nature's exit,
the foetus is extracted to be put on burning altars.
And whenever she has need of cruel, determined spirits,   560
herself she creates ghosts. Every human death is to her advantage.
She plucks from young men's faces the bloom of cheek
and from a dying boy cuts off a lock of hair with her left hand.
Often, even at a kinsman's funeral, the hideous Thessalian
bends over well-loved limbs and, while planting kisses, mutilates
the head and with her teeth she opens up the tight-closed
mouth and, biting off the tip of tongue which sticks
to parched throat, pours mumbles into icy lips
and sends a secret outrage to the Stygian shades.

When local rumour revealed her to Pompey, in the sky's   570
deep night—the time when Titan ushers in
midday beneath our earth—through deserted fields
he picks his way. His usual, loyal aides in wickedness

roamed round the broken-open graves and tombs
and spotted her, sitting far away on a precipitous crag
where Haemus slopes down, stretching out Pharsalian ridges.
She was trying out words unknown to wizards and the gods
of wizardry and shaping a spell for novel purposes.
Because she feared that wandering war might pass into another
sphere and the Emathian land lose such abundant bloodshed,   580
the witch forbade Philippi—defiled by spells
and by dreadful juices spattered—to shift the warfare,
soon to claim for herself so many deaths, soon to enjoy
the world's blood; she hopes to mangle corpses of slain
kings, to steal the ashes of the Hesperian race
and bones of noblemen and to acquire such mighty shades.
This is her passion and her sole concern: what can she grab from
    Magnus'
outstretched body? on which of Caesar's limbs swoop down?

Her Pompey's coward son addresses first:
'O glory of Haemonian witches, you have the power to reveal   590
Fate to the people and divert from their course events to come;
I beg that I may know for sure the end
prepared by the fortune of war. Not the lowest part
of the Roman multitude am I, Magnus' most illustrious son,
either master of the world or heir to ruin so immense.
Struck by doubts, my mind is frightened, but again is ready
to endure inevitable terrors. Take from events the power
to swoop down suddenly unseen. Either rack the deities
or spare the gods and from the shades extort the truth yourself.
Unbar the Elysian abodes and summon Death   600
herself: make her confess to me which ones of us she seeks.
Not unimportant is this task: it is worth your while to ask, even
for yourself, which way the gamble of such great destiny inclines.'
The wicked witch of Thessaly delighted in her fame's renown
so widely spread and in reply she said: 'If you were stirring
lesser fates, young man, it would be easy to compel the unwilling
gods to any course you chose. To my craft it is allowed,
when with their rays the constellations doom a single death,
to introduce delay; and though every star decree
old age, with drugs we cut in half the years.   610
But when from the world's first start has come down

a chain of causes, when all the Fates are troubled
if you want to make a change, and when humankind stands beneath
a single blow, then—we the throng of Thessaly admit it—
Fortune is the stronger. But if you are content to learn
events in advance, paths to truth both many and easy
will open up: for us the earth, ether, Chaos,
seas, plains, and rocks of Rhodope will speak.
But it is simple, in such abundance of fresh death,
to raise a single body from Emathian plains,   620
so the lips of a corpse just dead and warm
can speak out loud and clear, and no gloomy ghost
with sun-scorched limbs hiss indistinctly to our ears.'

She ceased and, with night's darkness doubled by her craft,
her dismal head concealed in a murky cloud, she wanders
through the corpses of the slain, thrown out, denied a grave.
Fast fled the wolves, fast fled the carrion birds, unfed,
tearing free their talons, while the witch of Thessaly
selects her prophet, and by examining innards chill
with death she finds a stiff lung's lobes, entire,   630
without a wound, and in a corpse she seeks a voice.
Many a dead warrior's fate now hangs in the balance:
whom does she wish to summon back to life above? If she had tried
to raise whole armies on the fields and restore them to the battle,
the laws of Erebus had given way, a multitude
had fought, drawn by her unnatural power from Stygian Avernus.
The corpse at last is chosen, one with pierced breast,
and is dragged along; a hook sunk in the dead man's rope,
the poor cadaver over rocks and stones is hauled to live
again, and it is placed below the high cliff of the hollow   640
mountain which ghastly Erichtho had condemned to her rites.

Sinking almost to the dark and hidden caves of Dis
the ground falls steep, a place oppressed by a forest
colourless with drooping leaves and shaded by the yew
impenetrable to Phoebus and with no crown facing heaven.
Within, the withered darkness and the colourless decay
from long night cavern-bound have no light unless
spell-conjured: the air stands stagnant not like this
in the jaws of Taenarus; grim limit of the unseen world

and ours, thus far the kings of Tartarus would not fear   650
to allow the ghosts. For though the seer of Thessaly
can force the Fates, who knows if she sees Stygian shades
by dragging them to her or making the descent herself?
With a Fury's crazy robes of many hues
she garbs herself, uncovered is her face with locks pulled back,
her bristling hair is bound with wreaths of vipers.

When she saw his comrades fearful and the youth himself
trembling with his gaze transfixed and lifeless face,
she says: 'Suppress the terrors conceived in anxious minds:
soon new life, soon life in genuine form will be restored,   660
so all, however fearful, may hear him speak.
Truly if I could show you Stygian lakes and the river-bank
which sounds with fires, if I could make appear
the Eumenides and Cerberus shaking his neck
shaggy with serpents, and the Giants with their hands bound back,
what cause for fear, you cowards, is the sight of timid ghosts?'

Then first she opens up the corpse's chest with fresh wounds,
and with boiling blood she fills it, from the innards washes off
the gore and applies generous doses of lunar poison.
With this is mixed whatever nature spawns   670
misbegotten. Here is the froth of rabid dogs,
here entrails of the lynx, here the hump of dire hyena
and the marrow of the snake-fed stag;
here is the remora, detainer of the ship mid-sea
though Eurus strain the rigging, and dragons' eyes,
and stones which sound when warmed beneath a breeding bird:
here is the Arabs' flying serpent and the viper born
in the Red Sea, the guardian of the precious oyster-shell,
the cast skin of still-living horned snake of Libya
and ashes of the phoenix burnt upon the eastern altar.   680
To this she added common poisons with names,
then put in leaves drenched in spells unspeakable,
and herbs her foul mouth spat on
at their birth, and venoms of her own creation.

Last comes her voice, bewitching the gods of Lethe
more potently than any drug, first composed of jumbled noises,

jarring, utterly discordant with human speech:
the bark of dogs and howl of wolves,
the owl's cry of alarm, the screech-owl's night-time moan,
the wild beasts' shriek and wail, the serpent's hiss;   690
it utters too the beating of the cliff-smashed wave,
the sound of forests, and the thunderings of the fissured cloud;
of so many noises was one voice the source. Then she speaks
in Haemonian incantation and pierces Tartarus with utterance thus:

  'I invoke the Eumenides, Hell's horror, and the Avengers;
I invoke Chaos, eager to disorder countless worlds;
I invoke the ruler of the earth, tormented for long future ages
by the drawn-out death of the gods; I invoke the Styx, and the
      Elysian fields
no witch of Thessaly may reach; I invoke Persephone, loathing sky
and mother; and the lowest form of our Hecate, through whom   700
the shades and I in silent utterance may commune;
I invoke the porter of the wide abode, who tosses human entrails
to the savage hound; I invoke the Sisters soon to spin a second thread
of life, and you, O ferryman of the blazing water,
old man already tired out by shades returning to me:
heed my prayers. Do I summon you with mouth sufficiently
abominable and polluted? Do I ever chant these spells
without consuming human entrails? How many times have I cut out
breasts filled by deity and washed them with warm brains?
Are there no babes, about to enter life, who laid   710
their head and heart upon your dishes? Then obey my prayer.
A soul I ask for, not one lying hid in the cave of Tartarus
and long accustomed to the darkness, but a soul on its way down,
life's light just fled, a soul still hesitating at the door
to pallid Orcus' chasm, a soul which, though he drain these drugs,
will join the dead once only. Let the ghost of a soldier with us
recently foretell all Pompey's future to the leader's son,
if civil wars have earned your gratitude.'

So she spoke; then raised her head and foaming lips,
and saw the ghost of an unburied corpse standing there,   720
fearing the lifeless frame and hated cage
of its old prison. It dreads to enter the opened breast
and innards and the entrails ruptured by a fatal wound.
What misery! The final gift of death is snatched from him unfairly

—to be beyond the reach of death. Amazed at this delay
allowed to Fate, enraged at death, Erichtho
lashes the unmoving corpse with a live snake,
and through earth's hollow cracks, bored by her spells,
she barks at the dead and shatters the silence of their realm:
    'Tisiphone and Megaera, untroubled by my voice,   730
do you not drive with your cruel lashes this unlucky soul
through Erebus' void? Now by your real names I will call you,
you Stygian she-dogs, and in this upper light
maroon you; through pyres, through burials I will chase you, vigilant;
I will banish you from graves and drive you off from funeral urns.
And Hecate, wan and wasted, I will show you to the gods as you are,
not as you usually visit them, false with different face,
and I will forbid you change your look of Erebus.
And girl of Henna, I will disclose the feast which holds you
underneath the earth's enormous weight, your lovers' bond   740
with night's gloomy king and the pollution you have suffered,
so foul that Ceres will not call you back. And you, the lowest
ruler of the world, your caverns I will burst and unleash Titan
and you will be struck by sudden daylight. Do you obey? Or
to Him must I appeal, at whose name the shaken earth
never fails to tremble, Him who can look upon uncovered Gorgon,
who can chastise the cringing Erinys with her own lashes,
Him who occupies a Tartarus to you unfathomable, Him in whose
     power
are you upper gods, Him who by the waters of the Styx can falsely
     swear?'

At once the frozen blood grew hot and warmed the blackened   750
wounds and ran into the veins and limbs' extremities.
At its pulse, the lungs beneath the chill breast quiver,
and into marrow disaccustomed steals new life,
mixed with death. Then all his frame pulsates, the muscles
strained; and the corpse lifts himself up from the ground
not gradually, limb by limb, but thrust away from the earth
and raised erect at one go. Uncovered are his eyes with gaping
stare: there was in him the look of someone not yet living,
already dying; the pallor and the stiffness both remain;
and he is stunned by his arrival in the world. But his sealed   760
lips sound with no muttering: voice and tongue are given him

only to reply. 'Speak', says the Thessalian witch,
'what I command and great will be your reward; for if you speak
the truth, I shall make you safe for all the world's eternity
from Haemonian craft; on such a pyre and with such wood
will I burn your limbs with Stygian spell
that no magicians will bewitch and make your ghost obey.
Think this worth the cost of second life: neither words nor drugs
will dare destroy your sleep of lengthy Lethe, once death
is given by me. The tripods and the prophets of the gods   770
are graced with obscure answers; he who seeks the truth
from ghosts and approaches bravely the oracles of relentless death,
let him leave certain. Do not hold back, I pray: give events their
        names,
give the places, give a voice through which the Fates can talk to me.'
A spell she added also to empower the shade to know
whatever she asks.

           With flowing tears the mournful corpse
said: 'Recalled from the silent river-bank,
myself I have not seen the grim threads of the Parcae,
yet this from all the ghosts I learnt,
that wild discord disturbs the Roman shades   780
and wicked war has shattered the underworld's repose.
Latian generals variously have left the Elysian abodes
and gloomy Tartarus: these have made plain
the intentions of the Fates. Grim were the faces
of the blessed ghosts: I saw the Decii, both son and father,
lives given to expiate war, and Camillus weeping,
and the Curii and Sulla complaining, Fortune, of you;
Scipio laments for his unlucky posterity, doomed to die
on Libyan lands; a greater enemy of Carthage,
Cato mourns the fate of his descendant who refuses slavery.   790
You alone among the holy shades I saw rejoicing,
Brutus, first consul when the tyrants were expelled.
Threatening Catiline exults, his fetters burst
and shattered, and savage Marii and bare Cethegi;
myself I saw rejoice those radical names:
the Drusi with their laws excessive, the Gracchi of enormous
        daring.
Their hands applauded, though eternal knots of iron

and Dis's prison confined them, and the guilty multitude
demands the fields of the blest. The lord of the stagnant
realm opens wide his pale abodes, he sharpens broken rocks   800
and hard steel for shackles and prepares the punishment
for the conqueror. Take back with you this consolation,
O young man, that in a calm retreat the shades await
both your father and your house, and in a cloudless region of the
     realm
keep a place for the Pompeys. And be not troubled by the glory
of a short life: the hour will come which levels
all the leaders. Make haste to die; exultant
in your mighty spirit, go down from tombs however small
and trample on the shades of the gods of Rome.
The question is, whose grave Nile and whose Tiber will lap   810
with waves: for the leaders, the battle concerns their burial alone.
Ask not about your own fate: though I keep silent,
the Parcae will grant you knowledge; a surer prophet will foretell
all to you in the fields of Sicily, your father Pompey, himself,
even he uncertain where to summon you or drive you back,
which zones, which regions of the world to bid you shun.
Unhappy men! Be in dread of Europe, Libya, Asia:
Fortune has distributed your graves between your triumphs.
O pitiable house, in all the world you will see nothing
safer than Emathia.'

               After so recounting destiny,   820
he mournful stands with silent face and asks for death once more.
Magic spells and drugs are needed for the corpse to die:
the Fates cannot regain his soul, their power
over him exhausted already at one go. Then the witch heaps up
a pyre with plenteous timber; the dead man comes to the fire.
Once the youth was laid upon the kindled heap, Erichtho left him,
finally permitting him to die, and goes as Sextus' companion
to his father's camp, and though the sky was taking on day's colour,
until they safely brought their steps within the tents,
night was told to hold back the day and gave them shadows thick.   830

BOOK SEVEN

Rising from the Ocean more slowly than eternal law summoned him,
grief-bringing Titan never drove his horses harder against the ether
and reversed his course, though the sky hurried him onwards;
he preferred to undergo eclipses and the toils of stolen
light, and he drew the clouds towards him, not as fodder for his flames
but to stop him shining clear on a Thessalian world.
  But the night—the final part of happy life for Magnus—
deceived his troubled sleep with an empty apparition:
he dreamt that, as he sat in his own theatre, he saw
the innumerable likeness of the Roman plebs,   10
and his name was raised to the stars by joyful
voices and the resounding tiers competed in applause;
such was the appearance and applause of the admiring people
long ago, when as a young man, at the time of his first triumph,
after conquering the tribes encircled by torrential Hiberus
and all the troops driven onwards by elusive Sertorius,
with the west pacified, revered in his plain toga as much
as in the one that adorns the chariot, with the Senate clapping
he sat, still a Roman knight. Perhaps at the end of success
his mind, distressed by troubles, fled back to happy times;   20
perhaps, through its usual obscurity, his repose foretold
the opposite of what he saw, bringing omens of great lamentation;
perhaps, when you were forbidden any more to see your ancestral
      abodes,
Fortune gave you Rome like this. Do not break his sleep,
watchmen of the camp, let no bugle strike his ears at all.
Tomorrow's repose, hideous and gloomy with the image of the day,
from every side will bring him deadly battles, war from every side.
How will the people have such sleep and such a joyous night?
O blessed would your Rome be, if she could see you even like this!
If only the gods above had granted to your fatherland and you,   30
Magnus, a single day when both of you, certain of your fate,
could have snatched the final pleasure of your love so great.
You proceed as if destined to die in Ausonia's city;

she, fully knowing that her prayers for you were always realized,
never thought this crime was part of destiny—
for her thus to lose even the grave of her beloved Magnus.
Joined in grief, young man and old and boy unbidden
would have wept for you, with loosened hair the crowd
of women would have torn their breasts, as at Brutus' death.
Now too, though they fear the unjust victor's weapons,   40
though Caesar personally announce your death, they will weep,
even while bringing incense, bringing laurel garlands to the Thunderer.
O how unhappy—their groans concealed their anguish;
they could not bewail you together in full theatre.

Day's first light had overcome the stars when the camp's throng
buzzed with mingled muttering and, while the Fates were dragging
the world to ruin, demand the battle-signal. Of the unlucky crowd
      most,
doomed not to see the day out, are grumbling around
their leader's tent itself and, fired by the mighty uproar,
bring on the hastening hours of imminent death.   50
A hideous frenzy comes upon them: each desires to precipitate
his own fate and the state's; slow and timorous is Pompey
called, too tolerant of his father-in-law, addicted
to world-rule in his desire to have beneath his sway
at once so many races from everywhere, in his dread of peace.
And more, the kings and peoples of the east protest that the war
is long drawn out, that they are detained far from their native lands.
Does it give you pleasure, O gods above, when universal ruin
is your plan, to add this guilt to our mistakes?
We charge to disaster, demanding warfare which will injure us;   60
in Pompey's camp, Pharsalia is their prayer.
The utterances of all were conveyed by the greatest master
of Roman eloquence, Tullius—under his civilian authority
fierce Catiline had trembled at the peace-making Axes.
He was enraged at warfare, because he longed for Rostrum
and for Forum, after enduring silence so long as a soldier.
His eloquence gave strength to their feeble cause:
   'This alone Fortune asks of you, Magnus, in return for all her many
favours—that you be willing to make full use of her; we leaders
of your camp and your kings together with the suppliant world   70
prostrate ourselves and beg you to allow the conquest

of your father-in-law. Shall Caesar mean war for humankind
for so long a time? Rightly do the nations who were tamed
by Pompey racing past resent that he is slow to conquer.
Where has your enthusiasm gone? or where your confidence in
    Fate?
Ungrateful man, are you alarmed about the gods? do you
    hesitate to trust
to them the Senate's cause? Of their own accord, the ranks will tear
your standards up and spring forward: you should feel shame to
    have won under compulsion.
If you are our bidden leader, if the war is waged for *us*,
give the men the right to fight on whichever field they wish.   80
Why do you keep from Caesar's blood the swords of all the world?
Hands brandish weapons; hardly anyone can wait for the signal
slow to sound: hurry, or your trumpets may leave you behind.
The Senate longs to know: does it follow you, Magnus, as soldier
or as retinue?'

        The leader groaned and felt that this was trickery
of the gods and that the Fates were hostile to his own intention.
He said: 'If you all wish it so, if the moment needs
Magnus the soldier, not Magnus the general, no more shall I detain
the Fates: let Fortune engulf the peoples in a single downfall,
let this day be the last for a large part of mankind.   90
But I call on you to witness, Rome, that the day of universal doom
was imposed on Magnus. The toil of war could have cost
you no wound; I could have handed over to the peace which he
    defiled
their leader, a prisoner, tamed without slaughter.
What frenzy for wickedness is this, O blind ones? Are men who are
intent on waging civil war afraid to conquer without blood?
We have taken from him the lands, we have barred him
from the entire sea, we have compelled his hungry troops to plunder
corn too early, we have made the enemy pray
rather to be overthrown by swords, to blend the deaths   100
of his men and mine. The war is more than half won
by the measures I have taken to prevent recruits from dreading battle,
if only they demand the signal, spurred by valour
and in fire of wrath. Simple fear of future evil
has sent many into utmost danger, but bravest is the man

who, quick to undergo ordeals if they loom close at hand,
can also postpone them. They wish to hand to Fortune
this our situation so successful, to surrender to the sword the crisis
of the world; they wish their leader to fight, rather than to win.
You, Fortune, gave to me the Roman state to govern: 110
take it back enlarged and keep it safe in blind warfare.
The battle shall be neither the reproach nor glory of Pompey.
In the gods' presence, Caesar, you prevail over me, with your
        unjust prayers:
the fight is on. How much crime and how much hardship
this day will bring upon the peoples! How many kingdoms will be
        overthrown!
How dark will Enipeus flow with Roman blood!
I wish that the first lance of deadly war may strike
this head, if it can fall without influence upon events
or the ruin of our party, since victory is no more welcome
to Magnus. Today, when the carnage is complete,   120
Pompey will be a name either hated by the people or pitied:
the conquered will have every hardship brought by final destiny,
the conqueror will have every crime.' So he speaks and grants
the people warfare and, as they rage with anger, he lets go
their reins; like this the sailor, conquered by violent Corus,
concedes control to the winds and, abandoning his skill, is swept along,
a useless cargo on his ship. The camp roars in a tumult
of agitated haste, and fierce spirits hammer
against their breasts with irregular blows. The paleness
of coming death is on many faces, a look like their fate.   130
It is clear that the day has come which will establish the destiny
of human life for ever, that the battle will decide
what Rome will be. Each man is unaware of his own dangers,
stunned by a greater dread. Who would fear for himself
if he saw the shore inundated by the deep or sea-water
on the mountain-tops and ether falling towards the earth
and the sun hurled down—widespread destruction? There is no time
to feel terror for themselves: they fear for Rome and Magnus.
Nor did they trust in their swords unless the sharpened point
sparked against the stone; then every lance is straightened   140
on the rock, they string their bows with better cords
and carefully filled their quivers with selected arrows;
the horseman extends his spurs and tightens his bridle-reins.

If I may compare men's labours with the gods,
not otherwise when Phlegra reared the raging Giants
did the sword of Mars grow hot upon Sicilian anvils
and Neptune's trident redden in the flames a second time
and Paean forge again his arrows after stretching out in death the
    Python,
did Pallas spread the Gorgon's locks across her Aegis,
did Cyclops make Pallenaean thunderbolts anew for Jupiter.   150

Yet Fortune did not refrain from the revelation
of disasters to come through various signs. As they made for
the fields of Thessaly, the entire ether blocked their approach: 153
it hurled down meteors in their faces and columns of immeasurable   155
flame and water-greedy cyclones mixed with fireballs
and with a rain of lightning made them close their eyes;
it knocked the crests from helmets, flooded hilts
with melted swords, dissolved the javelins it snatched,
and guilty blade smoked with the ether's sulphur; and hardly could   160
the standards be torn up from the ground, but with increased weight   162
they pushed down and overwhelmed the standard-bearer's head;
    adrip with tears,
only as far as Thessaly did they belong to Rome and to the state.
The bull brought forward to the gods smashed the altar,
ran away and headlong hurled himself into the fields of Emathia,
so no sacrifice was found for the ill-omened rites.
—But you, Caesar, what gods of wickedness, what Eumenides
did you invoke with ritual? What powers of the Stygian realm,
what horror of hell and Furies steeped in night   170
did you propitiate when soon to wage a wicked war so savagely?—
Now—who knows if it was by portents of the gods or if excessive fear
convinced them—to many people Pindus seemed to collide
with Olympus, and Haemus to sink into sheer valleys,
Pharsalia to emit nocturnal sounds of war,
a torrent of blood to permeate Ossaean Boebeïs;
they are amazed at one another's faces shrouded in darkness,
at the dimness of the daylight, at night brooding over helmets,
at departed parents and at ghosts of kindred blood
flitting before their very eyes. The frenzied people had   180
this one comfort, that the multitude is conscious of its wicked
prayer—it hoped for fathers' throats, for brothers' breasts—

and it rejoices in the portents, and thinks its mental turmoil
and its sudden madness is an omen of their wickedness.
What wonder is it, if mankind has been given a mind
foreboding ill, that people whose last day was waiting
trembled with distracted fear? The Roman visitor who lies
by Tyrian Gades, who drinks Armenian Araxes,
beneath whatever sky, whatever stars of universe,
he mourns, knows not the reason and rebukes his aching   190
mind, unaware of what he is losing on the fields of Emathia.
If those who tell can truly be believed, the augur sitting
on the Euganean hill, where Aponus emerges steaming
from the earth and wave of Antenor's Timavus is split,
said: 'The final day has come, the greatest issue is fought,
the wicked armies of Pompey and of Caesar clash';
perhaps he noted thunder and the ominous weapons of Jupiter,
perhaps he saw all ether and the poles resisting
the discordant sky, perhaps the gloomy deity in the ether
indicated battle in the sun's dark dimness.   200
Without a doubt the day of Thessaly was quite unlike
all the days that Nature unfolds: if through an expert augur
every human mind had noted the sky's strange signs,
Pharsalia could have been observed in all the world.
O mightiest of men—your Fortune gave displays
throughout the world, on your destiny the entire sky was intent!
Even among later races and the people of posterity, these events—
whether they come down to future ages by their own fame alone
or whether my devotion also and my toil can do anything
for mighty names—will stir both hopes and fears together   210
and useless prayers when the battle is read;
all will be stunned as they read the destinies, as if
to come, not past and, Magnus, still they will side with you.

The troops, as they descended, radiant from Phoebus' beams
facing them, flooded all the hills with light
and not randomly were launched upon the plains: the doomed ranks
stood in set array. Charge of the left wing was given
to you, Lentulus, with the fourth legion and the first,
then the best for war. To you, Domitius, keen to fight though the
          deity
is hostile, is granted the front of battle on the right.   220

But the central fighting strength was packed with bravest
troops brought from Cilician lands by their general
Scipio, in this region a soldier, but in Libya chief commander.
But next to the streams and pools of surging Enipeus
went the Cappadocians' mountain cohort and Pontic
horsemen, generous with the rein. But most of the dry ground
is held by tetrarchs and by kings and mighty tyrants
and by all the purple subject to the Latian sword.
There Libya sent Numidians and Crete
Cydonians, from there Ituraean arrows took their course,   230
there you, fierce Gauls, advanced against your usual enemy,
there Iberia moved its aggressive shields.
Snatch the nations from the victor, Magnus, and, by shedding
the world's blood all at once, put an end to all his triumphs.

It happened on that day that Caesar left his station,
on the point of moving troops to plunder crops, when suddenly
he sees the enemy descending to the level plains;
the moment he had prayed for a thousand times is presented,
when he can throw everything into the final hazard.
For he, sick of delay and blazing with desire for power,   240
had begun to condemn a civil war of brief extent
as a crime prolonged. When he saw the final battle
and the test between the leaders drawing near
and felt the destined downfall start to totter,
even his frenzy, so ready for the sword, for a short time
flagged and his mind so bold to guarantee
success stopped in doubt: his own destiny does not permit him fear;
Magnus' destiny does not permit him hope. He suppressed his dread,
and confidence springs forth, better for encouraging the host:
   'O soldiers, conquerors of the world, essence of my fortune,   250
the chance to fight so often longed for is here.
There is no need of prayers—now summon fate with sword.
How great will Caesar be?—in your hands it lies.
This is the day which I remember you promised me
by the waters of the Rubicon, the day we hoped for when we
      went to war,
the day for which we have postponed our return in triumph,   256
the day which must prove on the evidence of destiny which of us
      more justly   259

took up weapons: this is a battle bound to make the loser guilty.   260
If it was for me that you attacked your land with weapon and with flames,
fight fiercely now and with the sword put an end to blame:
once the judge of war is changed, no hand is clean.
Not for my sake is conflict waged, but so that you, I pray, may be
a free people and may hold power over all nations.
Personally I desire to return to ordinary life
and in plebeian garb to act the undistinguished citizen,
but provided that your power is universal, there is nothing I refuse
        to be.
Rule, and let me take the blame. And with no great bloodshed
do you realize your hope of the world: you will meet an army chosen 270
from Greek gymnasia, sluggish from devotion to the wrestling-floor
and with difficulty carrying their weapons, or barbaric babble
of a jumbled mob which cannot stand the trumpets, cannot stand
its own shout when the troops advance. Few hands of yours
will wage war against fellow Romans; most of the fight will rid
the world of these peoples and will crush the enemy of Rome.
Advance through cowardly races and infamous tyrannies
and with your sword's first stroke lay low the world;
let it be known that all the races led by Pompey's chariot
into Rome do not make up a single triumph.   280
Does it affect the Armenians which general holds sway
at Rome? Is there any barbarian who wants to put
Hesperia into Magnus' hands if it costs him any blood?
They hate all Romans and resent their masters,
those they know the more. By contrast, Fortune has entrusted
me to my own men's hands—witnessed by me
in so many wars in Gaul. Which soldier's sword shall I not
recognize? And when the quivering lance flies through the sky,
without mistake I shall declare whose arm propelled it.
But if I see the signs which never mislead   290
your leader—fierce looks and threatening eyes—
then you have won. I seem to look at streams of blood
and kings trampled on together and the Senate's
mangled body and nations swimming in an endless slaughter.
But I delay my destiny by detaining you with these words
when you are raging for the fight. Forgive me for putting off the
        battle;
I tremble with hope; never have I seen the gods so close to me,

about to give so much; only the plains' narrow strip of land
divides us from our prayers. I am the man, once war is over,
who will have the power to bestow the property of peoples and of
　　kings.　　　　　　　　　　　　　　　　　　　　　　　　　300
By what movement in the sky, by what star of heaven changing
　　course
do you, gods above, allow so much to the land of Thessaly?
Today provides either the reward or the penalty of war.
Picture the crosses, picture the chains for Caesar's side,
this head of mine placed upon the Rostra, my limbs flung far and
　　wide,
crime committed in the Saepta, and battles in the closed-in Campus:
we are waging civil war with a general of Sulla.
My anxiety is all for you—for me, a destiny will be ready
free from care and self-inflicted: the man who looks behind
before the enemy is conquered will see me stabbing my own guts.　　310
Gods—your cares have been distracted from the ether by the earth
and throes of Rome—give victory to the man who does not
think it necessary to draw the savage sword against the conquered,
who does not believe that fellow-citizens committed crime
because they bore opposing standards. When Pompey kept
your troops in a narrow place and denied your valour
room to move, with how much blood did he glut his sword!
Yet this I pray of you, soldiers: do not be keen to strike
an enemy's back; treat the man who flees as a citizen.
But, while their weapons glitter, let no image of affection　　　320
or glimpse of parents in opposing rank shake you:
disfigure with your sword the faces which demand respect.
If any man attacks his kinsman's breast with hostile
blade or if he violates no bond when he wounds,
let him count his unknown enemy's slaughter as a credit.
Level now the rampart and with fallen debris fill the ditches,
so the army can march out not straggling but in full companies.
Do not spare your camp: you will bivouac inside that rampart
from where the doomed army comes.' Hardly had Caesar finished
speaking, when each is drawn to his own task and hurriedly the men　　330
took up their weapons and ate their bread. They seize upon war's
　　portents;
rush on, trampling under foot the camp; take their stand in no
　　formation,

without their leader's tactics; everything they leave to Fate.
If in the deadly warfare you had placed so many fathers-in-law
of Magnus, so many seeking power over their own Rome,
they would not be rushing into battle with such headlong speed.

When Pompey saw the enemy's squadrons march out
straight ahead, allowing battle no delay—
the day appointed by the gods—he stood still with frozen heart,
stunned; and for a general so great to dread the fight like that   340
was ominous. Then he stifles his fears and, riding
on a lofty horse all along the line, he says: 'The day
your valour clamours for, the end of civil warfare
you demanded—it is here. Pour forth all your strength;
the final task of the sword remains and a single hour
drags down the nations. Whoever desires his land and house-gods dear,
his children, marriage-chamber, the ties he has left behind, must
          win them
by the sword: the god has set all prizes in the field in between us.
The better cause tells us to hope for favouring gods:
they themselves will steer the weapons through Caesar's guts,   350
they themselves will want to sanction Roman statutes with his blood.
If they planned to give my father-in-law world rule,
they could have hurried my old age to an end:
to preserve Pompey as leader is not the act of gods
angered with the people and with Rome. We have assembled
every capability of victory. Willingly have famous heroes
submitted to dangers; our soldiery is that of old, in its sacred image.
If to these times the Fates restored the Curii,
Camilli and the Decii vowing their lives to fate,
on our side they would stand. The races and innumerable cities   360
of the furthest east have assembled and stirred to battle hordes
in number never seen before: at a single moment all the world is
          ours to use.
All we races enclosed by the boundary of the zodiac,
as far as Notos and Boreas—we wield weapons.
Shall we not surround the dense-packed enemy
by pouring round our wings? Few are the sword-hands victory
requires, and of our squadrons most will wage war
with shouting only: for our army Caesar is not enough.
Imagine that your mothers, leaning from Rome's highest

city-walls with hair streaming, are urging you to battle;   370
imagine that the aged senators, prevented by their years
from joining the army, are laying at your feet their white and
    hallowed hair;
that Rome herself, in fear of a master, is coming to meet you;
imagine that the people now and the people of the future
bring their prayers combined: to be born in freedom is one
    throng's wish;
to die in freedom the other's. If after appeals so great,
there is a place for Pompey, a suppliant, with child and wife,
I would throw myself before your feet if I could do so with the dignity
of high office intact. Unless you conquer, Magnus will be an exile,
his father-in-law's laughing-stock and your disgrace: I pray that I
    escape   380
the worst destiny and degrading years at life's final pivot—
may I not in old age learn to be a slave.' At their general's words
so gloomy, their spirits blaze and Roman valour
is excited and they resolved to die in case his fears were true.

So from both sides the troops run forward with equal impetus
of anger: fear of tyranny arouses these, those the hope.
These sword-hands will achieve things that no future age
can make good nor humankind repair in all the years,
though it be free from warfare. That fight will crush
the future races, and it will rob of birth and sweep away   390
the people of the generation entering the world. Then all
the Latin name will be a fable: Gabii, Veii, Cora
hardly will be indicated by their dust-covered ruins,
the hearths of Alba and the house-gods of Laurentum,
an empty country which no senator inhabits except unwillingly
on night ordained, complaining of the decree of Numa.
It is not devouring time which has eroded and abandoned in decay
these memorials of the past: it is the crime of civil war we see,
so many empty cities. To what has the multitude of humankind
been reduced! We peoples born in all the world   400
are not enough to fill with men the town-walls and fields;
a single city holds us all. The cornlands of Hesperia are worked
by chained labourer, the house with its ancestral roof decaying
stands, about to fall on no one; and Rome, crowded
by no citizen of her own but filled with the dregs of the world,

we have consigned to such a depth of ruin that in a body so immense
civil war cannot now be waged. The cause of such a great catastrophe
is Pharsalia. The fatal names of Cannae and of Allia,
long cursed in the Roman calendar, must yield their place.
The dates of lighter disasters Rome has marked;   410
this day she wanted to ignore. O bitter Fates!
Air noxious to inhale, putrefying diseases,
maddening famine, cities given up to fires,
quakes which bring the walls of crowded cities tumbling—
all could be made good by these men who are dragged from
everywhere to a pitiable death by Fortune: as she deploys
and takes away the offerings of long ages, she stations on the plains
the peoples and the generals through whom to show you in your fall,
Rome, how mighty was your fall. What city held a wider sway
over the world or advanced more swiftly through prosperity?   420
Every war gave you nations, every year
Titan saw you advance towards twin poles
so that—because not much space of the eastern land remained—
for you the night, for you entire day, for you the ether sped,
and everything the wandering stars saw was Roman.
But the fatal day of Emathia, equivalent to all the years,
carried backwards your destiny. Thanks to that bloody day
India does not tremble at the Rods of Latium,
the girded consul does not lead the Dahae, forbidden to wander,
inside city-walls or lean on a Sarmatian plough,   430
and Parthia owes you savage retribution still and for ever,
and Liberty, in flight from the crime of civil warfare, has withdrawn
beyond Tigris and Rhine, never to return,
and wanders on, after our so many murderous attacks,
a blessing on Germany and Scythia, no longer mindful
of Ausonia—how I wish our people had never known her!
When Romulus first founded the city with the vulture's left-hand
flight and filled its walls from the notorious grove
until the ruins of Thessaly, you should have stayed in slavery, Rome.
Fortune, I complain about the Bruti. Why did we have   440
times of legality or years which took their names from consuls?
Fortunate are the Arabs and the Medes and eastern earth,
kept by the Fates beneath continuous despots.
Of all the peoples who endure tyranny, our situation is the worst:
we are slaves, and ashamed. Without a doubt, we have no

deities: since human life is swept along by blind chance,
we lie that Jupiter is king. Will he watch Thessalian
bloodshed from the lofty ether even though he holds his
    thunderbolts?
Will Jupiter, then, aim his fires at Pholoë, at Oeta,
at the grove of innocent Rhodope, at the pines of Mimas,   450
and let Cassius strike this head? He brought the stars
upon Thyestes, he doomed Argos to a sudden night:
for wielding swords which are alike, so many swords of brothers
and of fathers, will Thessaly be granted daylight by him? Human
affairs are cared for by no deity. Yet we have revenge
for this disaster, as much as gods may give to mortals:
the civil wars will create divinities equal to those above;
with thunderbolts and rays and stars Rome will adorn
the dead and in the temples of the gods will swear by ghosts.

With rapid charge they had reduced the space delaying   460
the fateful crisis and now, divided by a little strip of land,
they look to see where their javelins will fall or what hands   463
threaten death to them. That they might profoundly know   462
what horrors they would commit, they saw their parents   464
with opposing faces, their brothers' weapons close at hand—
and did not choose to change position. Yet numbness froze
every breast and icy blood congeals in their guts,
their piety is smitten, and entire companies
long held their javelins poised with arms outstretched.
May the gods give to you, Crastinus, not death—a penalty   470
awaiting everyone—but feeling in your corpse after death:
your hand hurled the lance which started fighting
and was the first to stain Thessaly with Roman blood.
O impetuous frenzy! When Caesar wielded weapons,
was there found a hand to act before his? Then air resounded,
shattered by the trumpets, the call to war declared by horns,
then bugles dared to give the signal, then the clamour reaches
the ether and bursts into the dome of furthermost Olympus
—from there the clouds keep far away, no thunders reach so far.
Haemus in re-echoing valleys took up the noise   480
and gave it back to caves of Pelion to reduplicate,
Pindus drives the roar, Pangaean rocks reverberate,
the crags of Oeta groan: men took fright at the utterances

of their own madness repeated by the entire earth.

Innumerable missiles are discharged with conflicting prayers:
some long to wound, some long to stick their weapons in the ground
and keep their hands undefiled. Chance swirls everything along
and Fortune, unpredictable, makes anyone she wishes guilty.   488
Then Ituraeans, Medes, and loose-clothed Arabs,   514
with their bows a threatening throng, steered their arrows at no target
but only at the air which hung poised above the plain;
from there falls death. But they stain their foreign steel
with no charge of wickedness; all the wrong stood condensed
around the Roman spears. The ether is screened by steel
and a night of weapons joined together hung above the plain.   520
   But how little of the destruction was performed by javelins   489
and flying steel! For civil hatred the sword alone   490
suffices and leads sword-hands into Roman guts.
Pompey's army, massed in dense-packed squadrons,
had joined their shields in a chain with shield-bosses side by side
and had taken up position with hardly space to wield hands
and weapons: crushed together, it feared its own swords.
With headlong onrush Caesar's frenzied army
attacks the dense formations; through weapons, through the enemy
it seeks a path. Where twisted coat of mail presents
its heavy chains, and breast lies safely hidden under covering,
even here they reach the guts: it is the furthest object   500
through so much armour that each blow reaches. Civil war
one line endures, the other wages; here chilled
the sword stands still, but every guilty blade on Caesar's side is hot.
And Fortune, not for long swaying the balance of so many issues,
swept away the wide-scale wreckage as Fate was racing on.

As soon as Pompey's cavalry deployed its wings
over all the plain and extended them along the battle's edge,
his light-armed troops, spread among the outer companies,
follow close and launch their savage bands against the enemy:
there every nation joins the battle with its distinctive weapon,   510
but all are seeking Roman blood; from here fly arrows,
firebrands, and rocks and slingstones melted by their passage
through the air, turned to liquid with their heated mass;   513
then Caesar, fearing his front line might waver   521

under this attack, keeps his cohorts sideways on behind the standards
and into the battle's flank where the enemy haphazardly was ranging
suddenly launches a column, his wings unmoved.
Forgetful of the battle, not embarrassed by their fear,
with headlong flight they made it clear that civil war
is never happily entrusted to barbarian hordes.
When first the charger, pierced by steel in his breast,
threw his rider on his head and trampled on his limbs,
all the cavalry left the plain and, with their bridles turned about,   530
they headlong charged at their own troops, a concentrated cloud.
Then the slaughter passed all limit and what followed was no combat
but war on one side waged with throats, with weapons on the other;
the one battle-line is not strong enough to slaughter all those
who can perish on the other side. I wish, Pharsalia,
that that gore which barbarian breasts shed may satisfy
your plains, that your springs may be dyed by no others' blood,
that this mass may cover all your fields with their bones.
Or if you prefer to be glutted with Roman blood,
then, I pray, spare these men: let the Galatians live, Syrians,   540
Cappadocians, Gauls, Iberians from the world's edge,
Armenians, Cilicians, for after civil war
these will be the Roman people. Once arisen, panic
spreads to everyone and destiny was granted speed for Caesar.

They came to Magnus' strength, his central squadrons.
The fighting which had flooded in random course across
all the fields halted here and Caesar's fortune came to a standstill.
Here the soldiers waging war were not assembled from the royal
auxiliaries but wielded weapons in their hands unasked:
that place contained their brothers and their fathers.   550
Here is your madness, your frenzy, your wickedness, Caesar.
Mind of mine, shun this part of battle and leave it to darkness
and from my words let no age learn of horrors
so immense, of how much is licensed in civil war.
Better that these tears and protests go unheard:
whatever you did in this battle, Rome, I shall not tell.
    Here Caesar, maddening the people and goading them to frenzy,
goes ranging round the troops, adding fires to spirits already blazing:
wickedness must not be missing in any section of his army.
He inspects their swords too, to see which wholly drip with blood,   560

which glitter, stained only at the very point,
which hand trembles as it grasps the sword, who wields his weapons
slack or taut, who supplies fighting at command,
who loves to fight, and whose expression alters when a fellow citizen
is killed. He visits bodies stretched upon the wide fields;
with the pressure of his hand he personally staunches many a wound,
which would have poured out all the blood. Wherever he goes
      round—
like Bellona brandishing her blood-stained lash
or like Mars, rousing the Bistonians, if with savage whips
he goads his steeds maddened by Pallas' Aegis—   570
there is a vast night of wickedness; slaughter follows
and the groans as of a voice immeasurable, and armour clatters
with the weight of falling breast, and swords on swords are shattered.
In person he supplies fresh swords, hands them weapons,
and orders them to mangle with their steel the faces of the enemy,
in person he advances the line, onward drives his army from behind,
with blow of inverted spear he rouses the reluctant,
forbids them to strike the masses and indicates the Senate;
well he knows which is the empire's blood, which are the guts
      of the state,
he knows the starting-point of his course to Rome, the spot to strike   580
as the Liberty of the world makes her final stand. Nobility mingled
with the Second Order and venerable persons are overwhelmed
by the sword; they slaughter Lepidi, Metelli,
Corvini along with famed Torquati, often leaders
of the state and greatest of men, with you excepted, Magnus.

There, covering your face with a plebeian helmet
and unknown to the enemy, what a weapon, Brutus, did you hold!
O glory of the state, O final hope of the Senate,
the last name of a family so great throughout the ages,
do not race too reckless through the enemy's midst,   590
do not hasten deadly Philippi upon yourself before its time,
doomed to die in a Thessaly of your own. Nothing do you
      achieve here,
intent on Caesar's throat: he has not yet reached the citadel
or gone beyond the peak of human law controlling everything;
he has not yet earned from Fate a death so distinguished.
Let him live and let him rule, so he may tumble, Brutus' victim.

Here perished all the glory of the fatherland: on the plains
in an enormous heap patrician corpses lie, with no plebeians among
    them.
Yet in the slaughter of famous men stood out the death
of battling Domitius, a man led by Fate through every   600
calamity: nowhere did Magnus' fortune collapse
without him. So often defeated by Caesar, he died
with his liberty intact: now happily he falls beneath
a thousand wounds, rejoicing not to have a second pardon.
Caesar saw him thrashing around in thick
blood and, taunting, said: 'Now, Domitius, my successor,
you abandon Magnus' army; the war is waged
without you now.' But the breath hammering at Domitius' breast
was strong enough for speech and he unlocked his dying lips:
'Caesar, because I see you not the master of the deadly   610
wage of wickedness but uncertain of your fate and lesser
than your son-in-law, I go free and peaceful to the Stygian shades
with Pompey still my leader: though I die, I can hope
that you will be subdued in savage war and pay
a heavy penalty to Pompey and to me.' No more said he;
life left him and thick darkness closed his eyes.

When the world is dying I feel shame to spend my tears
on the innumerable deaths and to follow individuals' destinies,
questioning, whose guts did the fatal wound
pass through? who trampled on his vitals spilling on the ground?   620
who faced the enemy and, dying, forced out with his breath
the sword thrust into throat? who collapsed when struck?
who stood firm while his limbs fell about him? who lets the
      weapons pass
right through the breast? or who was pinned by spear to the plain?
whose veins were drained of blood which split the air
and falls upon the armour of his enemy? who strikes his brother's
breast, cuts off the head and throws it far away
so he can plunder the familiar corpse? who mangles
his father's face and proves to those who watch by his excessive wrath
that the man he slaughters is not his father? No death deserves   630
its own lament; we have no space to grieve for individuals.
Pharsalia did not have those elements of battle
which other calamities had: there, Rome was ruined by the destinies

of warriors, here by entire peoples; a soldier's death there
was here a nation's death; here streamed Achaean blood,
Pontic and Assyrian—all that gore is stopped from sticking
and congealing on the plain by a torrent of Roman gore.
From this battle the peoples receive a mightier wound
than their own time could bear; more was lost than life
and safety: for all the world's eternity we are prostrated.   640
Every age which will suffer slavery is conquered by these swords.
How did the next generation and the next deserve
to be born into tyranny? Did we wield weapons or shield
our throats in fear and trembling? The punishment of others' fear
sits heavy on our necks. If, Fortune, you intended to give a master
to those born after battle, you should have also given us a chance
        to fight.

Now Magnus had realized that the gods and Roman destiny had
        changed
allegiance, unlucky man, reluctantly compelled by the whole
        calamity
to condemn his own fortune. He stood upon a mound in the plain
from a distance to gaze at all the destruction scattered   650
through the fields of Thessaly, otherwise hidden from view by
        warfare.
He saw so many weapons aimed at his own death, so many
bodies laid low and himself dying in so much blood.
But he does not choose—as is the custom of the doomed—to drag
        down everything
with him and plunge it into ruin and embroil the nations in his fall:
even now he persisted in believing the heaven-dwellers worthy
of his prayers that most of Latium's multitude would live on
after him and cherished this as consolation for his defeat.
'Refrain, gods,' he says, 'from overthrowing all the peoples.
With the world still standing and with Rome surviving, Magnus can 660
be ruined. If you choose to wound me more, I have
a wife and sons: so many hostages have I given to the Fates.
Is it not enough for civil war to crush both me
and mine? Are we a trivial disaster without the inclusion of the world?
Why mangle everything? Why work for universal ruin?
Now, Fortune, is nothing mine?' So he speaks and visits all
his troops, his standards, and his squadrons shattered now

in every part, and calls them back from racing into early death,
saying he is not worth so much. The general did not lack resolve
to go to face the swords and suffer death in throat or breast;   670
but he feared that, if Magnus' body lay prostrate, his soldiers
would not flee and that the world would crash down on its leader;
or else he wished to take away his death from Caesar's eyes,
uselessly, unlucky man! When your father-in-law wants to look at it,
your head must be presented, wherever in the world it is. But you
        too, wife,
were a reason for his flight, your face and the Fates' refusal
that he should die with part of himself missing. Then a steed is spurred
to carry Magnus from the battle, not fearing weapons from the rear
but going to meet his final destiny with enormous courage.
No sorrowing, no tears were there; his grief deserves respect,   680
with dignity maintained, a grief exactly fitting for you
to show in Roman hardships, Magnus. With unchanged face
you gaze upon Emathia: success in war never
saw you proud, adversity will never see you broken;
as far beneath him as faithless Fortune was in his happy days of
        three triumphs,
so is she in his days of misery. Now you have put aside the weight
of destiny, and you depart, free from care; now you have leisure
        to look back
on happy times; hope has vanished, never to be fulfilled;
now you may understand what you were. Escape the hideous battles,
call the gods to witness that none who stays to fight   690
now dies for your sake, Magnus. Like Africa, lamentable for her
        losses,
like guilty Munda and the calamity by Pharian flood,
so too, most of the Thessalian battle, after you, will be inspired
no longer now by Pompey's name so popular throughout the world
or eagerness for war, but by that pair of rivals always with us—
Liberty and Caesar; and once you had left the battle,
the Senate showed by dying that it was fighting for itself.
Does it not delight you to retire defeated from battle and not watch
this horror to the end? Look back at the squadrons covered
in foaming gore, at rivers muddied by the influx of blood,   700
and take pity on your father-in-law. With what heart will he enter
Rome, his luck the richer by those battlefields?
Whatever you suffer in unknown lands, an exile alone,

whatever you suffer subject to the Pharian tyrant,
trust the gods, trust the Fates' long-lasting favour:
to win was worse. Ban the sound of lamentation,
stop the people weeping, dispense with tears and grief.
Let the world do homage to Magnus' hardships as much as his
          successes.
Free from care, with no suppliant look, gaze upon the kings,
gaze upon the cities you possessed and the kingdoms you bestowed,   710
Egypt and Libya, and choose a land for your death.
     Larisa first was witness of your fall, first to see
your noble head, not subdued by destiny. With all her citizens
she poured forth her entire strength through her walls,
to meet you as in victory: with tears they promise gifts,
open up their homes and temples, long to be your partners in defeat.
It is clear that much endures of your mighty name,
that you, inferior only to yourself, could again impel to war
all the nations and again return to your former fortune.
But 'What need of peoples or of cities has a conquered man?' he says;   720
'Show your loyalty to the conqueror.' Caesar, you are walking still
in a lofty heap of slaughter through the guts of your fatherland,
but to you your son-in-law already grants the nations. His steed
          bears
Pompey off from there: tears and lamentation follow him
and the people's numerous reproaches against the cruel gods.
Now, Magnus, you have genuine proof and enjoyment of the
          popularity
you sought: the successful man knows not that he is loved.

When Caesar saw the fields drenched sufficiently with Hesperian
blood, thinking now that he should rein in his soldiers'
swords and hands, he granted life to worthless souls, to columns   730
whose death would have had no point. But to stop the camp
          inviting back
the routed men, to stop night-time rest dispelling panic,
he decides to move at once into the enemy's rampart
while Fortune glows, while terror is all-accomplishing,
without a fear that this order would be difficult for men weary
or by war exhausted. With no great encouragement
the troops were ready to be led to plunder: 'Victory complete is ours,
my warriors,' he said; 'there remains the payment for our blood,

which it is my task to show; I will not speak of bestowing
what each of you will give himself. Look: their camp is open wide,   740
full of every precious metal; here lies gold seized from
the western races; their tents confine the treasures of the east.
The massed wealth of many kings and Magnus
awaits its masters; hurry, soldiers, to precede the men
that you are chasing; all the riches which Pharsalia has made yours
are being stolen by the conquered.' What trench, what rampart   746/749
could withstand them as they sought reward of war and
     wickedness?   750
They race to know how large their wage of guilt is.
And for sure they found an enormous mass of bullion
heaped up from a plundered world to pay the costs of war;
but not enough for minds which wanted everything
was all the gold mined by the Iberian, disgorged by Tagus,
or gathered from the surface of the sands by wealthy Arimaspian;
though they seize it, they will think their wickedness sold cheaply.
Since they have pledged themselves in victory the Tarpeian
citadel and promised everything in their expectation of looting Rome,
the plunder of a camp is a cheat.

                        The wicked plebs takes   760
slumber on patrician turf and inhuman soldiers
lie on couches spread for kings, and on the beds of fathers,
beds of brothers, the guilty men laid down their limbs.
A maddened sleep harasses them and frantic dreams
revolve the battle of Thessaly in their tortured breasts.
Their savage crime is wide awake in everyone and in all their
     thoughts
they brandish weapons and they jerk their hands though no hilt is
     there.
I could think that the battlefield moaned, that the earth
breathed forth guilty spirits, that all the air was tainted
by the shades and the night of upper world by Stygian terror.   770
Victory exacts a hideous punishment deservedly, and slumber
brings on flames and hissing. The ghost of a murdered citizen
stands there; each man is tormented by a terrifying vision all his own:
he sees faces of old men, *he* the forms of younger men,
he in all his dreams is harried by his brother's corpse,
in *this* breast is his father— all these shades are in Caesar.

Just such were the faces of the Eumenides which Pelopean Orestes
saw when not yet purified upon the Scythian altar;
and he felt a mental turmoil no more thunderstruck than that
of Pentheus in his frenzy or Agave when she had ceased to rave.   780
On that night he is tormented by all the swords
which Pharsalia saw or which the day of retribution would see,
unsheathed by the Senate; he is lashed by the hellish monsters.
Yet his guilty mind forgives the unhappy man part of his punishment
because he sees the Styx, the shades and Tartarus thrust
into his dreams while Pompey is alive!

                      Though he suffered all of this,
when shining daylight revealed the losses of Pharsalia,
the appearance of the place in no way checks his eyes from fastening
upon the deathly fields. He sees rivers driven on
by gore and mounds of corpses high as lofty   790
hills, he watches heaps sinking into putrefaction
and counts the peoples of Magnus; a place for feasting
is prepared from where he can discern the faces and the features
of the dead. He is delighted that he cannot see the Emathian land
and that his eyes scan fields hidden underneath the carnage.
In the blood he sees his fortune and his gods.
And not to lose the joyful sight of his wickedness, in a frenzy
he refuses those unfortunates the pyre's flame and forces on to guilty
heaven the sight of Emathia. The Carthaginian who buried
the consul and Cannae lit by Libyan torches do not compel him   800
to observe the customs of humanity towards an enemy,
but, with his anger not yet glutted by the slaughter, he remembers
that they were his fellow citizens. We do not ask for individual
graves or for separate funeral-pyres: grant the nations
a single fire, let the bodies be burnt in a holocaust;
or if you enjoy punishing your son-in-law, heap up Pindus'
forest, raise up the woods packed with Oeta's oak,
let Pompey see the flame of Thessaly from his ship.
You achieve nothing by this anger: it matters not whether corpses
      disintegrate
by putrefaction or on the pyre; Nature takes back everything   810
in her kindly bosom, and bodies owe their own end to themselves.
These people, Caesar, if not consumed by fire now, will be consumed
together with the earth, together with the waters of the sea.

A shared funeral-pyre which will mingle stars with dead men's bones
awaits the universe. Wherever Fortune calls your spirit,
there will be these spirits too: into the breezes you will go no higher
than they, in no better place beneath the Stygian night will you lie.
Death is free from Fortune; Earth has room for all that she
has borne; the man who has no funeral urn is covered by the sky.
You——exacting punishment from the nations in corpses without
    burial—   820
why do you flee this carnage? Why do you desert these stinking fields?
Drink these waters, Caesar, breathe this air, if you can.
But the rotting hordes rob you of Pharsalian
fields, they rout the conqueror and possess the plains.

To the grisly fodder of Haemonian war came not only
Bistonian wolves but lions too, who left Pholoë
when they scented out decay of bloody slaughter.
Then she-bears left their lairs and loathsome dogs
their homes and houses: every keen-nosed creature
which senses air impure and tainted by carrion.   830
The birds which for a long time now had followed the camp
of civil war flock together. You birds, accustomed to exchange
Thracian winters for Nile, went later
to the mild south. Never was the heaven clothed with
such a cloud of vultures, never did more wings crush the air.
Every forest sent its birds and every tree
dripped with bloody dew from gore-stained wing.
Often on the victor's face and unnatural standards
fell gore or rotting flesh from the lofty ether,
as a bird let drop the limbs from its talons now exhausted.   840
Even so the entire horde is not reduced to bones and does not
    disappear
inside wild beasts, torn to shreds; they care not for the inmost
guts nor are they hungry to suck up all the marrow:
they barely taste the limbs. Most of the Latian multitude
lies there rejected; but sun and rains and lapse
of time dissolved and blended them with Emathian fields.

Thessaly, unfortunate land! With what crime did you so
hurt the gods that they inflicted on you alone so many deaths,
so many dooms of wickedness? What length of time will be enough

for distant ages to forget and to forgive you for the losses of the war?   850
Every crop will rise discoloured with tainted growth.
With every ploughshare you will desecrate the Roman shades.
First, new battle-lines will meet and for a second crime
you will offer your plains not yet dry from this blood.
Though we empty all our ancestors' graves—
the tombs still standing and those which have poured out
their funeral-urns, their framework overcome by ancient tree-root—
more are the ashes ploughed in the furrows
of Haemonian land, more the bones which rustic harrow strikes.
No sailor would have tied his rope to the Emathian   860
shore, no ploughman would have disturbed the land,
the grave of the Roman people, and the farmers would run away
from the haunted plains, no flocks would shelter
in the thickets, no herdsman would dare allow his herd
to pluck the grass which rises from our bones,
and you would lie unknown and bare, as if not supporting
human life because of ice or zone of excessive heat,
if you alone, instead of first, had borne the blasphemy of war.
O gods above, permit us to hate the guilty lands.
Why do you burden the entire world and so acquit it?   870
The carnage of the west, Pachynus' lamentable wave,
and Mutina and Leucas have made Philippi innocent.

BOOK EIGHT

Now beyond the gorge of Hercules and wooded Tempe,
seeking the deserted detours of the Haemonian forest
and driving on his steed, which was exhausted from the gallop and
    refused
to obey the spur, Magnus jumbles in uncertainty the traces of his
    flight
and intertwines his paths by wandering. He panics at the noise
of forests moving in the winds, and any of his comrades
who rejoins him from behind alarms him in his dread and terror
of attack. Though he has fallen from a lofty height,
he knows the price of his own blood is not yet cheap
and, remembering his fate, believes that he still has   10
a throat worth as much as he himself would give
for Caesar's severed head. Although he goes through wilderness,
the warrior's famous face does not allow him to conceal
his fate in safe hiding-places. Many who were heading for
the Pharsalian camp, when rumour had not yet disclosed his fall,
were stunned to meet their leader and were thunderstruck by his
    change
in luck: he scarcely was believed when he himself reported
his defeat. The presence of any witness of his hardships
is painful to Magnus. He would rather be unknown to all
the nations, pass in safety through the cities with an obscure   20
name; but from the unhappy man Fortune takes the penalties
of her prolonged support: she crushes his adversity with his renown's
enormous weight and overwhelms him with his former luck.
Now he thinks that honours were thrust on him too early,
and condemns the Sullan exploits of his laurel-crowned youth;
now in his fall the memory of Corycian fleets
and Pontic standards sickens him. So age too long
and life surviving after power destroy heroic
spirits. Unless the final day coincides with the end
of blessings, by speedy death forestalling sorrows,   30
former fortune brings disgrace. Is there anyone who dare

entrust himself to favourable Fates except with death available?

He reached the shore where the river Peneus,
already reddening with the carnage of Emathia, passed out into the
      sea.
From there a boat unequal to the winds and waves and hardly safe
on river's shallows carried him in trepidation out on to the deep.
Though at his oars Corcyra and the bays of Leucas
tremble yet, the lord of the Cilicians and the Liburnian land
crept on board the tiny boat, a timid passenger.
    He orders them to turn the sails towards the shores   40
of distant Lesbos, the land where you were hiding, Cornelia,
the sharer of his troubles, more sad than if you were standing
in the middle of Emathian plains. Forebodings stir up grim
anxieties, her sleep is shaken by trembling dread,
every night is full of Thessaly; and when the darkness is removed,
you run on to the rocks of a precipitous cliff, to the sea-shore's
edge; and looking out across the waves you are always first
to see the sails of an approaching vessel nodding far away
and yet you dare not ask at all about your husband's fate.
Look!—a ship which spreads its sails towards your harbours.   50
What it brings you do not know—as yet the height of fear for you
is a gloomy messenger of war and adverse rumour.
Here is your husband in defeat. Why waste the time of grief?
You are afraid, when already you could weep.
                          Then as the ship came near,
up she jumped and noticed the gods' cruel reproach:
the general disfigured by pallor, the white hair covering
his face, his clothing dirtied by black dust.
Night came over the unhappy woman and with its darkness took away
the sky and light, and anguish stopped her breath; all her limbs
give way, deserted by the muscles, her heart grew stiff, and long   60
she lies deceived by the hope that this is death. Now with the cable
fastened to the shore, Pompey moves across the empty sands.
When her loyal servants saw him close at hand,
they allowed themselves to censure Fate with nothing more
than stifled moans, and try in vain to lift
their semi-conscious mistress from the ground; Magnus clasps her
to his breast and revives her rigid frame with his embrace.

Once the blood returned to the surface of her body, she had begun
to feel Pompey's arms and to be able to endure
her husband's sorrowing face: Magnus tells her not to submit 70
to destiny and chides her excessive anguish like this:
    'Why do you, a woman, illustrious thanks to the name of ancestors
so great, shatter your noble strength at the first wound
of Fortune? You have an avenue to fame which will endure for
        centuries.
In this your sex, the only means of praise is not respect for the laws
nor warfare but an unhappy husband. Elevate your mind,
let your devotion fight with destiny: because I am defeated,
love me. Now I bring you greater glory,
because the Rods and the Senate's honourable throng
and the band of kings so great have left me: be the first and only one 80
to follow Magnus. The height of unincreasable anguish
is ugly while your husband is still alive: to mourn your man
should be the final act of loyalty. No losses have you
suffered from my war: Magnus lives on after the battles; it is
his fortune which has perished. Your tears are for the thing you loved.'
Rebuked by her husband's words, with difficulty she lifted from the ground
her feeble limbs, her lamentation bursting into protest so:
    'O how I wish that I had entered hated Caesar's marriage-bed,
an unlucky wife, bringing happiness to neither husband.
Twice have I harmed the world: the Erinys and the ghosts of the
        Crassi 90
were the attendants at my wedding; doomed to those shades,
I have brought the Assyrian disaster into the camps of civil war
and hurled the people headlong and have driven all the gods
from the better cause. O most mighty husband,
O husband too good for my marriage-bed, did Fortune have
such power over one so great? Why did I marry you if I was going
to make you miserable? I am guilty: now agree to punish me—
a punishment I willingly will suffer: to make the water gentler for you,
to make secure the loyalty of kings, to make all the world more ready
for your coming, scatter your companion on the sea. I had rather 100
paid for successful warfare with my life: now at least you can expiate
your disaster, Magnus. Cruel Julia, you have avenged
our marriage-bed with civil war; now, wherever you lie, come here,
exact the penalty and, placated by your rival's death,
spare your very own Magnus.' So she spoke and sank

into her husband's lap and melted the eyes of everyone
to tears. Hard Magnus' heart relents
and Lesbos blurred the eyes left dry at Thessaly.

Then the throng of Mytilene speaks to Magnus
on the shore now full: 'If our greatest glory will always be　　　　110
that we kept safe the pledge of such a mighty husband,
you too, we beg, bring honour to the city-walls devoted to you
by a sacred pact, bring honour to our friendly hearths by staying
a single night at least: make this a place which all the ages will revisit,
Magnus, which the Roman visitor will worship when he comes.
There are no better city-walls for you to enter in defeat:
all the rest can hope for favour from the victor, but these
already have their guilt. And what is more, our island lies upon the sea,
and Caesar has no ships. A large part of your chieftains, certain of
　　　the place,
will gather here; on this familiar shore your fate must be restored.　　　120
Take our temples' finery and the riches of the gods,
take our young men for service on the land or ships,
whichever is better; use the whole of Lesbos, as much as it can help.　　123
This charge alone remove from a land deserving well of you,　　　125
that you not seem to gain our loyalty when fortunate
and then reject it in misfortune.' Cheered in his adversity
by the great devotion of these men, rejoicing on the world's account
that loyalty exists, he said: 'I have shown to you
by no small pledge that no land in all the world deserves　　　130
more gratitude: with this hostage Lesbos held
my love; here was my sacred home, here my beloved house-gods,
here was Rome for me. To no other shores did I direct
my ship in flight, although I knew that Lesbos had, by keeping
safe my wife, already earned the wrath of Caesar,
not fearing to entrust to you a means so great
of pardon. But now it is enough to have made you guilty;
I must pursue my destiny through all the world.
Poor Lesbos, too fortunate with your everlasting name,
whether you teach the peoples and the kings to shelter Magnus　　　140
or whether you alone show loyalty to me. For I am resolved to seek
where in the world right and where wickedness exist. If any deity
is with me still, hear my final prayer:
grant that I meet peoples like Lesbos, who do not forbid a man

subdued in war from entering their harbours, though Caesar threatens,
or from leaving them.' He spoke and placed on board the ship
his sorrowing companion. You might have thought that everyone
was leaving the earth and soil of fatherland: such lamentation
rose from all the shore and angry fists were stretched into the ether.
And as they saw them leave, the people groaned, less   150
for Pompey, whose fortune had aroused their sorrow,
than for her, whom in all the time of war they regarded
as a fellow citizen. Were she heading for the camp
of a victorious husband, with difficulty would the mothers
have seen her off dry-eyed: with such deep love her purity had
     bound
some to her, her goodness others and the modesty of her virtuous
     face,
because in spirit she was humble, a guest irksome with no retinue,
because she lived as if her husband had been conquered when his
     destiny was still intact.

Already Titan had sunk into the sea to the middle of his fires:
he was not complete to those from whom he hid his orb nor
     those to whom   160
he showed it, if they exist. In Pompey's breast unsleeping troubles
turn now to the friendly cities of Roman alliance
and the fickle minds of kings, now to the pathless lands
of the world which lies beyond Auster and the excessive suns.
Often the distressing hardship of his anxieties and his loathing
of the future threw aside the weary tumult of his undecided breast,
and he consults the helmsman of the ship concerning all the stars:
by which does he identify the lands? what is his system in the sky
for cutting through the sea? by what star does he keep on course
     for Syria?
or which fire in the Plough directs him well to Libya?   170
The skilled observer of quiet Olympus to these questions says:
'We do not follow the stars which glide and slip
across the constellationed sky, deceiving wretched sailors
with heaven never standing still; but the never-setting pole star
which does not sink beneath the waves, the brightest star in both
     the Bears,
it directs our ships. Always when it rises to the heights
before me and the lesser Bear stands above the topmost yard-arms

we face towards the Bosporus and Pontus as it bends
the shores of Scythia. The lower Arctophylax sinks
from mast-top and the nearer to the sea Cynosura moves,   180
the ship is heading for the ports of Syria. From there Canopus
takes over, a star content to roam the southern sky,
afraid of Boreas: with it too on your left proceed
past Pharos and in mid-sea your ship will reach the Syrtes.
But to what destination do you bid our sails be set, with what rope
now the canvas stretched?' With wavering breast Magnus replied
to him: 'This alone you must see to in our journey over all the sea,
that your ship is always far from the Emathian
shores, that you leave Hesperia behind by sea and sky:
leave the rest to the winds. My companion and the pledge that I
        deposited   190
I have regained; before, I was certain which shores I desired;
now Fortune will provide a harbour.' So he speaks, but the other
turned the sails which hung in equal measure from the level
yard-arms and sent the ship to port; to cleave
Oenussae's rocks and the waves made rough by Chios, some ropes
he slackened toward the prow and some he tightened at the stern.
The waters sensed the change and made a different sound
with the ship's beak cutting through the sea and the keel
facing in a new direction. Not as deftly does the charioteer,
when with right-hand wheel he circles round the left-hand axle,   200
force the chariot close to the turning-post without touching it.

Titan showed the earth and hid the stars.
All those dispersed by Emathia's storm catch up
with Magnus; the first to meet him after he left Lesbos' shore
was his son; soon came the loyal band of chieftains.
Even when he was cast down by Fate and driven from the battle-line,
Fortune did not take from Magnus kings as his attendants:
the masters of the earth and the rulers of the east he has
as his companions into exile. Deiotarus, who had followed his leader's
scattered tracks, he orders to go to the remotest places of the world.   210
He says: 'Since the world, as far as it was Roman,
was lost at Emathia's disaster, it remains, most faithful of kings,
to test the loyalty of the east and of the peoples who drink
Euphrates and Tigris, still untouched by Caesar.
As you seek success for Magnus, do not be loath to enter

the distant homes of Medes and Scythian remotenesses,
to change your clime entirely, to bear my words
to the haughty son of Arsaces: "If your former pact
with me remains in force —the pact I swore by the Thunderer of
    Latium,
the pact your holy men ratified—fill your quivers,   220
stretch your Armenian bows with Getic strings.
Do this if, when I headed for the Caspian Gates and chased
the hardy ever-warring Alani, I ever let you freely
race across the Achaemenid plains and never drove you
trembling into Babylon's safety, O Parthians.
Beyond the lands of Cyrus and Chaldaea's kingdom's furthest parts,
where rapid Ganges and Nysaean Hydaspes reach the sea,
still nearer than Persia to the fire
of rising Phoebus was I: and though victorious everywhere,
I tolerated your sole absence from my triumphs;   230
alone among the kings of the eastern earth, the Parthian
approaches me on equal terms. And more than once the sons of
    Arsaces
survive by Magnus' help; who else was it who, following the wounds
of our Assyrian disaster, stifled Latium's righteous anger?
Now let Parthia, bound by all my services, break through
her boundaries and cross the bank forbidden through the centuries
and pass beyond Pellaean Zeugma. Conquer for Pompey, Parthians:
willingly will Rome be conquered." ' The king was not slow
to obey his difficult orders. He puts aside the marks of royalty
and disembarks, dressed in a cloak grabbed from a servant.   240
In dangerous times it is safe for a tyrant to simulate the beggar:
how much more secure, then, is the life a truly poor man leads than
the masters of the world! Once he has despatched the king upon
    the shore,
himself he passes through the Icarian rocks, avoiding Ephesus
and Colophon of tranquil sea and skirts the foaming
rocks of little Samos; the breeze breathes, flowing from the shore
of Cos; from there he speeds past Cnidos and abandons Rhodes
made famous by the sun and cuts short the mighty bays of Telmessus'
wave by a mid-sea course. The land of Pamphylia extends
to meet his ship: though he as yet has not dared to entrust himself   250
to any city-walls, you, little Phaselis, are first to be
approached by Magnus; your few inhabitants and your houses

drained of occupants stop you causing fear: the vessel's throng
was greater than your own. From here he spreads his sails again
and now sees Taurus, and Dipsus tumbling down from Taurus.

Could Magnus have believed that when he gave peace to the waves
he too would benefit? Along the shores of the Cilicians he flees,
safe in his tiny ship. A large part of the Senate follows him,
rallying around their fleeing leader, and at small Syhedra—
the harbour where Selinus sends and welcomes back his ships—   260
at a meeting of his chieftains Magnus finally unlocked his mournful
lips in these words: 'My companions both in battle and in flight,
the essence of our fatherland, although upon a naked shore
and in the land of the Cilicians surrounded by no troops,
your advice I ask and seek the starting-point of a new career,
offer me your mighty spirits. Not completely did I fall
on the fields of Emathia nor is my destiny so overwhelmed
that I cannot lift up my head and shake off the disaster
I have suffered. If the ruins of Libya could elevate Marius
to the Rods and return him to the Fasti which were full of him,   270
can Fortune hold me down, though struck by a lighter blow?
A thousand ships of mine are rolling on Greek waters,
a thousand generals; Pharsalia did not overthrow but scattered
my resources. But even on its own the fame of my achievements
waged through all the earth and my name which the world loves
can keep me safe. You must weigh for strength
and loyalty the kingdoms: Libya and the Parthians and Pharos,
which ruler best can help the Roman state.
But to you I will disclose the secrets
of my worries and which way the balance of my mind inclines.   280
I do not trust the youth of the tyrant of the Nile,
because loyalty in adversity requires mature years.
Then I fear the two-faced cleverness of the fickle Moor,
because the wicked son of Carthage, remembering his line,
menaces Hesperia and much in his foolish breast is
Hannibal, who stains the realm by indirect descent, connected with
Numidian ancestors: already, with Varus begging him for help,
he swelled with pride to see the Roman state in second place.
So come, companions, let us hurry to the eastern sphere.
Euphrates with his flood cuts off an enormous world;   290
the Caspian Gates set apart immeasurable retreats;

a different sky revolves Assyrian nights and days;
their sea of other-coloured wave is separate from ours;
they have an Ocean of their own. Fighting is their only passion.
Taller stands their war-horse on the plain and stronger is their bow;
neither boy nor aged man is slow to stretch the fatal
string; from no arrow is death unrealized.
They were the first to break Pellaean pikes with archery
and Bactra, the Medes' abode, and Babylon proud
of her walls, the home of the Assyrians. And our Roman javelins　　300
do not terrify the Parthians excessively: they boldly enter war,
after trying out their Scythian quivers on the day when Crassus fell.
They shower barbs which do not rely on iron alone:
their whistling weapons are steeped in lavish poison;
tiny wounds do harm and the slightest graze is death.
O how I wish my trust in the savage sons of Arsaces
were not so great! A fate too much a rival of our Roman
fate directs the Medes and the race is greatly favoured by the gods.
I shall let loose the peoples torn from this other land
and I shall summon and let fly the Orient from its abodes.　　310
But if eastern loyalty and barbarian treaties
fail us, let Fortune bear my shipwreck far beyond
connections of the ordinary world: I will not pray to kingdoms
I created. I shall have sufficient consolation for my death,
lying in another sphere, that my father-in-law has done nothing bloody
to these limbs and nothing holy. But reviewing all
the destinies of my life, always I was treated with respect
in that region of the world; how great I was beyond Maeotis,
how great beside Tanais, conspicuous in all the world!
What lands did my name enter with achievements　　320
more successful? From where did I return with greater triumph?
Rome, favour my plans! What greater joy could the gods
have ever given you than for you to wage a civil
war with Parthian soldiers and exhaust a race so mighty
and embroil it in our misery? When Caesar's armies
clash with the Medes, then Fortune must avenge either me
or the Crassi.'

　　　　So he spoke, but by their muttering he sensed
the warriors condemned his plan. Lentulus exceeded
all of them in his drive for excellence and loftiness

of anguish, and he offered utterances worthy of a recent consul: 330
   'Has the collapse at Thessaly so shattered your mind?
Has a single day doomed the destiny of the world? Is a dispute
so great decided in favour of Emathia? Does all the help
for this bloody wound lie useless? Are the Parthians' feet the only ones
left to you by Fortune, Magnus? What? Deserter of the world,
do you, detesting entire tracts of earth and sky,
seek heavens turned away from ours and foreign stars?—
Soon you will worship Chaldaean hearths and barbarian rites,
a slave of the Parthians.—Why is love of liberty alleged
as the reason for fighting? Why if you can be a slave do you deceive   340
the miserable world? Will he who shuddered to hear of you
when you were ruling the Roman state, will he who saw you leading
captive kings from forests of Hyrcania, from the Indian shore,
see you overthrown by Fate, humiliated, broken,
and will he madly raise his courage to attack the Latian world,
measuring himself and Rome alike by Pompey begging him for help?
Nothing worthy of your spirit and your destiny will you utter:
ignorant of converse in the Latin tongue, he will demand
that you entreat him with tears, Magnus. Must we suffer
this wound to our honour, that Parthia avenge before Rome   350
Rome's own Hesperian disaster? For civil warfare
she chose you as her general, for sure: so why do you spread
our wounds and unobserved disasters among the Scythian peoples?
Why teach the Parthians to change allegiance? Rome is losing
a consolation of her misery so great, that she endures no kings
but serves a citizen her own. Is it your delight to go through the world,
leading savage races against the city-walls of Rome, preceded
by the standards from Euphrates which were captured with the Crassi?
He alone of kings was absent from Emathia, while Fate concealed
its preference—so will he now challenge the resources   360
so immense of him reported victor? Will he want to join
his destiny with you, Magnus? His race inspires no such confidence.
Every people born in Arctic frosts is unsubdued
in warfare and a lover of death: the nearer you advance
towards the expanses of the east and warmth
of the world, the mildness of the sky makes the peoples soft.
There you see men in loose garments
and flowing clothes. Through the lands of Media,
upon Sarmatian plains, and the fields of Tigris stretching far

with level ground, the Parthian can be conquered by no enemy   370
thanks to his freedom of flight; but where the earth is swollen,
he will not scale the broken mountain-ridges, he will not wage war
through dim darkness, ineffective with his unsure bow,
he will not break through the river with a violent whirlpool by
    swimming it,
he will not, when all his limbs are drenched with blood
in battle, endure the summer sun beneath the torrid dust.
They have no ram, no war-engine, they have not the strength
to fill up trenches, but whatever can stop an arrow
will prove to be a wall against a Parthian in pursuit
Their battle is a skirmish, their warfare running away, their
    squadrons   380
roving, and their soldiers better at giving ground than driving back
    the enemy;
their weapons are bedaubed with tricks, their courage nowhere dares
to face fighting at close quarters but only from a distance to stretch
the bow-strings and to leave it to the winds to bear their wounds away.
The sword possesses strength and every race of warriors
wages war with swords; but the first assault disarms
the Medes and tells them to retreat with empty quiver.
No confidence in their hands have they, all in poison.
Do you believe them warriors, Magnus, who think it not enough
to face the battle's crisis with iron alone? Is it worth it,   390
to bid for scandalous assistance so you can die divided
by the entire world from your own land, so barbarian earth can settle
on you, so a tomb can cover you, small and lowly
yet enviable when Crassus still seeks burial?

   'But lighter is your lot, since death is the final penalty
and one not feared by warriors. Yet death is not Cornelia's
dread at the hands of the monstrous king. Barbarian lust is
surely not unknown to us, which blind and in the manner of the
    beasts
defiles with countless wives the laws and pacts of the marriage-torch,
where the secrets of the abominable chamber are exposed   400
among a thousand women? Frenzied on its feasts and undiluted wine,
the court dares sexual acts not specified
in any laws: in so many female embraces one man
is not exhausted in an entire night. In the chambers of the kings
lie their sisters and their mothers too, the sacred tie.

Among the nations the unhappy tale condemns the Thebes
of Oedipus for wickedness unwillingly committed:
how frequently the master of the Parthians is born from blood like
　　　this
combined, a son of Arsaces! If it is right for him to make his
　　　mother pregnant,
what shall I think forbidden him? Metellus' daughter so illustrious　　　410
will take her stand beside the barbaric bed, the thousandth wife,
although the royal lust, Magnus, to no other will be
more devoted, spurred on by cruelty and by the glory of her husbands:
to gratify the Parthian with more portents, he will know
that she was wife of Crassus too; as though already owed to the Assyrian
fates, she is dragged off as the captive of the old defeat.
Let the lamentable wound to our eastern destiny stick fast
and you will be ashamed not only to have sought assistance
from the deadly king but to have waged civil warfare first.
Among the peoples what greater reproach will there be against　　　420
your father-in-law and you than that, while you are joining battle,
vengeance of the Crassi disappears? All our leaders
should have launched an attack on Bactra and, to keep the troops
　　　anywhere
from idleness, should have exposed the northern quarter of the
　　　empire
to the Dacians and the squadrons of the Rhine, until deceitful Susa
and Babylon lay low, collapsed as tombs for the generals.
An end to the Assyrian peace we pray for, Fortune;
and if the civil war was finished at Thessaly
let the victor go to the Parthians. I could rejoice
in Caesar's triumphs over them alone of the races in the world.　　　430
When first you cross the chill Araxes, will the ghost
of the sorrowing old man, pierced by Scythian arrows,
not heap these words on you? "Do you come for treaties
and for peace? We unburied ghosts hoped that following our deaths
you would avenge our ashes." Then numerous reminders
of defeat will meet your eyes: the walls round which our generals
passed, their heads cut off, the place where Euphrates smothered
names so mighty and Tigris carried Roman corpses
down inside the earth and brought them out again. If through such
　　　scenes,
Magnus, you can go, then you can also placate your father-in-law,　　　440

seated in the midst of Thessaly. Why not turn your gaze upon the
    Roman
world? If you fear the realms extending to the south
and treacherous Juba, we make for Pharos and the lands of Lagus.
On one side Egypt is protected by the Libyan Syrtes, on the other side
the rapid river with its sevenfold flood drives back the sea.
The land is satisfied with its own blessings and has no need of trade
or Jupiter; all its confidence is in Nile alone.
The sceptre which boy Ptolemy holds he owes to you;
it was entrusted to your guardianship. Who would shudder at
the shadow of a name? His age is innocent. Justice, loyalty,   450
regard for the gods—do not look for these in an aged court;
nothing shames men grown accustomed to the sceptre: mildest is
    the lot
of realms beneath a new king.' Without another word
he drove their minds in this direction. Desperation, how much
liberty of speech you have! Magnus' proposal was defeated.

Then they left Cilician soil and swiftly steered
their ships to Cyprus; no other altars did the goddess prefer
to these, in memory of the Paphian wave, if we believe the deities
are born, if it is right to think that any of the gods had a beginning.
When Pompey left these shores, after travelling past   460
all the rocks of Cyprus which jut out southwards,
from there he turns with cross-wise current of the massive sea;
he did not reach the mountain welcome for its night-time light
and with battling sail he scarcely touched the lowest shores
of Egypt where the seventh river, the largest part
of divided Nile, races down into the shallows of Pelusium.
It was the time when Libra balances the level hours,
equal for one day, not more, and the light, diminishing,
repays to winter's night the compensation for its spring-time loss.
When he discovers that the King keeps himself at Mount Casius,   470
there he steers his course; neither Phoebus yet nor canvas is flagging.

Now with rapid course along the shore a scout on horseback
filled the frightened court with their visitor's arrival.
Hardly was there time for debate; yet all the freaks
of the Pellaean house assembled: Acoreus was among them,
kindly now in his old age and more restrained from feeble years—

he had his birth in Memphis, guardian of Nile, who rises up to cover
the fields, and foolish in its rites; while he was keeper of the gods,
more than a single Apis had lived the term of his own Phoebe—
his was the first voice of debate and he proclaimed the worth   480
and loyalty of Pompey and the sacred promises of the king's dead
    father.
But, better at persuading evil men and understanding tyrants,
Pothinus dared condemn Pompey to death
and said: 'Law and justice, Ptolemy, make many guilty;
loyalty, though praised, pays the penalty when it supports
the people Fortune crushes. Side with the Fates and gods,
and court the fortunate; avoid the failures. As stars are different
from earth and flame from sea, so profit is from right.
All the might of sceptres disappears if it begins to weigh
justice; regard for what is honourable overthrows citadels.   490
Unrestricted wickedness is the defence of hated tyrannies
and limit removed from swords. You cannot act brutally
without penalty unless you always do. Let him who wishes
to be good leave the court. Virtue and the highest power
are not compatible. The man ashamed of cruelty is always fearful.
Magnus has despised your years—he thinks you cannot
drive back even the defeated from our shore—but let him not
go unpunished. And do not let our visitor rob us of the throne;
remember you have closer ties: if you are tired of ruling,
then return the Nile and Pharos to the sister you rejected.   500
Let us in any case protect Egypt from the Latian troops:
whatever Magnus did not have while war was waged,
the victor also will not have. Now driven from the entire world,
with no confidence in his fortune left, he seeks a race
to share his fall. By the ghosts of civil war he is carried off.
And not only from his father-in-law's army does he run: he runs
    from
the faces of the Senate, of whom a large part gluts the birds of
    Thessaly;
and he dreads the nations he has left embroiled in shared
slaughter, and he fears the kings whose all he has engulfed,
and, the culprit of Thessaly, welcomed by no land,   510
he disturbs our world which he has not yet ruined.
To us is given, Ptolemy, a more just cause of grievance
against Pompey. Why do you stain secluded Pharos,

ever peaceful, with the guilt of war and make our fields
suspect to the victor? Why in your fall did you choose
this land alone on which to bring Pharsalian fate
and penalties your own? Already we have cause of guilt
which must be wiped out with the sword. Because by your persuasion
the Senate granted us the sceptre, with our prayers we supported
     your armies.

This sword, which Fate commands me to produce, I intended   520
not for you but for the loser; I shall strike your guts, Magnus;
I had preferred your father-in-law's: we are swept along
in the same direction as everything. Do you doubt that I need
     injure you
when it is allowed me? What confidence in our kingdom
brings you here, unlucky man? Do you not see our unwarlike people
with difficulty digging fields softened by receding Nile?
It is right to measure one's own realm and to admit one's weakness.
Ptolemy, can you prop up the fall of Magnus, the fall
beneath which Rome lies crushed? Dare you disturb the pyre
and Thessalian ashes and summon war into your realm?   530
Before the battle of Emathia we took the side of neither army:
do we now choose the camp of Pompey as the world abandons it?
Do you now challenge the victor's strength and acknowledged
     destiny?
In adversity it is right not to desert, but only for supporters in
     prosperity;
loyalty never chose the unfortunate to be its friends.'
All assented to the crime. The boy-king is delighted
at the unaccustomed honour—that his slaves permit him now
to issue orders so important. Achillas, chosen for the crime,
equips a tiny boat with swords and with associates
in horror, where the treacherous land juts out   540
with Casian sands and the Egyptian shallows tell of nearby
Syrtes.

     O gods above! Have Nile and barbarian Memphis
and the multitude so effeminate of Pelusian Canopus such
arrogance? Does the destiny of civil war so overwhelm the universe?
Does Roman fortune lie so low? In this disaster is there
any place for Egypt? Can the sword of Pharos be admitted?
Civil wars, observe at least this obligation:

provide kindred hands and fend off foreign horrors,
if Magnus by his name so famous has earned
to be the guilt of *Caesar*. Ptolemy, do you not dread   550
the downfall of a name so great, do you dare intrude your unclean
hands while heaven thunders, you vile eunuch?
Had he not been the conqueror of the world, had he not ridden
     three times
to the Capitol, were he not the lord of kings and champion of the
     Senate
and the victor's son-in-law, he was Roman, which might
have been enough for the Pharian tyrant: why probe our guts
with the sword? You do not know, presumptuous boy, you do not
     know
the situation of your fortune: now you hold the sceptre
of the Nile illegally; he who gave you power
has fallen in civil war.

                    Now had Magnus denied his sails   560
the wind and with the help of oars was making for accursed
shores; conveyed not far to meet him in a two-oared ship,
the wicked band hail him and, pretending that the realm
of Pharos was open to Magnus, they bid him come from the lofty
vessel's stern into their small boat, complaining of
the hostile shore and tides of two seas broken in the shallows
which stops the foreign fleets from touching land.
But if the laws of Fate and the approach of miserable
death, directed by decree of the eternal Order,
were not dragging Magnus, doomed to death, towards the shore,   570
not one of his companions lacked forebodings of the crime,
because had loyalty been pure, had the palace with devotion
true been opened up to Magnus, the bestower of the sceptre,
then Pharos' tyrant would have come with all his fleet.
But he yields to Fate and, when bidden leave his fleet,
obeys and chooses to prefer death to fear.
Cornelia headlong rushed towards the enemy boat,
the less prepared to be apart from her husband as he left
because she feared disaster. 'Stay behind, my reckless wife,
you too, my son, I pray, and watch my fortunes   580
far from shore, and on this neck put to the test
the tyrant's loyalty,' he said. But, deaf to his injunction,

frantically Cornelia stretched out both her hands: 'Where are you
    going
without me, cruel man? Am I deserted a second time,
kept away from Thessaly's disaster? Never with a happy omen are we
pulled apart, unhappy both. When you fled across the deep, you
    need not
have turned aside your ship, you could have left me in my hiding-place
in Lesbos, if it was your intent to keep me away from every land.
Or am I a satisfactory companion only on the waves?' When in
    vain she has
poured out these words, yet anxiously she hangs over the vessel's
    end   590
and in stunned terror cannot turn her gaze away;
she cannot look at Magnus. The fleet lay at anchor, anxious
about their general's fate, not fearing crime or weapons,
but afraid that with grovelling prayers Pompey would kneel before
the sceptre given by his own hand. As he prepared to step across,
a Roman soldier greets him from the Pharian boat,
Septimius, who—shame upon the gods!—had put aside the javelin
and was bearing the degrading weapons of the king, as his minion,
brutal, savage, cruel and no less fierce for bloodshed
than any wild beast. Who would not have thought that you took
    pity   600
on the peoples, Fortune, since this sword-hand had no part in war
and you had banished far from Thessaly his weapons so guilty?
You station far and wide your swords, so that in every part of the world
—alas!—a crime of civil war may be done for you. A dishonour
to the very conquerors, a story which will always shame
the gods: a Roman sword obeyed the king like this
and the boy of Pella cut your head off, Magnus,
with your own sword. With what reputation will posterity send
Septimius into the centuries? What name will this wickedness have
from those who call what Brutus did a crime?

                           Now the limit   610
of his final hour had come and, carried off into the Pharian boat,
he was not now his own master. Then the monsters of the king
prepare to bare the weapon. When he saw the swords close by,
he covered up his face and head, disdaining
to present them bare to Fortune; then he closed his eyes
and held his breath to stop himself from breaking

into speech and marring his eternal fame with tears.
But after murderous Achillas stabbed his side
with sword-point, with not a groan did he acknowledge
the blow and did not heed the crime, but keeps his body motionless,   620
and as he dies he tests himself, and in his breast he turns these
    thoughts:
'Future ages which never will be silent about the toils of Rome
are watching now, and time to come observes from all the world
the boat and loyalty of Pharos: think now of your fame.
For you the fates of lengthy life have flowed successful;
the people cannot know, unless in death you prove it,
whether you know how to endure adversity. Do not give way to
    shame
or resent the author of your fate: whatever hand strikes you,
think it your father-in-law's. Though they tear and mangle me,
still fortunate am I, O gods above, and no deity has the power   630
to deprive me of this. In life prosperity is changed:
death does not make a man unhappy. Cornelia sees this murder,
my Pompey too: with all the more endurance, pain of mine,
I beg, suppress your groans; my son and wife, if they admire
me in death, love me.' Such control of mind
had Magnus, he exercised this power over his dying spirit.

    But Cornelia found it harder to behold the brutal crime
than suffer it and with pitiable words she fills
the ether: 'O husband, it is I have killed you, wicked I:
distant Lesbos was the cause of delay fatal to you,   640
and Caesar has reached the shores of Nile first;
for who else has the right to do this crime? But whoever you are,
sent by the gods against that life, acting for Caesar's anger
or for yourself, you do not know, cruel man, where Magnus'
very guts are; you hurry and you rain down blows
where he, defeated, prays them fall. Let him pay a penalty
no less than death by witnessing my death first. Not free from blame
in war am I, because alone of matrons, his companion
through the waves and through the camps, deterred by no defeats,
I welcomed him when conquered—which even kings feared to do.   650
And this is my reward, my husband, to be left in the safety of the
    ship?
Traitor, were you being kind? As you approached your final destiny,
did I deserve to live? I shall die, and not by the favour of the king.

Allow me, sailors, to make a headlong leap or fit
the noose and twisted ropes around my neck, or let some comrade,
truly worthy of Magnus, drive the sword right through.
For Pompey he can do a service which he may then credit to Caesar's
weapons. O cruel men, do you restrain me as I race towards my
        destiny?
You still live, my husband, and Cornelia already is not
her own mistress, Magnus: they prevent me from summoning death,   660
for the victor I am saved ' So she spoke and fell among
her companions' arms and is carried off, as the ship in panic races off.

But, as the weapons sound on Magnus' back and breast,
the majestic beauty of his sacred features lasted,
his expression reconciled with the gods; and utmost death
changed nothing of the hero's bearing and his face: so say those
who saw the severed head. For cruel Septimius
in the very act of crime discovered a greater crime:
he rips away the covering, lays bare the sacred face
of Magnus, half-alive, he grabs the head still breathing   670
and puts the drooping neck across a bench.
Then he severs muscles, veins; and long he takes to break the knotty
bones; not yet was it an art to send heads rolling with the sword.
But after the severed neck was separated from the torso,
the Pharian minion claims this right, to carry it in his hand.
Roman soldier, contemptible and playing a supporting role,
do you with hideous sword cut off the sacred head of Pompey
not to carry it yourself? O destiny of deepest shame!
So that the ungrateful boy can recognize Magnus, that shaggy
hair by kings revered and locks which graced his noble   680
brow were grasped and on a Pharian spear—
while features are alive and sobs of breath impel
the mouth to murmur, while unclosed eyes are stiffening—
the head is fixed: when it commanded war, never
was there peace; it swayed the laws, the Campus and the Rostra;
with this face you stood proud, Roman Fortune.
And the sight of it was not enough for the monstrous tyrant:
he wants proof of his wickedness to survive. Then by their hideous
        art
the fluid is taken from the head, the brain removed
and skin dried out, and rotten moisture flowed away from deep   690

within, and the features were solidified by drugs instilled.

Last offspring, soon to perish, of the stock of Lagus,
degenerate and soon to yield the sceptre to your impure sister,
though you preserve the Macedonian in consecrated cave,
and the ashes of the kings find rest beneath a piled-up mountain,
though shades of Ptolemies and their disgraceful line
are enclosed in Pyramids and Mausoleums too good for them,
the shores strike Pompey, and his headless corpse is tossed
this way and that by shallow waters. Was it such a nuisance
to keep his body whole for his father-in-law?   700
With this good faith Fortune to the end maintained the destiny
so prosperous of Magnus, with this she summoned him in death
from the highest peak, and brutally in a single day she made him pay
for all the disasters from which she gave him so many years of
        freedom;
and Pompey was a man who never saw joy and hardship
mixed: when fortunate he was disturbed by none of the gods,
when miserable spared by none; at one go Fortune knocked him
        down
with the hand she had so long restrained. He is battered on the sands,
torn to pieces on the rocks while drinking in the water through his
        wounds,
the plaything of the sea, and when no distinctive shape remains   710
the single mark of Magnus is the absence of the torn-off head.

Yet before the victor could touch the sands of Pharos,
Fortune hurriedly prepared a grave for Pompey
so he should not lie without a tomb—or with a better one:
frightened Cordus ran down from his hiding-place towards the sea.
As quaestor he had been an ill-starred companion of Magnus
from the Idalian shore of Cinyrean Cyprus. Through the shadows
he dared advance and forced his fear, now overcome
by loyalty, to seek the corpse amidst the waves
and draw it to the land and drag Magnus on to the shore.   720
A mournful Cynthia offered too little light through the thick
clouds; but the torso, differing in colour from the whitened water,
is visible. He holds his general in a tight embrace
as the sea snatches him away; then, overcome by such a massive
        burden,

he awaits the waves and with the sea's assistance pushes forward
the corpse. When now it sat upon the dry sea-shore,
he bent over Magnus, poured tears into every
wound, and to the gods and stars obscure he says:
   'Your Pompey, Fortune, does not ask for costly pyre
heaped high with frankincense; he does not ask that smoke enriched   730
should carry eastern perfumes from his body to the stars;
or that the loyal necks of Romans should bear their Parent;
or that his funeral procession should display his ancient triumphs;
or that the Fora should resound with mournful song; that all the army,
grieving and with weapons cast down, should pass around the fires.
Give Magnus the lowly coffin of a plebeian funeral
to tip the mangled body into dry fires;
let the miserable man not be without timber or a lowly burner.
Let it be enough, O gods, that Cornelia does not lie
with loosened hair and, as she embraces her husband, does not
        command   740
the torch to be placed beneath, but that she, unhappy wife, is missing
from the final tribute of the pyre, though she is not yet far from shore.'
   So the young man speaks and sees far off some tiny fires
without a guard cremating a body worthless to its kin.
From there he seizes flames and draws from underneath the limbs
the half-burnt timbers. 'Whoever you are,' he said, 'uncared-for ghost
and dear to kinsman none, but luckier than Pompey,
grant pardon that a stranger's hand disturbs your pyre
once it is built; if any feeling after death remains, then willingly
you give up your pyre and allow these losses from your grave,   750
and feel ashamed that you are burnt when Pompey's remains are
        scattered.'
So he speaks and filling up his cloak with burning ashes
flies back to the torso which, almost carried off by the waves,
was hanging on the edge of the shore. The topmost sand he
        moved aside
and, trembling, placed in tiny trench the fragments of a broken vessel
he had gathered at a distance. No timber rests upon
the noble corpse, the limbs lie on no pile:
Magnus is received by fire laid beside, not underneath, him.
   Sitting near the flames, he said: 'O mightiest
commander, crowning majesty of the Hesperian name,   760
if this pyre is more repulsive to you than tossing on the sea

or than unburied body, then turn aside your shade
and mighty spirit from my ceremonials; Fate's injustice
directs that this be right; to prevent any outrage
by monster of the sea, by beast, by birds, by savage Caesar's
rage, accept all that you can, a tiny flame,
kindled by a Roman hand. If Fortune grant return
to Hesperia, ashes so sacred will not rest
in this spot, but Cornelia will receive you,
Magnus, and pour you from my hand into the urn.   770
Meanwhile let me mark the shore with a little rock,
to be a signal of your grave; if anyone by chance should want
to placate you slain and give in full the honours of death,
let him find the ashes of your torso and let him recognize the sands
to which he must restore your head, Magnus.' After saying this,
he stirs the feeble flames by adding fuel.
Magnus is consumed and into the slow fire he drips,
feeding pyre with melting flesh. But now the daylight sent ahead
of dawn had struck the stars: he breaks the sequence
of the funeral and, stunned, he seeks his hiding-place upon the shore. 780
What punishment do you dread, you fool, for this crime?
For this, loquacious fame has welcomed you for all the years to come.
The burial of Magnus' bones his wicked father-in-law will praise:
just go, confident of pardon, and confess his burial,
demand the head.—Devotion forces him to complete
the ceremonial. He grabs the bones, half-burnt and not yet
separated enough from the muscles and full of scorched marrow;
he quenches them in sea-water and, heaped together, covered them
with a little earth. Then to stop a gentle breeze uncovering
and carrying off the ashes, with a rock he presses down the sand,   790
and to prevent a sailor's interfering with the grave by fastening
a mooring-rope, he inscribed the sacred name with half-burnt stick:
'Here lies Magnus.'

              Are you happy, Fortune, to call this
Pompey's tomb, in which his father-in-law preferred
he should be buried rather than have no funeral at all? Reckless hand,
why do you thrust a grave on Magnus and confine his roaming
shade? He is buried where furthest earth floats
on Ocean flowing back; the name of Rome and all its empire
is the limit of his grave for Magnus; cover up the rock: it is brimming

with reproach against the gods. If all of Oeta belongs to Hercules 800
and all of Nysa's ridges make room for Bromius, then why
has Magnus a single stone in Egypt? He can occupy
all the fields of Lagus if his name is fixed
to no turf. Let us peoples be in doubt and tread on none
of Nile's sands in terror of your ashes, Magnus.
But if you think the rock is worthy of such a sacred name,
then list his exploits so immense, memorials of his mightiest deeds,
fierce Lepidus' upheavals and the Alpine war,
the conquered army of Sertorius when the consul was recalled,
the chariots he drove while still a knight, trade secure 810
for the nations and Cilicians frightened of the sea; the conquest
of the barbarian world and nomad races and all the realms
which lie in the east and in the north. Say that always after warfare
he returned to the toga of the citizen, that, content with driving
    chariots
three times, he waived his claim to many triumphs for his fatherland.
What grave can hold all this? A pitiable tomb arises,
not full of any honours or the sequence of his annals
so immense; and Pompey's name, which people were accustomed
    to read
above the lofty roof-tops of the gods and arches built
with enemy's plunder, is not far from the lowest sand, placed so low 820
upon the grave that stranger may not read it standing upright,
that Roman visitor would pass it by if it were not pointed out.

Land of Egypt, guilty in civil war's destiny,
not without cause for sure did the song of Cumae's prophet
warn that the soldier of Hesperia was not to touch
Pelusian shores of Nile and the banks swollen in summer.
Brutal land, for a crime so terrible what should I ask for you in prayer?
May Nile be detained in the region where he rises and turn back
his waters, and may barren fields be in need of winter rains,
and may you disintegrate entirely into crumbling sands of Ethiopia. 830
We have admitted into Roman temples your Isis
and half-divine dogs and rattles bidding grief
and Osiris, whose mortality you prove by mourning him:
but *you*, Egypt, keep our shades in your dust.
    You, too, O Rome, though already you have given a temple
to the savage tyrant, have not yet fetched Pompey's ashes;

still the general's ghost in exile lies. If the earliest generation
feared the victor's threats, now at least receive
your Magnus' bones, if they rest in that hateful land,
not yet dislodged by waves. Who will fear the tomb?   840
Who will dread to move a ghost deserving sacred rites?
I wish that Rome would order me perform this crime and be
    prepared
to use my arms: enough and O too greatly blessed
if it were my luck to tear up the remains and bear them
to Ausonia, to violate a general's so-called tomb.
Perhaps when Rome wishes to demand from the gods
an end to barren furrow or to deadly Austri
or to excessive fires or to earth which shakes the houses,
on the gods' advice and command, Magnus, you will pass
into your Rome and your ashes will be carried by the highest priest.   850
For who will travel to Syene, parched by scorching
Cancer, and to Thebes, dry beneath the rainy Pleiads,
as tourist of the Nile, who will make for the expanse of deep
Red Sea or Arab ports as barterer of eastern
merchandise, Magnus, and not be diverted by your grave's
venerable rock and by the ash perhaps disturbed on the surface
of the sands, not be commanded to placate your shade
and to prefer you to Casian Jupiter? In no way will that grave
impair your fame: if you were buried in temples and in gold
you would be a less precious shade. Now you are like the highest
    deity.   860
Fortune, do you lie in this grave? More majestic than the victor's
altars is the sea-lashed rock beside the Libyan waters.
Often people who deny Tarpeian gods their frankincense
venerate the thunderbolt enclosed by the Etruscan turf.
One day this will be to your advantage, that no lofty pile
with marble mass arose, to last into the future.
No lengthy time will scatter the heap of tiny
dust, the tomb will fall, and of your death
the evidence will vanish. A happier age will come,
when the people pointing out that rock will not be believed;   870
and Egypt in the eyes of the crowds of our descendants will be
    perhaps
as false about the grave of Magnus as Crete about the Thunderer's.

BOOK NINE

But his shade did not lie in Pharian embers
nor did the scanty ash imprison such a mighty ghost;
it leapt up from the tomb and, leaving half-burnt limbs
and the ignoble pyre, it heads for the Thunderer's dome.
Where dark air—all that space opening out between the earth
and paths of the moon—is linked to starry skies,
live the half-divine shades, who, innocent in life,
are enabled by their fiery excellence to bear the lower
ether, their spirit gathered into the eternal spheres:
somewhere people laid in gold or buried with incense   10
do not reach. There, when it had filled itself with real
light and marvelled at the wandering planets and stars
fixed in the sky, it saw the depth of the night beneath which
lies our day and laughed at the insults to its torso.
From here it flitted above the fields of Emathia, the standards
of blood-stained Caesar and the fleets dispersed upon the sea
and, avenging wickedness, it settled in the sacred breast
of Brutus and stationed itself in the mind of invincible Cato.

He had hated Magnus too, when the outcome hung in the balance
and it remained doubtful whom civil wars would make   20
the master of the world, although he had gone to war, a follower
rushed on by his fatherland's authority and by the Senate's command;
but after the Thessalian disaster, now with all his heart
he supported Pompey. He took into his care his fatherland
when it lacked a guardian, revived the people's trembling limbs,
restored the swords thrown down by coward hands,
he waged a civil war without desiring power
or fearing slavery. In warfare he did nothing
for himself: his party after Magnus' death was wholly
that of freedom. As his side was dispersed around the shores,   30
to stop the victory of Caesar grabbing it with rapid strike,
he headed for the seclusion of Corcyra and in a thousand ships
he took away with him the fragments of the Emathian collapse.

Who would think that on so many vessels travelled troops
in flight? Or that for conquered ships the sea was too narrow?
    Then he made for Doric Malea and Taenarus, accessible to the shades,
and Cythera from there, and with ships urged on by Boreas
he shuns the shores of Greece and follows the Dictaean shores
as the waves give way. Then, when Phycus dared to bar its harbours
to the fleet, he overthrew and pulverized the town, deserving savage   40
plunder, and from here he glides on gentle breezes over the deep
to your shore, Palinurus (since not only in Ausonian
water have you memorials, but Libya proves
that its tranquil harbours satisfied the Phrygian helmsman).
Then the vessels spreading sail afar upon the deep
kept their spirits in suspense: were they bringing partners
in misfortune or enemies? The victor's speed makes everything
terrifying and there is no vessel he is not thought to be aboard.
But those ships were bearing grief and lamentation
and misery which would even move the tears of stern Cato.   50

For after uselessly Cornelia with her prayers had stopped
the sailors and her stepson's flight, in case the torso, driven back
by chance from the Pharian shore, returned towards the sea,
and after flame revealed the pyre of an improper burial,
she said: 'So, Fortune, I was not fit to kindle
my husband's pyre, to throw myself full stretch across
his icy limbs, to tear and burn my hair
and to lay out the limbs of Magnus scattered by the sea,
to pour generous tears on all his wounds,
to fill my robes with bones and tepid cinders   60
to gather whatever I could from the extinguished tomb
to sprinkle in the temples of the gods. The pyre
blazes without any funeral honour; some Egyptian hand perhaps
performed this duty, painful to the shade. How good it is
that the ashes of the Crassi are unburied! To Pompey this fire came
by the greater malice of the gods. Shall I always have a like experience
of misery? Shall I never be permitted to perform the proper rites
for husbands? Shall I never beat my breast beside urns not empty?
Yet what need of graves have you, my pain; do you
require any props? Wicked woman, do you not carry Pompey   70
in all your heart? Does not his image stick in the core of your
guts? The woman who will live on and survive can go and seek

her husband's ashes.
Yet now the fire which far away from here still gleams
with meagre light, rising from the Pharian shore, presents
something, Magnus, of you to me; already has the flame subsided,
and the smoke which carries Pompey off at sunrise
is vanishing, and hateful winds are pulling tight my canvas.
I do not wish to leave the Pelusian shores, if that is believable.   83
Now not more dear to me is any land which, conquered,   78
granted Pompey triumphs, is the chariot traversing
the lofty Capitol; Magnus the successful has faded from my breast: 80
him possessed by Nile I want and my complaint is that I do not
cling to the guilty land; the crime commends the sands to me.   82
You, Sextus, seek the hazards of warfare and move   84
your father's standards through the world; these orders
Pompey left for you, stored up in my charge:
"When the fatal hour has condemned me to death,
take up, O sons, the civil war and never,
while someone of my stock remains on earth,
let Caesars have the chance to reign. By the glory of my name,   90
impel the sceptres or the cities strong in their own
liberty: to you I leave this party and these troops.
Whichever Pompey comes on to the waves will find
a fleet, and my successor will bring war to all
the nations of the world: only keep your spirits undaunted
and mindful of your father's rights. One man alone will it be right
to obey, if he takes the side of freedom—Cato."
My promise to you, Magnus, I have discharged, your orders I have
carried out; your trick has worked: deceived, I have lived on,
so I should not, a traitor, carry off the words entrusted to me.   100
But now, husband, I will follow you through empty Chaos,
through Tartarus, if any such exists; how far away the death to which
I am consigned is doubtful: before that, I will take revenge on my life
itself for being long-lived. It was able to watch your murder, Magnus,
without escaping into death: pounded by my beating it will perish,
into tears it will dissolve: never shall I resort to swords
or nooses or to the headlong plunge through empty space:
it is disgraceful after you to be unable to die from grief alone.'
After speaking so, she veiled her head with cloak of mourning
and resolved to suffer darkness and withdrew into the hollows   110
of the ship, and hugging close her savage pain

she enjoys her tears and loves her grief in her husband's stead.
Unmoved was she by waves and Eurus shrieking
in the rigging and by cries arising at the height of danger,
and making prayers the opposite of the scared sailors
she lay composed for death and sided with the gales.

Cyprus first with foaming waves receives the ship;
from there Eurus, in possession of the sea but now less violent,
drove it to the land of Libya and the camp of Cato.
Grim, since in great terror the mind feels forebodings,   120
Magnus saw his father's comrades and his brother
from the shore; then he races headlong deep into the waves:
'Brother, tell me where our father is; is the crown and head of the
      world
still standing or are we felled—has Magnus taken to the shades
the Roman destiny?' So he speaks and so his brother in reply:
   'O you are fortunate, driven into other regions by fortune,
you only hear the crime; these eyes of mine are guilty, brother,
because they could look upon my father. Not by Caesar's weapons
      did he meet
his death, nor did he die at the hands of an agent worthy of his fall:
in the power of the vile king who holds the Nile's lands,   130
relying on the gods of hospitality and on his generous gift
towards the king's ancestors, he fell, the victim of the kingdom he
      had given.
Myself I saw them tearing at our great-hearted father's breast,
and not believing that a Pharian tyrant could have so much power,
I thought his father-in-law already stood on the Nile's shore.
But I was not affected so much by our aged father's
blood and wounds as by the leader's head paraded
through the city, which we saw held high with javelin driven
through; it is said that this is kept for the eyes of the cruel
conqueror, that the tyrant wanted proof of his crime.   140
But whether dogs of Pharos or the ravenous birds tore
his body apart or the stealthy fire which we saw
disposed of it, I know not. Whatever injustice of Fate
carried off those limbs, for those crimes I forgive the gods:
I complain about the part preserved.' When Magnus heard
such words, he did not vent his pain into groans
or tears but, raging with a son's indignant love, declares:

'Sailors, hurry down your ships from the dry sea-shore;
let the fleet by rowing burst forth against the opposing winds.
Generals, come with me (nowhere in civil warfare   150
has there been so great a prize) to bury the unburied shade,
to sate Magnus with the blood of the eunuch tyrant.
Shall I not engulf in sluggish Mareotis the rotting flesh of Pella,
Alexander's body from its sanctuary uncovered?
Shall not Amasis, torn out from the pyramid tombs,
and the other kings go floating down the rushing Nile for me?
Let all their tombs pay penalty for you unburied, Magnus.
Isis, power in the eyes of the world, from her tomb I shall evict
and Osiris clothed in linen I shall scatter through the crowd   159
and I shall burn the head by placing gods beneath it. The land will
        pay   161
this penalty to me: I shall leave the fields devoid of cultivators,
nor will there be anyone to benefit from rising Nile; you will be
        sole lord
of Egypt, father, when I have driven out the gods and peoples.'
He had spoken and was fiercely hurrying the fleet towards the waves;
but Cato praised and curbed the young man's wrath.

Meanwhile, when Magnus' death was heard of, all along
the shore the ether sounded, struck by lamentations;
without a parallel, unknown to any age, was that grief
—that whole nations should mourn the death of one great man.   170
But when Cornelia was seen, as she left the ship,
worn out by tears, with loosened tresses spread across her face,
still more they wail, their blows again redoubling.
When first she came to the shores of allied land,
she gathered Magnus' garments and his medals and his weapons
and his armour stamped with gold, which he once had worn,
and the embroidered toga, garments three times
seen by highest Jupiter, and she put them on the funeral fire.
In her sorrow those were Magnus' ashes. All devotion
takes up her example and pyres rise on all   180
the shore to offer fire to the shades of Thessaly.
So when the Apulian prepares to make the grass grow high
on plains grazed bare and to renew the winter's fodder
and warms the land with fire, then together Garganus
and Voltur's fields and warm Matinus' pastures glow with light.

Yet not as pleasing to the ghost of Magnus
is all the crowd which dares to reproach the gods
and criticizes them for Pompey as are Cato's words,
few in number but coming from a breast filled with truth.
'A citizen has died', he says, 'far inferior to our ancestors   190
in knowledge of the limit of power, but valuable in this age yet
which has no respect for justice; without harming
liberty, he was powerful; alone when masses were prepared
to be his slaves, he kept from office; he was ruler
of the Senate—but it still ruled. He demanded nothing by right of
          war
and what he wanted to be given, he wanted to be able to be
          denied him.
He did own excessive wealth, but paid in more than
he kept back. He did seize the sword, but he knew how to lay it
          down.
He did prefer warfare to the garb of peace, but once in armour
          peace he loved.
The general liked to take up power—and to resign it.   200
His home was pure and free from luxury, never corrupted
by its master's prosperity. Illustrious, revered by the world
is his name and of great benefit to our Rome.
Long ago, when Marius and Sulla were admitted, the true guarantee
of liberty disappeared: with Pompey taken from the world,
now even the bogus guarantee has gone. Now tyranny will be no
          shame,
nor will there be a screen for power nor will the Senate be a mask.
How fortunate he was—his final day came to meet him in defeat,
the wickedness of Pharos brought to him the swords he should
          have sought!
Perhaps you could have lived on under the tyranny of your
          father-in-law.   210
To know how to die is the warrior's best lot, the next to be
          compelled to die.
And if by fate I fall into another's power, make Juba,
Fortune, behave like this to me; I do not decline to be kept
for the enemy, provided that he keeps me with my head cut off.'
By these words greater honour in his death came
to the noble ghost than if the Roman Rostrum had resounded
with the general's praises.

Meanwhile discord of the masses rumbled,
weary of the camp and warfare after Magnus' death;
then Tarcondimotus raised the signal for deserting
Cato. As he ran away with hurried fleet, Cato followed   220
to the edge of shore and censured him with words like these:
    'O Cilician, never pacified, again do you proceed
to plunder on the seas? Fortune has removed Magnus:
now as a pirate you return to sea.' Then he gazed at all
the warriors in crowded commotion; one of them, disclosing
his intent to flee, addresses the commander with words like these:
'We—give pardon, Cato—were led to fight by love
of Pompey, not of civil war; we turned partisan
out of goodwill. The man the world preferred to peace lies dead;
our cause has disappeared: allow us to return   230
to our native house-gods, deserted homes, and children dear.
What end to battle will there be if it is not Pharsalia
or Pompey? Phases of our lives have gone for nothing:
let our death pass into safety, let our old age see ahead
its rightful flames; the civil war hardly can provide
burial for just its leaders. No barbarian tyranny
awaits the conquered; brutal Fortune does not threaten me
with Armenian or Scythian yoke: I pass into the power
of a citizen in toga. Whoever was second while Magnus was alive,
he to me will be the first. To the sacred ghost the highest honour   240
will be paid; a master I shall have, as defeat compels,
but I shall have no leader, Magnus: you alone I followed to war,
after you I shall follow destiny; for it cannot be right for me to hope
for success, nor would it be allowed. Everything is in the power
of Caesar's fortune; victory has scattered wide the weapons of Emathia;
for us losers, confidence is limited—in all the world he is
the only one who could, if he would, offer safety to the conquered.
Civil war is wickedness with Pompey dead, though while he lived
it was loyalty. If, Cato, you will always follow
public laws and the fatherland, then let us seek the standards   250
which a Roman consul holds.' So he declared,
and leapt upon a ship, accompanied by the riot of his soldiers.
    It would have been the end for the Roman State, and all the mass
was seething on the shore, between one slavery and the next:
from the leader's sacred breast the words burst out:
'So was it with a similar wish that you waged war, young men,

were you too in favour of masters, and were you the troops
of Pompey not of Rome? Now that you are not labouring for tyranny,
now that you live and die not for your leaders but yourselves, now that
you win the world for no one, now that it is safe for you to conquer,   260
you run away from war, and with your neck devoid of one you
          seek a yoke
and do not know how to live on without a king. Now the cause
          of danger
is one worthy of warriors. Pompey was allowed full use of your
blood: now do you refuse your fatherland your throats and swords
when liberty is near? From three masters Fortune has now
left just one. You should feel ashamed: the palace of the Nile
and the bow of Parthian soldier have done more for legality.
Away with you, degenerates, despise the gift of Ptolemy's weapons.
Who would think *your* hands were guilty of any bloodshed?
Caesar will believe that readily you ran away from him,   270
Caesar will believe that you were first to flee from Emathian
          Philippi.
Go, free from fear; with Caesar as your judge you have deserved
to live, subdued by neither siege nor weapons.
O loathsome slaves, following your former master's death,
to his heir you pass. Why do you not wish to earn
a reward greater than life and pardon? Carry off across the waves
the unlucky wife of Magnus, the daughter of Metellus,
lead away the Pompeys and surpass the gift of Ptolemy.
Whoever carries my head, too, to the hated tyrant
will give it for no small reward: those soldiers by the price   280
of my neck will know that they did well to follow my standards.
So, to it—buy your reward with massive bloodshed:
a coward's crime is mere flight.' He spoke, and summoned back
all the ships from mid-sea, just as when the swarms
together leave the wax which brings forth young
and do not intertwine their wings, forgetful of the honeycomb,
but each flies independently and now no longer sips lazily
the bitter thyme: the sound of Phrygian brass rings out,
and, stunned, they stop their flight, return to their pursuit
of flower-bearing toil and love of scattered honey: 290
the shepherd free from worry on the grass of Hybla now rejoices
that the riches of his hut are safe. So by Cato's utterance
endurance of rightful warfare was impressed upon the warriors.

And now he resolved with war's exertion and chain of labours
to occupy their minds, not used to bearing inactivity.
First the soldiers are exhausted on the sea-shore's sands.
Their next task is against the city-walls and the defences
of Cyrene: though shut out, with no anger does he avenge himself;
the only penalty exacted from the conquered was that Cato
    conquered them.
Next he resolved to head for Libyan Juba's kingdom bordering   300
the Moors, but Nature blocked their journey by interposing
the Syrtes: yet she, his daring valour hopes, will give way to him.
    The Syrtes, perhaps, when Nature gave the universe
initial shape, were left in doubt between the sea and land
—because the land neither sank down far to let in waters
of the deep nor defended itself against the sea,
but by ambiguous condition of the place it lies, an impassable tract,
where sea is broken on the shallows and land is severed
by the deep and waves sound, cast up after many a shore·
so badly did Nature abandon this part of herself   310
and not require it for any purpose, Or perhaps the Syrtes once
were filled to a greater depth of ocean and swam deep down,
but greedy Titan, feeding his sun-rays on the sea,
drew up the waters near the torrid zone;
and now the sea still struggles with Phoebus as he dries it up;
soon when ruinous time brings near his rays,
the Syrtes will be land; since already the wave which floats on top
is shallow, and water far and wide diminishes and soon will run out.

When first the sea, urged by oars, thrust onward all the burden
of the fleet, Auster growled, black with thick-packed rain.   320
Raging against his own realms, with a whirlwind he defended
the sea invaded by the fleet and drove the waves far from
the Syrtes and broke up the water by inserting shore.
Then it seized the canvas on any ships with mast erect
and ripped them from the sailors, and with ropes in vain attempting
to withhold the sails from Notus, they surpassed the vessel's length
and bellied out beyond the prow. If anyone with forethought
has fastened all the sails aloft to yard-arm's top
he is overcome, swept off course with his naked rigging.
A better lot befell the fleet which chanced upon deep waves   330
and was tossed on indisputable sea. Whichever ships, relieved

by chopping down their timbers, made the crushing blast flow over
     them,
the tide carried off at liberty, rolling them towards
the winds; in victory it thrust them towards Auster, who resisted.
The shallows leave these vessels stranded and the land, cut short
by ocean, smashes them: exposed to doubtful destiny,
one part of ship is grounded, the other floats upon the waves.
Then as the ships were driven further aground, the sea became
     more shallow
and the land rose up to meet them often: although the waves are
     struck
by the Auster, yet often they do not surmount the mounds of sand.   340
On the sea's surface, far from all the fields, rises up
a ridge of dust still dry, untouched by water;
the unlucky sailors halt, and though their vessel sticks to ground
they see no shores. Like this the sea seizes some;
the majority of ships obeyed the steering and the tiller,
safe in flight, and allocating sailors with experience of the place,
unharmed they reach the sluggish lake of Triton.

This lake, the legend goes, is dear to the god heard by ocean
all along the shore as he blows across the surface with his windy shell;
this lake is dear to Pallas too, who when born from her father's head   350
alighted upon Libya first of lands (since it is nearest
to the sky, as by its heat alone is proved) and in the pool's
calm water saw her face and set her footsteps on its edge
and called herself 'Tritonis' from the water that she loved.
Next to it the silent river Lethon glides along,
carrying oblivion, the legend goes, from channels of the underworld;
and the garden of the Hesperides, once guarded by
unsleeping dragon, poor now its branches have been robbed.
Spiteful is anyone who takes away from aged time its glory,
who summons poets to the truth. There was once a golden wood,   360
its branches heavy with their riches and with tawny shoots,
a band of virgins, guardians of the shining grove,
and the snake with eyes condemned never to sleep
curled round the timbers bent down by ruddy metal.
Alcides took from the trees their prize and from the grove
its task, when he left the branches destitute without their load
and carried back to Argos' tyrant gleaming apples.

So driven from these places and cast ashore by the Syrtes,
the fleet did not reach beyond the Garamantian waves
but with Pompey as its leader stayed in the parts of better   370
Libya. But Cato's energy, not knowing how to linger,
ventures to expose his troops to unknown races
and on land to go around the Syrtes, trusting in his army.
This course was urged by the same winter which had barred the sea;
and to men who feared excessive fires rain gave hope that the season
would moderate their journey, made cruel neither by the Sun
nor by harsh frost, with Libya's sky on one side and winter on the
     other.
And so he speaks, about to set his foot upon the barren sands:
   'O men who have decided on one source of safety—following my
       camp
to die with neck unconquered, prepare your minds   380
for a mighty task of heroism and for the highest toils.
We march towards the barren plains and burnt-up places of the
     world
where Titan is excessive and waters scarce in springs,
where dry fields are caked with deadly snakes.
Hard is the path towards legality and love of crashing fatherland.
Let any come through Libya's centre and attempt the pathless lands
who are decided not to pray for escape, who are satisfied
to march. For it is not my intention to deceive
anyone or onwards lead the mass by concealing the risk.
I want as my companions men attracted by the very dangers,   390
who think it fine and Roman to endure even the bitterest,
with me their witness. But the soldier who requires a guarantee
of safety and is captivated by life's sweetness, let him take
the fairer path to be his master's slave. Provided I am first to tread
the sands and first to place my footsteps in the dust,
let the heat of ether strike me, let the serpent full
of poison come to meet me: test your dangers in advance
by my fate. Whoever sees me drinking, let him thirst,
and let him swelter, whoever sees me heading for the shade of trees,
and whoever sees me on horseback at the head of companies of foot,   400
let him feel weak: if it is known by any difference whether I go
as a general or a soldier. Serpents, thirst, and heat of sand
are sweet to heroism; endurance in adversity rejoices;
happier is courage whenever it costs itself a great price.

Libya alone with its brood of evils can show
that it is honourable for warriors to have fled.' So he fires
their frightened minds with heroism and with love of toils
and takes the journey not to be retraced on desert track;
and Libya, soon to shut his sacred name in a little tomb,
laid its hands upon the destiny of Cato, who was above worry.   410

The third part of the world is Libya, if you want to trust
in rumour altogether; but, if you go by winds and sky,
it will be a part of Europe. For Nile's shores are not
more distant than Scythian Tanais from furthest Gades,
the point where Europe runs away from Libya and by their curve
the shores have made a place for Ocean; but the greater region
goes to make up only Asia. For, while together those
send forth Zephyr, the latter, bordering on the left side
of Boreas and on the right side of Notus, goes off into the east,
sole mistress of Eurus. The fertile part of Libya's land   420
inclines towards the west; but even this is broken up
by no springs: from infrequent Aquilones it receives the northern
showers and refreshes its fields while we have cloudless skies.
For no riches is it harmed; not for bronze and not for gold
is it melted; pure and faultless in its soil,
it is earth to the core. The people's only source of riches
is Maurusian timber: its benefit they did not know
but lived content with foliage and shade of the citrus-tree.
Into the unfamiliar grove have gone our axes,
and from the world's extremity we sought feasts and tables.   430
But all the coast surrounding the roaming Syrtes,
stretched beneath excessive day and next to scorched
ether, parches crops and with its dust kills off
Bacchus and, powdery, is bound together by no roots.
The mild climate needed for life is missing and down in that land
there is no concern for Jupiter; the zone is inert with nature
sluggish and it does not feel the seasons on its unploughed sands.
This soil so inactive yet sends up infrequent grasses
which the hardy race of Nasamonians collect, who, naked, occupy
the fields closest to the sea and are fed by the savage Syrtes   440
on the losses of the world. For on the sea-shore's sands the plunderer
lies in wait and, though no vessel touches harbour, with wealth
he is familiar: in this way the Nasamonians trade

with the entire world, in shipwrecks.
                                        By this route
his hardy energy bids Cato march. There his troops, untroubled
by gales, fearing no storms on land, endured
sea-terrors. For more violently on dry shore
than on the sea does Syrtes take the Auster's blast
—he does greater damage on land. Libya does not smash
the rising wind with mountains in his path or drive him back with
            crags   450
and scatter him and slacken him from whirlwind into liquid breezes;
he does not rush upon the woods and grow exhausted twisting
aged timbers: all the soil lies open, and, progressing freely,
he inflicts Aeolus' fury on all the sands,
and violently drives in circles a cloud
which bears no rain, its dust awhirl: most of the earth
is lifted up and hangs suspended with the whirlwind never unwound.
The impoverished Nasamonian sees his kingdom floating in the wind,
his home pulverized; the cottage flies away, torn off roof first,
uncovering the Garamantian. No higher does the fire   460
bear aloft what it consumes; and the height which smoke can rise to
and mar the day is equalled by the dust which occupies the air.
Then too, more violently than usual, the wind attacks
the Roman army and the tottering soldiers cannot stand firm
on sands which even as they tread on them are torn away.
It would shake the earth and shift the world from its position
if a craggy Libya with solid frame and sturdy bulk
confined the Auster in caverns hollowed out;
but, because with shifting sands it is easily disturbed,
by resisting nowhere it remains stable and the deepest earth   470
stands firm because the topmost earth gives way. With violent force
the wind sent whirling warriors' helmets, shields, javelins,
and with vigour carried them through the great sky's expanse.
Perhaps they were a prodigy in a land remote
and far removed, and races there fear weapons fallen
from the sky and think that what was torn from human arms
was sent down by the gods. In this way, without a doubt,
those objects fell for Numa offering sacrifice, which
on patrician neck our chosen young men bear: Auster or Boreas
had robbed the peoples who carried our holy shields.   480
With Notus torturing the world like this the Roman troops lay down,

afraid they would be swept away; they fastened tight their clothing
and they clutched the earth and lay there not by weight alone
but with an effort, hardly unaffected by the Auster even so;
it rolled above them mighty heaps of sand, enveloping
the warriors with earth. Hardly were the soldiers strong
enough to raise their limbs, embedded in the mighty mass of dust.
A great rampart of piled-up sand fettered even
those still standing, and they were held immobile as the ground rose.
It shattered walls, knocked down their stones, and carried them afar   490
and at a distance dropped them, in an amazing disaster:
those who saw no houses saw portions of them tumbling down.
    And now their entire path is hidden and gone are all the
       land-marks: 493
they found their way by constellations, yet constellations incomplete   495
are what the horizon ringing the Libyan region shows,
and it conceals many with the sloping rim of the earth.
And when the heat released the air which wind had whirled around
and the day was set on fire, with sweat their limbs are dripping,
their mouths are dry with thirst. A tiny stream was sighted far away   500
in a shallow channel: this a soldier snatched with difficulty
from the dust, into his helmet's gaping bowl he poured it all
and to his general held it out. Every throat was caked
with dust, and as the general himself held the smallest drop of liquid
he aroused envy. He said: 'Degenerate soldier, did you consider
me the only one in this multitude devoid of heroism?
Did I seem so soft and so unequal to the first
heat? How much more do you deserve that punishment,
to drink while the people thirst!' Roused by anger so,
he knocked the helmet down, and there was water enough for all.   510

They had come to the temple, the only one among the Libyan tribes
which the rough Garamantians possess. There stands the oracle-giver,
Jupiter, as tradition says, but not shooting thunderbolts
or like our own, but Ammon with his twisted horns.
There the Libyan tribes have not put wealthy temples,
and treasure-chambers are not bright with eastern gems.
Although for peoples of the Ethiopians and wealthy tribes
of Arabs and the Indians, Jupiter Ammon is the only god,
still he is poor and occupies a shrine profaned
through ages by no wealth and, a deity of the ancient ways,   520

he defends his temple against Roman gold.
That there are gods in the place is proven by the lone green forest
in the whole of Libya. For all the land that with its parched
dust separates burning Berenicis from warm Leptis
knows no leaves: Ammon has taken the forest for himself.
The cause of the wood is a spring right there which binds
the crumbly earth and with its waters tames the sands, uniting them.
Here too there is no obstacle to Phoebus when the day stands
poised at the zenith; the trees protect their trunks with difficulty:
so short is the shadow driven by the rays towards the centre.   530
It has been discovered that this is where the circle
of the higher solstice strikes the middle of the zodiac.   532
But whatever race you are, cut off from us by Libya's fire, for you   538
the shadow falls towards the south when for us it goes towards the north.
The slowly-moving Cynosura climbs into your sight, you think
the dry Wain is plunged into the deep, and no star have you
at the zenith, always safe from sea; both poles are far away
and the constellations' speed sweeps everything right through the
      sky.   543
They do not move aslant: Scorpio rises no more erect   533
than Taurus, Aries does not give his rising-time to Libra,
Astraea does not order Pisces to go down slow;
Chiron matches Gemini and rainy Aegoceros is the same
as blazing Cancer and Leo rises no more than the Urn.   537

Before the doors were standing peoples sent by the east;   544
by horned Jupiter's advice they were seeking unknown destinies;
but to the Latian general they gave way, and his companions beg
Cato to try out the deity spoken of throughout the Libyan
world, to pass a judgement on the reputation of so long an age.
The most encouragement to pry into the future using the voice
of gods came from Labienus. 'Chance', he said, 'and the fortune   550
of our path have brought to us the mouth of a deity so mighty
and the god's advice: we can profit from so great a leader
through the Syrtes and learn the outcome given to war.
For I cannot believe the gods would grant their secrets
and speak the truth to any more than sacred Cato.
It is certain that your life is ever steered according to celestial
laws: you are a follower of God. Look—a free opportunity to speak
with Jupiter is given you: inquire about the destiny of wicked

Caesar, scrutinize the future character of your fatherland:
will the people be permitted to enjoy self-rule and the rule of law   560
or is the civil war all waste? Fill your breast
with sacred voice; as a lover of strict excellence, at least
ask what excellence is, demand a model of rectitude.'

He, filled with the god he carried in his silent mind,
poured forth from his breast words worthy of the shrine:
'What question, Labienus, do you bid me ask? Whether I prefer
to meet my death in battle, free, to witnessing a tyranny?
Whether it makes no difference if our lives be short or long?
Whether violence can harm no good man and Fortune wastes her
      threats
when virtue lines up against her, and whether it is enough to wish for 570
things commendable and whether what is upright never grows by
      its success?
We know the answer: Ammon will not plant it deeper in me.
We are all connected with the gods above, and even if the shrine
      is silent
we do nothing without God's will; no need has deity of any
utterances: the Creator told us at our birth once and always
whatever we can know. Did he select the barren sands
to prophesy to a few and in this dust submerge the truth
and is there any house of God except the earth and sea and air
and sky and excellence? Why do we seek gods any further?
Whatever you see, whatever you experience, is Jupiter.   580
Let those unsure and always dubious of future events   ·
require fortune-tellers: no oracles make me certain,
certain death does. Coward and brave must fall:
it is enough that Jupiter has said this.' So declaring
he departed from the altars with the temple's credit intact,
leaving Ammon to the peoples, uninvestigated.

He carries his own javelins himself, on foot he marches in front of
the panting soldiers' faces, he does not command them to bear
the hardships but shows them how, and on no necks reclining
is he carried or seated in a carriage; of sleep he was most frugal,   590
the last to take the water which, when at last a spring is found,
the troops, desiring liquid, are made to watch; he stands aside
until the camp-followers have finished. If great renown
is won by real merit, if excellence is examined naked

with success removed, whatever in any of our great ancestors
we praise—was luck. Who has earned a name so mighty
by favourable battle, who by blood of nations?
This triumphal march through the Syrtes and remotest parts of Libya
I would rather make than climb the Capitol three times
with Pompey's chariot, than break Jugurtha's neck.   600
Look—it is the real father of his country, who most deserves
your altars, Rome: you will never be ashamed to swear by him
and you will make a god of him, now, one day,
if you ever stand with neck unfettered.

                        Now thicker
is the heat and they tread the furthest zone made
in the southern sky for mortals by the gods, and water
is more scarce. In the desert's midst, a single spring was found
with ample water but which a crowd of serpents occupied, so many
that the place could hardly hold them. Parched asps were stationed
on the edge and in the waters' midst were thirsty dipsads.   610
The commander, when he saw his men would perish if they left
    the spring,
addresses them: 'Soldiers, terrified by empty semblance
of death, do not hesitate to drain the safe waters.
Harmful is the serpents' poison when mingled with the blood;
they have venom in their bite and with their fangs they threaten
    doom;
your drinks are free from death.' He spoke and drained the
    questionable
poison; and in all the Libyan sand, that was the only spring
from which he for himself demanded water first.

Why the Libyan air abounds in such great plagues,
prolific in death, or what hidden Nature   620
has mingled with her harmful soil, no care or toil of ours
can know; except that a legend, spread throughout the world,
has deceived the centuries in place of the real reason.
In the furthest parts of Libya, where the burning earth
receives the Ocean heated by the sinking sun,
lay wasting wide the fields of Medusa, Phorcys' daughter,
not protected by the forests' foliage, not softened by the furrow,
but rough with stones its mistress's face had looked upon.

It was in this body first that harmful nature brought forth
savage killers; snakes born from that throat   630
poured out their shrill hisses with their darting tongues.
They lashed Medusa's neck itself—she was delighted;   633
the serpents, in the manner of women's hair, hung loose   632
across her back and rose erect across her brow in front,   634
and when the locks are combed the vipers' poison flows.
This is the only part of ill-fated Medusa which all
may look upon unharmed. For who had time to fear the monster's
gaping mouth and face? Who that looked directly at her
was allowed by Medusa to die? Hesitant fate she hurried on,
forestalling fear; the limbs were dead while breath remained,   640
and the shades were not discharged but stiffened underneath the
    bones.
The locks of the Eumenides aroused only madness;
Cerberus calmed his hissing at Orpheus' singing;
Amphitryon's son looked at the Hydra as he conquered it:
this monster her own father Phorcys, the second god
upon the waters, feared; her mother Ceto, too, and even
her sister-Gorgons; she could threaten sky and sea
with unaccustomed lethargy and make earth overlie the universe.
From heaven birds fell down with sudden weight,
the beasts were fastened to their rocks, entire tribes   650
of Ethiopians, living near, grew stiff in marble.
No living thing could undergo the sight of her; the snakes themselves
attempted to avoid the Gorgon's face by stretching backwards.
She turned to stone the Titan, Atlas, who stood beneath
the Pillars of the West; and long ago, when heaven
feared the Giants supported on Phlegraean snakes,
she raised them up as mountains and the Gorgon on the centre
of Pallas' breast concluded the frightful battle of the gods.
To this place was carried Perseus, born of Danae's womb
and rain enriched, by Parrhasian wings of the Arcadian   660
inventor of the cithara and oily wrestling-floor.
Suddenly in flight he raised the Cyllenian scimitar,
the scimitar already red with another monster's blood—
the guardian of the heifer loved by Jupiter was laid low—
then the virgin Pallas brought assistance to her winged brother.
She made a bargain for the monster's head, and ordered Perseus
on the border of the Libyan land to turn towards the rise of Phoebus

and to cleave the Gorgon's realm with backward flight,
and in his left hand put a shield bright with tawny bronze
in which she bade him look at petrifying Medusa.   670
She in slumber, which was soon to bring eternal rest in death,
was not submerged entirely: a large part of her hair keeps watch,
the snakes stretched forward from the locks defend the head;
the rest are lying fully on her face and on the darkness of her eyes.
Herself does Pallas guide the anxious man, and with Perseus turned
     away
she steers the Cyllenian scimitar which trembles in his hand
and ruptures the wide junction of the snaky neck.
What a look the Gorgon had, her head cut off
by the wound of hook-shaped weapon! How much poison I must
     think
her mouth breathed out and how much death her eyes shot forth!   680
Even Pallas could not watch, and though Perseus looked away
his features would have frozen had Tritonia not spread out
the dense tresses and veiled the face with snakes.
In this way the winged hero seized the Gorgon and flew into the sky.
He in fact was shortening his path and passing through the air
on a nearer course if he cut right across Europe's cities:
Pallas told him not to harm the fruitful lands,
to spare the nations. For who would not look up to see the ether
at such a mighty flyer? With the Zephyr the winged one turns his
     course
and travels over Libya which, sown with no cultivation,   690
is open to the stars and Phoebus: the orbit of the sun afflicts
and burns the soil; and in no other land does night
fall into sky more loftily and block the path of the moon
if she forgets her wandering swerve and runs straight through
the constellations, without fleeing north or south to avoid the
     shadow.
Yet that barren land and fields productive of no good
catch the venom from the gore of dripping
Medusa, a hideous dew from wild blood
which heat promotes and boils in the crumbling sand.

Here the gore, which from the dust was first to push a head,   700
raised up the Asp inducing sleep with swollen neck:
here the blood more plentifully fell with a drop of thick

poison; in no other serpent is it more concentrated.
This in its need for heat does not pass into icy regions
of its own accord but crosses desert as far as Nile;
but—shall we ever feel ashamed of gain?—from there to here
are brought the Libyan deaths and we have made the Asp a
    commodity.
But the mighty Haemorrhois which will not let
its victims' blood stand still unfolds its scaly coils,
and Chersydros, born to live in the fields of Syrtes,   710
land and sea, and Chelydros, drawn along with smoking track,
and Cenchris, which will always glide along a direct path:
it is tinted on its dappled belly with more marks
than Theban serpentine adorned with tiny flecks.
Ammodytes, of the same colour as the parched sands and
    indistinguishable
from them; Cerastes moving with twitching spine;
and Scytale, the only one to slough its skin while frost
lies sprinkled still; and Dipsas parched;
and dangerous Amphisbaena, which moves towards both its heads;
and Natrix, tainter of the water; and flying Jaculus;   720
and Parías, content to cut a path with its tail;
greedy Prester stretching wide its foaming mouth;
the putrefying Seps, dissolving bones along with body;
the Basilisk which pours forth hisses terrifying all
the beasts, which harms before its poison and orders the entire crowd
far out of its way and on the empty sand is king.
You Dragons too, with golden lustre gleaming,
who glide as harmless deities in all the lands,
blazing Africa makes you fatal: with wings you drive
the lofty air, and following entire herds you coil   730
around the mighty bulls and burst them with your lashes;
not even the elephant is saved by his size: everything you consign
    to death,
you have no need of poison to doom to painful end.

Among these perils Cato with his hardy troops proceeds
along his dry journey, witnessing so many grim casualties
among his soldiers, and unfamiliar deaths with tiny wound.
The young man Aules, standard-bearer of Etruscan blood,
stepped upon a Dipsas, which twisted back its head and bit him.

Hardly was there pain or a sensation of a bite, and even death's
appearance is not malignant and the injury does not look threatening. 740
Look—the silent venom creeps along, and devouring fire
eats away the marrows and with hot decay it sets the guts ablaze.
The poison drinks up moisture spread around
the vital parts and starts to parch the tongue
on his dry palate; there was no sweat to pass across
the tired frame, the stream of tears recoiled from the eyes.
Not the glory of the state, not the authority of saddened Cato
could stop the burning warrior from boldly scattering
the standards and in his frenzy seeking far and wide
the waters which the thirsty poison in his heart demanded. 750
If he were hurled into Tanais or Rhône or Po, if he were
drinking Nile when it wanders through the fields, he would burn.
Libya assisted in his death, and a less deadly reputation
has the Dipsas when it is helped by scorched lands.
Deep he probes for channels in the arid sand;
now he returns to the Syrtes and takes the waves in his mouth,
and the sea-water gives him pleasure but yet does not suffice.
And he is not aware of the type of doom and death by poison,
but thinks it thirst; and he steeled himself to open with his sword
his swelling veins and fill his mouth with blood. 760
    Cato bids the standards be hurried off without delay: none was
      allowed
to learn that thirst had so much power. But death more grim
than that was in full view: a tiny Seps was fastened to
the leg of miserable Sabellus; as it clung with cunning fang
he tore it off and with his javelin pinned it to the sands.
It is a serpent small in size, but so much bloody death
no other brings. For the skin nearest to the wound
burst, shrank back, uncovered pale-coloured bones;
and now as the cavity gapes, the wound is bare without a body;
the limbs are drenched with pus, the calves have melted, the knee 770
was bare of covering, and even every muscle of the thighs
dissolves, and the groin drips with black decay.
The membrane which binds the belly burst apart, and out melt
the entrails; and not as much as there should be from an entire body
melts into the ground, but the savage poison boils
the limbs down; death shrinks the whole into a tiny pool of venom.
All that makes a human being is uncovered by the unholy nature

of the killer: 779
the muscles, ligaments, the rib-cage, the chest-cavity,   777
and everything concealed by vital organs lay exposed
in death. His shoulders and his strong arms drip away,   780
his neck and head dissolve: no more quickly in the hot Auster
will snow melt and disappear or wax yield to the sun.
A little thing I mention, that the body was consumed and dripped
          with pus:
this a flame can also do; but what funeral pyre ever removed the bones?
They too disappear and with the crumbling marrow
allow no trace of rapid death to remain.
Among Cinyphian plagues the prize for injury is yours:
they all remove life, but you alone the corpse.
    Look, there comes a form of death the opposite of liquefaction.
Nasidius, a farmer of the Marsian land, a scorching   790
Prester struck. A fiery redness set alight his face,
and swelling strains the skin, confounding all his features,
their shape destroyed; now larger than his entire body
and exceeding human size, the pus is exuded over all
his limbs as the poison exerts its power far and wide;
the man himself is out of sight, buried deep in bloated body,
and his breast-plate cannot hold the swelling of his bursting chest.
Not so does the foaming mass of water overflow
from a blazing cauldron; sails in the Corus curve
into bellies not as vast. No longer can the shapeless mass   800
and torso with its jumbled bulk contain the swollen limbs.
Untouched by beaks of birds and destined to provide for wild beasts
a banquet not without danger, they did not dare consign the body
to the tomb but ran away as it still grew, its limit not yet fixed.
    But greater sights are offered by the Libyan killers.
A cruel Haemorrhois sank its fangs into Tullus,
a noble youth and an admirer of Cato.
And as the pressure of the Corycian saffron generally streams
from entire statues all together, so all his limbs
at once emitted ruddy poison instead of blood.   810
His tears were blood; gore flows abundantly
from whatever openings moisture uses; his mouth and spreading
nostrils run with it; his sweat turns red; all his limbs
are awash with his copious veins; his entire body is one wound.
    But, unlucky Laevus, your blood, frozen by a serpent

of the Nile, stopped your heart, and you do not evince the bite
with any pain but in a sudden darkness receive
death and in sleep go down to join your comrades' ghosts.
With death as swift those poisons do not infect the cups,
the ones which pretend to be Sabaean twigs and which when ripe   820
the Saïtae, gatherers of doom, pluck from the hideous trunk.
   Look—from afar a savage serpent, called by Africa
the Jaculus, twists round the trunk of a barren oak and hurls itself
and pierces through the head of Paulus and his temples and escapes.
Poison played no part this time: death came with the wound and
    took him.
They found out how slowly the bullets whirled from the sling fly,
how sluggish a whizzing Scythian arrow shrieks by.
   What good is it that the Basilisk is pierced by miserable Murrus'
spear? The poison swiftly runs along the weapon and attacks
the hand; he straight away unsheathes his sword and strikes   830
the hand and in one go he severed it entirely from the shoulder,
and as he gazes at the pitiable pattern of his own death
he stands safe as his hand dies. Who would have thought the Scorpion
brought doom or had the strength to bring on speedy death?
He, threatening and cruel with his knotted tail erect,
won glory by defeating Orion, as heaven witnesses.
Who would fear to tread upon your hiding-place, Salpuga?
To you too the Stygian sisters give power over their threads.

In this way neither shining day nor black night gave them rest—
the ground on which they lay was suspected by the miserable men.   840
For neither piled up leaves composed their beds
nor did their couches rise on straw, but on the ground they roll,
their bodies exposed to death, and by their warmth
they attract the killers chill with night-time cold,
and among their limbs they nurture mouths for a long time harmless
while the poison is inert. And, with the sky their guide, they do
    not know
the measure or the limit of their journeyings: often they complain
and shout: 'Gods, give back to us in our distress the battle which
    we fled,
give back Thessaly. Why do we, a band sworn to the sword,
endure inactive deaths? In place of Caesar, Dipsads   850

fight; Cerastae finish off the civil war.
Our desire is to go to ruddy zone and region scorched
by horses of the sun; I wish to attribute my death to ethereal causes
and to die at heaven's hands. No complaint have I against you,
Africa, or against you, Nature: you removed from the nations
the place which bore so many freaks and gave it to the serpents,
and you condemned the soil to be intolerant of Ceres, denying it
farmers, and you willed that the poisons should find no human beings.
We have come into the lands of snakes: exact the penalty,
whichever of the gods you are who, in hatred of our trafficking,   860
have broken off a region with a scorching zone on this side, and
        on that
the shifting Syrtes, and have in the space between set forms of death.
Through the haunts of your retreat the civil war advances,
and the soldier, sharing in your knowledge of the secret region,
strikes upon the barriers of the world. Perhaps still worse
awaits us, once inside: fires and hissing waters meet,
the sky sinks down; but beyond that land
there lies none except the dismal realm of Juba,
known to us by rumour. We shall long, perhaps,
for this land of serpents: this climate has a consolation: 870
something still lives here. I do not seek the fields
of my fatherland or Europe or Asia, which sees other suns:
but Africa—in what part of the sky, in what land
did I leave you? At Cyrene even now the winter stiffened:
have we reversed the order of the year with our tiny journey?
We go towards the opposing pole, we are evicted from the world,
we turn our backs for Notus' blasts; now perhaps Rome herself
is beneath my feet already. This comfort in our doom
we ask for: let our enemy come here, let Caesar follow
where we flee.' In this way, tough endurance lightens   880
its complaints. They are forced to undergo such mighty hardships
by the heroism of their leader: stretched out on the naked sand
he keeps watch and at every hour challenges Fortune.
He—just one man—is there at every death; wherever he is summoned
he flies and confers a mighty service, greater than preservation,
strength to meet with death; and in his presence they were ashamed
to die with groans. What power could any pestilence
have against him? In others' breasts he conquers misfortunes
and as spectator shows that mighty pain is powerless.

Reluctantly and late did Fortune weary of such mighty dangers   890
and give assistance to them in their distress. A single race
inhabits earth unharmed by the savage serpents' bite—
the Psylli of Marmarica. Their tongues are as effective
as potent drugs, their blood itself is safe with power to resist
the venom, even without incantation. The nature of their soil
has bidden them live free among the serpents.
They benefit from placing their abode in the midst of poison:
that peace with death is given them. So great is their reliance
on their blood that, when a little toddler falls down upon the ground,
in their dread of any adulteration caused by union with a stranger,   900
they test the suspect offspring with a deadly Asp.
And as the bird of Jupiter, when it has brought forth from the
     warm egg
unfeathered young, turns them towards the rising of the sun:
those which can endure the rays and undergo the daylight
with direct glance are kept for heaven's use;
but those who flinch from Phoebus lie neglected: so the Psyllus has
a guarantee of origin if a baby does not shudder
when he touches snakes or plays with serpents handed him.
That people, not content with their own safety only,
keeps watch for strangers, and against the deadly creatures   910
the Psyllus gives assistance to mankind. At that time they were
     following
the Roman standards and as soon as the commander ordered
     shelters to be erected,
first the sand surrounded by the rampart's length they purify
with incantation and with words which drive away the snakes.
The camp's extremities are enclosed by a medicated fire.
Here elder hisses, foreign galbanum sweats moisture;
and tamarisk, not blessed in foliage, and eastern costos
and powerful panacea and Thessalian centaury
and sulphur-wort and thapsos from Mount Eryx crackle in the flames;
and larch they burn and abrotonum, troublesome to serpents   920
with its smoke, and the horns of stag born far away.
So the night is made safe for the warriors. But, if anyone draws on
     his doom
by daytime plague, then are the marvels of the magic people seen:
a mighty battle of the Psylli and the poison gulped.
For first he marks the limbs by touching with saliva

it checks the venom and confines destruction in the wound;
then many a spell does he recite with foaming tongue
in continuous murmur, and the speed of the wound gives
no time for breath nor does death allow even the shortest silence.
And often the destruction, though lodged within the black marrow,   930
is charmed away by incantation; but if the venom heeds
more slowly and when summoned out and told to leave resists,
then leaning over the pale wounds he licks them,
sucking out the poison with his mouth, and, biting, drains the frame
and efficaciously from the icy body draws forth death
and spits it out; and for the Psylli it is easy even
by the poison's taste to know which serpent's bite he has overcome.

Lightened then by this assistance, at last the Roman
soldiers in the barren fields wander far and wide.
Twice had Phoebe lost her flames, twice regained her light,   940
and as she rose and vanished she saw Cato wandering over sands.
And now for him the dust started to congeal more and more
and Libya thickened and began to turn into earth again,
and now afar, here and there, the foliage of trees began to raise itself,
and rustic huts of heaped-up piles of straw began to rise.
What great rejoicing that better land was reached had the miserable
       men
from their first sight, in front of them, of savage lions!
Leptis was nearby: in its quiet halting-place
they passed a winter free from rains and heat.

When Caesar left, satiated with the slaughter of Emathia,   950
he renounced the other burdens of anxiety, intent upon his
       son-in-law
alone. Following his traces scattered uselessly
on land, with rumour as his guide, he goes towards the waves
and coasts along the Thracian straits, water swum
in love, and Hero's towers on the melancholy shore
where Helle, daughter of Nephele, conferred upon the sea its name.
Nowhere does a smaller wave of water separate
Asia from Europe, although with narrow course
the sea divides Byzantium and oyster-bearing Calchedon
and Propontis races from a tiny mouth, carrying the Euxine.   960
And admiring glory, he seeks Sigeum's sands,

Simois' waters, Rhoeteum renowned for its Greek tomb
and the ghosts that owe so much to bards.
He walks around a memorable name—burnt-out Troy—
and seeks the mighty traces of the wall of Phoebus.
Now barren woods and trunks with rotting timber
have submerged Assaracus' houses and, with roots now weary,
occupy the temples of the gods, and all of Pergamum
is veiled by thickets: even the ruins suffered oblivion.
He sees Hesione's rock and Anchises' marriage-chamber hiding   970
in the woods; the cave where the adjudicator sat; the place
from which the boy was snatched to heaven; the peak
where Naiad Oenone grieved; no stone is without a story.
Unwittingly, he had crossed a stream creeping
in dry dust—this was Xanthus. Oblivious, he placed
his footsteps in the deep grass: the Phrygian local tells him
not to tread upon the shade of Hector. Scattered stones
were lying there, preserving no appearance of anything sacred:
the guide says: 'Have you no respect for the Hercean altars?'
O how sacred and immense the task of bards! You snatch everything 980
from death and to mortals you give immortality.
Caesar, do not be touched by envy of their sacred fame;
since, if for Latian Muses it is right to promise anything,
as long as honours of the Smyrnaean bard endure,
the future ages will read me and you; our Pharsalia
shall live and we shall be condemned to darkness by no era.
When revered antiquity had filled the leader's sight,
he raised a sudden altar with a heap of turf and poured
into the incense-burning fires prayers not unfulfilled:

   'Gods of the ashes, you who live in Phrygian ruins,   990
and household gods of my Aeneas, now preserved
in Lavinian abodes and Alba and on whose altars
the Phrygian fire still shines; and Pallas looked upon
by no male, the memorable guarantee in the hidden temple:
upon your altars the most glorious descendant of the Julian clan
offers holy incense and he solemnly invokes you in your
former home. Grant me a prosperous passage for the future:
I shall restore the people; in gratitude the Ausonians will give back
their walls to the Phrygians, and Pergamum will rise Roman.'

So he spoke, returned to his fleet and opened all his sails   1000

to Corus following, and with the gale impelling him
he was keen to compensate for his delays at Ilium and he sails
past mighty Asia and leaves behind him Rhodes with foaming sea.
With Zephyr never slackening the ropes, the seventh night
reveals the shores of Egypt by the flames of Pharos.
But day arose and hid the night-time lamp
before he entered calm waters. There he finds the sea-shore
full of uproar, voices jumbled up in murmur indistinct,
and, fearing to entrust himself to a suspect power,
he kept his ships away from land. But a minion of the king,   1010
bearing a dreadful gift, sailed out into the mid-sea:
he brings the head of Magnus, wrapped in Pharian cloth,
and first he justifies the crime with utterance unspeakable:
'Conqueror of the earth and greatest of the Roman race, and safe—
although you do not know it yet—with your son-in-law killed,
the Pellaean king lets you off the toils of battle
and of sea and shows the one thing missing from Emathian
warfare. In your absence, civil war has been accomplished for you:
Magnus, as he sought to repair the ruins of Thessaly,
lies low by our sword. With a pledge so mighty, Caesar,   1020
we have bought you; by this blood our pact with you was struck.
Receive the realms of Pharos, gained without slaughter;
receive power over Nile's flood; keep for yourself whatever
you would give for Magnus' neck; and consider as a vassal
worthy of your camp the one who has been given by the Fates
such mighty power against your son-in-law. And do not think this
    service
worthless because it was accomplished with an easy killing.
He was his grandfather's guest-friend; he restored the sceptre
to his banished father. Why say more? For such a mighty deed
you will find a name, or else, you may consult the world's opinion.   1030
If it is a crime, then you admit your debt to us is greater
because you do not commit this crime yourself.' So he spoke, exposed
and held aloft the covered head. Already his appearance, drooping
in death, had altered the form of the familiar face.

Caesar at the first sight did not condemn the gift
and turn away his eyes; he lingered till he could believe the face;
and when he saw the confirmation of the crime and thought it now
was safe to be the loving father-in-law, he poured out tears which fell

not of their own accord, and squeezed out groans from his happy
breast, not able to conceal his mind's conspicuous joy   1040
except by tears, and he destroys the tyrant's savage
service, preferring to lament his son-in-law's torn-off head
than be in debt for it. The man who trampled on the Senate's
limbs with face unmoved, who saw the fields of Emathia
with dry eye, to you alone, Magnus, does not dare
refuse laments. O harshest share of destiny!
Did you, Caesar, chase this man with wicked warfare,
a man for whom you had to weep? Does the pact of families united
touch you now? Do your daughter and your grandson bid you
     grieve now?
Do you believe that this benefits your camp among the people   1050
who love the name of Pompey? You are touched perhaps
by envy of the tyrant, and feel pain that another had such power
over captive Magnus' guts, and you complain that warfare's
revenge has vanished and your son-in-law has been taken
from the power of his proud conqueror. Whatever impulse made
you weep, it was far removed from true affection.
With these feelings, I suppose, you scour the lands and seas,
that your son-in-law should nowhere die in hiding. O how happy
that his death has been removed from your control! How great
the crimes which cruel Fortune spared our Roman shame   1060
in not allowing you, you traitor, to show mercy to Magnus
while he was still alive! Yet with these words he dares to deceive,
and by his brow gains credence for the pretended grief:
     'Minion, from my sight remove your king's
disgusting gift. Your crime deserves worse
from Caesar than from Pompey; the one reward
of civil war—to grant survival to the conquered—
we have lost. But if his sister were not hated
by the Pharian tyrant, to the king I could have given back
what he deserves, and in return for such a present to your brother,   1070
Cleopatra, could have sent your head. Why did he wield the secret
sword and thrust his weapons into our struggle?
Did we then create authority for the Pellaean sword
on the fields of Thessaly? Was freedom for your realms my aim?
I could not bear Magnus ruling the world of Rome with me:
Ptolemy, shall I bear you, then? Uselessly have we embroiled
the nations in civil warfare if in this world there is

any other power than Caesar, if any land belongs to two.
I should have turned my Latian prows from your shore:
regard for my reputation stops me, in case I seem not to condemn   1080
blood-stained Pharos but to fear it. And do not think that you
deceive the conqueror: for me too was such a welcome
ready on the shore; it is the fortune of Thessaly which means
that my head is not conveyed like this. We waged war
with greater risk, assuredly, than could be feared:
I dreaded exile, my son-in-law's threats, Rome:
the penalty of rout was Ptolemy. But we spare his youth,
excuse his crime. Let the tyrant know that for this slaughter
nothing more than pardon can be given. Bury in the tomb
the mighty leader's head, but not in such a way that earth   1090
merely hides your guilt: offer incense to his rightful grave,
placate the head and gather up the ashes dispersed
upon the shore and to the scattered shade grant a single urn.
Let the ghost sense the arrival of his father-in-law and let him hear
my words of loving protest. Since he prefers everything to me,
since he prefers to owe his life to his Pharian vassal, the nations
have been deprived of a day of happiness, our reconciliation
has been lost to the world. My prayer has found no favouring gods—
my prayer that, after laying down successful weapons, I might
          embrace you
and ask from you your old affection and your staying alive,   1100
Magnus, and to be your equal, satisfied with a reward
quite worthy of my toils. Then in lasting peace
I could have helped you in defeat forgive the gods;
you could have helped Rome forgive me.' And with these words
he did not find a comrade for his tears, nor did the multitude believe
his protest: they hide their groans and veil their hearts
with happy brow, and cheerfully—O happy liberty!—they dare
to gaze upon the bloody crime though Caesar grieves.

BOOK TEN

As soon as Caesar, in pursuit of Pompey's head,
reached land and trod the dreadful sands,
the general's fortune and the destiny of guilty Egypt
fought: would Lagus' kingdom be subdued by Roman
force or would the sword of Memphis remove the head
of conqueror and conquered from the world? Your ghost assisted him,
Magnus: your shade rescued your father-in-law from bloodshed,
to stop the Roman people loving Nile after your death.
From there he passes untroubled into the Paraetonian city,
which was following his standards through the bond of such a
     savage crime.   10
But from the growling of the crowd, complaining that the Rods
and Roman power are invading their own, he sensed discordant
breasts and feelings unreliable: not for him
had Magnus died. Then with his face always concealing fear,
undeterred he visits the gods' abodes and temples of ancient
deity which declare the Macedonians' might
of old, and charmed by no delights, not by gold
or by adornment of the gods, not by city-walls,
he eagerly descends into the cavern hollowed out for a burial-place.

There the crazy offspring of Pellaean Philip   20
lies, the lucky bandit, seized by destiny avenging
the earth: in a sacred shrine they laid the warrior's limbs
which should have been dispersed through all the world; Fortune
spared his shade, and to the last his kingdom's destiny endured.
For if Liberty had ever restored the world to itself,
he had been kept for mockery, born as an example
not serviceable to the world—to show that lands so many
could be under one man's sway. He left the bounds and hiding-places
of his Macedonians, despising Athens conquered by his father,
and, driven by the thrust of Fate through Asia's peoples,   30
rushed on amid human devastation and drove his sword
through all the nations, unfamiliar rivers he disturbed—

Euphrates with the blood of Persians, Ganges with the blood of
    Indians:
an evil deadly to the earth, a thunderbolt
which struck all the peoples equally, a star baneful
to humankind. He was preparing to advance his fleet to Ocean
by the outer sea. No obstacle to him was flame or waves
or barren Libya or Ammon of the Syrtes.
Following the world's slope, he would have gone into the west
and past the poles and drunk Nile from his source: 40
his final day blocked his path and only Nature
could impose this limit on the crazy king;
jealously he took away with him the power with which
he had captured all the world, and, leaving none as heir
of his entire fortune, he exposed the cities to be torn apart.
But in his own Babylon he fell, dreaded by the Parthian.
How disgraceful! the people of the east more closely feared
the pikes than now they fear the javelins. Although we rule
as far as Arctos and the homes of Zephyr, although we dominate the
    lands
beyond the back of blazing Notus, in the east we shall yield   50
to the master of the Arsacids. Parthia, not lucky
for the Crassi, was a quiet province of tiny Pella.

Now coming from Nile's Pelusian flood,
the unwarlike boy-king had allayed his people's wrath.
With him as hostage, Caesar was secure
in the Pellaean court, when Cleopatra bribed the guard
to undo the chains of Pharos, and in a little two-oared boat
she entered the Emathian halls without Caesar's knowledge—
the disgrace of Egypt, deadly Erinys of Latium,
promiscuous to the harm of Rome. As much as the Spartan woman   60
with her harmful beauty knocked down Argos and the homes of Ilium,
so Cleopatra swelled the madness of Hesperia.
With her rattle she alarmed the Capitol, if such a thing can be,
and she attacked the Roman standards with unwarlike Canopus,
in her intent to lead a Pharian triumph with Caesar as a captive;
and doubtful was the outcome on the Leucadian flood:
would a woman—not even Roman—rule the world?
This spirit she acquired from that night which first in bed
united Ptolemy's impure daughter with Roman generals.

Who would not excuse your crazy love,   70
Antony, when fire devoured Caesar's stubborn
heart? Even in the midst of madness, in the midst of frenzy
and in the court inhabited by Pompey's shade,
while drenched with blood of the Thessalian slaughter, adulterously
he shared his anxieties with Venus and combined with war
illicit union and progeny not born from wife.
O the shame! Forgetting Magnus, he gave you brothers,
Julia, from a loathsome mother, and he let
the routed party gather strength in Libya's furthest realms
while he spends time disgustingly on love beside the Nile,   80
since he prefers to make a gift of Pharos, not to conquer for himself.
Relying on her looks, Cleopatra comes to him, gloomy
without tears, adorned with simulated grief
as far as was attractive, her hair spread out as if torn,
and she began to speak like this: 'O most mighty Caesar, if nobility
is anything, I, the most illustrious daughter of Pharian Lagus,
driven from my father's sceptre, an exile for eternity
unless your hand restores me to my destiny of old,
I as queen embrace your feet. Come to our people
as a favourable star. I shall not be the first woman to rule   90
the Nile's cities: with no distinction of sex
Pharos knows how to bear a queen. Read my dead father's
final words: shared rights to power he gave me
and a marriage-chamber with my brother. The boy himself loves
his sister, if only he were free; but his emotions and his swords
are subject to Pothinus' sway. Nothing of my father's power
do I seek to gain myself: free our house from guilt
and shame so great, remove the minion's murderous forces
and tell the king to be a king. How great the swelling
which the slave bears in his mind! He tore off Magnus' head   100
and now he threatens you—but may the Fates avert this far away!
It was scandalous enough for the world and for you, Caesar,
that Pompey was the crime and the credit of Pothinus.'
Uselessly she would have tried to influence the stubborn ears of Caesar:
her face supports her prayers, her impure beauty finishes her speech.
She bribes the judge and spends an unspeakable night.

Once the general's truce was gained and bought by mighty gifts,
a banquet celebrated the joys of such great events

and with a huge commotion Cleopatra displayed
her own extravagance, not yet transferred to Roman generations.   110
The place itself was equal to a temple which an age
more corrupt would hardly build; the panelled ceilings
showed her riches, thick gold concealed the beams.
The house shone, not encrusted with veneers of marble
on the surface; in its own right, not useless, stood the agate
and the purple stone; in all the palace onyx
in abundance was trodden on; ebony of Meroë does not veil
the door-posts huge but stands in place of ordinary timber,
the support, not the adornment, of the house. The halls are clothed
by ivory, and Indian tortoise-shells, stained by hand,   120
are inlaid in the doors, their spots embellished with abundant
      emeralds.
Jewels glitter on the couches and the furnishings are tawny with
      jasper.
The coverlets are gleaming: most of them, long steeped
in Tyrian dye, took on their stain from more than a single cauldron;
some shine embroidered with golden feathers, some blaze with
      cochineal,
following the method of mingling heddles on Pharian looms.
Then the numerous servant crowd and multitude of attendants:
some were marked out by their blood of different colour, others
by their age; this group had Libyan locks, another locks so blond
that Caesar said that in no fields of the Rhine   130
had he seen such glowing hair; some were of a scorched complexion
with curly heads and wore their hair receding from the forehead;
and there were boys unfortunate, enfeebled by the sword,
castrated of their manhood: opposite there stands a stronger
age-group, yet with hardly any down darkening their cheeks.

There the rulers took their places; so does Caesar, power greater
than they; and with excessive make-up on her harmful beauty,
not content with her own sceptre nor with her brother-husband,
loaded with the Red Sea's booty, on her neck and in her hair
Cleopatra wears a fortune and she strains beneath her finery.   140
Her white breasts shine through the Sidonian thread
which, tightly made by Seres' comb, the Nile's needle
loosens, opening up the strands by stretching out the cloth.
Then they set on snowy tusks round tables cut

in Atlas' forest, such as Caesar never saw,
not even when he captured Juba. O what madness, blind
and frantic with ostentation—to reveal one's treasures
to a man waging civil war, to inflame the mind
of a guest bearing weapons. Even though it were not he, ready
in abominable warfare to seek riches in the ruin of the world;   150
put there the generals of old, names of an age of poverty,
Fabricii and solemn Curii, let here recline that
consul brought grimy from his Etruscan plough:
he will wish to lead a triumph like this for his fatherland.
They poured the banquet on to gold what land, what air,
what sea and Nile supplied, what luxury, made mad
by empty ostentation, sought through all the world
without hunger's command; they served many birds
and many beasts—the gods of Egypt, and crystal-ware provides
Nile water for their hands, and huge jewelled cups   160
received the wine, but not of Mareotic grape,
but noble, fierce Falernian which Meroë
had aged in not many years, compelling it to foam.
They put on garlands twined with flowering nard
and never-failing rose, and on to their dripping locks
they poured much cinnamon—whose scent had not yet faded
and which had not lost its flavour in a foreign country—
and cardamom brought fresh from nearby harvest.
Caesar learns to squander the riches of a plundered world;
it shames him to have waged a war against his impoverished
     son-in-law   170
and he prays for pretexts to fight the Pharian peoples.

When exhausted pleasure set a limit to the banqueting
and to Bacchus, Caesar starts to prolong the night with
lengthy conversation and he addresses linen-clad Acoreus,
reclining in the highest seat, with friendly words:
'Old man, devoted to the sacred rites and not abandoned by the gods,
as proven by your age, expound the origins of Pharos' race,
the situation of its lands, the customs of the multitude,
the rituals and shapes of the gods; express whatever
is carved on the ancient shrines, reveal the gods   180
who are willing to be known. If your ancestors taught
their mysteries to Cecropian Plato, what visitor ever more deserved

to listen so or could better comprehend the universe?
For sure, I was brought to Pharos' cities by report about my
　　　son-in-law,
but still report about you too; always in the midst of battles
I found time for higher things, for regions of the stars and sky,
nor will my own year be worsted by Eudoxus' calendar.
But though there lives within my breast such enormous energy
and love of truth, there is nothing I would rather know
than the causes of the river which lie hidden through so many ages　　190
and its unknown source: let me have a hope assured of seeing
the springs of Nile, and I will abandon civil war.'

He finished; holy Acoreus in reply began like this:
'To me it is permitted to disclose the secrets of my mighty ancestors,
Caesar, up to now unknown to the profane multitudes.
To keep silent about such mighty miracles—let that be piety for others;
but I consider it the heaven-dwellers' wish that this work should have
a universal passage and their sacred laws become the knowledge
　　　of the people.
To the planets which alone regulate Olympus' speed
and which run counter to the sky, a different power was given　　200
by the first law of the universe. The sun divides the periods of time,
replaces day with night, and with his powerful rays forbids
the stars to proceed and stays their roaming course by halting them;
Moon with her alternations mingles Tethys and dry land;
chilly ice and zone of snow to Saturn have been given;
master of the winds and unpredictable thunderbolts is Mars;
under Jupiter is the mild climate and air which is never clouded;
but the seeds of all things fruitful Venus
holds; the Cyllenian is ruler of the wave immense.
When he is in the part of heaven where Leo's stars　　210
meet Cancer, where Sirius displays his scorching
fires and where the Circle is, the shifter of the changing year,
containing Aegoceros and Cancer, under which lie hidden
Nile's openings—when the master of the waters has struck these
with his fire directly overhead, then with fount unleashed
Nile emerges, just as Ocean attends, summoned
by increases of the moon, and he does not narrow his growth
until the night has regained the summer hours from the sun.

　　'False was the belief of the ancients, that snows of Ethiopians help

Nile to expand into the fields: no Arctos is there in those   220
mountains and no Boreas. Your proof of this: the simple colour
of the people burnt by sun and Austri hot with vapours.
In addition, every river's head, set running
by the melted ice, swells as spring begins at the snow's
first dissolution: Nile neither makes his waters rise
before the rays of the Dog nor confines his river with his banks
before Phoebus matches night with Libra as the referee.
That too is why he does not even know the laws of other waters,
and why he does not swell in winter, when, with sun removed afar,
the water lacks its usefulness: told to bring moderation   230
to an excessive clime, he emerges in the midst of summer
beneath the scorching zone; and to stop the fire from shattering the
    earth,
Nile is there to help the world and swells to meet the blazing
face of Leo, and when Cancer scorches its own Syene,
he is there, in answer to appeal, and does not free the fields
from his waters until Phoebus slopes towards the autumn
and Meroë makes the shadows longer. Who can give the causes?
Like this did mother Nature tell Nile to run; like this
it is essential for the world. False too was antiquity when it attributed
these waters to the Zephyrs: fixed are the seasons of their blast,   240
continuous their days, and long their power over the air,
either because they drive the clouds down from the western sky
across the Notus and compel the rains to settle on the river;
or because they strike the waters of Nile as he bursts through the
    shore
so frequently and with continuous billows forces him to halt:
he, with his progress checked, with the barrier of sea facing him,
seethes on to the fields. Some people think that there are
air-holes in the earth and mighty fissures in its hollow frame.
Here deep down the water passes to and fro invisibly,
summoned back from Arctic chill beneath the middle region,   250
when Phoebus is directly over Meroë, and the scorched earth
has attracted the waters there; Ganges and Po are brought
through a secret region of the world: then Nile, spewing all the rivers
from a single source, delivers them through not a single stream.
There is a report that from the overflowing Ocean which encloses
all the lands Nile far off bursts out violently
and that the salt of the sea is weakened by the lengthy course.

Moreover, we believe that Phoebus and the sky are fed
by Ocean: this, when sun has touched the claws of hot Cancer,
he seizes and he raises up more water than the air   260
can digest; this the nights fetch back and discharge into Nile.
But I—if it is right for me to solve such a great dispute—
Caesar, I believe that certain waters, long ages after the completion
of the universe, burst out from the shaken veins of earth
not by God's intention; that certain waters at the actual construction
of the universe originated with the whole—and these the Creator
and the crafter of the world himself controls beneath a fixed authority.

    'Your desire to know Nile, Roman, was shared
by tyrants Pharian and Persian and of Macedon,
and no age is there which has not wished to grant the knowledge   270
to the future—but up to now its natural power of hiding is victorious.
Alexander, greatest of the kings, adored by Memphis,
begrudged Nile his secret and sent his chosen band through furthest
reaches of the land of Ethiopians: they were hindered by the ruddy
zone of scorched sky; they saw Nile steaming.
To the west and to the world's extremities came Sesostris
and drove his Pharian chariot across the necks of kings;
yet he drank your rivers, Rhône and Po,
before he drank Nile from his source. The mad Cambyses
penetrated the east as far as the people of long life,   280
and after running short of food and feeding off the slaughter of his
        men
he returned with you, Nile, undiscovered. Lying legend
has not dared to speak about your source. Wherever you appear
you are a puzzle; and no race can take the glory
of rejoicing in possession of Nile. Your streams
I shall disclose, as far as God, concealer of your waters, Nile,
has granted me to know you. You rise from the middle region;
venturing to raise your banks in the face of blazing Cancer,
direct you go towards Boreas and the middle of Boötes with your
        waters;
with bends your course is turned towards the west and east,   290
now favouring the people of Arabia, now the sands of Libya,
and first to see you are the Seres, yet these too seek your source,
and with a foreign flood you strike the fields of the Ethiopians,
and the world knows not in whose debt it is for you.
Nature has revealed your hidden head to none, has not allowed

the people to see you in your infancy, Nile, has made remote
your hiding-places and preferred the amazement of the peoples
to their knowledge of your origins. Yours is the right to rise
at the very solstice, to grow thanks to a winter out of season
and to bring a winter of your own; to you alone is it allowed   300
to roam through both the hemispheres. In one is sought your origin,
in the other the finish of your water. Far and wide by your divided
stream is Meroë surrounded, fruitful for her black farmers,
rejoicing in her foliage of ebony; though she is leafy
with many a tree, she has no shade to moderate the summer,
so directly does that line of the world strike Leo.
From there you travel past the zones of Phoebus, suffering no loss
of waters, and for a long time you traverse the barren sands,
now concentrating all your strength into a single stream,
now wandering and breaking up the bank, which readily gives
    way to you.   310
Again your sluggish channel summons back the splintered waters
where Egyptian lands are separated from the peoples of Arabia
by Philae, gateway of the realm. Then, as you cut through
the wilderness where trade-routes join the Red Sea and our own,
a gentle glide leads you onward. Who would think, to see you flow
so quietly, that you, Nile, can arouse the wholesale
anger of your violent flood? But when sheer paths
and plunging cataracts have met your flow
and you take offence that any rocks bar your flood, which is
forbidden nowhere, then with your foam you challenge the stars,   320
everything is roaring with your waters, and, as the mountain rumbles
loud, your foaming stream grows white with waves unwilling.
Next is the mighty land which our venerable antiquity
calls Abatos—when struck it feels the first attack—
and the rocks, which it is agreed to call the river's veins
because they are the first to give clear signs of fresh swelling.
Next has nature set mountains round your roaming waters
and they keep you away from Libya, Nile; between them in a deep
valley your water goes, silent now with former habit regained.
Memphis first allows you plains and open country   330
and forbids your banks to set a limit to your growth.'

Like this, secure as if in safety of peace, they spent
the passage of midnight. But Pothinus' insane mind,

once now stained with sacred slaughter, did not rest
from planning crimes: since Magnus' murder, he now thinks
that nothing is a crime; the shade lives on beneath his breast
and the avenging goddesses give him frenzy for new horrors.
He thinks his lowly hands are worthy to shed that blood too
with which Fortune plans to drench the conquered Fathers:
and the punishment for civil war, the Senate's vengeance,   340
was almost granted to a slave. Fates, avert this crime
afar, that this neck should be severed without Brutus there.
The Roman tyrant's punishment is being added to the wickedness
        of Pharos
and the warning lost. Presumptuous, he makes plans not sanctioned
by the Fates: he does not try to entrust the murder to hidden trickery
but challenges the undefeated general with war unsheathed.
His misdeeds gave him so much spirit that he ordered
Caesar's head to be cut off and your father-in-law united with you,
        Magnus;
and he tells his loyal slaves to take these words
to Achillas, his associate in Pompey's murder.   350
Him the unwarlike boy had put in charge of all his forces
and given the sword to use against everyone and against himself alike,
retaining no authority for himself. 'Now lie', he said,
'on your soft couches, spend your time in comfortable slumbers:
Cleopatra has attacked the palace; and Pharos has been
not just betrayed but given away. Do you alone hold back from
        running
to the bedroom of your mistress? The guilty sister is marrying her
        brother—
the Latian general she has already married—and racing to and fro
        between
her husbands she possesses Egypt and she whores to gain Rome.
Cleopatra has been able to capture the old man with magic: 360
put your trust in the boy, you wretch—if a single night unites them
and he once experiences her embraces with impure heart
and deeply drinks of loathsome love beneath the name of affection,
he will give to her both me and your life too, perhaps,
between kisses. On crosses and in flames we shall pay the price,
if he finds his sister beautiful. No help remains on any side:
on this the king her husband, on this is Caesar the adulterer.
And we are guilty, though I admit it, in the eyes of such a savage judge:

which of us who have not touched her does Cleopatra
not consider guilty? By the crime which we performed together,   370
the crime we did in vain, by our alliance struck in Magnus' blood,
I call you, come; stir up war with sudden uproar,
charge; let us cut short with death the night-time marriage-torches
and let us kill our cruel mistress on her couch itself,
whichever man she lies with. And let the Hesperian leader's fortune,
which has raised him up and set him over the world,
not deter us from the exploit: we share his glory;
Magnus makes us exalted too. Look upon the shore,
which gives us confidence for wickedness; consult the defiled
waves about the power we have; and look on Pompey's grave   380
of scanty dust, not covering all his parts.
The man you dread was this man's equal. We are not illustrious in
    blood—
what does it matter?—and we do not control kingdoms or the
    wealth
of nations: for wickedness, we are of mighty destiny. Those men
    Fortune
draws into our hands: look—there comes another
victim, nobler. With a second murder let us placate
the peoples of Hesperia: Caesar's throat drained dry can give me
this advantage, that the Roman people love those guilty
of the murder of Pompey. Why do we shudder at the name so great
and forces of the general? Once he has left them off,   390
he will be a common soldier. This night will end the civil wars
and give the people offerings to their dead and send down to the
    ghosts
the head which still is owing to the world. Fiercely attack
Caesar's throat; let Lagus' soldiers do this for their king,
the Roman soldiers for themselves. Refrain from delay.
Full with feasting, soaked with wine, and ready for Venus
you will find him: be bold: the gods above will grant to you
all the many prayers of Catos and of Bruti.'

                                        Achillas was not slow
to obey persuasion to crime: he gave the signals for moving camp
not loud, as usual, and he did not betray his troops   400
by blast of any trumpet: impetuously he snatches up
all the tools of savage war. Most of the multitude were of

the Latian people; but such immense forgetfulness had seized
their minds—the soldiers were corrupted into foreign ways—
that they marched beneath a slave general, at the bidding of a minion,
when it was scandalous for them to hearken to the Pharian tyrant.
No loyalty, no duty have the men who follow camp, and their hands
are up for sale; there lies right—where pay is nearest:
they earn a little cash and offer to attack Caesar's throat
not for themselves. In the name of Right! where does   410
the lamentable destiny of our empire not find civil warfare?
Troops kept away from Thessaly are raging in their native way
on Nile's shore. What more could Lagus' house have dared,
had it welcomed you, Magnus? Every sword-hand, I suppose,
gives to the gods above what it owes, and it is not right for any Roman
to be missing. Like this the gods resolved to tear asunder
Latium's body: the nations do not split to support
the father-in-law and son-in-law; civil war is stirred
by a minion and Achillas has taken on a Roman's role;
and if Fate does not ward off their hands from Caesar's blood,   420
their side will win. Both were present speedily
and the court, distracted by the feasting, lay exposed
to every plot and Caesar's blood might have been shed
among the royal cups and his head have settled on the table.
But they fear the panicky confusion of warfare in the night,
in case the murder, performed in disorder and left to fate,
drags you down, Ptolemy. So mighty was their confidence in the sword
they did not hurry on the crime; the ease of this greatest deed
they scorned; to the slaves it seemed that to let that hour
for killing Caesar pass was a loss they could retrieve.   430
He is preserved to pay the penalty in open light;
a single night was granted to the general and Caesar lived
thanks to Pothinus, reprieved till Phoebus' rise.

Lucifer looked down from the Casian rock and sent
the daylight into Egypt, warm even in the earliest sun,
when far off from the walls is seen an army, not wandering
or with scattered companies but such as comes with straight array
towards their full-strength enemy: ready to experience and to inflict
close-quarters fighting, on they rush. But Caesar does not trust
the city-walls and he defends himself with the doors of palace closed,   440
submitting to an ignoble hiding-place. And the entire court

was not open to him, hemmed in as he was: his forces he had
    gathered
in the smallest portion of the house. Both wrath and dread
affect his spirit: he fears attack; is angry at his fear.
Just so a noble beast hidden in a tiny prison
bites the barrier and breaks his frenzied teeth;
and no differently would your flame rage in the caves
of Sicily if Etna's summit, Mulciber, were blocked.
The daring man who recently beneath Thessalian Haemus' rock
was not afraid of all Hesperia's chiefs   450
or Senate's battle-line or the general Pompey, though his cause
forbade him to hope, who promised himself a destiny not deserved,
took fright at the wickedness of slaves and inside the house
is overwhelmed by weapons. The man whom the Alani would not
    have outraged
nor the Scythian nor the Moor who ridicules the wounded stranger,
this man for whom the Roman world's expanse is not enough
and who would think the Indians with Tyrian Gades a tiny kingdom,
like an unwarlike boy or a woman in a captured city,
seeks the safety of a house; his hope of life he places in a threshold
    shut,
and with uncertain path he roams and wanders through the halls,   460
yet not without the king: he takes him everywhere with him
to exact retribution and welcome atonement should he die
and, if the weapons and the firebrands run out, to launch your
head against your slaves, Ptolemy. Like this, the barbarian of Colchis
is believed to have waited for her father, dreading vengeance
for the kingdom and her flight, ready with her sword
and brother's head together.
                 Yet extremities compel
the general to try the hope of peace, and a minion of the king
was sent to rebuke the savage slaves with their absent
tyrant's words, asking on whose authority they stirred up war.   470
But neither universal law nor agreements sanctioned by the nations
    were
powerful enough to stop the king's ambassador and
    intermediary of peace
from falling by the sword. Yet who assesses such an act   472A
worthy of placing in the tally of your wickedness,
Egypt guilty of so many horrors? Not the land of Thessaly

or mighty realms of Juba, not Pontus or the impious standards
of Pharnaces or the region surrounded by chill Hiberus,
not barbarian Syrtis, has ventured the amount of wickedness
your luxury has performed.
                              War on every side oppresses him
and now the weapons fall upon the house and shake the building.
No ram have they to shift the threshold at a single blow   480
and to smash the house, no machine of war,
nor is the task to flames entrusted; but the soldiers, blind
of purpose, separate, surround the enormous building
and nowhere does the force attack with all its strength.
The Fates say no and Fortune maintains the function of a wall.

What is more, by ships as well the palace is assailed, where
the house of luxury projected into the middle of the waves
with bold retaining wall. But everywhere is Caesar present
in defence: he repulses these attacks with sword and these with fire,
and while blockaded—so great is his firmness of mind—he performs   490
the work of a besieger. He commands that firebrands dipped in pitchy
fat be hurled against the vessels linked together for the fight;
and the fire was not slow along the ropes of tow, along
the planking wet with wax; and simultaneously
the sailors' benches and the topmost yard-arms caught alight.
Already are the half-burnt vessels nearly sunk into the water,
already are the enemy and their weapons swimming. And not
on ships alone did fire settle; but the dwellings which were near
the sea caught fire from its far-reaching heat
and the Noti nurtured the calamity, and the flame, struck   500
by a whirlwind, ran through the dwellings as swiftly
as a meteor often races with its trail in the ether,
though lacking fuel and burning thanks to air alone.
That destruction for a little time recalled the people
from the besieged palace to help the city. And the period
of calamity Caesar did not waste in sleep but in blind night
he leapt aboard the ships, successful always in his use
of headlong speed of warfare, and he seized his opportunity
and now took Pharos, the gateway of the sea. An island once,
in the days of prophet Proteus, in mid-sea it had stood,   510
but now it is very close to the Pellaean walls.
To the general it afforded twin benefits in warfare.

He deprived the enemy of a passage out, and the outlet to the deep,
and when he saw the mouth of ocean free for reinforcements,
Caesar did not postpone further the destiny and punishment
which Pothinus deserved. But not with anger due—
not by cross, not by flames, not by wild beasts' tooth did he take him:
what a crime! his neck drooped, struck badly by the sword;
he died by Magnus' death. And, more, Arsinoe was kidnapped
in a plot prepared by her slave Ganymedes and came   520
to Caesar's enemies; as Lagus' offspring she is mistress
of the camp which lacks its king, and pierced the tyrant's
terrifying slave Achillas with a sword of justice.
A second victim, Magnus, now is sent down to appease your ghost;
but Fortune thinks this not enough. Far be it that
that should be the sum of your revenge. Not himself the tyrant
is enough as retribution, not all the royal house of Lagus:
until his country's swords reach Caesar's guts,
Magnus will be unavenged. But the frenzy did not disappear
once the author of the madness was removed; again they go   530
to fight, now under the command of Ganymedes, and they wage
many battles with favourable warfare. That single day could
have passed into glory and the centuries because of Caesar's utmost
        danger.

With his soldiers massed around him in the tiny jetty's space
while he prepares to transfer fighting on to empty vessels,
the Latian general is suddenly encircled by all war's
terror: on this side ships densely line the shore,
on this the infantry are leaping at his rear. No path of safety is there,
not flight, not heroism; hardly can he even hope for honourable
        death.
With no routed army or heaps of massive carnage,   540
Caesar then was on the point of defeat, but without bloodshed:
captured by conditions of the place, he is perplexed; and doubtful
whether to fear or pray to die, he looked back at Scaeva in the
        crowded
line, Scaeva who already had earned the fame of everlasting glory
on your fields, Epidamnus, when after the walls were breached
he alone blockaded Magnus as he trod upon the ramparts.

EXPLANATORY NOTES

BOOK 1

1–7 The subject of the poem is announced.

1 *worse than civil wars*: because Pompey and Caesar were not only fellow citizens but related to one another by marriage.

4 *the pact of tyranny was broken*: the so-called First Triumvirate, in which Pompey, Caesar, and Crassus agreed to co-operate politically with each other. The pact, made in 60 BC, broke down in the late 50s.

6–7 *of standards … javelins*: the standards (*signa*), eagles (*aquilae*), and javelins (*pila*) are all distinctively Roman equipment.

8–32 Lucan regrets the civil war when Rome might have been conquering the rest of the world.

12 *wars which would bring no triumphs*: a triumph could be earned only by a victory over a foreign enemy.

15–18 Lucan refers to east, west, south, and north in turn by means of periphrases; 'Titan' and 'the star' both denote the sun.

20 *Nile's birth*: a topic of fascination to the Romans; Lucan includes a discussion of the subject in book 10.

31 *Pyrrhus*: king of Epirus, who inflicted several major defeats on Rome in the third century BC.

the Carthaginian: i.e. Hannibal, who waged the Second Punic War against Rome, 218–201 BC.

33–45 Lucan declares that the civil war and other terrible events which followed are made worthwhile by Nero.

39 *the Carthaginian's shade*: i.e. Hannibal's ghost, imagined as awaiting revenge for his defeats at the hands of the Romans. Lucan refers to the battle of Thapsus in 46 BC fought in Africa not far from Carthage.

41 *Caesar*: i.e. Nero.

    the famine of Perusia: a town in Italy (mod. Perugia) where Augustus besieged Mark Antony's brother Lucius for several months in 41 BC.

42 *the struggles of Mutina*: in 44 BC Mark Antony besieged Decimus Brutus in the city of Mutina; in 43 BC the consuls came to Brutus' aid and ended the siege but were killed by Antony in battle nearby.

43 *the slave wars*: Pompey's son Sextus with his fleet partly manned by slaves was defeated in the Sicilian seas in 36 BC.

45–66 In a prayer to Nero, Lucan looks forward to his deification and asks him to inspire his poetry.

50 *the transference of the sun*: when his father the sun handed his chariot to Phaethon, disaster followed: the world was set on fire and Phaethon died. The story is told in Ovid, *Met.* 2. 19–332.

57 *feel the weight*: for the association of weight with divinity cf. Homer, *Il.* 5. 837–9.

62 *warring Janus*: the gates of Janus' temple in Rome were only closed in time of peace.

64–5 *the god who has control of Cirrha's secrets*: i.e. Apollo; his shrine at Delphi is here referred to, Cirrha being a nearby town.

66 *you are enough*: Roman poets conventionally asked for divine inspiration from Apollo, Bacchus, and other deities; Lucan here compliments Nero by treating him as a god.

67–120 *The causes of the war 1*: the collapse of all great things such as Rome is fated and inevitable and the First Triumvirate could never last long; Crassus' death, following Julia's death, removed the last obstacle to war.

79 *her chariot*: a two-horse chariot (*bigae*), whereas the sun's was pictured as a four-horse chariot.

83 *Fortune*: a central concept and force in the poem: see Introduction, ii. 5.

85 *made common property of masters three*: again the First Triumvirate is referred to, cf. above, 1. 4 n.

91 *all the constellations*: the twelve signs of the zodiac.

95 *with a brother's blood*: Romulus is said to have killed his brother Remus in a quarrel about the new city-walls of Rome.

97 *Asylum*: Romulus' original foundation from which Rome grew: a refuge for slaves and criminals.

101 *Isthmus*: of Corinth, the narrow neck of land which connects the Peloponnese with mainland Greece.

105 *Carrhae*: an important city in the Assyrian empire (mod. Harran), site of the defeat of Crassus by the Parthians in 53 BC.

118 *Sabine women*: Romulus and the Romans carried off the Sabine women, who reconciled their husbands with their fathers when they were about to enter battle.

120–57 *The causes of the war 2*: Lucan introduces his two protagonists, Pompey and Caesar.

121–2 *fresh exploits . . . Gallic conquests*: Pompey had celebrated three triumphs, over Numidia (81 BC), Spain (71 BC), and Asia (62 BC), and had overcome the pirates, who had caused havoc to shipping throughout the Mediterranean, off the coast of Cilicia in 67 BC; more recently, Julius Caesar had conquered Gaul.

123 *Magnus*: 'the Great'; Lucan much more often calls Pompey 'Magnus' than 'Pompeius': Magnus was a name given him early in his career, in 81 BC, after victories in Sicily and Africa.

124 *your fortune*: on Caesar's special relationship with Fortuna see Introduction, ii. 5.

129–30 *years declining towards old age*: in fact, Pompey was only six years older than Caesar.

130 *through long experience of civil life*: Pompey's previous experience of active warfare had been fourteen years earlier, in his victory over Mithridates of Pontus in 63 BC.

132 *generous to the crowd*: Pompey staged shows and games to entertain the people, for example at the opening of his theatre, Plutarch, *Pomp.* 52.

133 *the theatre he had built*: Pompey built Rome's first stone theatre in 55 BC.

135 *the shadow of a great name*: Lucan alludes to Pompey's nickname Magnus ('The Great') when he uses the word 'great' (*magnus*).

155 *its own precincts*: the part of the sky from where it came.

158–82 *The causes of the war 3*: the luxury brought by Rome's military superiority and empire caused a breakdown in law and morality, according to Lucan. Cf. Sallust, *Bell. Cat.* 10–11.

167 *the bane of every nation*: lit. 'the thing because of which every nation perishes', i.e. luxury objects.

176 *laws and rulings of the plebs*: technically laws (*leges*) were passed by the entire people including the patricians, whereas 'decrees of the people' (*plebiscita*), the normal form of legislation and binding on the whole people, were passed by popular assemblies in which no patrician cast his vote. The legislation mentioned in 177 introduced by consuls, not tribunes, was a shocking deviation.

183–227 Caesar sees a vision of Rome, then crosses the Rubicon.

185 *Rubicon*: a small river in north Italy flowing into the Adriatic Sea not far from Ariminum (mod. Rimini). It formed the boundary between one of Caesar's provinces, namely Gallia Cisalpina, in which he was permitted to move with his army, and Italy, in which he was not.

188 *tower-crowned head*: in Roman visual art, cities were often represented wearing such crowns.

196 *Phrygian house-gods of Iulus' clan*: the household gods (*penates*) brought from Troy to Italy by Aeneas, father of Iulus (also called Ascanius) and ancestor of Julius Caesar.

197 *Mysteries of Quirinus, who was carried off to heaven*: Quirinus was Romulus, founder of Rome, who was said to have been deified (Ovid, *Fast.* 2. 491–512). The Quirinalia were celebrated on 17 February.

198 *Jupiter of Latium, seated in lofty Alba*: Jupiter was also worshipped (as *Iuppiter Latiaris*) at a temple on the Alban Mount in Latium.

199 *hearths of Vesta*: the Vestal Virgins tended the sacred fire supposedly brought from Troy by Aeneas in the temple of Vesta in Rome.

213 *The ruddy Rubicon*: the river is reddish in colour.

217 *winter was strengthening it*: Caesar crossed the Rubicon in January 49 BC.

228–61 Moving swiftly, Caesar takes Ariminum; Lucan presents the inhabitants' suppressed terror.

229 *Balearic sling*: the inhabitants of the Balearic islands (modern Majorca and Minorca) were famous for their skill with the sling and fought in Roman and Carthaginian armies.

230 *Parthian's arrow shot over his shoulder*: the Parthians were famed not only for their dexterity with the bow, which included shooting on horseback, but in particular for the notorious 'Parthian shot', the arrow launched while the Parthian was fleeing.

231 *Ariminum*: a city in Umbria on the Adriatic coast about 9 miles south of the Rubicon. From here the *via Flaminia* led to Rome. It was a strategic point for Caesar's operations in Etruria and Picenum.

238 *the impious alarm*: i.e. of civil war.

245 *towering among his troops*: probably on horseback.

253 *Latium*: here used for 'Italy'.

254 *movements of Senones*: the Senonian Gauls crossed the Alps, established themselves on the Adriatic coast, and in 387/ 6 BC captured Rome.

255 *the Libyan war-god*: lit. 'Mars of Libya', meaning Hannibal. Ariminum played an important role in the Second Punic War, remaining loyal to Rome.

260 *mid-sea is mute*: Lucan probably refers to the so-called Halcyon days, calm days in midwinter when the halcyon was believed to nest: Ovid, *Met.* II. 741–8.

261–95 The arrival at Caesar's camp of Curio the former tribune, expelled from Rome by the Senate, strengthens Caesar's resolve.

266 *the turbulent tribunes*: the tribunes of the people Quintus Cassius and Mark Antony, who supported Caesar, were threatened by the consuls Marcellus and Lentulus and forced to flee for their lives.

267 *violating their rights*: the tribunes of the people were sacrosanct, that is, it was an offence to lay hands on them.

276 *I extended your command*: Curio as tribune vetoed proposals to termi-
nate Caesar's command in Gaul.

283 *for twice five years*: Caesar's Gallic command lasted for some ten years.

286 *no long triumphal march*: for Caesar's expectation of a triumph for
his victories in Gaul see *Bell. Gall.* 8. 51. In fact he did not celebrate
such a triumph until 46 BC (Livy, *Per.* 115).

287 *the consecrated laurel crown is not required by the Capitol*: the climax
to the triumphal march was the general's dedication of his laurel
crown and spoils to Jupiter at the temple on the Capitoline.

289, 290 *father-in-law, son-in-law*: through Pompey's marriage to Caesar's
daughter Julia (above, 111).

293 *the Elean race-horse*: Elis was a city-state in the Peloponnese where
the Olympian Games were held. Lucan refers to the chariot-race,
the most prestigious event.

296–351 Caesar addresses his soldiers with a rousing speech appealing
to their shared experience of warfare and speaking scornfully and
savagely of Pompey.

301 *in northern fields*: i.e. in Gaul and Britain.

313 *verbose Marcellus*: Lucan evokes all three Marcelli: Gaius Claudius Marcellus, consul in 50 BC; Gaius Claudius Marcellus, consul in 49 BC;
Marcus Claudius Marcellus, consul in 51 BC. All are recorded as
opposing Caesar.

those empty names, the Catos: the plural is used here as a sign of Caesar's
contempt: the Cato is Marcus Porcius Cato, see Glossary.

316 *his age does not allow it*: though the minimum age in law for celebrating
a triumph was 30, Pompey obtained a triumph over King Hiarbas
of Numidia when he was only 25.

318 *his limitation of grain through all the world*: in 57 BC Pompey was put
in charge of the corn-supply with virtually absolute powers for five
years; some sources suggest that Pompey created a corn-shortage
in order to be given such great powers, e.g. Plutarch, *Pomp.* 49.

319–23 *Who does not know ... Milo the accused?*: at the trial in 52 BC of
Titus Annius Milo, accused of murdering the politician Publius Clo-
dius Pulcher, Pompey stationed soldiers in and around the Forum,

though this was contrary to law, supposedly to prevent disturbances, but obviously as a form of intimidation: thus Cicero did not dare deliver his defence speech. Caesar emphasizes Pompey's lawlessness here.

336 *wandering Cilicians*: Caesar refers disparagingly to Pompey's victory over the pirates, whose base was in Cilicia in Asia Minor.

336–7 *Pontic battles . . . by barbaric poison*: a disparaging reference to Pompey's victory over King Mithridates of Pontus, who is described as 'war-worn' because he had been fighting Rome for some forty years and had already suffered defeats at the hands of Sulla and Lucullus; that the battles are said to be 'with difficulty finished off' is a further sneer at Pompey, unable (Caesar implies) even to finish off a campaign against this war-weary king, except by un-Roman resort to poison.

352–91 The centurion Laelius, evidently fictitious, rallies the wavering troops with a rousing speech.

356–7 *the post of first centurion*: the *primipilus* was the centurion in command of the first cohort and thus the senior centurion of the legion.

358 *oak-leaves*: the civic crown, *corona ciuica*, was awarded to a soldier who had saved the life of a fellow citizen in battle: Gellius 5. 6. 11–15.

370 *subdued with oar the Ocean's swollen waves*: he alludes to Caesar's crossing from Gaul to Britain.

371 *curbed . . . the foaming Rhine*: Caesar built a bridge across the river, *Bell. Gall.* 4. 16–17.

381 *Etruscan Tiber*: the River Tiber rises in Etruria (Tuscany).

392–465 A catalogue of Caesar's troops as he prepares to march on Rome. The catalogue was a *topos* of epic.

396 *Leman*: Lake Geneva.

397 *Vosegus*: a chain of mountains in north-east France, dividing Lorraine from Alsace, the modern Vosges.

398 *Lingones*: a people who lived near modern Langres (north-east France).

399 *Isara*: a river in Gaul (mod. Isère) which flows into the Rhône.

402 *blond Ruteni*: a people in the Rouergue (south-west France).

403 *Atax*: a river (mod. Aude) in Gallia Narbonensis (south France).

404 *Varus, now Hesperia's boundary, the frontier advanced*: the Varus (mod. Var) was another river in Gallia Narbonensis. By Lucan's time, this rather than the Rubicon was considered the boundary of Italy (e.g. Mela 2. 72).

405 *the harbour sacred under the name of Hercules*: the Portus Herculis Monoeci (mod. Monaco).

407 *Corus, Zephyr, Circius*: these wind-names seem problematical: Corus is a north-west wind, Zephyrus the west wind, and Circius a north-west wind, yet the context requires Circius to be anything other than a north-west wind; Lucan should have named the east or south-east winds common in the area. Some suppose Lucan's Circius to be the mistral; most consider him confused here.

409 *the stretch of changing shore*: probably the Belgian coast.

412–16 Because the Mediterranean is virtually tideless, the tides of the Atlantic Ocean provoked much interest and speculation about their cause: cf. Mela 3. 2.

414 *the lesser star*: the moon, hence the mention of 'lunar hours'.

416 *to drink the waves which feed him*: for the idea that the sun was fuelled by the sea cf. 10. 258–9.

420 *the Nemetes*: a German people on the Rhine near Speyer.

the Atyrus: a river (mod. Adour) in south-west France, rising in the Hautes-Pyrénées and flowing through the territory of the Tarbelli (Landes) into the Atlantic.

422 *Santoni*: a people in Saintonge (south-west France), north of the Garonne.

423 *Bituriges*: a people in the region of Avaricum (mod. Bourges).

Suessones: (usually Suessiones) a people of Gallia Belgica (northern France and Belgium) who lived to the west of the Rhine and gave their name to Soissons; they were noted for their tall stature and the length of their weapons.

424 *Leuci*: a people of south-eastern Gallia Belgica on the upper Moselle.

Remi: a people of Gallia Belgica whose chief town is modern Reims in northern France.

425 *Sequani*: a people of Gallia Belgica near Besançon, west of the Jura range.

426 *Belgae*: one of the main peoples of Gaul; their territory was bounded by the Seine, Marne, Rhine, and North Sea.

427 *Arverni*: modern Auvergne. Lucan (and, later, Sidonius Apollinaris) states that the Arverni claimed brotherhood with the Romans; several other sources (e.g. Cicero, *Ad Att.* 1. 19. 2, *Ad Fam.* 7. 10. 4, Caesar, *Bell. Gall.* 1. 33, Tacitus, *Ann.* 11. 25) give the same information about the neighbouring Aedui.

428 *Nervii*: a people of Gallia Belgica, north of Cambrai.

429 *the treachery of Cotta's murder*: Lucius Aurunculeius Cotta, an officer of Caesar in Gaul who was ambushed and killed in the winter of 54/53 BC (see Caesar, *Bell. Gall.* 5. 26–37).

430 *Vangiones*: a people of Germany near modern Worms.

430-1 *your loose-worn breeches, Sarmatians*: a nomad tribe in the Danube region, described by Ovid as wearing flowing trousers, *Trist.* 5. 10. 34.

431 *Batavi*: a German people whose territory lay between the Maas and the mouth of the Rhine (now Holland).

432 *Cirta*: a river in Gaul (mod. Hérault).

433-4 *the Rhône . . . sweeps the Arar to the sea*: the River Arar (mod. Saône), known for its sluggishness (Caesar, *Bell. Gall.* 1. 12), flows into the Rhône at Lyons.

435 *Cebennae*: modern Cévennes, a range of mountains in southern Gaul extending north to Lyons.

441 *Treviri*: a people through whose territory flowed the River Moselle. From the ancient name is derived modern Trier.

442 *Ligures*: a people of the Maritime Alps called *capillati* or *comati* from their long hair.

442–3 *Long-Haired Gaul*: Gallia Comata, the last part of Gaul to be conquered by Rome, as opposed to the other parts where Roman man-
ners, including short hair, had been adopted.

445–6 *Teutates, Esus, Taranis*: probably the names of three Celtic gods.

446 *the slab*: the altar.

Diana of the Scythians: the worship of Diana among the Tauri in
Scythia allegedly involved human sacrifice; cf. 3. 86 n., 6. 74–5 n.

447 *Bards*: poets of Gaul.

450 *Druids*: the high-priests of the Gauls.

457 *in another sphere*: evidently a reference to the Druid belief in the
transmigration and immortality of the soul; see e.g. Caesar, *Bell.
Gall*. 6. 14.

459 *Arctos*: the constellation nearest the Pole Star and so representing
the north.

463 *the curly-haired Cauci*: also called Chauci, a people of northern Germany on the lower Weser; Juvenal 13. 64–5 mentions the curly hair
of Germans.

466–86 *The scene at Rome 1*. False rumours about Caesar terrify the people.

468 *he occupies the nearest towns*: after Ariminum, Caesar took Arretium
(Arezzo), Pisaurum (Pesaro), Fanum (Fano), Iguvium (Gubbio), and
Auximum (Osimo): Caesar, *Bell. Civ*. 1. 11–12.

474 *Mevania*: a town in Umbria (mod. Mevagna) near the River Clitumnus
(Clitunno) famous for its white cattle.

476 *Nar*: a river of central Italy (mod. Nera) between Umbria and Sabine
land which flowed into the Tiber near Ocriculum (Otricoli).

481–2 *the peoples . . . Elbe*: i.e. German, the Elbe being a river in Germany.

486–522 *The scene at Rome 2*. The Senate leads the flight from Rome
in panic.

488 *the Fathers*: the name often given to the senators (Latin *patres*).

489 *the dreaded declaration of war*: Caesar (*Bell. Civ*. 1. 5. 3) calls the declaration of emergency powers against public enemies *Senatus consultum
ultimum*.

493–509 Lucan here adapts the standard description of the captured and sacked city, a *topos* in writers of history and epic, to make an ironic point: Rome is not (yet) sacked. The paradoxical behaviour of the citizens is conveyed especially succinctly in 504, 'flee towards war'.

522–83 Worse to come is predicted by the terrible prodigies and portents recounted by Lucan. To list prodigies was another standard descriptive set-piece used by writers in various genres. Cf. Virgil, *Georg.* 1. 464–88, a passage capped by the prediction of civil war after the assassination of Caesar; Ovid, *Met.* 15. 779–806, influenced by Virgil.

534 *from northern parts*: signifying Caesar's approach from the north.

535 *the head of Latium*: probably meaning Jupiter's temple on the Capitol in Rome.

544 *Mycenae of Thyestes*: the rulers of Mycenae in the Peloponnese, the brothers Atreus and Thyestes, had a terrible feud which culminated in Atreus' killing Thyestes' sons and serving them up to him at a feast: the sun is said to have hidden his face in horror (cf. Ovid, *Pont.* 4. 6. 47–8). The subject was treated in a play by Lucan's uncle Seneca, *Thyestes*.

548 *savage dogs*: see Glossary s.n. Scylla.

549 *From Vesta's altar*: the extinction of the fire on Vesta's altar was regarded as a terrible omen, which symbolized the end of the Roman race; cf. Plutarch, *Numa* 9. 5–6.

550 *the Latin Festival*: a festival in honour of Jupiter, celebrated annually on the Alban Mount, which culminated in a night-time bonfire.

552 *the Theban funeral-pyre*: an allusion to the funeral-pyre of the Theban brothers Eteocles and Polyneices who killed each other fighting for power: their bodies were burnt on the same pyre but the flame split in two, showing that their hostility lasted after death.

552–3 *the earth sank down its pivot*: the earth is thought of as centred around a central axle.

556 *Native Gods*: the Di Indigetes, of whom little is known, probably but not certainly local gods.

564 *Cumae's prophetess*: the Sibyl of Cumae (in the Bay of Naples) who features in Virgil, *Aen.* 6.

566 *Galli*: self-castrated eunuch priests of Cybele.

575–6 *the weapons of fierce Lycurgus*: the mythical King Lycurgus slighted Bacchus and was punished by a madness in which he killed his wife and child and cut off his own leg.

576–7 *on resentful Juno's order caused Alcides to shudder*: on his return from the Underworld Juno sent a madness (here personified as Megaera) upon Hercules, under the influence of which he killed his wife and children, a story told in Greek tragedy by Euripides and by Seneca in his play *Hercules Furens*.

580 *From the Campus the shade of Sulla*: Sulla was buried in the Campus Martius in Rome: Appian, *Bell. Civ.* 1. 106.

582–3 *Marius burst his tomb ... waters of the Anio*: possibly an allusion to Sulla's treatment of Marius' remains: he broke open the grave then threw Marius' body into the River Anio: Cicero, *Leg.* 2. 56, Valerius Maximus 9. 2. 1. The names of both Marius and Sulla bear overtones of civil war.

584–638 Therefore the decision is taken to consult the Etruscan prophet, Arruns, who purifies the city. But the sacrifices go badly and Arruns prophesies doom to come.

585 *prophets from Etruria*: divination was an Etruscan art; cf. Ovid, *Met.* 15. 558–9.

586 *Luca*: a town in Liguria (mod. Lucca).

587–8 For a description of the different types of divination see the entry in the *Oxford Classical Dictionary*, 2nd edn. (1970), 356–7.

590–1 *accursed flames*: kindled by ill-omened types of wood.

591 *progeny of barren womb*: possibly the offspring of a mule or more generally births by parthenogenesis (virgin birth).

593 *chief priests*: the *pontifices* and other priests.

594 *ceremony*: a ceremony of ritual purification (*lustrum*).

595 *Pomerium*: the empty space outside Rome's walls, part of the city's religious boundary.

596 *in Gabine manner*: an ancient way of wearing the toga derived from Gabii, an ancient Latin town of religious importance, cf. Virgil, *Aen.* 7. 612.

598 *Troy's Minerva*: i.e. the Palladium (an image of Pallas Athene = Minerva) brought by Aeneas from Troy and ultimately deposited in the temple of Vesta. Cf. 9. 993.

599 *keepers of . . . mystic verses*: the College of Fifteen Priests (*Quindecimviri*) were the custodians of the Sibylline books which contained oracles in verse.

600 *Cybele . . . bathed in little Almo*: once a year a statue of Cybele was bathed in the Almo, a small river near Rome. The College of Fifteen Priests presided over the cult of Cybele.

602 *the Seven festive at the banquets*: the *Septemviri Epulones*, the priests in charge of the Feast of Jupiter.

the Titian brethren: a college of priests at Rome, traditionally associated with Titus Tatius, king of the Sabines in Romulus' time.

603 *the Salians*: priests of Mars who kept the sacred shields and whose name came from the ritual dances (Latin *salio*, 'I leap') they performed during their procession through Rome.

604 *the Flamens*: fifteen priests dedicated to particular gods and chosen from the noblest families of Rome. They wore a conical cap.

608 *holy places*: a place where lightning had struck was considered sacred and called a *bidental*, so named from the sacrifice of animals (*bidentes*) there.

610 *salted grains*: the ground barley mixed with salt thrown on the victims at sacrifices.

611 *The victim long resisted*: it was considered a sign of the gods' anger (hence 'displeasing') for the victim to struggle.

621 *in its hostile half*: for purposes of divination, the two parts of the liver were labelled for friends and for enemies. The 'hostile half' here is thus associated with Caesar.

625 *the caul betrays its hidden things*: the membrane which normally hides the intestines was open.

628 ·*a second head*: a serious omen portending the increase of Caesar's prosperity at Pompey's expense.

636 *Tages*: an Etruscan said to have sprung from the earth and taught the Etruscans how to foretell the future.

639–72 The Roman philosopher and astrologer Figulus foresees from Mars' prominence and the entire configuration of the sky terrible civil war. Housman points out in his Astronomical Appendix (pp. 325–7) that on virtually every count Lucan's astronomy here is wrong.

639 *Figulus*: Publius Nigidius Figulus, a contemporary of Cicero who was a Pythagorean philosopher and famed astrologer.

640 *Egyptian Memphis*: in Roman times, the Egyptians were especially renowned for their skill in astrology and divination.

653 *rains rivalling Deucalion's*: Deucalion and his wife were the only humans to survive the Flood sent by the gods to punish mankind's wickedness. At Germanicus, *Aratea* 562 Deucalion is used to denote Aquarius, the water-carrier: so it seems that Lucan is making a recherché allusion here.

656 *the fierce Nemean Lion*: the constellation of Leo, identified with the lion in the Nemean forest (in Greece) killed by Hercules.

659 *Gradivus*: one of Mars' titles.

673–95 A Roman matron in a prophetic frenzy foretells the main events of the civil war. This episode is designed to recall, and contrast with, Virgil's description of Amata's feigned Bacchic frenzy at *Aen.* 7. 373–405.

675 *Lyaeus of Ogygia*: Bacchus was called Lyaeus (Greek = 'the loosener', a reference to the effect of wine); Ogygian = Theban, referring to Bacchus' birth from Semele, daughter of Cadmus, king of Thebes.

678 *O Paean*: one of the names of Phoebus Apollo, literally 'healer'.

682 *war without an enemy*: i.e. a foreign enemy.

685 *him*: i.e. Pompey, whose death and decapitation is described in book 8.

686–8 *over seas . . . Emathia's battle-lines*: the battle passed from Thessaly (= Emathia) to North Africa: the mention of the Syrtes and Libya foreshadows Cato's march through the deserts of Libya in book 9. Cato's forces were defeated at the battle of Thapsus in 46 BC.

687 *Enyo*: a goddess of war.

689–90 *over . . . Alps and . . . Pyrenees*: reference to the warfare in Spain between Caesar and Pompey's sons, who were defeated by Caesar at the battle of Munda in 45 BC.

691 *impious war waged in the Senate's midst*: a reference to the assassination of Caesar by Brutus, Cassius, and others outside the Senate-House in 44 BC.

692 *The factions rise again*: in place of Pompey and Caesar, Brutus and Cassius against Antony and Augustus, and subsequently Augustus against Antony.

694 *already have I seen Philippi*: Lucan (here and at 7. 854ff. and 9. 270) along with other authors (Manilius 1. 908–13, Ovid, *Met.* 15. 824, and later Florus 2. 13. 43, Juvenal 8. 242–3) follows Virgil (*Georg.* 1. 489–90) in linking the battles of Pharsalia and Philippi, which were both (at the time when Virgil was writing) in the Roman province of Macedonia. This is no geographical error, but a tribute to Virgil.

BOOK 2

1–15 A wish for ignorance of the future.

16–233 The people's reaction to the portents and prophecies is described. One old man recalls at length the civil wars between Marius and Sulla.

17 *put a dismal end to business*: in times of emergency the Senate declared a cessation of judicial and all public business (*iustitium*). Cf. 5. 32, 116.

19 *purple robe*: one of the marks of high office.

36 *who would bring reproach*: because the mothers' prayers would not be answered and so the gods would be seen to ignore a suppliant's prayer.

46 *Cannae, Trebia*: two famous battles in the Second Punic War in which Hannibal defeated the Romans, at Cannae in Apulia in 216 BC and at Trebia in Cisalpine Gaul in 218 BC.

49–50 *lines of Medes, Achaemenid Susa*: evidently a reference to the Parthians, whose empire had earlier belonged to the Medes, then the Persians. Achaemenes was the founder of the Persian dynasty; Susa was the capital city of the Achaemenids.

50 *the Massagetae*: a people from between the Caspian and Aral Seas.

52 *Suebi*: a people of Germany living east of the Elbe.

54 *Dacian, Getan*: two peoples living on the lower Danube, linked again by Lucan at 3. 95.

55 *the eastern quivers*: Lucan is probably referring to the Parthians, whose characteristic weapon was the bow and arrow.

63 *to stop them both*: i.e. to keep freedom.

69–70 *his Teutonic and his Libyan triumphs*: references to Marius' victories over the Teutones and Ambrones in 102 BC and his defeat of Jugurtha, king of Numidia in North Africa in 105 BC.

70 *hid his head in muddy sedge*: reference to Marius' hiding in the marshes of Minturnae in Latium in 88 BC.

76–83 Lucan has worked into his poem the story told by Plutarch, *Marius* 39.

90 *Jugurtha, whom he had paraded in a triumph*: Jugurtha king of Numidia, after resisting the Romans for a long time, was finally defeated by Marius, who celebrated a triumph over him, in which Jugurtha was exhibited, in 104 BC.

91 *trod on Punic ashes*: when Marius arrived in Africa he landed near Carthage. For the idea of Marius and Carthage offering one another mutual consolation cf. Velleius 2. 19. 4.

93 *Libyan wrath*: probably = 'a wrath like Hannibal's'. Some see the phrase as an allusion to the myth of Antaeus, told in 4. 593–655, a giant of North Africa who gained extra strength from contact with his mother the earth.

94–5 *he set free bands of slaves*: returning from Africa, on his arrival in Etruria in 87 BC Marius proclaimed freedom to the slaves (Appian, *Bell. Civ.* 1. 67).

119 *Baebius*: Marcus Baebius, torn to pieces in 87 BC.

121 *Antonius*: Marcus Antonius, consul 99 BC, a great orator and one of Sulla's supporters, was killed in 87 BC by the tribune Publius Annius, who took the head to Marius at table.

124 *the decapitated Crassi*: Publius Licinius Crassus, a father and son bearing the same name, both opponents of Marius, died in 87 BC, according to some accounts.

Fimbria: Gaius Flavius Fimbria, one of Marius' most violent followers.

125 *the cruel prison oak-post*: probably the oak-post in the prison at Rome to which prisoners were chained.

126 *Scaevola*: Quintus Mucius Scaevola, Pontifex Maximus, killed in 82 BC by the younger Marius when seeking refuge in the temple of Vesta. This incident has been transferred by Lucan from after Sulla's return to Italy to the period before the death of Marius.

130 *the seventh year*: i.e. his seventh consulship in 86 BC, after a gap of thirteen years. He died at the start of his seventh consulship.

134 *Sacriportus*: after the deaths of Marius and his ally Cinna, Sulla returned from Asia and defeated the younger Marius at Sacriportus in Latium in 82 BC with great loss of life.

135 *Colline Gate*: the northern gate of Rome, site of a fierce battle in 82 BC between Sulla and those favouring the Marian cause, mainly the Samnites led by Telesinus and Lamponius, at which thousands of men are said to have fallen.

138 *exceeding the Caudine Forks*: narrow mountain-passes in the mountains near Caudium, a town in Samnium, where a Roman army had been defeated by the Samnites in 321 BC.

151 *brothers fell as brothers' prizes*: a reference to the acquisition by Lucius Domitius Ahenobarbus (a Sullan) of his brother Gnaeus' (a Marian) estates in Apulia. Lucan conceals this adverse comment on Nero's ancestor in a generalization.

163 *the Bistonian tyrant's stables*: Diomedes, king of the Bistonians in Thrace, was said to have fed his mares on the flesh of strangers.

164 *Antaeus' doorposts*: Antaeus the Libyan giant was said to have killed all comers after wrestling with them. Lucan incorporates the fight between Antaeus and Hercules into his epic, 4. 581–660.

165 *in Pisa's palace*: Oenomaus, king of Pisa in Elis, put to death the suitors of his daughter Hippodameia.

173–4 *the ghost of Catulus*: Quintus Lutatius Catulus, formerly an ally of Marius, became an opponent and committed suicide in 87 BC on being prosecuted by Marius' nephew Marcus Marius Gratidianus.

174 *as victim Marius*: a reference to the savage death of Marcus Marius Gratidianus, adopted into the Marian family (described by Livy, *Per.* 88, Florus 2. 9. 26), evidently in revenge for the death of Catulus. Catiline is said to have presided over this episode.

193 *Praeneste's Fortune*: Praeneste (mod. Palestrina) is a town about 23 miles south-east of Rome, where there was a famous temple of Fortune. Because it was loyal to Marius, Sulla ordered the town to be besieged; it was sacked and many inhabitants killed in 82 BC.

197 *Rome's Sheepfold*: an enclosed place (also called Saepta) in the Campus Martius where polling took place, the scene of Sulla's massacre of all the Samnite prisoners immediately after the battle of the Colline Gate (see 2. 135). Lucan identifies the prisoners not as Samnites but as soldiers of Marius, which renders Sulla's action even more horrific.

222 *Fortunate*: Sulla added the title Fortunate (*Felix*) to his name in 82 BC, believing himself the special favourite of Venus.

tomb: on Sulla's tomb see above, 1. 580 n.

234–325 Lucan introduces two of the Republican protagonists, Brutus (who is not developed in the poem as it survives) and Cato (who takes on the role of leader after Pompey's death in book 8: book 9 is devoted to him). Brutus visits Cato at night and they converse.

237 *Parrhasian Helice*: the constellation of the Great Bear, also called Helice from the Greek word meaning 'to turn' because it turns around the Pole. See Ovid, *Fast.* 2. 153–92, *Met.* 2. 405–507. It is called Parrhasian from the legend of its origin: the girl Callisto was loved

by Jupiter and turned into a bear. The legend was set in Arcadia;
Parrhasian = Arcadian, Parrhasia being a region in Arcadia.

238 *his kinsman Cato*: Brutus' mother was Cato's step-sister. Later, in 45
BC, Brutus married Cato's daughter Porcia.

278 *an unofficial leader*: Pompey held no magistracy at this time.

326–91 Marcia, who had been Cato's wife, comes straight from her second
husband Hortensius' funeral to ask Cato to renew their marriage-
bond. Impressed by her loyalty, Cato agrees and they do so in Brutus'
presence with the simplest of ceremonies. The episode reveals Cato's
austerity.

327–8 *hallowed Marcia*: daughter of Lucius Marcius Philippus she was Cato's
wife and bore him three children. Cato then passed her to Hortensius
and after his death received her back again. See Plutarch, *Cato the
Younger* 25. 4–5, 52. 3.

328 *Hortensius*: Quintus Hortensius Hortalus, consul 69 BC, a famous
Roman orator and rival of Cicero. He died in 50 BC.

355 *white woollen band*: white wool bands, or 'fillets', were hung on the
doorposts of the bridegroom's house.

356 *customary torches*: carried in procession as the bride went to the groom's
house.

   couch: the wedding-couch or marriage-bed, usually in the *atrium*.

358 *the matron*: the matron of honour.

   towered crown: a symbol of Cybele, worn by the bride.

359 *preventing her . . . lifted over*: the bride was lifted over the threshold
by the bridegroom.

360–4 Lucan describes the bride's apparel: flame-coloured veil, long white
robe with belt around the waist, necklace, and covering of the upper
arms.

367 *The purple*: the purple colour in the costume of the *matrona*.

368 *The usual jokes*: ribald songs called Fescennine verses sung outside
the marriage-chamber (cf. Catullus 61. 122).

369 *in Sabine fashion*: this custom was said to originate with the Sabines.

371 *witness*: a functionary at a wedding, originally an augur who took the omens.

380–1 *This was the character ... of austere Cato*: Cato was a strict Stoic; descriptions of his character can be paralleled in Stoic texts (such as Seneca's *Letters*).

386 *in the manner of the Roman citizen of old*: Cato adopted the earlier custom of wearing the toga without a tunic or undergarment.

387 *Venus*: = sexual intercourse.

392–438 Pompey withdraws to Campania, the coastal area including the Bay of Naples, to make Capua the base of his operations throughout Italy. This gives Lucan the opportunity to describe the Apennine mountains running up the middle of Italy and the rivers that flow from them.

393 *the Campanian walls of the Dardanian settler*: i.e. Capua, capital of Campania, said to have been founded by Capys, one of the Trojans who accompanied Aeneas from Troy: see Virgil, *Aen.* 10. 145.

399 *the Lower and Upper Seas*: the Lower Sea is the Tyrrhenian and the Upper Sea the Adriatic.

405 *On to the left flank*: i.e. falling into the Adriatic.

408 *Eridanus*: the Po (see Glossary).

411 *the story says*: Lucan refers to the story of Phaethon son of Helios/ Phoebus = the Sun, who drove his father's chariot too close to the earth and set fire to it. He was struck by Jupiter's thunderbolt by way of punishment and fell into the Eridanus (the Po), where his sisters as they mourned him were changed into poplar-trees dripping tears of amber. See Ovid, *Met.* 2. 1–366.

421 *the mountain's right-hand slopes*: now comes a list of rivers which flow into the Tyrrhenian Sea.

430 *Umbrians, Marsians, Sabine*: the Umbri, Marsi, and Sabini were three peoples of central Italy to the north, east, and north-east of Rome respectively.

434 *Lacinium's temple*: Lacinium (mod. Capo di Colonne) is a promontory in southern Italy near Croton where there was a temple of Juno.

438 *Sicilian Pelorus*: a promontory in north-eastern Sicily (mod. Punta di Faro).

439–77 Caesar progresses through northern Italy with success after success as Pompey's generals are routed.

439–40 *only by shedding blood*: apparently Caesar met little resistance; Lucan adapts this to his characterization of Caesar.

456 *earth again struck open*: for an earlier storm launched by Aeolus see the opening episode of Virgil's *Aeneid*, 1. 50–156.

462 *frightened Libo's flight*: Scribonius Libo, father-in-law of Pompey's son Sextus. One of Pompey's generals in Tuscany, he abandoned his post at Caesar's approach to join the consuls in Campania.

463 *Thermus' rout*: the praetor Quintus Minucius Thermus, commander of the garrison at Iguvium, a town in Umbria, was forced to withdraw because the inhabitants' allegiance shifted to Caesar.

464 *Sulla*: Faustus Cornelius Sulla, son of Sulla the dictator, son-in-law of Pompey. He crossed over to Greece on Caesar's approach.

469 *Lentulus expelled*: Publius Cornelius Lentulus Spinther, a former consul, fled before Caesar's advance from Asculum, a town in Picenum.

474 *a most stalwart company*: the reference is to a legion lent by Pompey to Caesar in Gaul in 53 BC to make up for losses in Gallic campaigns; the legion was recalled to Italy in 50 BC to face a possible Parthian war (Caesar, *Bell. Gall*. 6. 1).

478–525 Domitius at Corfinium. Pompey's general Domitius Ahenobarbus (an ancestor of the emperor Nero), stationed in Corfinium in Samnium (modern Popolo), attempts to impede Caesar's progress by breaking the bridge. But he is unsuccessful and as Caesar prepares to besiege the town the gates open and Domitius is surrendered to Caesar by the people. Caesar spares him, though Domitius would rather die. For Caesar's account see *Bell. Civ*. 1. 16–23.

478 *Domitius*: Lucius Domitius Ahenobarbus, an ally of Cato and later of Pompey; his death is described in 7. 597–616.

480 *the recruits . . . dark-clothed Milo*: the troops who had been stationed around the Forum at Milo's trial, cf. 1. 323. Milo is described as 'dark-clothed' (*pullato*, accepting the emendation of *polluto*, 'polluted')

because of his appearance in court wearing the dark clothes of mourners to gain sympathy.

505–6 *towers which will move their mighty stones*: i.e. movable towers, also used by Caesar at 3. 455–8.

506 *the siege-shed*: also called 'penthouse' or 'mantelet'—a shed under which besieging soldiers could protect themselves from missiles thrown by the besieged as they worked under the walls. See Vegetius, *De re militari* 4. 15.

507–8 *the troops dragged out their general, a captive*: according to Caesar (*Bell. Civ.* 1. 19–20) Domitius' troops mutinied on learning of Domitius' plan to flee from Corfinium.

526–95 Pompey's speech to his troops. This is a complacent and boastful speech in which Pompey reviews his past achievements and minimizes the importance of Caesar's invasion of Italy. Pompey's reliance on the past only serves to reveal his present weakness. Moreover, Lucan deliberately introduces some unconvincing points into his speech (e.g. 561 below) as part of his characterization of Pompey.

542 *Lentulus*: Publius Cornelius Lentulus Sura, a fellow conspirator with Catiline, had lost his seat in the Senate.

543 *Cethegus*: see Glossary.

545 *Metelli*: the name evokes Lucius Caecilius Metellus, who as consul successfully opposed the Carthaginians in the First Punic War and when high priest rescued the Palladium, a sacred image of Pallas, from a fire in the temple of Vesta in 241 BC; Quintus Caecilius Metellus Macedonicus, consul in 143 BC and censor in 131 BC, subduer of the Celtiberians and opponent of the Gracchi; and his four sons, all of whom reached the consulship.

547 *Lepidus by Catulus was brought low*: Marcus Aemilius Lepidus, a former follower of Sulla, was an eminent figure, consul in 78 BC, who was in 77 BC declared an enemy by the Senate. He then marched on Rome and was defeated just outside the city by Quintus Lutatius Catulus, his colleague as consul, and Pompey.

Carbo: Gnaeus Papirius Carbo was one of the leaders of the Marian faction. During the wars with Sulla he was defeated and fled from Italy; he was put to death on Sicily by Pompey in 81 BC.

548 *Axes*: symbol of the Republic's might, used to behead prisoners, cf. 7. 64n.

554 *the enemy who felled Spartacus*: i.e. Crassus. Spartacus was a Thracian captive who escaped from a gladiatorial training-barracks and led an army of slaves which defeated several Roman armies. Crassus as praetor defeated and killed him in 71 BC.

561 In any case, Pompey was only six years older than Caesar (cf. 1. 129–30 above); moreover, a small troop of veterans was valued over a larger number of raw recruits.

570 *he fled from the chill waters of the Rhine*: Caesar's retreat from Germany into Gaul, Caesar, *Bell. Gall.* 4. 19.

578 *the pirates*: Pompey in 67 BC overcame the pirates in three months and settled them on plots of land in Cilicia (cf. 1. 346).

581 *the king*: Mithridates VI, king of Pontus, whom Sulla brought to terms but was unable to eradicate. He was defeated by Pompey in the Third Mithridatic War and finally committed suicide in the Crimea in 63 BC.

588 *Baetis*: a river in the south of Spain (mod. Guadalquivir), which falls into the Atlantic north of Gades (mod. Cádiz). This is evidently a reference to Pompey's campaigns against Sertorius.

590 *Arab*: a reference to Pompey's campaigns in Syria and Palestine.

591 *Colchians . . . fleece*: an allusion to the story of the Golden Fleece stolen from Colchis by Jason and the Argonauts.

592 *Cappadocians*: Pompey restored Ariobarzanes I, king of Cappadocia, to his kingdom in 63 BC.

592–4 These names all refer to Pompey's eastern campaigns and his subsequent 'settlement of the east', his reorganization of the eastern part of the Roman empire into annexed provinces and client states.

593 *Sophene*: an area on the left bank of the upper Euphrates.

596–627 Pompey's speech fails to inspire his men to fight. Because of their silent and unenthusiastic response he retreats to Brundisium, which Lucan then describes.

609 *Brundisium*: modern Brindisi, a town in Calabria on the Adriatic coast on the heel of Italy.

611–12 *fugitives ... defeat*: legend said that Brundisium was founded by Cretans who fled with the Athenian Theseus, who failed to use the white sails which would have indicated his success to his waiting father but instead used the black sails which indicated failure. Cf. Catullus 64. 212–48.

624 *Illyrian Epidamnus*: the old name for a Greek city in Illyria on the Adriatic normally called Dyrrachium in Roman times, cf. 6. 14 (mod. Durrës). It was the usual landing place for those crossing from Brundisium, being the start of the Via Egnatia.

628–49 Pompey sends his son Gnaeus Pompeius to Asia to request the assistance of his allies, the eastern kings.

633 *Euphrates and Nile*: i.e. go to summon help from the kings of Parthia and Egypt.

636 *Pharian kings*: Cleopatra and Ptolemy.

637 *my Tigranes*: Tigranes I, king of Armenia, re-established on his throne by Pompey.

Pharnaces: Pharnaces II, son of Mithridates VI, was given the Bosporan kingdom in the Black Sea by Pompey.

638 *both Armenias*: Armenia Maior, the whole plateau to the east of the Euphrates and Armenia Minor, a small kingdom to the west of it.

640 *the marsh of Maeotis*: the sea of Azov, when frozen, was said to be crossed by Scythian nomads on wagons.

645 *who mark the Latian calendar with your names*: i.e. the consuls, whose names were used to identify the year in the list or calendar. In this case, Lucius Cornelius Lentulus Sura and Gaius Claudius Marcellus, 49 BC.

650–79 Caesar pursues Pompey to Brundisium and tries to cut off Pompey's access to the sea.

666 *lofty Eryx*: a high mountain in Sicily.

667 *Gaurus*: mountains in Campania, near the foot of which lay Lake Avernus.

670–1 Caesar's activities here are described in *Bell. Civ.* 1. 25: briefly, he made wooden rafts, which he secured with anchors at the four corners and then fortified with parapets and towers.

673 *the arrogant Persian*: Xerxes, king of Persia 486–465 BC, when invading Europe built a bridge of ships across the Hellespont from Abydos on the Asiatic side to Sestos on the European side, about one mile in width.

677 *Mount Athos*: a mountain projecting from Chalcidice in Macedonia. Through its isthmus Xerxes ordered a canal to be cut for his ships: remains of the canal can still be seen.

680–703 With difficulty Pompey leaves Italy.

683–7 For Caesar's account of Pompey's activities see *Bell. Civ.* 1. 26: Pompey armed large merchant-ships and used them to ram Caesar's works; fighting occurred almost every day.

686 *ballista*: a military machine for shooting stones, not actually using the same mechanism as a catapult: described by Vitruvius 10. 11.

691–2 *Virgo . . . Phoebus*: apparently a date in the autumn and just before dawn; other sources place this in the spring and during the night. The Claws are those of Scorpio, which extended into the sign Libra and hence designate Libra here.

693–703 For Caesar's account see *Bell. Civ.* 1. 27–8.

704–36 Caesar enters Brundisium which welcomes him; Pompey's fleet loses two ships as he escapes safely.

710 *the Euboean wave which batters Chalcis*: Lucan compares the narrow passage out of the harbour with the Euripus or Straits of Euboea separating Chalcis, a city on the island of Euboea, from Attica.

715 *the Pagasaean ship*: the Argo, built at Pagasae in Thessaly.

716 *Cyanean Rocks*: when the Argo passed between the Clashing Rocks, Symplegades, or Cyanean Islands, at the very mouth of the Black Sea, the rocks closed and struck off the stern of the Argo.

718–19 *Symplegas . . . for ever fixed*: if any ship passed safely through the Clashing Rocks it was fated that the rocks would never again move.

BOOK 3

1–35 As Pompey is crossing to Epirus, the ghost of Julia appears to him in a dream. This dream, at the moment when Pompey is leaving his country for ever, balances the vision at the moment of Caesar's entry into Italy at 1. 185–203.

11 *like a Fury*: because she is to haunt him throughout the civil war, she says (below, 30–4).

16 *the ferryman of scorched Acheron*: Charon, who ferries the souls of the dead across Acheron and other rivers of the Underworld. Acheron's epithet 'scorched' is borrowed from another river of the Underworld, 'Phlegethon', lit. 'Fiery'.

18–19 *all three Sisters . . . the Parcae*: i.e. the Fates. Normally Atropos breaks the threads, while Clotho and Lachesis spin and measure; here Lucan has the latter two abandon their regular tasks to assist Atropos, thus indicating the massive scale of slaughter in the civil war.

22–3 *to drag her mighty husbands down always to disaster*: Cornelia's first husband Publius Licinius Crassus died with his father at the battle of Carrhae in 53 BC.

23 *into a warm tomb*: the usual period of mourning for a spouse was ten months (see Ovid, *Fast.* 1. 36); however, Julia's complaint is unfounded, for it was two years after her death that Pompey remarried.

33–4 *civil war will make you mine*: i.e. you will die.

35–45 Pompey arrives in Epirus, more determined on war despite the omens of disaster.

36 *He*: Pompey.

39–40 i.e. if there is no consciousness after death, this ghost is a delusion which should not alarm me; if there is awareness after death, then death is nothing terrible. For these ideas cf. Plato, *Apology* 40 C.

46–70 Caesar makes sure of Italy's loyalty by securing the corn-supply: he sends Curio to Sicily to bring corn.

60–1 Cf. 2. 435–8, where Lucan says that Sicily was once linked to Italy.

65 Sicily and Sardinia were two of Rome's great sources of corn.

71–112 Caesar marches to Rome and is received in fear by everyone including the senators.

75–6 *scenes of war ... paraded ahead of him*: in the triumphal procession the victorious general was preceded by his captives and spoils and placards portraying the lands, cities, and rivers captured.

84 *the sheer citadels of Anxur*: a town (later called Tarracina) in Latium on the Appian Way 65 miles south-east of Rome.

85 *Pomptine marshes*: the area to the south-east of Rome crossed by the Appian Way.

86 *the lofty grove ... Scythian Diana's realm*: the town of Aricia below the Alban Mount on the Appian Way about 16 miles from Rome. Nearby was a grove and temple of Diana; the priest was by custom a runaway slave who took this position by killing his predecessor. Lucan likens this cult of Diana to that of Scythian Diana among the Tauri (in the Crimea), described in Ovid, *Pont.* 3. 2.

87 *Latian Rods*: an allusion to the Latin Festival celebrated by the Roman consuls, here referred to by their rods of office, on the Alban Mount, cf. 1. 550 n., 5. 402 n.

96 *your leader*: Pompey.

101 *they equate his wishes with his power*: lit. 'they think he wants to do whatever he is able to do', i.e. they presume the worst.

103 *The Palatine halls of Phoebus*: Caesar calls a meeting of the Senate not in the Senate-house but in the Temple of Apollo on the Palatine hill.

105 *the sacred chairs*: the chairs of office, properly called curule chairs (cf. 107), occupied by the consuls and praetors, who had sided with Pompey.

111–12 *his sense of shame exceeded Rome's self-degradation*: lit. 'that he blushed to command more things than Rome blushed to submit to'.

112–68 Metellus the tribune resists Caesar's soldiers who are robbing the Treasury. His fierce words incite Caesar's threats. Metellus is then urged by Cotta to give way and the Treasury is ransacked.

114 *aggressive Metellus*: Lucius Caecilius Metellus, one of the tribunes and a supporter of Pompey; for his ancestry cf. 2. 545n.

115 *Saturn's temple*: the location of the public treasury of Rome, at the foot of the Capitoline hill.

125 *sacred blood*: because Tribunes were sacrosanct, cf. 1. 267.

126–7 *the tribune's curses followed Crassus*: Gaius Ateius Capito as tribune in 55 BC opposed Crassus' expedition against the Parthians and pronounced curses on him as he was leaving Rome (Plutarch, *Crassus* 16). The defeat and death of Crassus were regarded by many as the result of his disregarding Capito's warnings.

132–3 i.e. Caesar can get resources from his war in Gaul and has no need to rob the treasury of Rome, which now enjoys a kind of 'peace', being free from foreign wars. Lucan here contrives a pointed contrast between war and peace.

143 *Cotta*: an unidentified Aurelius Cotta, tribune in 49 BC, or possibly Lucius Aurelius Cotta, consul in 65 BC.

146 *perishes by freedom*: i.e. by asserting freedom, e.g. in speaking too freely to the tyrant.

147 *if willingly you do whatever ordered*: for the thought cf. 4. 487.

157–8 *wealth from Punic Wars*: after the First Punic War the Carthaginians paid Rome 1,200 talents, after the Second 10,000 talents.

158 *from Perseus*: the last King of Macedonia, conquered in 168 BC. A huge booty was paid into the Roman treasury.

Philip: Philip V, King of Macedon, father of Perseus, conquered by the Romans in 197 BC; again, a large indemnity (1,000 talents) was exacted.

159 *the Gaul*: Brennus, the leader of the Gauls who captured Rome in 387/6 BC; after receiving a large ransom of gold, the Gauls fled and Camillus recovered the gold for Rome.

160 *Fabricius*: Pyrrhus, king of Epirus, tried in vain to bribe Gaius Fabricius Luscinus in the early third century BC.

162 *Asia's wealthy peoples*: probably a reference to treasures from Antiochus XIII, king of Syria, and Attalus III, king of Pergamum, which passed to Rome in 64 BC and 133 BC respectively.

163 *Minoan Crete . . . Metellus*: Crete, in the mythological past the kingdom of Minos, was subdued by Quintus Caecilius Metellus Creticus in 68/7 BC.

164 *Cato . . . Cyprus*: Cyprus became a Roman province in 58 BC: from here Marcus Porcius Cato brought back some 7,000 talents.

166 *carried before Pompey in his triumphs*: Pompey's triumphs over Mithridates VI, king of Pontus, Tigranes II, king of Armenia, and Aristobulus, king of Judaea. See 1. 121–2 n., 6. 817–18 n.

168 *then for the first time Rome was poorer than a Caesar*: subsequently it often happened that the State was poorer than the Emperor (Caesar).

169–297 A catalogue of Pompey's forces, gathered from the east, i.e. Greece and Asia. The catalogue was a standard feature of epic poems.

171–3 First, troops from Phocis (for which Lucan erroneously writes Phocaea; cf. the reverse error at 3. 340, 5. 53), an area in central Greece around Delphi. Amphissa and Cirrha are both towns in the area and Parnassus the mountain above Delphi.

174–5 Troops from Boeotia in central Greece: the Cephisus is an important river and 'Cadmean' Dirce a spring near Thebes, the city founded by Cadmus.

176–7 Troops from Elis (see 1. 293 n.); the waters of the River Alpheus supposedly passed under the sea to rise in Sicily (cf. Virgil, *Ecl.* 10. 4–5).

177–8 Arcadian troops: Maenalus is a mountain in Arcadia in the Peloponnese.

178 Thessalian troops: Trachis was a town and Oeta a mountain in southern Thessaly, where the dying Hercules climbed on to his own funeral pyre.

179 *Thesprotians*: from Epirus.

179 *Dryopes*: a people of Thessaly.

179–80 *Selloi . . . Chaonian hill*: from Chaonia in Epirus near Dodona, where the oak-tree oracle of Jupiter was destroyed in 219 BC.

182 *Phoebus' dockyards*: probably a reference to the town of Apollonia in Epirus (Phoebus = Apollo).

183 *Salamis*: a reference to Athens' part in the victory over the Persians at the battle of Salamis in 480 BC off the island of Salamis in the Saronic Gulf, when Athens was a great naval power.

184 *dear to Jupiter*: because he was born there.

185–6 Cnossos and Gortyn were two of the hundred cities of Crete, whose inhabitants were famed for their skill in archery. The 'eastern arrows' are those of the Parthians.

187 *Dardanian Oricos*: a Greek town on the coast of Epirus, founded by the Trojan Helenus, a son of Priam.

188 *Athamanians*: people living on the mountains of Epirus.

Enchelians: inhabitants of Epirus, where Cadmus retired and was changed into a snake; *enchelus* is the Greek word for an eel. Cf. Ovid, *Met*. 4. 563–603 for Cadmus' metamorphosis.

190 *Apsyrtos*: an island in the Adriatic Sea off the coast of Illyria where the Colchian princess Medea was said to have killed her brother Apsyrtus.

191–2 i.e. Thessalians: Peneus was a river and·Iolcos a port, from which the Argonauts sailed for Colchis, supposedly the first sea voyage by man.

200–2 *Cone . . . Peuce*: an island at the mouth of the Danube; Peuce was a large island some distance from the mouth—see Strabo 7. 3. 15, p. 305.

203–13 Asia Minor. Mysia was a region of Asia Minor, in which was Troy, Mount Ida, and the River Caicus; Arisbe was a small town in the Troad, Pitane a sea-port of Mysia, Celaenae a city of southern Phrygia, at the sources of the rivers Marsyas and Maeander. The story referred to is Pallas' invention of the flute: when she threw it away, the satyr Marsyas of Celaenae picked it up, challenged Apollo, and was beaten and flayed by the god (Ovid, *Fast*. 6. 693–710, *Met*.

6. 400). The Pactolus and Hermus are rivers of Lydia said to have sands of gold.

211–13 By the Trojans' 'usual bad omens' Lucan means being always defeated in war. Caesar boasted descent from Iulus = Ascanius, son of Aeneas.

214–17 Syria: Orontes, the River Asi; Ninos, i.e. Nineveh, the famous city whose site in Lucan's day was in Parthia (it is possible that Lucan has confused it with the city Ninus in Commagene); Damascus, a city on a plain and therefore exposed to winds; Gaza, a city on the sea-coast of Palestine, Idume, an area west and south of the Dead Sea; Tyre, a city on Syria's coast, either 'unstable' from earthquakes (Seneca, *Nat. Qu.* 6. 1. 13) or 'fickle' as at Virgil, *Aen.* 1. 661; Sidon is near Tyre: both produced valuable purple dye from shellfish.

218–19 The Phoenicians from Tyre and Sidon (= Phoenicia), who were the great sailors of the ancient world, used the Little Bear (Cynosura) for navigation while the Greeks used the Great Bear (Ovid, *Fast.* 3. 107–8).

220–4 Lucan (wrongly) means that the Phoenicians invented the alphabet, before Egypt (represented by Memphis, mod. Cairo) had invented papyrus for writing on, made by interweaving papyrus reeds, and while it was still using hieroglyphics carved on stone.

225 *Tarsus*: a city of Cilicia founded by Perseus.

226–8 Places in Cilicia: Corycus was a city, famous for its cave; Mallus and Aegae were ports; the Cilician pirates settled by Pompey after his conquest of them became his allies.

233 *the Pellaean commander*: Alexander (see Pella in Glossary), who stopped in his conquest of the world at the Eastern Ocean.

237 A reference to sugar-cane; cf. *Periplus of the Red Sea* 14 for the import of sugar-cane from India.

240–1 The Brahmin ceremony of self-immolation, burning alive.

244–5 Troops from Asia Minor; Amanus is a mountain in Cilicia; the Niphates a mountain chain in Armenia from which the Tigris flows.

246 *Choatrae*: a people of Scythia.

247–8 i.e. by Arabs Lucan apparently means people from south of the equator: cf. Pliny, *Nat. Hist.* 6. 87 about the Ceylonese ambassadors' surprise at the direction of shadows.

249 *Orestae*: a people of Illyria. As this seems not to deserve the adjective 'furthest', the text may well be wrong here; Shackleton Bailey may be correct to emend with Scaliger to *Oretae*.

250 *Carmanian leaders*: Carmania was a country to the north of the Persian Gulf at its eastern end.

250–2 In contrast with us, for whom the Bear does not set at all and Bootes sets slowly.

253–5 Lucan says that the only part of the zodiac which passes perpendicularly over Ethiopia is the projecting hoof of Taurus. This implies that Ethiopia lies further south than any other part of the zodiac, which (as Housman explains, pp. 327–9) is a mistake arising from a misconception about the location and orientation of the zodiac.

260 i.e. Euphrates resembles the Nile in fertilizing the land with its flood-waters.

261–3 The Tigris was thought to disappear into the earth and reappear, cf. 8. 438–9, Seneca, *Nat. Qu.* 3. 26. 4, 6. 8. 2, *Med.* 723.

266 *content . . . two*: i.e. by killing Crassus, the third rival for power.

267 *Bactros*: a river of Bactriana (Central Asia).

270 *Moschi*: a people of Scythia.

272 *Halys . . . Croesus*: a river, the boundary of Lydia and Media. The oracle given to Croesus, king of Lydia, said that if he crossed the river he would destroy a great empire; this proved to be his own, not the enemy's. See Herodotus 1. 53.

277–9 i.e. the Black Sea, by pouring into the Mediterranean a large body of water, deprives the Pillars of Hercules (= Gibraltar) of the boast of being the only place where Ocean enters the Mediterranean. The Sea of Azov (= Maeotis) was supposed to have an outlet to the Arctic Ocean.

280–3 Scythian peoples: Essedonians from near the Sea of Azov; Arimaspi rich in gold; Arii, a people of Persia; Massagetae, who opened veins in their horses when hungry to suck the blood; Geloni east of the Tanais.

284 *Memnonian:* = 'eastern', because Memnon was son of Aurora, the dawn.

285–6 *his soldiery counted by thrown weapons:* a story about Xerxes depicts him as able to count the number of troops in his army only by ordering them to throw their weapons and then counting these weapons.

286 *the avenger:* Agamemnon, who raised an enormous fleet to recover his brother Menelaus' wife from Troy.

292–5 North Africa. Jupiter was worshipped in the form of a ram at Ammon in Libya; the Marmaridae lived between Cyrenaica and Egypt.

298–355 Caesar marches to Massilia, which refuses to admit his army.

301 *Phocaean warriors:* Massilia was founded by Greeks who emigrated from Phocaea in Asia Minor.

306 *Minerva's bough:* the olive branch, sacred to Minerva, goddess of Athens, and a symbol of peace.

314–15 i.e. let no external race embroil itself in this your civil war.

328 *The end of crime:* the crime = civil war. It will be the end of civil war if fighting is entrusted to none but citizens, as opposed to non-Romans; for the citizens' shared blood will forbid them to fight.

330–2 Cf. Valerius Maximus 2. 6. 9 for Massilia's rule that no one should enter the town armed.

340 *Phocis:* Phocis is here put erroneously for Phocaea, cf. 5. 53 n.

350 *Saguntum:* a city near the Mediterranean coast of Spain, besieged for eight months by Hannibal in 219 BC; this siege was regarded as the immediate cause of the Second Punic War.

355–98 Caesar angrily declares that he will besiege Massilia, and commences his works.

389 *not compelled:* i.e. by Pompey.

399–452 Caesar cuts down the sacred grove, striking the first blow of the axe himself. Lucan incorporates into this passage an epic set piece expected of him, namely the felling of trees, ll. 440–5. Typically he alters the usual context from seeking wood for a funeral pyre to seeking wood for siege-works, with a hint of Caesar's vindictive megalomania. For the tree-felling *topos* see Homer, *Il.* 23. 108–26, Ennius, *Ann.* 175–9 Skutsch, Virgil, *Aen.* 6. 176–82, 11. 133–8.

402–3 *Pans, Silvani, Nymphs*: all deities who inhabit the countryside.

423 *Phoebus is in mid-sky*: the priest fears to enter the grove at any time of the day (including noon) or night.

441 *Dodona's wood*: i.e. the oak, cf. 6. 427n.

442 *cypress*: often used in Roman funerals.

448–9 *Often their good fortune . . . the unlucky*: i.e. Lucan suggests that the jubilation of the blockaded soldiers is unfounded, because the guilty (Caesar) is protected by his good fortune.

453–96 Caesar leaves for Spain, giving orders that the siege of Massilia is to continue. Caesar's army unsuccessfully attempts to take the city.

455 *ordering continuation*: Caesar's legate Gaius Trebonius was put in charge of the siege of Massilia.

458 *with unseen cause*: they were on rollers.

459–61 i.e. seeing the tall structure wobble, the Massilians thought that the earth itself was shaking.

475 *tortoise*: a military formation in which a group of men advanced, protected by their overlapping shields held above their heads.

497–508 The Massilians take the offensive and destroy the ramp.

499–500 *boldly broke out*: according to Caesar, this sortie took place while the Massilians had been granted a truce: *Bell. Civ.* 2. 13–14.

509–762 The Romans now attack Massilia from the sea, reinforced by the arrival of the fleet of Caesar's admiral, Decimus Brutus. A sea battle follows, in which Brutus and the Romans are victorious. Naval battles do not feature prominently in surviving Latin epic, although

Ennius included one in his *Annales* (book 14) and Virgil adapted this in the games of *Aen.* 5, which include a ship race.

516 *Stoechades*: islands in the Mediterranean just east of Massilia, mod. Îles d'Hyères.

518 i.e. the men too old for military service and the boys too young: 'lads' translates *ephebi*, denoting boys of 16–20 years, a Greek word, appropriately, for the young men of a Greek colony here.

530 *triremes*: light ships with three rows of oars, used for warfare.

530–1 i.e. quadriremes, ships with four rows of oars.

531–2 i.e. quinquiremes, ships with five rows of oars.

533 *Liburnian galleys*: small, light, fast warships.

535 *the praetorian ship of Brutus*: the admiral's flagship.

542 *sweep the blue*: an epic phrase, occurring in Catullus 64. 7, Virgil, *Aen.* 3. 208; for similar phrases see Ennius, *Ann.* 377 Skutsch, Virgil, *Aen.* 5. 778.

600 i.e. to take Telo's place at the helm.

609–33 Such an incident is told of one of Caesar's soldiers in Suetonius, *Jul.* 68. 4.

619–20 A reversal of what might be expected normally.

682–3 *kept alive in covered sulphur*: the flame concealed the thin coat of sulphur with which the torches were smeared. On the compressed expression here see D. R. Shackleton Bailey, 'Lucan revisited', *PCPhS*, NS 33 (1987), 79.

696 *Phoceus*: a young man of Massilia, evidently invented by Lucan; his name recalls Phocis/ Phocaea cf. 3. 340n., 5. 53n.

710 *Balearic thong*: i.e. sling, cf. 1. 229.

747 *you can still outlive me*: the Romans had a horror of children dying before their parents, cf. Cicero, *Nat. Deor.* 2. 72.

753–6 According to Caesar, *Bell. Civ.* 2. 7 five Massilian ships were sunk and four captured.

BOOK 4

1–47 The war in Spain: Caesar fights Pompey's generals Afranius and Petreius near Ilerda, without success. Lucan's account is a compressed version of Caesar's (*Bell. Civ.* 1. 37–55 and 59–87); Lucan is not interested in precise details of military manœuvres.

4 *Afranius and Petreius*: Lucius Afranius, partisan of Pompey who served under him against Sertorius in Spain and in the Mithridatic War; Marcus Petreius too had considerable military experience. Together they conducted the war in Spain for Pompey.

8 *energetic Asturians*: from the region now called Asturias in Spain.

9 *light-armed Vettones*: a people of Lusitania (now Portugal).

9–10 *Celts . . . Iberians*: i.e. the Celtiberians, inhabiting the Aragon area. See also on Pompey's troops Caesar, *Bell. Civ.* 1. 39.

12 *Ilerda*: a city (mod. Lérida) in Hispania Tarraconensis on a hill over the river Sicoris (mod. Segre).

20 *Cinga*: a river in Hispania Tarraconensis, the modern Cinca, which flows from the Pyrenees into the Ebro.

28–31 On Caesar's night-time manœuvres to advance his camp secretly cf. *Bell. Civ.* 1. 41–2.

36 *This side*: i.e. Caesar's.

37 *that side*: i.e. Pompey's.

45 Lucan has apparently conflated the relief of the soldiers attacking the mound with the relief by the cavalry of the ninth legion's attack on Ilerda, described by Caesar at *Bell. Civ.* 1. 45–6.

48–120 Caesar's camp is flooded by the spring rains and famine ensues. Lucan's description of the flood is influenced by Ovid's deluge (*Met.* 1. 262–347) and by Stoic ideas of the final cataclysm (e.g. Seneca, *Nat. Qu.* 5. 18. 2).

54 *star-dipping heaven*: i.e. the western sky, where the stars supposedly dipped in the Ocean.

56–7 *the spring-time carrier of fallen Helle*: i.e. the Ram (Aries), who carried Helle and Phrixus on his back over the sea; Helle fell off and her name was given to the sea, the Hellespont (sea of Helle). Lucan means when the sun had entered Aries, in March.

59 *day had won*: i.e. after the vernal equinox.

61 *took flames in Eurus*: i.e. the moon grew red.

62 *Nabataean*: = Arabian = eastern. Cf. Ovid, *Met.* I. 61, 5. 163, Juvenal II. 126.

76–103 The storm and its effects are described by Caesar, *Bell. Civ.* I. 48.

81 *drank the Ocean*: for the belief that rainbows drank the Ocean's water cf. Plautus, *Cur.* 131a.

106 *the world's lowest part*: the southernmost of the world's five zones, cf. Virgil, *Georg.* I. 240–3; thus the reference in 109 is to the signs of the zodiac between the tropics.

110–11 *Neptune ... second jurisdiction*: after the dethronement of Saturn, his three sons Jupiter, Neptune, and Pluto drew lots to decide dominion over earth, sea, and the underworld. Neptune drew the second lot.

121–47 The flood recedes, Caesar crosses the Sicoris and Petreius retreats from Ilerda.

134–5 For the Britons' use of this kind of coracle and Caesar's use of it now cf. *Bell. Civ.* I. 54.

147 *through their love of death*: cf. I. 458–62. Caesar tells us that Petreius and Afranius planned to raise troops in Celtiberia (= central Spain), *Bell. Civ.* I. 61.

148–253 Caesar pursues the Pompeians and cuts them off from the mountains. The proximity of the two camps leads to fraternization, which is cut short by Petreius' massacre of all Caesar's soldiers in his camp.

149–50 On the crossing of the river see Caesar, *Bell. Civ.* I. 54.

172–82 For Caesar's account of the fraternization see *Bell. Civ.* I. 74–5.

188 *as a private citizen*. i.e. no longer a general.

213–15 i.e. if they cannot be champions of the Senate by defeating Caesar, they can at least prove their loyalty to the senatorial cause by not yielding without fighting.

219 *with no discrimination*: for the idea of a hierarchy of slaves, cf. Tacitus, *Agr.* 31. 3.

254–336 The Pompeian troops flee back towards Ilerda but Caesar cuts them off from the water. The Pompeians' ordeal of thirst is described.

259 *The generals*: i.e. Petreius and Afranius, commanders of the Pompeians.

287–8 *skin . . . bone*: when a wound ceases to bleed the flesh shrinks and draws in the skin towards the bones.

298 *Asturian gold*: a reference to the Asturian gold-mines in Hispania Tarraconensis (Spain). The miner is 'pallid' from being underground and the same colour as his gold, cf. Silius Italicus 1. 231–3.

319–20 Several opponents of Rome are said to have poisoned the rivers and springs: Pyrrhus (King of Epirus), Jugurtha (King of Mauretania), Mithridates, Juba.

322–3 *aconite which grows on the Dictaean rocks*: cf. Theophrastus, *Hist. Plant.* 9. 16. 4 for sources of aconite.

337–401 Afranius on behalf of the Pompeians asks Caesar to accept their surrender; he is successful and his troops are dismissed by Caesar and return home.

344–62 Afranius' speech: cf. Caesar, *Bell. Civ.* 1. 84.

355–6 i.e. 'do not pardon us because we fought against you, but because we were the people you could conquer'.

364 *war-service*: cf. Caesar, *Bell. Civ.* 1. 86: 'Pledges were given by Caesar that no harm would be done and none forced to take oath of allegiance against his will.'

380 *agate*: lit. myrrhine-ware; *murra* was a highly prized mineral from which vases were made, perhaps agate.

393 *Happy is the man*: the wording here, *felix qui potuit*, echoes Virgil *Georg.* 2. 490; cf. 319 'O how blessed are those', *o fortunati*, which echoes Virgil, *Georg.* 2. 458 *o fortunatos*.

397 *colonists*: in contrast with Caesar's soldiers, who after the war would be formed into military colonies planted in the enemy's country. Thus to be defeated is portrayed as a benefit.

399–400 *one . . . one*: Caesar, Pompey.

402–47 Meanwhile Caesar's legate Antonius is being besieged by the Pompeians in Illyria on the shores of the Adriatic. His troops try to escape on three rafts.

404 *Salonae*: an important city in Illyria (mod. Solin), capital of Dalmatia, a Roman colony, near mod. Split.

405 *Iader*: evidently a river near Salonae; only a town on the Illyrian coast by this name is known to us (mod. Zadar).

406 *Antonius*: Gaius Antonius, not to be confused with his brother Marcus Antonius (Mark Antony).

406–8 Antonius' position was on the island of Curicta (mod. Krk) off the coast of Illyria.

415–16 *comrades and general Basilus on the shore of land opposite*: Caesarian troops under Dolabella were stationed on the mainland and had been joined by Lucius Minucius Basilus, admiral of Caesar's fleet.

433 *Octavius*: Marcus Octavius, one of Pompey's admirals.

438 *the scare*: a rope strung with red feathers used by hunters to scare and confine game. The smell of the feathers mentioned below derived either from the red dye or from the birds whose feathers were used.

440–1 *Molossian . . . Spartan . . . Cretan hounds*: hunting dogs, cf. Seneca, *Phaedr.* 31–43.

448–73 The Pompeians set an underwater trap, which catches the third raft; there follows a fight between the trapped men and Pompeian ships.

448 *Pompey's Cilicians*: originally pirates, cf. 3. 226–8 n.

452–4 According to Florus (2. 33) the first and second rafts escaped, carried over by high tide, but the third was caught by the underwater boom.

462–3 *men of Opitergium*: a Roman colony (mod. Oderzo), near Venice.

463 *ships*: i.e. Octavius' ships, Pompey's fleet.

465 *Vulteius*: Florus (2. 33) tells us he was a tribune in Caesar's army; nothing more is known of him.

472 *a full cohort*: i.e. 600 men.

474–581 Vulteius, captain of the captured raft, urges his men to kill one another rather than be taken alive. His men do as he urges. The Stoic theme of suicide as an escape from slavery is introduced here.

493 *friends*: from the two rafts which had reached safety.

504 *with our elders and our children*: they are deprived of the glory of killing these too. A perverse notion, typical of Lucan's love of inversion and paradox.

526–7 *the sign of Leda*: i.e. Gemini, the 'Twins', namely Castor and Pollux, the twin sons of Jupiter and Leda. The time is June, midsummer.

528 *Thessalian arrows*: i.e. the constellation Sagittarius, 'the Archer', supposedly formed by Chiron, the Centaur who had lived in Thessaly. At this time of year Sagittarius, the opposite sign to Gemini, sinks in the day and rises in the night.

529 *Histrians*: a people of the Danube.

549–51 *from Cadmus' seed ... wounds*: after Cadmus killed the dragon near the spring of Dirce, at Thebes, he sowed its teeth in the ground; from them sprang up soldiers who killed one another. See Ovid, *Met*. 3. 101–26.

551 *the Theban brothers*: Polynices and Eteocles, the sons of Oedipus and descendants of Cadmus, who killed one another in battle.

552–6 *in Phasis' plains ... *: in the land of Colchis, Jason's task was to kill the 'unsleeping' dragon which guarded the Golden Fleece, to plough the earth with fire-breathing bulls, and to sow the dragon's teeth in the ground. The 'Earth-born' men who sprang up killed one another through Medea's spells. See Ovid, *Met*. 7. 104–42.

561–2 Lucan presents an inversion of what is normal: the attacked parts of the body themselves attack the weapons.

581–660 Caesar's lieutenant Curio sails to Africa and on his arrival at the river Bagrada is told the story of the fight there between Hercules and the giant Antaeus. The episode permits Lucan to include a description of a wrestling match, a variant on the boxing match in ancient literature, e.g. the beginning of book 2 of Apollonius of Rhodes' *Argonautica*, in Theocritus' *Idyll* 22 and in Virgil, *Aen.* 5. 362–86.

583 *Lilybaean*: = Sicilian, Lilybaeum being a town on the westernmost promontory of Sicily (mod. Marsala), facing the coast of Africa.

585 *the famous anchorage*: famous both from its association with Hercules (in the story which follows) and from Scipio Africanus's station there in the Second Punic War.

586 *Clipea*: a town on the coast of North Africa (mod. Kelibia), east of Carthage.

588 *Bagrada*: a river of North Africa near Utica (mod. Majerda).

590 *the kingdom of Antaeus*: Strabo (17. 3. 8, p. 829) mentions 'the tomb of Antaeus' in the area.

612 *threw down*: both strip themselves prior to wrestling.

Cleonae: a town in Argolis near Nemea; the lion Hercules killed is often called the Nemean lion.

634 *in the waters of Inachus*: a river in Argos near which was the marsh of Lerna where Hercules killed the Hydra.

637 *his savage stepmother*: Juno, wife of Jupiter, Hercules' father, who persecuted the offspring of Jupiter's liaisons with mortal women, in this case Alcmena.

639 *when he supported Olympus*: when Hercules was seeking the apples of the Hesperides, Atlas offered to fetch them if Hercules would support the sky in his stead, then refused to take back the burden until forced to by Hercules.

656–8 *a greater name*: a reference to the 'Cornelian camp', *Castra Cornelia*, named after Publius Cornelius Scipio Africanus the elder, who landed here in 204/3 BC and defeated two Carthaginian leaders (Hasdrubal and Syphax), so alarming the Carthaginians that they recalled Hannibal from his campaign in Italy to deal with Scipio.

661–714 Curio defeats Varus, the Pompeian commander in Africa.

667 *under Varus' rule*: Publius Attius Varus, cf. 2. 466, 8. 287. Cf. Caesar, *Bell. Civ.* I. 31, where Varus' raising two legions in Africa is mentioned.

670 *their Juba*: King Juba of Numidia, who owed his throne to Pompey. Moreover, there possibly existed a personal enmity between Curio and Juba because Curio had proposed a law for reducing Juba's kingdom to a province, mentioned below, 687–92.

673 *on the middle line*: i.e. the central line of the ancient world, which ran through Rhodes and Alexandria; Juba's kingdom lay entirely to the west of this line, which here designates its eastern boundary.

677 *Autololes*: a fabulous people on the Mauretanian (Atlantic) coast of Africa.

Gaetulians: a people of north-west Africa.

680 *Mazaces*: a people of Numidia.

682 *Massylian race*: a people of Numidia.

684 *Arzucian hunter*: an African.

685–6 Thus Pliny, *Nat. Hist.* 8. 54 on how the Gaetulians catch lions by throwing clothes over their heads.

689 *in his year*: i.e. 50 BC, when Curio was a tribune.

694 *at this rumour of the king*: i.e. that he was preparing his forces (687).

695–9 *because his army … right*: Curio's troops were not veterans of Caesar's campaigns on the Rhine but the Pompeians captured at Corfinium, who had surrendered their leader Domitius to Caesar (see 2. 507–8).

698 *the old*: leader, i.e. Domitius (see previous n.).

701 *so he speaks*: for Caesar's version of Curio's speeches see *Bell. Civ.* 2. 31–2.

708 *the shows*: i.e. the gladiatorial shows.

713–14 For Curio's defeat of Varus according to Caesar see *Bell. Civ.* 2. 34–5.

715–98 Curio is tricked and defeated by King Juba and kills himself. Cf. Caesar's account, *Bell. Civ.* 2. 38–43. In this section Lucan incorporates the topos of the untrustworthiness of Africans. The presentation of the episode as Hannibal's revenge upon the Romans is another standard theme of rhetoric and an important strand in the poem: see Ahl 107–12.

719 i.e. his only fear is that the enemy will hear of his approach and retreat before he can fight them, if he is incautious enough to let report of his planned attack reach the enemy.

724 *their cleverer enemy*: the ichneumon (or Egyptian rat): cf. Pliny, *Nat. Hist.* 8. 88.

725 *with the shifting shadow*: i.e. its tail.

734 *the troops*: i.e. the infantry.

788–90 i.e. the killing of Romans by Romans will be like a propitiatory sacrifice to the ghost of Hannibal and the Carthaginians, who had suffered greatly at Roman hands.

799–824 Lucan addresses Curio, reviewing his life, especially the part he played in provoking the civil war. This extended apostrophe of a character in the poem is a favourite technique of Lucan.

802 Evidently a deliberate echo of Curio's words at 1. 289–90.

824 An echo of Virgil's words at *Aen.* 6. 621–2.

BOOK 5

1–64 The meeting of the Senate in Epirus: Lentulus urges the Senate to appoint Pompey to the command of the war. This the Senate does and goes on to bestow honours on allied peoples.

4 *Atlas' daughter*: 'daughter' for 'daughters', the seven Pleiades, daughters of Atlas, the constellation which sets in the middle of November.

5 *the day ... Calendar*: i.e. 1 January 48 BC. The year was known by the names of the consuls, who took up office on 1 January.

6 *Janus*: hence our 'January', the month of Janus.

8 *both consuls*: i.e. the consuls of 49 BC, Lucius Cornelius Lentulus Sura and Gaius Claudius Marcellus (cf. 2. 645n.).

12–14 i.e. the Senate in exile is not part of Pompey's army but a body in its own right with its own authority.

13–14 *Axes bared legally*: the axes were the consuls' symbols of office, thus the reference is to the presence of both consuls: see below.

14 *The venerable Order*: i.e. the Senate.

23–4 *icy wagon of Hyperborean Bear*: i.e. the north, the Hyperboreans being a legendary people of the far north.

28 *Camillus lived at Veii*: when the Gauls sacked Rome in 387/6 BC the Roman Senate convened at Veii, about 9 miles from Rome, and appointed Camillus as dictator in the emergency.

34 *whoever is not an exile is here*: the implication is that the pro-Caesarian Senators in Rome are the real exiles, not the Senators with Pompey.

38–9 *the enemy . . . waves*: a reference to the deaths on the raft of Vulteius described in 4. 402–581.

50 *Phoebean Rhodes, the mistress of the sea*: the island of Rhodes off Asia Minor had a large temple and colossal statue of Apollo, identified with the Sun. The island was renowned for seafaring.

51 *uncouth soldiers of chill Taÿgetus*: i.e. the Laconians: Taÿgetus is a mountain range in Laconia in the Peloponnese.

53 *Phocis freed . . . Massilia*: Phocaea in Asia Minor, not Phocis in central Greece, was the mother city of the colony of Massilia: for the same blurring cf. 3. 340.

54 *Sadalas and valiant Cotys*: Cotys king of Thrace and his son Sadalas assisted Pompey with some cavalry.

55 *Deiotarus*: King of Galatia, who also brought cavalry to help Pompey.

Rhascypolis: chief of a Thracian tribe, who also brought cavalry to Pompey. Cf. Caesar, *Bell. Civ.* 3. 4.

57 *sceptred Juba*: Juba's position as king was confirmed by the Senate.

60–1 *the Pellaean diadem*: a reference to the Egyptian king, Ptolemy XIII (see Pella in Glossary; the first Ptolemy was a Macedonian).

63 *the sister*: Cleopatra VII: her brother Ptolemy seized the kingdom of Egypt from her and he was then recognized as king by Pompey.

64 *father-in-law*: Caesar: the crime of killing Pompey is taken away from him by the Egyptians who perform the deed.

64–120 *The Delphic oracle 1*: Appius goes to consult the oracle at Delphi about the result of the war (also Valerius Maximus 1. 8. 10, Orosius 6. 15. 11): Lucan describes the oracle. Here, Lucan incorporates a Virgilian epic feature of the consultation of an oracle; cf. *Aen.* 3. 84–120, where Aeneas consults Apollo's oracle at Delos.

67 *Appius*: Appius Claudius Pulcher, censor in 50 BC, took Pompey's side in the civil war. He had an interest in divination and wrote a work on augury.

71–2 i.e. Delphi was supposed to be the centre of the earth: the stone called the omphalos (navel) was in the temple of Apollo.

73 *Bromius*: i.e. Bacchus.

74 *triennial rites*: i.e. occurring every other year, as the Romans counted inclusively, cf. Ovid, *Met.* 6. 587–8.

75–6 In the great flood Mount Parnassus was the only part of the earth left showing above the waters: cf. Ovid, *Met.* 1. 316–29.

79 *Paean*: Apollo.

81 *Themis*: the goddess to whom the oracle at Delphi once belonged, Aeschylus, *Eum.* 2–3.

93 *all Divinity*: meaning the supreme being, cf. Seneca, *Ep.* 107. 10, Lucan 9. 580.

93–6 Lucan here expounds the Stoic doctrine of the 'spirit of the world', *anima mundi*, cf. 9. 578–80, Virgil, *Aen.* 6. 724–34.

97 *virgin's breast*: i.e. the Pythia, the prophetess at Delphi.

108 *the Tyrians*: on consulting the oracle, evidently after an earthquake (cf. 3. 217), the Tyrians were told to found the colony of Gades (Strabo 3. 5. 5, p. 169).

109 *the sea of Salamis*: in the war between the Greeks and Persians the oracle advised the Athenians to put their trust in 'wooden walls'.

This was interpreted as ships and in 480 BC the Athenian fleet conquered Xerxes' fleet at Salamis, an island in the Saronic Gulf not
far from Athens (see Herodotus 7. 140–3).

109–10 Several countries, including Egypt, were saved from famine by
following the oracle's instructions.

111 *the poisonous air*: probably a reference to the plague of Thebes which
was ended on the oracle's advice by the banishment of the murderer
of Laius.

114 *forbade the gods to speak*: the oracle seems to have been largely ignored
during the late Republic and early Empire (cf. Juvenal 6. 555–6).
Some see in Lucan's words here an allusion to Nero's supposed aboli-
tion of the oracle; but such stories seem apocryphal.

120–97 *The Delphic oracle 2*. Appius asks that the oracle be opened. The
priestess tries to dissuade him but is forced to utter a prophecy.
The god enters her and she foretells Appius' death before the battle
of Pharsalia.

120 *the tripods*: a tripod was a three-legged stand used in temples to support
a bowl for offerings, incense, etc.; the word often refers especially
to the tripod in Apollo's temple at Delphi, in which the Pythian
priestess apparently seated herself to prophesy.

125 *Phemonoe*: said to be the name of the first priestess of Apollo at Delphi:
her name means 'prophetic mind'.

134 *Python*: = Delphi. The sanctuary was attacked by Gauls in 279 BC.

144 *white woollen band*: the band (*infula*) was a sign of priesthood, cf. Virgil,
Aen. 10. 537–8.

Phocis' laurel: Phocis was the area of Greece in which Delphi was
situated.

183 *the prophetess of Cumae in her Euboean retreat*: i.e. the Sibyl, whose
cave was at Cumae in Campania, Italy. Cumae was founded by
Chalcis, a town of Euboea, the island to the north-east of Attica
and Boeotia in Greece.

185–6 *selected . . . the destiny of Rome*: i.e. she wrote the Sibylline books
pertaining to the Romans alone.

194–6 This is a prophecy of his death, because Appius died and was buried on Euboea.

198–236 *The Delphic oracle 3*. After Lucan has addressed the oracle (a typical example of apostrophe: see Introduction, iii. 4), the narrative resumes with the emergence and collapse of the prophetess and Appius' misinterpretation of the oracle.

207 *again returning to vengeance of the Bruti*: just as Marcus Junius Brutus will participate in the assassination of Caesar, so his ancestor Lucius Junius Brutus expelled the tyrant Tarquins in 509 BC (see Glossary).

232 *rocky Carystos*: a town on the south coast of Euboea noted for its marble.

233 *Rhamnus*: on the east coast of Attica, facing Euboea, where Nemesis, the goddess of retribution, was worshipped.

235 *Euripus with waves shifting course*: the Euripus was the narrow strait of water between Euboea and Boeotia very dangerous to ships as the tides ebb and flow more often here, seven times in 24 hours (Pliny, *Nat. Hist.* 2. 219).

236 *Aulis, treacherous to fleets*: the tide carries ships from Chalcis towards Aulis, on the coast of Boeotia, through these dangerous waters.

237–99 Caesar's troops mutiny in their wish for peace. According to Suetonius, Caesar's troops never mutinied during his ten years' campaigns against the Gauls but more than once during the civil wars. This mutiny occurred at Placentia in north Italy (mod. Piacenza).

260 For the same idea cf. Seneca, *De Ira* 10. 4: 'Upon the individual soldier the commander may unsheathe all his sternness, but leniency is necessary when the whole army deserts.'

273 *guiltless in our poverty*: because Caesar's soldiers have gained nothing from the blood they have shed.

286 *which crime*: i.e. the massacre of opponents and seizure of their property.

300–73 Caesar quells the mutiny with a menacing speech and the ringleaders are executed. The speech shows Caesar's power over his men: it is frightening how he can turn them from mutiny to the execution of their fellow-soldiers and even to volunteering for death.

334 *now Roman citizens*: i.e. no longer soldiers but ordinary citizens.

339 *than it now rises*: because of their flow.

345 *Labienus*: Titus Labienus fought under Caesar in the Gallic wars in which he was Caesar's second-in-command, but early in the civil war changed sides and was appointed by Pompey as one of his legates in the campaign in Greece.

349–51 i.e. the act of desertion rather than joining the enemy is the prime and irrevocable act of treachery in Caesar's eyes.

358 *civilians*: as 'soldier' and 'civilian' were antithetical, mutually exclusive, terms in Latin, for Caesar to call his mutinous soldiers 'civilians' is in effect to disband them (cf. Tacitus, *Ann.* I. 42).

374–402 Caesar sends his army to Brundisium with orders to raise a fleet there and himself goes to Rome where he is made dictator and consul.

374 *Brundisium*: cf. 2. 609.

    ten encampments: i.e. after ten days' march.

375 *Hydrus*: a river in Calabria, running through the town of Hydruntum (mod. Otranto).

376 *Taras*: Tarentum, a town on the inside of Italy's heel (mod. Taranto).

    Leuca: a town in Calabria at the southern point of the heel.

377 *Salapian swamp*: Salapia was a town in northern Apulia (mod. Salpi), sitting on a lagoon.

    Sipus: another name for Sipontum (mod. Manfredonia), a town on the coast of Apulia, just north of Salapia.

378 *fruitful Apulian Garganus*: a mountain and promontory in northern Apulia, famous for its oak-forests, Horace, *Odes* 2. 9. 7.

380 *Dalmatia*: on the east coast of the Adriatic, north of Epirus, modern Yugoslavia.

    Calabria: a region in south-east Italy including the 'heel'.

383–4 *as dictator . . . the calendar*: i.e. he assumed the offices of dictator (which he resigned eleven days later: *Bell. Civ.* 3. 2) and consul (here referred to as 'the highest office'). He had already been consul, hence is said to honour the consulship by the addition of his dictatorship.

392–4 Lucan describes a mock-election: the elections for the consulship took place on the Campus Martius, where the people assembled in their centuries to cast their votes: here the people are not permitted to vote, but the rest of the ceremony, including the naming of the tribes, is observed in a sham.

395–6 Unfavourable omens could stop ceremonies such as elections: here observation of the sky is prohibited and unfavourable omens, such as thunder and the owl, are ignored.

397–9 Lucan alleges that from this time consuls are chosen simply to give a name to the year. He generalizes the practice of consuls' holding office for very short periods of time.

400–2 A reference to the Latin Festival, presided over by the consuls (see 1. 550n.), held in honour of Jupiter Latiaris on the Alban Mount, site of the Trojan foundation of Alba Longa. The implication is that Jupiter no longer deserves to be worshipped in this way because of his failure to prevent Rome's capture by Caesar.

403–60 Caesar goes to Brundisium and although it is not the time of year for sailing urges his men to set sail. This they do and are becalmed. At last they cross over to Epirus.

406 Cf. 2. 610–15 for Brundisium's shape and Cretan connection.

420 *Phaeacia*: the fabled land which Ulysses visited, located in antiquity on the island of Corcyra, i.e. Corfu.

421 Caesar's ships were heavy transport ships reliant on their sails, whereas Pompey's ships were manoeuvrable war-ships with rowers.

428 *with sheets to port*: the 'sheets' were the ropes which tied the two lower corners of a sail to the ship.

436 *the Bosporus binding Scythian waves*: i.e. the Straits of Kerch between the Black Sea and the Sea of Azov, cf. Herodotus 4. 28, Strabo 2. 1. 16, p. 73, 7. 3. 18, p. 307.

440 *Bessi*: a Thracian tribe, nomadic according to Lucan.

455 *every hope of shipwreck*: the sailors are so desperate they prefer the prospect of shipwreck in a storm to that of dying becalmed.

458 *curving waters*: the surface was no longer flat but marked by the dips and peaks of the waves.

460 *Palaeste*: a town on the coast of Epirus.

461–503 Caesar camps at Dyrrachium and sends messages to Antony requesting him to send over immediately the forces remaining in Italy so that he can proceed with the war.

462–3 *Genusus, Apsus*: rivers of Macedonia between Dyrrachium and Apollonia.

473–5 Lucan refers to the fact that Pompey and Caesar met for the last time at Luca, two years before the death of Julia and her second child.

479 *rehearsing Leucas*: a reference to the battle of Actium, which Antony lost in 31 BC to Octavian (Augustus). Lucan hints that Antony's delay (to be described shortly) amounts to treachery.

504–59 *Caesar and the storm 1.* Caesar demands that Amyclas take him in his small boat to Italy; Amyclas warns him of the imminent storm but agrees. Various versions of the story are told by Plutarch, *Caes.* 38; Appian, *Bell. Civ.* 2. 57; Dio 41. 46; Valerius Maximus 9. 8. 2; Florus 2. 35–7. Storms were part of the furniture of Greek and Roman epic (see Morford 20–36) and Lucan includes in his poem four set-piece storms in all (see Introduction, iii. 3). Of these, the storm in book 5 is both the most elaborate and the closest to the traditional literary storm (for an analysis see Morford 37–44). This storm is not integral to the narration of events; in fact, in practical terms it is a failure, because Caesar does not complete the crossing to Italy; however, Lucan incorporates it primarily as an illustration of Caesar's megalomaniacal belief in himself.

507 i.e. the first watch served for three hours, after which the second watch took over.

509 *too bold even for a slave*: because slaves have nothing to lose and therefore will attempt anything.

524 *the rope*: kept at the bottom of the fire, presumably soaked in pitch, to stop the fire going out altogether.

535 Housman inserted a line here, to mend the text, which was subsequently refined by Shackleton Bailey.

549   *reddened with the sign of winds*: an echo of Virgil, *Georg.* I. 430–1.

555   *crow's pacing of the shores*: cf. Virgil, *Georg.* I. 388–9.

560–93   *Caesar and the storm 2.* Caesar and Amyclas embark. As the storm rises, Amyclas urges Caesar to turn back but Caesar orders him to maintain his course.

572   *Corus' sea*: Latin poets spoke of the sea as belonging to the wind blowing over it.

579–80   i.e. 'if you refuse to head for Italy because the gods forbid you, then head for Italy when I order you'.

593–653   *Caesar and the storm 3.* The storm increases in violence and rages. Typically Lucan pushes the conventions beyond the norm for epic.

620–4   A reference to Deucalion's flood.

622   *the Second Realm*: i.e. Neptune's. Cf. 4. 110–11 n

652   *Ambracian coast*: Ambracia (mod. Arta) was the area around the Ambracian Gulf, south of Epirus.

653–77   *Caesar and the storm 4.* Caesar declares his readiness to die, if this is the appointed time, provided he remains feared by the world. Immediately his boat is carried safely to shore.

664   *my inscription* the inscription on a tombstone (epitaph) giving details of a man's ancestry and career.

668   *as an ordinary man*: lit. 'as a private citizen', i.e. not yet as a monarch. Cf. 2. 564.

678–702   *Caesar and the storm 5.* On his return to camp, Caesar's soldiers reproach him for leaving them and for risking his life. A sign of the men's devotion to him.

684   *by unwilling gales*: as shown by their returning Caesar unharmed to dry land.

703–21   Caesar's troops in Italy now cross over to Epirus.

703   *the generals in Italy*: i.e. Antony and Caesar's other captains.

716   *the letter*: migrating birds often take formations in the shape of letters, e.g. an inverted V.

719 *Lissus*: a town on the coast of Macedonia.

720 *Nymphaeum*: a port on the coast south of Lissus.

721 *made a harbour*: the harbour of Nymphaeum was exposed on one side but with a change in the wind became safe for Caesar's ships, cf. Caesar, *Bell. Civ.* 3. 26.

722–815 Pompey decides to send his wife Cornelia to the island of Lesbos for safety: as she wakes he tells her of his decision and she expresses her reluctance and sorrow, faints and is taken on board ship. This scene is juxtaposed with the storm scene to contrast the frail, human Pompey with the fearless, superhuman Caesar. The deep pathos evoked by Lucan by the scene between Pompey and Cornelia will be recalled when they next see one another, at the start of book 8.

727 *lawful Venus*: i.e. married love.

771–2 She wants to die at the same time as Pompey; this is her wish, as a devoted wife. She cannot describe her lot as 'carefree' if it involves surviving Pompey.

BOOK 6

1–28 Caesar marches to capture Dyrrachium but is anticipated by Pompey: description of Dyrrachium. According to Caesar, *Bell. Civ.* 3. 41, Caesar was first to arrive at Dyrrachium and cut Pompey off.

3 *their paired adversaries*: an image from gladiatorial fights.

17 *Taulantian*: the Taulantii were a people of Illyria, near Dyrrachium.

the Ephyraean walls: Ephyra was the ancient name of Corinth; Corinth founded Corcyra; and Dyrrachium was a joint colony of Corinth and Corcyra.

29–117 Caesar surrounds the city and Pompey's forces with vast earthworks. Pompey suffers plague in his camp and Caesar famine in his. Thus Lucan reverses the normal situation: it is usually the besieged not the besiegers who suffer famine.

42 *ring*: a ring of nets thrown around the wood to prevent the quarry from escaping.

48 *the walls of Ilium*: the walls of Ilium (= Troy) were said to have been built by Apollo and Neptune, Ovid, *Met.* II. 199–204.

50 *Babylon*: the city had brick-built walls, Ovid, *Met.* 4. 57–8, Juvenal 10. 171, of huge extent, Herodotus I. 178.

55 *Sestos to Abydos*: two towns facing each other across the Hellespont. Xerxes bridged the Hellespont, 2. 673 and n.

56 *Phrixus' sea*: Phrixus was the brother of Helle whose fall into the sea gave the Hellespont its name. Cf. 4. 57 and n.

57 *Ephyra*: Corinth.

57–8 *the wide realms of Pelops*: i.e. the Peloponnese.

58 *sparing ships long Malea's curve*: Lucan alludes to Nero's plans for cutting a Corinthian canal, on which work began in AD 67, Pliny, *Nat. Hist.* 4. 10, Suetonius, *Nero* 19. 2.

62 *casualties of both Thessaly and Libya*: at the battles of Pharsalia and Thapsus.

66 *mad Pelorus barks*: a reference to the dogs of Scylla on the coast of Sicily near Pelorus. Cf. I. 548–9.

67–8 *Caledonian Britons* . . . : i.e. Britons in Scotland do not notice disturbances on the south coast at Rutupiae (Richborough) in Kent.

74–5 *as much as separates . . . Aricia . . . from . . . Rome*: i.e. about 16 miles. For Aricia and Diana cf. 3. 86–7. Diana may be Diana of Mycenae here because of the similarities with the cult of Diana/Artemis among the Tauri, Strabo 5. 3. 12, p. 239, of which the priestess was Iphigeneia, the daughter of Agamemnon king of Mycenae (thus Euripides' play *Iphigenia in Tauris*, cf. Ovid, *Trist.* 4. 4. 63–82). Cato (*Origines* fr. 71 Peter = 3. 4 Chassignet) suggests that Iphigenia and her brother Orestes came to Rhegium in South Italy to expiate their mother's murder but supplies no connection with Aricia.

76–7 Again, 16 miles. The walls are the walls of Rome.

91 *Nesis*: an island on the coast of Campania (mod. Nisita) of volcanic origin.

97 *the Sacred Disease*: erysipelas, sometimes called Ignis Sacer ('Sacred Fire'): a redness of the skin caused by inflammation, eruption or ulceration (Celsus 5. 26. 31B).

110 *he*: Caesar.

118–262 Pompey attempts to break through Caesar's rampart but is driven back by the heroic efforts of one man, Scaeva. This passage permits Lucan to include his version of an *aristeia*, a traditional feature of epic in which the focus is on the exploits of one hero. Scaeva's *aristeia*, however, is gruesome in the extreme, again conveying the horror of civil war.

126 *Minicius' fort*: the name may derive from the commander of the fort, Minucius, Appian, *Bell. Civ.* 2. 60.

129 *Latian Birds*: Roman Eagles, i.e. the standards.

144 *Scaeva*: Marcus Cassius Scaeva, a common soldier in the Gallic Wars, during which he achieved promotion to the rank of centurion. For his desperate bravery at Dyrrachium see Caesar, *Bell. Civ.* 3. 53, Valerius Maximus 3. 2. 23.

147 *the Latian vine-staff*: the symbol of office of Roman centurions. The 'lengthy ranks' were the ranks of ordinary soldiers.

169 *something more than death*: i.e. victory.

173 *with himself*: he threatens to jump down on them.

177–8 *flimsy skull*: thus Housman; the Latin could refer to the skull or the helmet.

198 *falarica*: a heavy spear-like weapon hurled by hand or machine, here the latter, hence the reference to the 'twisted cords' of the ballista. Also at Virgil, *Aen.* 9. 705.

200 *ballista*: see 2. 686n.

214 *Gortynian*: Gortyn was a city in Crete.

220–3 *the Pannonian bear*: a scene in the amphitheatre is here described, a fight between a Libyan and a bear brought from Pannonia, a Roman province to the north-east of Italy, south and west of the Danube.

226–7 i.e. the warriors could not have rejoiced more if they had seen Caesar himself wounded.

228 *He*: Scaeva.

240 *His*: Scaeva's.

256 *naked-breasted Mars*: Mars was often depicted with spear and shield but no armour.

258–9 *Iberians, Cantabrians, Teutones*: the first two were peoples of Spain, the last a German people. Had Scaeva conquered a foreign race he could have celebrated a triumph; hence the mention of the 'Thunderer's temple', below, the temple of Jupiter Capitolinus in Rome where the spoils were hung in the culmination of the triumphal procession. A triumph was not permitted for a victory over a Roman enemy.

263–313 Pompey attacks at another point and successfully breaks out of the blockade. Caesar is furious and seeks a battle but Pompey does not press home his advantage. For Caesar's account of the fight, cf. *Bell. Civ.* 3. 62–70.

269 *twofold warfare*: on land and sea.

285 *Torquatus*: Lucius Manlius Torquatus, a follower of Pompey, cf. Caesar, *Bell. Civ.* 3. 11.

287 *Circaean gale*: of Circeii in Latium, Italy, a town with a promontory; the area was associated in mythology with Circe the sorceress.

293 *Henna*: a town in the middle of Sicily.

294 *Enceladus*: the giant supposedly buried under Mount Etna, so the cause of its eruption. Cf. Virgil, *Aen.* 3. 578–82.

300 *their general*: Pompey.

302 *a Sulla*: as opposed to Pompey, as being more bloodthirsty.

306–13 Lucan reviews future events of the war which might have been avoided: the battle of Thapsus near Utica (46 BC), the battle of Munda (45 BC), Pompey's death (described in book 8), Juba's death (46 BC), the death of Metellus Scipio, descendant of Scipio the conqueror of Carthage (cf. 2. 472 and n.), and Cato's death (46 BC).

313 *Pharsalia could have disappeared from destiny*: i.e. might never have happened.

314–32 Caesar heads for Thessaly and Pompey pursues him, rejecting advice to return to Italy.

320 *following Caesar's model*: i.e. armed.

331 *Candavia*: a mountain-range beginning in Epirus, separating Illyricum from Macedonia.

333–412 Description of Thessaly. This is one of Lucan's geographical set pieces; its inclusion reflects his rhetorical training. His material here is drawn from earlier writers such as Herodotus 7. 129; cf. Ovid's description of Tempe and the rivers of Thessaly at *Met.* 1. 567–82. It subdivides as follows: 333–49 the ring of mountains surrounding the plains of Thessaly, and the valley of Tempe; 349–59 cities; 360–80 rivers; 381–94 peoples and heroes; 395–412 inventions, especially those connected with war.

333–4 *crag of Ossa* . . . : i.e. south-east.

335–6 . . . *Pelion*: i.e. north-east. In fact, Lucan appears to have reversed the true positions of Ossa and Pelion.

337–8 . . . *wooded Othrys*: i.e. south.

339–40 *Pindus* . . . : i.e. west. The Iapyx is the north-west wind which helps the crossing from Italy to Greece.

341–2 *at Olympus' foot* . . . : i.e. north.

346 *Tempe's passage*: the narrow valley of Tempe in northern Thessaly between the mountains Olympus and Ossa is the only path to the sea for the rivers of the Thessalian plains. It was thought that before the formation of Tempe their waters had covered the country in a huge lake, Herodotus 7. 129. 3.

348 *by Hercules' hand*: cf. 8. 1 and n.

349–50 *sea-born Achilles*: Achilles' mother was the sea-goddess Thetis and Phthia, part of Thessaly, was his kingdom.

351 *Phylace*: its king was Protesilaus, famed for jumping ashore first at Troy.

352 *Rhoetean shores*: i.e. Trojan, Rhoeteum being a promontory and city in the Troas.

Pteleos: a port in Thessaly.

352–3 *Dorion . . . the Pierides*: where Thamyras challenged the Muses (here called the Pierides) to a contest in song: he lost and was deprived of his sight and musical powers, cf. Homer, *Il.* 2. 594–5 (though Homer locates this Dorion in the Peloponnese), Statius, *Theb.* 4. 181–4. The Muses were called the Pierides because they were associated with Pieria, near Mount Olympus.

353–4 *Meliboea . . . quiver*: from where came Philoctetes, who was given Hercules' quiver as a reward for kindling Hercules' funeral pyre.

355 *Larisa*: see 7. 712 n.

356 *Argos once renowned*: i.e. Pelasgian Argos in Thessaly, not Argos in the Peloponnese.

357–9 *Thebes, Echion, Agave, Pentheus*: Thebes in Phthia; Agave came from Thebes in Boeotia; Echion was her husband. According to the Bacchic legend Agave tore her son Pentheus to pieces while in Bacchic frenzy. Lucan's account of Agave's exile is unparalleled in surviving ancient texts. It seems strange that he calls Phthian Thebes 'Thebes of Echion' as Echion is always associated with the Boeotian Thebes. Possibly Lucan is reproducing a myth (unknown to us) in which Agave and Echion founded or ruled over Phthian Thebes after leaving Boeotia.

363 *kidnapped Isis' father*: i.e. the river-god Inachus, father of Io, who was abducted by Jupiter and transformed into a heifer; she was identified with the Egyptian goddess Isis: Ovid, *Met.* 1. 583–750.

363–4 *almost your son-in-law, Oeneus*: the river-god Achelous had been promised Deianeira, the daughter of Oeneus, but was defeated by Hercules and had to give her up to him: Ovid, *Met.* 9. 1–97.

364 *the Echinades*: a group of islands in the Ionian Sea off the coast of Acarnania, said to have been nymphs who were hurled into the sea by angry Achelous: Ovid, *Met.* 8. 573–89.

365–6 *stained with Nessus' blood Evenus . . . Meleager*: on the banks of the Evenus, which passes by Calydon, the city ruled by Meleager, the centaur Nessus was killed. For Nessus' death see Ovid, *Met.* 9. 101–33 and below, 391–2 n.

366–7 *Spercheus . . . Malian*: a river entering the Malian Gulf.

368 *Amphrysus*: on the banks of this river Apollo served King Admetus as a shepherd.

369 *Anaurus*: a Greek name meaning 'without air'.

380 *terror for the gods*: the gods were afraid to break an oath sworn on the waters of the Styx, cf. 749.

385 *Magnetes*: inhabitants of the eastern part of Thessaly.

   Minyans: they lived round Iolcos in Thessaly; most of the Argonauts were Minyans.

386–7 *Pelethronian caves*: part of Mount Pelion.

387 *Centaurs, Ixion*: Ixion wished to make love to Juno and was deceived by Jupiter with a cloud: the union of Ixion and the cloud produced the Centaurs.

388–94 Individual centaurs are mentioned, cf. Ovid, *Met.* 12. 210–535, the battle of the Lapiths and the Centaurs.

391 *Pholus*: entertained Hercules on his travels.

391–2 i.e. Nessus, who tried to rape Deianeira while conveying her across the river Evenus but was killed by Hercules with an arrow tipped with the poison of the Lernaean Hydra.

393 *Chiron*: i.e. the constellation Sagittarius, which appears in winter.

394 *greater Scorpio*: Scorpio takes up more space than any other constellation of the zodiac.

396 *struck by the trident of the sea*: in the contest between Athena (Minerva) and Poseidon (Neptune) to name Athens, Poseidon struck the rocks and produced a horse. This contest was variously situated in Attica and (as here) in Thessaly.

400 *from Pagasaean shore*: the Argonauts sailed from Pagasae near Iolcus on the Bay of Volos, cf. 3. 193–7 for the Argo's departure.

402 *Ionos*: an ancient king of Thessaly.

410–12 The Aloadae, Otus and Ephialtes, sons of Poseidon and Aloeus' wife, were of enormous size and piled up mountains to climb to heaven: Homer, *Od.* 11. 305–20.

413–506 Both sides pitch camp and await battle. Pompey's son Sextus goes to consult Thessalian witches about the outcome: their powers are described. Thessaly was a classic locale for witches, and these are classic witches: this is another Lucanian *tour de force*. Roman writers of all periods show an interest in the supernatural; this is particularly evident in Neronian writers.

420 *Sextus*: younger son of Pompey by his wife Mucia.

421–2 After he was outlawed in 43 BC Sextus occupied Sicily and used it as a base for blockading Italy: his plundering of supplies to Rome earned him the name of pirate. His father's triumphs at sea were over the pirates.

425 *Delos' tripods*: Delos was evidently an oracle-centre early in the archaic period, cf. *Homeric Hymn to Delian Apollo* 131–2.

426 *Dodona*: the oracle of Zeus/Jupiter in Epirus, said to use one or more bronze cauldrons in prophecy.

427 *earliest fruits*: i.e. acorns, from Dodona's oak-trees.

442 *the Colchian stranger*: Medea. Cf. Ovid, *Met.* 7. 222–31 for a description of Medea in Thessaly.

450 *Babylon of Perseus*: Perses, son of Perseus and Andromeda, ancestor of the Persian dynasty, ruled in Babylon.

455–6 *the promise* ... : i.e. hippomanes, said to be a swelling growth on the head of a new-born foal: if it was bitten off and eaten by its mother, she would rear the foal: Pliny, *Nat. Hist.* 8. 165. Hippomanes was used in magic and witchcraft, cf. Virgil, *Aen.* 4. 515–16.

458–91 A list of impossible things (*adynata*) achieved by the witches now follows.

460 For the power of the 'twisted thread' cf. Virgil, *Ecl.* 8. 73–9.

474 *Nile does not rise in summer*: as it normally did, cf. 10. 228–37.

475 *Maeander*: a river in Asia Minor with a winding path, from which is derived the word 'meander'.

475–6 *Rhône, Arar*: the characteristics of these two rivers in Gaul are reversed, cf. 1. 433–4.

477 *Olympus*: so high it towered above the clouds, cf. 2. 271.

488–90 Cf. Virgil, *Ecl.* 8. 71.

498 *one particular deity*: usually regarded as Demiurgus, creator of all other gods (cf. 745 n.).

499–506 A commonly occurring idea in classical texts is that witches could render the moon's light dull and draw it down from the sky (cf. Virgil, *Ecl.* 8. 69, Seneca, *Med.* 787–92) and that the moon then shed poisonous foam on plants which the witches used in magic.

507–69 Lucan describes Erichtho, the most foul and extreme of the Thessalian witches. He caps his set piece on witches in general with a *tour de force* of gruesomeness and hideousness.

515 *life*: = the fact that she is living.

534–5 *the torch held by the parents*: it was the parents' duty to set alight the funeral pyre of their own children.

538 *preserved in stone*: in a stone sarcophagus. Cf. Pliny, *Nat. Hist.* 2. 211, 36. 131.

542 *the pallid nails*: lit. 'growths'; the nails continue to grow after death.

545 *the crosses*: where slaves were executed.

570–88 Sextus Pompey goes to Erichtho in the middle of the night and finds her casting spells to keep the war in Thessaly, to provide her with corpses.

589–623 *The necromancy 1.* Sextus Pompey asks Erichtho to reveal to him the outcome of the war and Erichtho replies, agreeing to do so. The following scene of necromancy (prophecy by a corpse) is probably the most horrific of all descriptions of necromancy in ancient writers. He takes the 'standard' features and elaborates them, taking many of them to extremes. There are a number of literary debts and influences here, including Ovid's description of the Underworld (*Met.* 4. 432 ff.), Seneca's necromancy scene in *Oedipus* (530–658: similar setting, preparations, etc.) and portrayals of witches, such as Medea in Ovid (*Met.* 7). But above all, the scene should be read with Aeneas' consultation of the Sibyl in *Aen.* 6 in mind throughout. Lucan has inverted a number of the features of Virgil's account, thus conveying his horror of civil war, e.g. hero Aeneas is replaced by worthless Sextus and dignified Sibyl by foul Erichtho; instead of the living visiting the Underworld, a dead man is brought back to life to prophesy; the optimistic prophecy of the future is replaced by a pessimistic view of Rome's past.

617–18 In these lines Erichtho alludes to various magic skills, e.g. geomancy, aeromancy, necromancy, hydromancy.

617 *Chaos*: here = the Underworld, see 696 n.

619 *such abundance of fresh death*: it is traditional to criticize Lucan for not noticing that no fighting has yet taken place in Thessaly; cf. 626 n.

624–41 *The necromancy 2*. Erichtho selects a suitable corpse.

626 *corpses of the slain*: the origin of these corpses is not clear as there has been no fighting yet in Thessaly.

631 *without a wound*: its lung must be undamaged so the corpse can be made to speak.

636 *Stygian Avernus*: here = the Underworld. Lake Avernus near the Bay of Naples was the entrance to the Underworld which Aeneas used in Virgil, *Aen.* 6.

638 *a hook*: Lucan adapts to his necromancy scene the Roman practice of dragging the bodies of executed criminals with a hook.

642–56 *The necromancy 3*. Description of the dreadful setting for the necromancy and of Erichtho's preparation for the rite.

644 *the yew*: the yew is often associated with death and the Underworld, e.g. Ovid, *Met.* 4. 432.

654 *of many hues*: the inverse to the pure white robes of holy sacrifice is in other texts black robes (e.g. Seneca, *Oed.* 551–3); the multicoloured robes here seem to be an alternative inversion, possibly inspired by the multi-coloured robes evidently worn by Furies in dramatic performances. For multi-coloured threads/material in magic, cf. Virgil, *Ecl.* 8. 73–4, 77, *Ciris* 371–2, Petronius, *Satyr.* 131.

656 *wreaths of vipers*: with snakes for hair, she resembles the Gorgons or the Furies.

657–66 *The necromancy 4*. She reassures Sextus Pompey and his companions.

657 *the youth*: Sextus Pompey.

660 *life in genuine form*: so that the corpse will not appear as a ghost, but as a real man brought to life again.

662–3 *river-bank which sounds with fires*: the rivers of the Underworld include among others the Styx and Phlegethon (or Pyriphlegethon), a river of fire.

665 *the Giants with their hands bound back*: like the Titans their brothers, the Giants were confined in Tartarus after their battle with the gods.

667–84 *The necromancy 5*. Erichtho's magic brew is applied to the corpse. For other descriptions of a witch's brew cf. Medea in Ovid, *Met.* 7. 262–78 and Seneca, *Med.* 675–736; Lucan's goes beyond these.

669 *lunar poison*: for the magical foam shed by the moon see 499–506 n.

672 *entrails of the lynx*: cf. the belief that the urine of lynxes changes into stones (Ovid, *Met.* 15. 413–15).

hump of dire hyena: the hump was formed by the union of neck and spine (Pliny, *Nat. Hist.* 8. 105).

673 *snake-fed stag*: for the enmity of stags and snakes, cf. Pliny, *Nat. Hist.* 8. 118.

674 *remora*: in Greek, echeneis, literally 'ship-holder', the sucking-fish believed to delay ships.

676 *stones which sound*: Lucan refers to the eagle-stone, supposedly found in the nests of eagles: Pliny, *Nat. Hist.* 10. 12, 36. 149.

677 *the Arabs' flying serpent*: identity unknown to us. Housman lists other ancient references to this creature.

677–8 *the viper born in the Red Sea*: reference unknown to us.

679 *horned snake of Libya*: the Cerastes; cf. 9. 716.

680 *ashes of the phoenix*: it rose again from its own ashes: see Herodotus 2. 73, Tacitus, *Ann.* 6. 28, Ovid, *Met.* 15. 392–407.

685–718 *The necromancy 6*. Lucan describes Erichtho's voice: after the catalogue of magical substances, a catalogue of weird noises. Then Erichtho invokes the powers of the Underworld to release the corpse's soul to her. Cf. Medea's invocation, Seneca, *Med.* 740–51.

695 *the Avengers*: avenging goddesses, cf. Statius, *Theb.* 5. 60.

696 *Chaos*: variously conceived as the abyss from which all things arose and as one of the gods of darkness; in the latter sense here, as at Virgil, *Aen.* 4. 510.

697 *the ruler of the earth*: i.e. Pluto; in the division of the world, Jupiter received Heaven, Neptune the Sea, and Pluto the Underworld.

tormented: Pluto is tormented either because the gods do not die and therefore do not enter his realm as his subjects or because he wishes to die and regrets that he is immortal.

700 *the lowest form of our Hecate*: Hecate had three manifestations: as the moon in the sky, as Diana on earth, and as Hecate in the Underworld, cf. Ovid, *Met.* 7. 194 'three-formed Hecate'. She is called 'our' here because of her association with witches.

704 *ferryman*: Charon.

715 *Orcus*: another name for the god of the Underworld.

716 *will join the dead once only*: she specifies that it is a recent corpse whose soul has hardly entered the Underworld; hence it will join the dead only once because it has not yet joined them.

719–49 *The necromancy 7.* On the soul's refusal to enter the body, Erichtho utters terrible threats to the powers of the Underworld: to the Furies; Hecate; Persephone; Pluto; the unnamed deity (see 745n.).

733 *Stygian she-dogs*: she will not call them by their customary names, the Eumenides or Erinyes, but by the titles used in incantations, 'Stygian she-dogs'.

736 *Hecate*: see 700n.

739 *Henna*: a town in Sicily; from a nearby meadow Persephone was abducted by Pluto.

739–41 *feast, bond, pollution*: the 'feast' is the pomegranate seeds, which doomed Persephone to spend half her time in the Underworld. The reference of the 'bond' and the 'pollution' is unknown.

742–3 *lowest ruler of the world*: Pluto's realm was the lowest of the three (see 697n.).

745 *Him*: as at Statius, *Theb.* 4. 515–17, the necromancer threatens the powers of the Underworld with the invocation of a supreme deity

who is not named. Various identifications have been suggested, e.g. Demiurgus or Creator, and from the Graeco-Egyptian magic papyri Hermes, Osiris, and Typhon/Seti.

749 *who . . . can falsely swear*: i.e. without punishment, unlike the other gods. Cf. Virgil, *Aen.* 6. 323–4.

750–76 *The necromancy 8.* In response to these threats the corpse comes to life and Erichtho addresses him, promising never to call him up again.

759 *already dying*: the corpse is returning to life by reversing the stages of dying.

770 *tripods*: i.e. oracles: tripods were part of the apparatus of prophecy.

776–820 *The necromancy 9.* The corpse reports the sadness of the Roman shades at the civil war, the joy of the shades of those Romans who were prepared to attack their fellow countrymen, and hints that Pompey and his sons will die soon. This passage is evidently designed as an inversion of the parade of future Roman heroes shown to Aeneas in the Underworld by his father Anchises, Virgil, *Aen.* 6. 756–885. Some of the plurals in these lines are generic, i.e. 'Curius and his sort'.

777 *silent river-bank*: of Lethe in the Underworld.

787 *Sulla . . . Fortune*: Fortune was Sulla's guardian god (hence he took the name Felix, cf. 2. 221) and Sulla's faction was to be worsted in the civil war.

788 *Scipio*: cf. 306–13 n.

790 *Cato*: Marcus Porcius Cato the censor, 234–149 BC, who demanded the destruction of Carthage. His great-grandson was the Cato of the civil war.

795 *those radical names*: the Latin word *popularis* combines the meanings of 'favourites with the masses' and 'pursuing a political programme designed to favour the masses (as opposed to the élite)'; to be described as a *popularis* was generally an insult.

796 *the Drusi*: a reference to Marcus Livius Drusus, tribune in 122 BC, and his son of the same name, tribune in 91 BC, who took up some of the measures of the Gracchi.

805–6 *the glory of a short life*: i.e. Caesar's short-lived rule.

809 *the gods of Rome*: a reference to deified emperors, of whom Julius Caesar was the first.

813–14 Evidently Lucan planned an episode in a later book which either was not written or does not survive in which the ghost of Pompey appeared to his son, as did Anchises to Aeneas in the *Aeneid*.

817–18 Lucan says that Pompey and his sons will die in lands over which Pompey had triumphed. Pompey dies in Egypt, Gnaeus in Spain, and Sextus in Miletus (Asia). Pompey's triumphs were awarded for victories over Numidia, Spain, and Asia. Thus Libya here stands for Africa.

820–30 *The necromancy 10*. Erichtho burns the corpse and Sextus returns to camp.

BOOK 7

1–44 Pompey's dream on the night before the battle of Pharsalia is described. Lucan will balance this with Caesar's dream after the battle towards the end of the book (776–86).

3 The ancients thought that the sun itself moved from west to east and that its apparent daily movement from east to west was caused by the motion of the sky. Lucan suggests that on the day of the battle the sun tried to travel faster than usual eastwards to avoid rising.

9 *his own theatre*: Pompey built the first stone theatre at Rome (near the Campus Martius) in 55 BC.

12 *tiers*: lit. 'wedges' of seats in the theatre.

14 *his first triumph*: Pompey's first triumph was over Numidia in 79 BC, his second triumph over Spain in 71 BC, and his third over the east in 61 BC.

17–18 *plain toga . . . the chariot*: the plain white toga worn by Roman citizens after the age of puberty, here contrasted with the purple toga (*toga picta*) worn by the triumphing general as he processes in his triumphal chariot.

19 *a Roman knight*: Pompey was designated consul for 70 BC while still a knight, not having passed through the regular career-structure.

34 *her prayers for you*: for Rome's prayers for Pompey's recovery from illness in 50 BC realized cf. Juvenal 10. 283–6, Cicero, *Tusc. Disp.* 1. 86, Plutarch, *Pomp.* 57.

42 *the Thunderer*: i.e. Jupiter Capitolinus: Lucan appears to envisage the celebration of Caesar's victory in a triumph or thanksgiving.

45–85 At sunrise Pompey's troops demand battle and Cicero addresses Pompey on their behalf, urging him to fight immediately. This episode is unhistorical, as we know (e.g. Plutarch, *Cic.* 39) that Cicero was not present at Pharsalia; however, he is useful for Lucan as a representative of both troops and Senate. Neither Cicero's advice nor his motive does him or the Republican cause any credit.

64 *Axes*: symbols of authority of the consul, cf. 2. 548 n.

79 *our bidden leader*: cf. 5. 46–7.

85–150 Pompey replies. Against his better judgement, compelled by the pressure, he gives the signal for battle. The episode in general shows Pompey's weakness (he knows it is better to wait but his craving for popularity causes him to give way) and his speech in particular shows his pessimism and lack of confidence.

92 *was imposed*: i.e. had it forced on him rather than choosing it himself.

92–3 *cost you no wound*: i.e. could have been brought to a successful conclusion by different tactics, such as attrition.

119 *victory is no more welcome*: i.e. than defeat.

133 *what Rome will be*: a free state or a monarchy.

139–43 Description of men preparing for battle is a set feature of epic, cf. Virgil, *Aen.* 7. 624–40, where the Latins arm themselves.

140–1 *every lance is straightened on the rock*: these are reusable weapons, retrieved from battle and straightened before repeat use.

146 *upon Sicilian anvils*: i.e. in the forge of Vulcan and the Cyclopes under Mount Etna (cf. 150).

150 *Pallenaean*: Pallene was the later name of Phlegra, in Chalcidice in Macedonia, northern Greece.

151–213 The portents and signs of the day are described. This is a set-piece by Lucan, used to heighten tension. Cf. 1. 522–83 with n. For the portents before Pharsalia, cf. Florus 2. 13. 45; Appian, *Bell. Civ.* 2. 68. In Valerius Maximus (1. 6. 12) the portents occur during Pompey's march to Thessaly.

164 i.e. thereafter they became Caesar's private property.

176 *Boebeïs*: a lake in Thessaly at the foot of Mount Ossa.

192–6 For this story of the augur, Gaius Cornelius, see Plutarch, *Caes.* 47 and Gellius 15. 18.

193 *the Euganean hill*: near Patavium (mod. Padua).

   Aponus: a hot spring with medicinal qualities (mod. Abano Terme).

194 *Antenor's Timavus*: a river going to the Adriatic, not far from Patavium; Antenor was the founder of Patavium, cf. Virgil, *Aen.* 1. 242–4.

195 *The final day has come*: taken from Virgil, *Aen.* 2. 324.

214–34 Pompey's battle formation is described. Cf. Caesar, *Bell. Civ.* 3. 88, Plutarch, *Pomp.* 69, Appian, *Bell. Civ.* 2. 76.

218 *Lentulus*: this is not necessarily accurate: according to Appian, Lentulus was in charge of the right wing.

219 *Domitius*: Lucius Domitius Ahenobarbus: see above, 2. 478.

227 *tetrarchs*: the name given to certain minor rulers in eastern kingdoms, originally a name given to one of four rulers.

228 *the purple*: = royalty.

230 *Cydonians*: Cydonia was one of Crete's chief towns.

   Ituraean arrows: the Ituraei were a people of northern Palestine especially skilled in archery and horsemanship, cf. 3. 213 ff.

231 *fierce Gauls*: probably the Allobroges who went over to Pompey's side, Caesar, *Bell. Civ.* 3. 59–61.

234 *put an end to all his triumphs*: by removing all peoples whom he could defeat.

235–336 Caesar sees Pompey's army ready for battle and is delighted. He delivers a rousing speech to his soldiers and inspires them to immediate action. The presentation of two balancing speeches of opposing generals was a traditional feature in battle-narratives; Lucan uses it here to contrast the characters of Caesar and Pompey. Caesar appeals to his soldiers' self-interest, whereas Pompey moves from patriotism to his own situation.

254 *you promised me*: cf. 1. 386–8.

266 *ordinary life*: lit. 'private life', as opposed to holding military and/or political office.

267 *in plebeian garb*: 'plebeian' is here used in the loose, not the technical, sense.

279 *chariot*: in the triumphal procession.

285 *those they know the more*: i.e. Pompey, because of his conquests in the east.

306 *Saepta*: the voting enclosure on the Campus Martius.

    battles in the closed-in Campus: cf. 2. 197; a reference to Sulla's butchery of prisoners there.

307 *a general of Sulla*: Pompey, who first came to prominence fighting for Sulla, cf. 1. 326, 'Sulla's pupil'.

315–17 A reference to the battle at 6. 263–313.

323–5 i.e. 'Kill those who confront you whether they are your kinsmen or not and your act will count as a crime and hence to your credit with me.'

326 *Level now the rampart*: probably a piece of rhetorical embroidery: it is contradicted by Caesar, *Bell. Civ.* 3. 89; Appian, *Bell. Civ.* 2. 74 confirms it, but he was probably using Lucan as his source.

337–84 Pompey is appalled to realize that the fatal battle has come and delivers a speech to his soldiers, a speech which ends gloomily with an uninspiring picture of defeat. The soldiers resolve to fight to the death.

357 *our soldiery is that of old*: his army is like that of the early Republic, with nobles and senators serving as soldiers. Cf. 2. 566.

368 *for our army Caesar is not enough*: it appears that Pompey's troops out-numbered Caesar's by a factor of two to one.

385–459 Lucan reflects on the devastating effect of the battle on his own times. This is a method of heightening the tension prior to his description of the battle itself.

392 *Gabii, Veii, Cora*: Veii was a town in Etruria, Gabii and Cora towns in Latium. Gabii was a by-word for a ghost-town, cf. Horace, *Ep.* I. 11. 7. For Veii cf. on 5. 28, Propertius 4. 10. 27–30.

394 *Laurentum*: an ancient town in Latium.

396 *the decree of Numa*: the reference is to the celebration of the 'Latin Festival' (*feriae Latinae*) at Alba Longa by night. For Numa see Glossary.

402–3 *worked by chained labourer*: a reference to the large estates (*latifundia*) on which large teams of slaves worked.

407 *civil war cannot now be waged*: because there are not enough citizens left to wage a *civil* war.

408 *Allia*: a river about 11 miles from Rome, the site of a battle when the Roman army was annihilated by the Gauls under Brennus in 387/6 BC. The day of this defeat, 18 July, was an 'unlucky' day in the Calendar.

422 *twin poles*: probably the furthest east and west, referring to the rising and setting of the sun, cf. Seneca, *Ben.* 3. 33. 3.

425 *the wandering stars*: i.e. the planets (see D. A. Kidd, 'Lucan VII. 423–425', *Mnemosyne*, 4th ser., 19 (1966) 42–5).

429 *the girded consul*: a reference to the traditional ceremony of the founding of a new colony in which the consul, with his toga tucked up, drove a plough to mark the circuit of the walls.

433 *Tigris and Rhine*: these two rivers are here used to denote the boundaries of the Roman empire.

436 Lucan wishes that Rome had never known liberty, because she loses it with such pain.

438 *from the notorious grove*: the first population of Rome was established by Romulus in a grove as an asylum for criminals. Cf. Virgil, *Aen.* 8. 342.

447–8 i.e. will he watch and do nothing despite the thunderbolts in his hand?

450 *Mimas*: a mountain range on the Erythrean peninsula of Ionia, opposite the island of Chios.

451 *Cassius*: Gaius Cassius Longinus, one of Caesar's murderers, a supporter of Pompey. (Not the Cassius of 2. 266.)

451–2 For the sudden darkness (caused by an eclipse) at Argos see 1. 544 n.

457–9 Lucan refers to the practice of deification of dead emperors which began with Julius Caesar.

460–84 The battle begins. The initial horror of the two sides is broken by Crastinus, one of Caesar's soldiers, who starts the battle.

470 *Crastinus*: an old soldier of Caesar serving as a volunteer in Caesar's army, cf. Caesar, *Bell. Civ.* 3. 91.

485–505 At first missiles are thrown, then the armies close and hand-to-hand fighting takes place.

506–44 Pompey's cavalry divides and he deploys his light-armed troops to attack. Caesar uses some cohorts he has kept to the rear to reinforce his front line and turns Pompey's cavalry back in confusion. This section contains an intervention by the poet (535–43) in which he expresses two alternative wishes: (1) that only foreign blood be spilt at Pharsalia; (2) that no foreign blood of the races soon to be incorporated into the Roman state be spilt at Pharsalia.

543 *these will be the Roman people*: a reference to the extension of Roman citizenship under the Principate.

545–85 Caesar attacks the centre of Pompey's army and meets real resistance here from Romans. After expressing his unwillingness to do so, Lucan describes the horrors perpetrated by Caesar's army.

568 *her blood-stained lash*: the image here may be drawn from Virgil, *Aen.* 8. 703.

569–70 Mars, carried in his chariot, rouses his own Thracians against the race helped by Pallas.

575 *faces*: he supposedly told his men to aim at the faces of young patricians, Florus 2. 50.

582 *the Second Order*: the knights; the senators were the First Order in the Roman state.

586–96 Lucan addresses Brutus, urging him to wait until Caesar has seized power to kill him. This is a typical intervention by the poet using apostrophe (direct address) of one of the characters in his poem. Both here and at 2. 323–5 Brutus is characterized as passionate and fiery. It is likely that in the complete poem Brutus would have reappeared, perhaps in a prediction of the assassination of Caesar.

587 *what a weapon*: i.e. the weapon with which to kill Caesar.

592 *doomed to die*: Brutus committed suicide at the battle of Philippi in 42 BC.

593–4 For the idea cf. 2. 562–5.

597–616 The death of Domitius. This is included because Domitius was Nero's ancestor (see Introduction, i. 2) and altered to glamourize his death: in fact, Domitius was killed by cavalry (Caesar, *Bell. Civ.* 3. 99) or by Antony (Cicero, *Phil.* 2. 71; cf. Postgate's observation that at 3. 609 ff. Lucan changes the achievement of an Atilius to a Massaliote soldier so that his own maternal ancestors should not be on Caesar's side: Heitland, p. liii). The implication in 597–8 that Domitius is a patrician is either wrong (the family did not attain patrician status until the early principate: Suetonius, *Nero* 1. 2) or flattery of Nero. Lucan includes the fiction of Caesar's scornful words to Domitius and Domitius' fearless last words: collections of the last words of the famous were made in antiquity; they were thought to reveal a man's true character.

600 *Domitius*: Nero's ancestor. Cf. 2. 478–525 n., 2. 478 n., and Introduction, i. 2.

604 *a second pardon*: cf. 2. 511, Suetonius, *Jul.* 34. 1.

606 *my successor*: Domitius had been appointed by Pompey and the Senate to succeed Caesar to the command in Gaul; cf. Caesar, *Bell. Civ.* 1. 6.

617–46 Lucan describes the slaughter in general, declining to name individuals because of the massive scale and significance of the battle. This is very effective rhetorically.

647–727 Pompey flees from the battle. Pompey's motives are depicted as admirable (although a less charitable view is also possible, that he despaired too soon of the Republic), including his request to the gods to stop the carnage. Lucan apostrophizes Pompey and describes his warm reception at Larisa, a town of Thessaly. This is very similar to Valerius Maximus' account, 4. 55. Contrast Caesar's account of Pompey's flight, according to which he did not stop in Larisa but hurried straight to the sea, *Bell. Civ.* 3. 96.

677 *Then a steed is spurred*: cf. Caesar's account of Pompey's departure from battle, *Bell. Civ.* 3. 96.

690 *none who stays to fight*: the fighting continued after Pompey's departure, see Caesar, *Bell. Civ.* 3. 97.

691 *Africa, lamentable for her losses*: Scipio, Cato, and Juba waged war in Africa after Pompey's death.

692 *Pharian flood*: a reference to the Alexandrian War, 48–47 BC.

711 *Libya*: here stands for Numidia.

718 *yourself*: i.e. your former self.

727 *the successful man knows not that he is loved*: a generalization (*sententia*) rounds off the paragraph devoted to Pompey, meaning that you only know your true friends in adverse situations, 'A friend in need is a friend indeed.'

728–60 Caesar captures Pompey's camp.

755 *Tagus*: a major river of the Iberian peninsula, flowing into the Atlantic Ocean in modern Portugal.

756 *Arimaspian*: cf. 3. 280n.

760–86 The soldiers lie down to sleep but are haunted by terrible dreams; Caesar experiences more nightmares than everyone else. This episode balances the account of Pompey's dream at the start of the book.

761 *on patrician turf*: for Caesar's account of the luxurious tents of some of the Pompeians see *Bell. Civ.* 3. 96, cf. Plutarch, *Pomp.* 72.

772 *flames and hissing*: i.e. the Furies with burning fire-brands and snaky hair.

776 *all these shades are in Caesar*: while each individual soldier sees some of the ghosts, Caesar sees them all.

777–8 *Pelopean Orestes . . . Scythian altar*: Orestes was a descendant of Pelops (his great-grandson) through Atreus and Agamemnon; he was chased by the Furies after killing his mother Clytemnestra, as far as the Crimea, where he was purified at the altar of Tauric Diana in Scythia.

780 *Pentheus, Agave*: both experienced mental disturbance, Pentheus when under the influence of Bacchus, his mother Agave afterwards when she returned to her senses and realized she had torn her son to pieces. Cf. 6. 357–9 n. For Pentheus' illusions see Euripides, *Bacch.* 918–22; for Agave's awakening from madness *Bacch.* 1264–301.

786–824 Caesar breakfasts on the battlefield, delighting in the sight of the corpses whose burial he has forbidden. This is the climax to Lucan's horrific characterization of Caesar, and typically incorporates the author's apostrophe of Caesar. (Contrast Appian's account, *Bell. Civ.* 2. 81, in which Caesar is simply said to eat Pompey's supper.)

792 *counts*: according to Caesar, *Bell. Civ.* 3. 99, 15,000 Pompeians died at the battle of Pharsalia.

799–801 *The Carthaginian . . . enemy*: after the battle of Cannae the Roman consul Aemilius Paullus, who was killed in the battle, was buried by Hannibal with all honour, Livy 22. 52. 6.

803 *his fellow citizens*: *ciues* as opposed to *hostes* (enemies), whom he there- fore hates more fervently than enemies; for the same sentiment see Suetonius, *Vit.* 10. 3.

811 *bodies owe their own end to themselves*: i.e. they decay naturally.

812 *consumed by fire*: i.e. in the conflagration which Stoics believed would end life on earth. Cf. too Ovid, *Met.* 1. 256–8, Seneca, *Ad Marc.* 26. 6, *Nat. Qu.* 3. 13. 2.

825–46 The beasts and birds devour the unburied corpses. A grisly piece of description.

832 *You birds*: i.e. cranes who migrate each winter. Cf. 3. 199–200, 5. 711–16.

845 *lies there rejected*: i.e. by the birds.

847–72 Apostrophe to Thessaly. Lucan addresses Thessaly with pictures of future finds of relics of the battle which will make it impossible to forget and with images of how Thessaly would be spurned if it were the only arena of civil war. This makes a doomy ending to book 7.

853 *for a second crime*: the battle of Philippi; crime = civil war.

871–2 Lucan refers to subsequent episodes of the civil war: 'carnage of the West' = the battle of Munda in Spain; the wars with Sextus Pompey, ended by the battle of Naulochus and Mylae off the coast of Sicily, here denoted by the name of another part of Sicily, the southern promontory Pachynus; 'Mutina' refers to the war with Antony, 43 BC; the battle of Actium fought near the promontory of Leucas; 'Philippi' probably embraces both the battle of Pharsalus and that of Philippi.

BOOK 8

1–32 Pompey flees from the battlefield. Book 8 is devoted to Pompey; in this opening episode we meet him fearful and fleeing, in contrast with 7. 677–89.

1 *the gorge . . . Tempe*: according to legend Hercules formed the valley of Tempe, cf. 6. 347–8.

24 *honours*: the consulship of 70 BC. At the age of 36 Pompey was not yet entitled to hold the consulate.

25 *Sullan exploits of his laurel-crowned youth*: the triumph (hence 'laurel-crowned') Pompey celebrated, contrary to Sulla's wishes, over Iarbas, king of Numidia, probably when Pompey was aged 25. This too was illegal, as Pompey was still an *eques* and not a senator, as required.

26 *Corycian fleets*: a reference to Pompey's victory over the Cilician pirates in 67 BC.

27 *Pontic standards*: a reference to his victories over Mithridates VI, king of Pontus, in the Third Mithridatic War (66–64 BC).

33–108 *The reunion of Pompey and Cornelia*. Pompey reaches the shore of Thessaly and sets sail for Lesbos to rejoin Cornelia. The scene immediately shifts to Lesbos, where Cornelia haunts the cliffs, looking out for news of Pompey. When she sees Pompey arrive Cornelia faints; he embraces her and revives her. Then he rebukes her for her weakness and she in reply blames herself for his misfortune and offers to die. Her speech moves everyone, including Pompey, to tears. The literary inspiration of Cornelia watching the sea is provided by Catullus 64. 126–7 (Ariadne watching for Theseus' sails); Ovid, *Her.* 2. 121–30 (Phyllis gazing at the sea for a sight of Demophoon's ship); and the story of Ceyx and Alcyone (Ovid, *Met.* 11, esp. 463–73 and 710–15). This episode shows the bond of Pompey and Cornelia, last seen together at the end of book 5 (722–815), an episode here echoed in several features: Pompey's tears, Cornelia's faint, the physical affection they show towards each other.

72–3 *of ancestors so great*: Cornelia was descended from the Scipios.

90 *Twice have I harmed the world*: she was first married to Publius Crassus, son of the triumvir Marcus Crassus: both died at the battle of Carrhae in 53 BC; her second marriage was to Pompey.

92 *the Assyrian disaster*: i.e. the battle of Carrhae, in Assyria.

109–58 The people of Mytilene welcome Pompey and offer him sanctuary; he thanks them for their loyalty and declares his intention to move on. His departure with Cornelia provokes deep grief. The speech of the Mytilenaeans (110–27), welcoming Pompey, shows their loyalty to him and illustrates the devotion he continues to inspire, even in defeat. This scene is prefigured in book 7 by Pompey's reception at Larisa in Thessaly (7. 712–27).

118 *already have their guilt*: in Caesar's eyes, by sheltering Cornelia and receiving Pompey.

159–201 Pompey converses with the helmsman and tells him only to sail away from Thessaly and the West and to leave their course to Fortune. In this passage Lucan shows Pompey's rootedness in the past, his inability to look ahead, and his reluctance to make decisions. The half-set sun represents symbolically Pompey's indecisiveness. Contrast the scene in Virgil, *Aen.* 10. 159–62, where Aeneas is firmly in control. Lucan also takes the opportunity to include astronomical lore in the helmsman's speech.

160–1 i.e. the Antipodes: it was a matter of debate in antiquity whether or not the Antipodes existed.

175 *both the Bears*: the Greater Bear (Ursa Major) and the Lesser Bear (Ursa Minor).

178 *the Bosporus*: the narrow strait connecting the Black Sea with the Mediterranean, dividing Europe and Asia.

179 *Arctophylax*: = Bootes, cf. 2. 722.

181 *Canopus*: a star in the constellation Argo, also called Berenice's Hair, invisible in Italy, cf. Manilius 1. 216–17, Pliny, *Nat. Hist.* 2. 178.

189 *by sea and sky*: i.e. by steering and by observing the stars.

195 *Oenussae's rocks*: the islands of Oenussae lay east of Chios.

196 i.e. he set a new course south or south-east.

202–55 Pompey sends King Deiotarus to seek help from Parthia and himself proceeds along the coast of Asia Minor. Deiotarus is here presented as an epitome of loyalty. No other source reports Deiotarus' mission to the Parthians and it may be Lucan's invention. If so, it is designed to show not only Deiotarus' loyalty but also Pompey's desperation—the idea of seeking help from Parthia, Rome's archenemy, is misguided, almost mad. In particular, ll. 232–4 sound ill after 1. 10–12 and 7. 431. (Cf. Lentulus' speech below, 331–453.)

205 *his son*: Sextus.

209 *Deiotarus*: cf. 5. 55.

218 *the haughty son of Arsaces*: Orodes II, of the Arsacid dynasty, who defeated Crassus at Carrhae in 53 BC.

225 *Babylon*: cf. 1. 10. Ctesiphon was really the capital of the Parthians.

233–4 After the battle of Carrhae, Pompey dissuaded the Senate from continuing the Parthian war.

237 *Pellaean Zeugma*: Zeugma was a town on the Euphrates with a bridge over the river, the boundary of the Parthian and Roman empires, at a place currently in eastern Turkey; it was called Pellaean because it was supposedly founded by Alexander.

244 *the Icarian rocks*: Icaria was an island in the Sporades group in the Aegean Sea, west of Samos. Pompey avoids the calm water near the coast because of his fear of cities and instead takes the rocky strait between Icaria and Samos.

244–5 *Ephesus and Colophon*: cities on the coast of Asia Minor.

246 *Samos*: an island in the Aegean off the coast of Asia Minor.

247 *Cos*: another island.

 Cnidos: a city on the coast of Asia Minor, not far from Rhodes.

247–8 *Rhodes made famous by the sun*: cf. 5. 50–1.

248–9 *Telmessus' wave*: the city of Telmessus on the southern coast of Asia Minor gave its name to the bay on which it stood.

249 *The land of Pamphylia*: an area along the southern coast of Asia Minor.

251 *Phaselis*: a city and port of Lycia.

252–3 Phaselis' population is presumably away fighting.

255 *Dipsus*: evidently a waterfall, possibly to be identified with the River Catarrhactes.

256–327 *The Senate meeting 1*. Pompey and the Senators hold a meeting at Syhedra. Pompey addresses them in a speech weighing up three possible destinations, Libya, Egypt, and Parthia, and urges them to take refuge with the King of Parthia. In the context of book 8 Pompey's speech has to fail, hence Lucan has written into it flaws and weaknesses, e.g. Pompey's expression of his misgivings about Parthia at 306–8 and 311–16. Pompey's speech was almost certainly a standard exercise in the rhetorical schools at this date (it was a little later, in Quintilian's time: 3. 8. 33).

257 *the Cilicians*: here stands for the pirates, settled in Cilicia by Pompey.

259 *Syhedra*: a small town in Cilicia.

260 *Selinus*: a river in Asia Minor.

269 *the ruins of Libya*: i.e. Carthage. Marius returned from Carthage to take power again, cf. 2. 88–93. Pompey's use of a Marian analogy is hardly reassuring, given Marius' savagery on his return to Rome.

270 *the Fasti which were full of him*: the consuls' names were recorded in the Fasti; Marius was consul seven times.

277 *Libya*: i.e. Numidia, under King Juba.

281 *the youth of the tyrant*: Ptolemy XIII was 13 years old.

283 *the fickle Moor*: Juba, King of Numidia.

286 Juba's descent from Hannibal is not elsewhere attested, though the two families may have been linked by marriage in the past.

293 *their sea*: the Red Sea, perhaps here confused with the Persian Gulf.

294 *an Ocean of their own*: the Indian Ocean.

298 *Pellaean pikes*: the pike, *sarisa*, was the national weapon of Macedonian soldiers, therefore stands for 'formations, phalanxes' here.

299–300 *Babylon proud of her walls*: cf. 6. 50.

322 *Rome, favour my plans!*: the fact that Pompey uses exactly the words of Julius Caesar as he crossed the Rubicon (1. 200) indicates that Pompey is now not significantly different from Caesar in his monomaniacal tendencies.

326–7 *Fortune must avenge either me or the Crassi*: i.e. if the Parthians defeat Caesar, Pompey will be avenged for his defeat by Caesar; if Caesar defeats the Parthians, the Crassi will be avenged for their defeat by the Parthians.

327–455 *The Senate meeting 2*. Lentulus replies, at considerable length, to Pompey's speech. Lentulus represents the Senate (cf. 5. 15–47). This too may have been a standard topic in the Roman education system: Lucan presents a *tour de force*, designed to win the argument convincingly, by appeals to heart and head, in short by pulling out all the stops. Lentulus opposes Pompey's suggestions and advocates Egypt as a refuge. His proposal wins.

330 *a recent consul*: Lentulus had been consul in 49 BC.

334–5 i.e. to grovel at.

341 *he who shuddered*: any Parthian.

351 *Rome's own Hesperian disaster*: i.e. the battle of Pharsalia.

402–3 *not specified in any laws*: i.e. too awful to be anticipated by law-makers.

406–7 *Thebes of Oedipus*: where Oedipus unwittingly slept with his mother.

413 *her husbands*: Pompey and Crassus the younger.

416 *the old defeat*: the battle of Carrhae, actually only five years earlier.

419 *first*: i.e. before the war against the Parthians.

425 *Susa*: cf. 2. 49, an Achaemenid city, subject to the Parthians.

426 *the generals*: i.e. the Crassi.

432 *the sorrowing old man*: i.e. Crassus.

438–9 See 3. 261–3 n.

447 *Jupiter*: i.e. rains.

448 *The sceptre*: Aulus Gabinius, a supporter of Pompey, proconsul of Syria, restored Ptolemy XII Auletes (father of the boy-king Ptolemy) to the throne of Egypt in 55 BC. Pompey was appointed guardian of the boy.

449–50 Lentulus means that Ptolemy is not a real king; but his words, 'the shadow of a name', repeat Lucan's description of Pompey at 1. 135.

456–71 Accepting Lentulus' opinion and the Senate's vote, Pompey sails towards Egypt via Cyprus, intending to meet Ptolemy. This is not a simple narrative of a journey, for Lucan takes the opportunity to weave in mythology about Venus' birth and astronomical lore.

457 *the goddess*: Venus, born from the foam at Paphos on Cyprus.

463 *the mountain*: i.e. Pharos with its light-house, an island off the coast of Egypt.

464 *the lowest shores*: i.e. the easternmost.

467 *Libra*: i.e. the Scales, the sign of the autumn equinox.

470 *Mount Casius*: a mountain on the Egyptian coast near the most easterly mouth of the Nile.

472–542 *The Egyptian court*. At the news of Pompey's approach Ptolemy's court consider what action to take. Lucan presents only one speech (by contrast with the true debate in the Roman Senate), that of Pothinus, who urges Pompey's assassination. Everyone agrees and Achillas is despatched to perform the crime. The question of Pompey's fate was a topic debated in the schools of rhetoric: Quintilian 7. 2. 6, cf. 3. 8. 55–8. Whereas the speech advocating the murder of Pompey is attributed to Theodotus of Chios in other sources (Plutarch, *Pomp*. 77, Appian, *Bell. Civ*. 2. 84), in Lucan it is put into the mouth of Pothinus the eunuch, partly for economy in the poem as a whole (in book 10 Pothinus urges the murder of Caesar) and partly to shed the most uncomplimentary light on the Egyptian court.

477 *guardian of Nile*: taken to be a reference to the Nilometer, the well at Memphis which marked the height of the river's waters (see Strabo 17. 1. 48).

478 *foolish in its rites*: the Egyptians worshipped animal gods, to Roman scorn.

479 *Apis*: the bull, associated with the moon (here Phoebe), supposed to be permitted to live only for a fixed period of time. Cf. Pliny, *Nat. Hist*. 8. 184–6.

483 *Pothinus*: a eunuch in Ptolemy's court.

500 *the sister you rejected*: although Cleopatra was supposed to share the throne with her brother he had driven her from power.

502 Reference to the fact that Egypt did not fight on Pompey's side (or Caesar's).

512 *more just cause of grievance*: i.e. than any other nation.

517 *we have cause of guilt*: because Pompey has chosen Egypt as a refuge.

519 *with our prayers*: if not with troops.

542–60 Lucan curses Egypt, with apostrophe first of the gods then of Ptolemy. Lucan typically inserts such apostrophes at moments of high drama and significance, to heighten the tension.

552 *while heaven thunders*: it is inappropriate for Ptolemy to interfere while heaven is showing its wrath.

553–4 *ridden . . . to the Capitol*: i.e. in triumph.

559 *illegally*: because the right to the throne depended on Pompey.

560–662 *The murder of Pompey*. On Pompey's arrival a small boat is sent to carry him to the shore. Pompey enters the boat and is murdered. Cornelia laments his death. This section contains a whole gamut of emotions: including Pompey's command to Cornelia to stay behind; Cornelia's wild speech to be with him; Pompey's dying thoughts; Cornelia's lamentation. Throughout, Pompey's thoughts are of his popularity, fame, and reputation and he consciously behaves nobly so as not to damage them. Cornelia again shows herself utterly devoted to him, reproaching and blaming herself, desperate to share his fate. This scene recalls the earlier scene on the beach at Mytilene (33–108) in which Lucan shows the empathy between husband and wife and in which Cornelia faints and reproaches herself for Pompey's situation.

566 *tides of two seas*: the two bays on either side of the Casian promontory.

568–71 Lucan leaves out part of his argument: 'if the laws of fate . . . were not dragging Magnus [he could have escaped because] not one . . . '.

597 *Septimius*: he had served as a centurion under Pompey when Pompey cleared the Mediterranean of pirates (Plutarch, *Pomp*. 78, Caesar, *Bell. Civ.* 3. 104), hence 'with your own sword' below, 608.

the javelin: the distinctively Roman weapon, as 1. 7.

607 *the boy of Pella*: the boy-king Ptolemy.

610 *what Brutus did*: murder Caesar.

627–8 Pompey envisages feeling shame at being dispatched by the Egyptian king and his minions.

634 *admire*: as opposed to grieve at: Pompey equates admiration with love (not for the first time).

646–7 *Let him pay . . . my death first*: Cornelia suggests that for Pompey to witness her death will be like death to him. She wants to punish him with this sight because he seems to welcome death as a release.

663–91 Septimius cuts off Pompey's head and gives it to Achillas who takes it to Ptolemy, who has it embalmed. The decapitation of Pompey by a Roman soldier is shocking and violent but Lucan's sense of deepest outrage is saved for his description of the foreign practice of embalmment.

673 i.e. to decapitate at one stroke.

675 *the Pharian minion*: Achillas.

692–711 Lucan contrasts the fate of the dead Ptolemies and that of the dead Pompey, in a savage denunciation full of anger.

692 *soon to perish*: Ptolemy died shortly afterwards, in the Alexandrian War against Caesar (*Alexandrian War* 33).

693 *impure sister*: Cleopatra. Lucan refers to the Egyptian practice of brother–sister marriage.

694 *the Macedonian*: Alexander the Great, buried at Alexandria.

695 *the kings*: the Pharaohs.

697 *Mausoleums*: here = vast tombs. The name arose from the tomb of Mausolus, satrap of Caria in the fourth century BC, which was one of the seven wonders of the world.

712–93 *The burial of Pompey*. Cordus, a follower of Pompey, gives the body a makeshift funeral and tomb. Cordus is another invention of Lucan: according to Plutarch (*Pomp.* 80) Pompey was buried by his ex-slave Philippus. Lucan presents Cordus as another example of the devotion and loyalty inspired by Pompey.

717 *the Idalian shore of Cinyrean Cyprus*: Cinyras was a mythical king of Cyprus. Idalium was a mountain-city in Cyprus.

730 *frankincense*: it was customary to throw frankincense on the funeral pyres of the wealthy.

732 *the loyal necks of Romans*: Romans would carry the funeral bier.

their Parent: more usually 'Father of his Country' (*Pater Patriae*).

735 *with weapons cast down*: Lucan seems to envisage the troops throwing their weapons on to the pyre.

737 *dry fires*: i.e. not fed by incense.

759 *he*: Cordus.

793–822 Lucan laments Pompey's grave and lists his achievements which should appear on the epitaph. In effect Lucan here delivers a funeral oration (*laudatio funebris*) over Pompey.

794–5 i.e. it is greater vengeance for Caesar that Pompey is buried like this, in a tomb too lowly, than that he be not buried at all.

801 *Bromius*: Dionysus/ Bacchus; the mountains of Nysa were his territory.

808 *fierce Lepidus' upheavals*: see 2. 547n.

   the Alpine war: Pompey's wars with the Alpine tribes when marching against Sertorius through the Alps.

809 *when the consul was recalled*: in fact, Metellus was not recalled from his long years fighting Sertorius, nor was he consul at this time; Lucan represents the situation to Pompey's credit.

810 *chariots*: of triumph.

817 *the sequence of his annals*: a reference to his three consulships.

823–72 Lucan curses Egypt in a passage which reveals Roman xenophobia; imagines himself retrieving Pompey's remains personally; envisages the homage to Pompey where he lies; and finally raises the possibility that Pompey did not die at all.

824 *Cumae's prophet*: the Sibyl.

829 *be in need of winter rains*: because there would be no water from the Nile; usually the Nile supplied all the water needed.

831 *Isis*: her temple stood in the Campus Martius.

832 *half-divine dogs*: Anubis, a god portrayed with a dog's head on man's body.

   rattles: the sistrum, used in the worship of Isis, cf. 10. 63.

833 *Osiris*: the husband of Isis; his death and resurrection was celebrated yearly.

835–6 *a temple to the savage tyrant*: very soon after his death, Julius Caesar was deified, a cult established, and a temple built.

848 *excessive fires*: i.e. a heat-wave, as at 1. 646–7 and 9. 375.

852 *Thebes*: in southern Egypt.

858 *Casian Jupiter*: Jupiter was worshipped on Mount Casius, see 470 n.

859 *buried in temples*: like a hero.

863 *Tarpeian gods*: i.e. the gods worshipped on the Capitol at Rome, as opposed to the older Etruscan rites.

864 A reference to the *bidental*, see 1. 608 n.

872 *Crete*: the Cretans were regarded as liars especially in their claim that Jupiter was buried there (as if an immortal god could be buried anywhere . . .).

BOOK 9

1–18 *The apotheosis of Pompey*. The spirit of Pompey leaves his ashes and flies up to the abodes of the Blessed. The reference is to the moon's orbit, the region believed by the Stoics to be inhabited by the souls of the wise.

5 *dark air*: it was thought that the air above the earth was dark until it reached the fiery ether.

11 *it*: Pompey's spirit.

18 *Brutus, Cato*: Cato continued Pompey's role by taking command of the Pompeian campaign in Africa and Brutus by his part in the assassination of Caesar.

19–50 Cato takes charge of Pompey's forces and retreats to Corcyra and then to Africa. In this passage Lucan introduces the main character of book 9.

19 *He had hated Magnus too*: Cato had hated Pompey in addition to Caesar.

28 *fearing slavery*: Cato did not fear slavery because as a Stoic he could at any time resort to suicide.

32 *a thousand*: probably 300, in fact.

37 *Cythera*: a large island south-west of Cape Malea.

39 *Phycus*: a town on a promontory on the coast of Cyrenaica in Africa.

42 *Palinurus*: a reference to the town of Paliurus on the coast of Africa east of Cyrene, associated by Lucan (apparently wrongly) with Aeneas' helmsman after whom Cape Palinurus on the coast of southern Italy was named.

51–116 Cornelia laments on board ship near the Egyptian shore.

52 *her stepson*: Sextus, son of Mucia.

66 *by the greater malice of the gods*: it was worse for Pompey to have this wretched burial than none at all. Cf. 8. 761–3, 793–5.

68 *urns not empty*: i.e. containing ashes.

83 *if that is believable*: i.e. that a woman does not fear enemy land.

79 *chariot*: i.e. triumphal chariot.

86 *for you*: for Sextus and Gnaeus.

91 *sceptres*: i.e. kingdoms.

117–66 Cornelia's ship reaches Cato's camp. Pompey's sons meet: Sextus tells Gnaeus of their father's death and Gnaeus wishes to go to Egypt to recover the body and take revenge. Cato restrains him.

121 *Magnus*: Gnaeus, who has been with Cato.

132 *the victim*: i.e., in Caesar's eyes, atoning for his giving the kingdom to Ptolemy.

159 *Osiris clothed in linen*: linen was used in ritual to wrap Osiris' dismembered limbs.

161 *by placing gods beneath*: wooden effigies used as fuel.

167–217 Cornelia lands and performs rites over Pompey's clothes and weapons; Cato delivers a funeral oration for Pompey.

177 *embroidered toga*: the garb of a triumphing general, purple and gold, hence 'three times seen by Jupiter', i.e. Jupiter Capitolinus, whose temple on the Capitol was the final point of the triumphal procession.

181 *the shades of Thessaly*: the soldiers follow Cornelia's lead and mourn their comrades who died at the battle of Pharsalia.

182–5 *the Apulian*: a reference to Apulian farmers burning stubble. Garganus, Voltur, and Matinus are all mountains in Apulia, southern Italy.

197 *paid in*: to the state treasury.

217–93 Mutiny. The troops desert, declaring that they followed Pompey and did not wish to fight in a civil war; Cato shames them into remaining. This episode shows the soldiers' personal devotion to Pompey and is also an important illustration of Cato's iron character.

219 *Tarcondimotus*: a Cilician king.

235–6 A reference to Pompey's paltry burial.

239 *a citizen in toga*: i.e. Roman.

251 *a Roman consul*: Caesar was one of the consuls. Cf. 5. 389.

256 *with a similar wish*: i.e. as the Caesarians.

265 *From three masters*: i.e. the triumvirs (cf. 1. 4), of whom now only Caesar was left.

268 *the gift of Ptolemy's weapons*: i.e. Pompey's murder, which brings Roman troops one stage nearer to liberty.

271 *Emathian Philippi*: i.e. the battle of Pharsalia; see 1. 694 n., also 6. 581, 7. 871–2.

276 *reward*: i.e. by betraying Pompey's wife and sons and Cato to Caesar, as explained in the following lines.

278 *the Pompeys*: Sextus and Gnaeus.

288 *Phrygian brass*: a reference to cymbals, called 'Phrygian' from their association with Cybele, at whose sound bees were thought to congregate (cf. Virgil, *Georg.* 4. 64).

291 *Hybla*: a mountain of Sicily famed for its honey.

294–318 Cato keeps his troops occupied on various tasks and sets out to sail to King Juba. This gives Lucan an opportunity to describe the Syrtes which lie in between, with a display of learning in presenting theories about their formation.

298 *though shut out*: in fact, the inhabitants opened the gates to Cato.

319–47 A storm arises and destroys some of the ships. For discussion of this storm, one of four in Lucan's poem, see Morford 48–9, who notices echoes of the storm which opens Virgil, *Aen.* 1 and of the storm in the Syrtes described by Apollonius Rhodius, *Arg.* 4. 1240–9.

347 *Triton*: an inland lake not far from the coast and perhaps once connected to the coast by a river.

348–67 Lucan recounts legends connected with Lake Triton, including the Garden of the Hesperides. This mythical interlude provides variety from the terrors of nature and the horrors of war in general. The association of Cato with this area of legend visited by Hercules exalts him on to a similar level with the Stoic hero.

350 Pallas was born straight from her father Jupiter's head.

355 *river Lethon*: in Cyrenaica, a long way east of Lake Triton; it is possible that Lucan has conflated Syrtis Major, near Cyrenaica, with Syrtis Minor, near which was Lake Triton.

357 *the garden of the Hesperides*: variously located in Cyrene and beyond Mount Atlas. Hercules' twelfth labour was to steal the golden apples, guarded by the sleepless dragon.

365–7 *Alcides . . . Argos' tyrant*: the twelfth labour of Hercules (= Alcides) imposed by Eurystheus, king of Argos.

368–410 The fleet anchors off the coast of Libya. Anxious not to lose time, Cato plans to take the army across land. He persuades his men with a rousing speech, which outlines the dangers they will face (snakes, thirst, and sand: these are met in the reverse order). The speech conveys Cato's character: his patriotism, his endurance, and his determination, in the pursuit of freedom and virtue.

370 *Pompey*: i.e. Gnaeus Pompey.

394 *to be his master's slave*: i.e. to join Caesar.

398–402 i.e. Cato says he will set an example by sharing all the hardships. It will be permitted for his men to complain of thirst, heat, exhaustion if they see Cato taking advantage of his position. But as he will not, they will have no cause of complaint.

406 *to have fled*: from Pharsalus: they will redeem themselves by facing the dangers of Libya.

409 *soon to shut*: after Cato's suicide at Utica following the battle of Thapsus (46 BC).

411–510 A description of Libya and the hazards it presents to Cato and his men, including heat, wind, and thirst. Lucan's geographical description, reflecting the tastes of the rhetorical schools, is a *tour de force* which incorporates his fourth 'storm', the Libyan dust-storm (445–92), on which see Morford 49–50. The section also illuminates Cato's self-denying steely character, in his refusing to drink even a drop of water.

416 *Ocean*: the Mediterranean.

417–20 i.e. Europe and Libya have the source of the west wind; Asia and Europe share the north wind; Asia and Libya the south wind; Asia alone has the east wind.

417 *those*: Europe and Libya.

418 *the latter*: Asia.

427 *Maurusian*: = Mauretanian (Moroccan).

436 *Jupiter*: in his capacity as god of rain and water.

454 *Aeolus' fury*: i.e. the full force of the winds: see Glossary s.n. Aeolus.

478–9 *those objects . . . chosen young men*: the sacred shield of Numa which supposedly fell from the sky and the eleven exact replicas Numa had made; these were looked after by the Salian priests, drawn from patrician families, and carried annually in a procession through Rome, cf. 1. 603.

510 *water enough for all*: i.e. none equally: everyone was satisfied because no one was drinking.

511–37 They arrive at the temple of Jupiter Ammon: Lucan describes the god and the place. Since this temple would not readily have been on Cato's route, it seems that Lucan has adapted his material to include an episode which gives Cato credit and contrasts with Appius' consultation of the Delphic oracle in book 5. Moreover, in this passage Lucan includes exotic astronomical matter, ascribing to the Tropic of Cancer phenomena which occur at the equator: on the astronomical details and text here see Housman's Astronomical Appendix, pp. 329–33.

524 *Berenicis*: the region round Berenice in Cyrenaica.

531–2 *the circle of the higher solstice*: the Tropic of Cancer.

540 *climbs into your sight*: whereas for us it is always visible.

533–7 A piece of bravura: into five lines Lucan has worked the twelve signs of the zodiac in their opposing pairs, while making the point that at the equator all twelve signs rise at the same height and take the same time to rise and set. Astraea is Virgo; Chiron Sagittarius; Aegoceros Capricorn; and the Urn is that held by Aquarius.

544–86 Labienus urges Cato to consult the oracle but he declines. This episode contrasts with Appius' consultation of the Delphic oracle at 5. 64–236, above all in Cato's refusal to consult the oracle. Lucan presents Cato as delivering an oracle himself, as he voices the Stoic belief in fate and predestination.

550 *Labienus*: cf. 5. 345 n.

587–604 Cato's endurance is shown as they continue on their march: Lucan pronounces a eulogy of Cato as the epitome of virtue.

596 *was luck*: lit. 'was Fortune', i.e. was Fortune's gift.

600 *break Jugurtha's neck*: Jugurtha was strangled in prison soon after Marius' triumph in 104 BC.

604–18 *The snakes of Africa 1*. They come to a spring full of snakes, which Cato pronounces safe to drink from.

619–99 *The snakes of Africa 2*. By posing the question why Libya abounds in snakes, Lucan is able to introduce the story of Medusa and Perseus which presents the origin (*aition*) of the snakes; this mythological material gives some relief from the narrative of Cato's march and hardships.

626 *Medusa, Phorcys' daughter*: Phorcys, an old sea deity, was the father of the three Gorgons.

628 *looked upon*: and therefore turned into stone.

636–7 *only part ... unharmed*: it is possible to look at her hair safely, as opposed to her face, which brings instant death.

644 *Amphitryon's son*: Hercules' mortal father was Amphitryon.

655 *the Pillars of the West*: a mountain in north-west Africa near Gibraltar supported by Atlas, one of the Titans, cf. Ovid, *Met.* 4. 656 for Atlas' transformation into a mountain.

656 *the Giants supported on Phlegraean snakes*: i.e. at the battle of Phlegra, the Giants had snakes as legs.

657–8 *the Gorgon on the centre of Pallas' breast*: Pallas' shield (the aegis) had a portrayal of the Gorgon's head at its centre.

659 *To this place*: 'the furthest parts of Libya', described in 624–8.

660 *rain enriched*: Jupiter impregnated Danae in the form of golden rain.

660–1 *Parrhasian wings . . . wrestling-floor*: the Arcadian inventor is Mercury, from Arcadia; Parrhasia was a region of Arcadia; Perseus was wearing Mercury's winged sandals. Cf. 2. 237n.

661 *cithara*: a lyre.

663 *the scimitar already red*: Mercury had already used it to kill Argus (see below), Ovid, *Met.* 1. 716–19.

664 *the guardian*: Argus, the many-eyed monster set by Juno to watch Jupiter's paramour Io, whom she had transformed into a heifer.

665 *her winged brother*: both Perseus and Pallas were children of Jupiter.

692–5 'Night' here is the shadow of the earth: the earth at the equator casts its shadow highest on the sky, so the moon becomes eclipsed if it follows a straight path as opposed to oblique.

700–33 *The snakes of Africa 3*. A catalogue of the snakes of Africa. This is a *tour de force* of learning, which reflects Lucan's interest in natural history. In particular, Lucan may have drawn material from a work of the second-century-BC poet Nicander, whose *Theriaca* is a didactic poem about snakes and other poisonous creatures. The Latin didactic poet Aemilius Macer, a contemporary of Ovid, wrote an imitation of Nicander's poem on snakes, which suggests that the topic was in vogue under the early Principate. That it remained of interest is confirmed by Lucian's brief *On the Dipsades* (mid-second century AD). Many of the snakes' names are Greek words which express their nature.

708 *Haemorrhois*: lit. 'flowing blood'.

710 *Chersydros*: lit. 'dry land and water'.

711 *Chelydros*: lit. 'water-tortoise'.

712 *Cenchris*: a fish marked with many small specks, like millet (*kenchros* in Greek).

714 *serpentine*: a sort of stone with snake-like markings.

715 *Ammodytes*: lit. 'sand-ducking'.

716 *Cerastes*: a horned snake, cf. 6. 679.

717 *Scytale*: lit. 'club'.

717–18 *while frost lies*: i.e. in spring as opposed to summer.

718 *Dipsas*: a snake whose bite caused thirst (*dipsa* in Greek).

719 *Amphisbaena*: lit. 'going both ways'.

720 *Natrix*: 'swimmer' in Latin.

Jaculus: 'javelin' in Latin.

721 *Parias*: a red-brown snake.

722 *Prester*: 'sweller'.

723 *Seps*: 'putrefier'.

724 *Basilisk*: a snake with markings on the head like a crown, lit. 'kinglet'.

727 *Dragons*: a snake worshipped in the east. Cf. Pliny, *Nat. Hist.* 8. 32–7.

734–838 *The snakes of Africa 4*. As Cato marches through the desert, many of his soldiers are killed by the snakes. Their deaths are described. Lucan ends this section by adding scorpions and ants to the list of hazards. In this he broadly follows the pattern of Nicander's *Theriaca*, of which the bulk is devoted to snakes and antidotes but which ends with sections on spiders and scorpions.

747 *the glory of the state*: the Roman standard, which resembled an eagle.

787 *Cinyphian*: Cinyps, a river in Libya, hence = Libyan, African.

790 *the Marsian land*: an area of central Italy near the Fucine lake. It is interesting to note that Marsic magicians were famous for cures to snake-bites, though not so here, it seems.

808–9 *saffron . . . statues*: apparently an allusion to showering the audience in the theatre with saffron.

815 *unlucky Laevus*: Laevus means 'unlucky', e.g. Horace, *Ars* 301.

820 *Sabaean twigs*: Saba, a town in Arabia, was renowned for its incense, here referred to as 'twigs', Pliny, *Nat. Hist.* 12. 52. Cf. [Seneca] *Herc. Oet.* 376, 793, Virgil, *Aen.* 1. 416.

821 *Saïtae*: the people of Saïs, a town in the Nile delta.

836 *defeating Orion*: Orion was stung to death by a scorpion which then became a constellation.

837 *Salpuga*: a venomous ant, cf. Pliny, *Nat. Hist.* 29. 92.

839–89 *The snakes of Africa 5*. The men complain of their sufferings caused by the snakes. Cato attends the dying.

865 *the barriers of the world*: i.e. the gates of the west.

877 *for Notus' blasts*: the south wind was supposed to rise at the equator, which they imagine they have crossed.

890–937 *The snakes of Africa 6*. The Psylli, a local people, help them, by warding off the snakes and sucking out the poison from their wounds. Lucan displays his interest in two further branches of learning here, ethnography and medicine.

893 *the Psylli*: said to be snake-charmers as well as immune from poison, Pliny, *Nat. Hist.* 7. 14.

902 *the bird of Jupiter*: the eagle.

919 *Mount Eryx*: a mountain in Sicily.

938–49 Cato and his men arrive at Leptis. Here ends the part of the book devoted to Cato, with a respite from troubles.

950–99 Meanwhile Caesar pursues Pompey but stops at Troy, where he goes sightseeing, visiting places mentioned in the story of the Trojan War (in Homer's *Iliad* especially). This episode takes us back in time, to events contemporary with the opening of book 8. This sightseeing tour describes places with which Lucan and his readers may have been familiar; in any case the combination of antiquarianism and travel-writing reflects Roman intellectual interests. This passage includes the famous apostrophe to Caesar promising him immortality through Lucan's poem, which some scholars use as evidence for the title *Pharsalia*.

954–5 *water swum in love*: the Hellespont, swum by Leander of Abydos in his love for Hero of Sestos on the other side who gave him a signal from her tower.

956 *Helle*: because it was called the Hellespont after her, after she fell in from the back of the Golden Ram.

959 *Calchedon*: in Asia Minor on the Bosporus, nearly opposite Byzantium.

960 *Propontis, Euxine*: the Sea of Marmara, joined to the Euxine (the Black Sea) by the narrow Bosporus.

961 *Sigeum's sands*: a promontory near Troy.

962 *Simois' waters*: a river running near Troy.

Rhoeteum: a place near Troy famous for the tomb of Ajax.

963 *to bards*: Homer, above all.

965 *the wall of Phoebus*: Apollo and Poseidon built the city-wall for Laomedon, king of Troy.

967 *Assaracus*: king of Phrygia, son of Tros, grandfather of Anchises, great-grandfather of Aeneas.

970 *Hesione's rock*: here Hesione, daughter of Laomedon, king of Troy, was exposed to the sea-monster and rescued by Hercules.

Anchises' marriage-chamber: where Anchises and Venus made love; Aeneas was born from their union.

971 *the adjudicator*: Paris judged which of the three goddesses, Juno, Minerva, and Venus, was the most beautiful.

972 *the boy*: Ganymedes, son of Tros, abducted by Jupiter to be his cup-bearer.

973 *Oenone*: a nymph, loved by Paris. Because he deserted her for Helen, she refused to cure his battle-wound, until it was too late. Finding him dead she was stricken by grief and killed herself.

975 *Xanthus*: a river near Troy.

979 *Hercean altars*: when Zeus (= Jupiter) was regarded as the god of the house he was called Zeus Herceus.

984   *the Smyrnaean bard*: Homer, whose birth-place was said to be Smyrna on the west coast of Asia Minor.

991   *my Aeneas*: Julius Caesar claimed descent from Aeneas through Iulus, Aeneas' son.

992   *Lavinian abodes*: Lavinium was founded by Aeneas.

993   *the Phrygian fire*: the flame brought by Aeneas from Troy to Italy.

993   *Pallas*: the image of the goddess Pallas, known as the Palladium, emblem of the safety of Troy, in the temple of Vesta.

1000–34   Caesar travels on to Egypt. On his arrival a soldier of Ptolemy meets him with the head of Pompey.

1005   *the flames of Pharos*: the light-house at Alexandria.

1035–108   Caesar weeps feigned tears over Pompey, reproaches Pompey's murderers and tells them to appease his shade. This passage includes an apostrophe by Lucan to Caesar condemning his hypocrisy.

1067   *to grant survival to the conquered*: an element of Caesar's policy was to spare his enemies when they fell into his hands (*clementia*).

1100   *ask . . . your staying alive*: ask you to go on living.

BOOK 10

1–19   Caesar visits the tomb of Alexander the Great in Alexandria.

8   i.e. if Caesar also were assassinated in Egypt, this might be thought to make up for Pompey's murder. Cf. 386–9 for the same idea.

9   *Paraetonian city*: Alexandria.

20–52   Lucan's outburst against Alexander. He invites us to link him with Caesar.

20   *the crazy offspring*: Alexander the Great.

29   *Athens conquered by his father*: Philip II conquered Athens at the battle of Chaeronea in 338 BC.

34   *thunderbolt*: note that Julius Caesar is compared with a thunderbolt, 1. 151–7.

40 *drunk Nile from his source*: Lucan apparently envisages Alexander circumnavigating the world to find the source of the Nile. The source of the Nile was unknown in Alexander's day and in Lucan's—and a matter of great interest in both.

48 *the pikes*: weapons used by Macedonian troops, here contrasted with the javelins, the characteristic Roman weapons (cf. 1. 7).

51 *the master of the Arsacids*: i.e. Alexander. Arsaces, the first king of the Parthians (mid-third century BC), founded the dynasty called the Arsacids. Of course, in Alexander's time, there were no Arsacids; however, Lucan means here that although Rome rules a vast empire to the north, west, and south, in the east Rome will always be inferior in her achievements to Alexander's achievements in that region.

52 *Pella*: the capital city of Macedonia, mentioned here to create a contrast with Rome: in the east, the nation which defeated Rome (in the persons of the Crassi) was a mere province of Pella.

53–106 First Ptolemy then Cleopatra approach Caesar. Cleopatra appeals to Caesar to rid the court of Pothinus. Caesar is won over by her. The passage includes an emotional tirade against Cleopatra by Lucan.

57 *the chains of Pharos*: chains across the mouth of the harbour.

58 *Emathian*: here = Macedonian, and so Alexandrian.

60 *the Spartan woman*: Helen, wife of Menelaus king of Sparta, abducted by the Trojan Paris, and so the cause of the Trojan War between the Trojans and the Greeks (also called the Argives) who were led by Menelaus' brother Agamemnon, king of Argos.

63 *rattle*: cf. 8. 832 n.

75 *Venus*: see 2. 387 n.

77 *brothers*: Cleopatra and Caesar had one son, Caesarion.

81 He spends his time acting to secure Cleopatra's kingdom for her instead of pursuing Cato and the Pompeians.

98 *the minion*: Pothinus (cf. 8. 483 n.).

107–35 *The banquet 1*. Lucan describes the luxurious setting of the banquet and the attendants.

112 *would hardly build*: because steeped in luxury it would have priorities other than temples, e.g. palaces, baths.

116 *the purple stone*: probably porphyry, a type of marble.

117 *ebony of Meroë*: cf. 302–4.

124 *Tyrian dye*: i.e. purple: the production of Tyrian purple involved steeping the fabric consecutively in two different dyes. Tyre was a city on the Phoenician coast.

125 *cochineal*: a scarlet dye.

126 *mingling heddles*: technical vocabulary from weaving referring to the threads, also called 'leashes'.

134–5 *a stronger age-group*: boys or young men not castrated.

136–71 *The banquet 2.* Description of Cleopatra's beautiful and luxurious appearance and of the extravagant riches of the banquet.

139 *the Red Sea's booty*: pearls.

144–5 *round tables cut in Atlas' forest*: citrus-wood tables from Mauretania (cf. 9. 427).

152 *Fabricii*: see 3. 160n.

152–3 *that consul*: Lucius Quinctius Cincinnatus, who was saluted consul while he was ploughing (458 BC).

162 *Falernian*: a wine which when produced in Italy required several years' fermentation.

164 *nard*: a perfumed plant, the source of an expensive perfume.

172–92 *The banquet 3.* Caesar asks Acoreus about the Egyptian gods and the source of the Nile.

174 *linen-clad*: the appropriate garb for the priest of Isis.

179–80 The reference is to hieroglyphics.

182 *Plato*: Plato (*c.*429–347 BC) is said to have travelled to many places, including Egypt.

what visitor ever more deserved: i.e. than I do.

187 *my own year*: the Julian Calendar, named after Julius Caesar and introduced by him in 45 BC, adapted from the calendar established by
Greek astronomers. (Book 10 is set in 48 BC.)

Eudoxus' calendar: Eudoxus of Cnidus was a Greek mathematician
and astronomer of the fourth century BC.

193–331 *The banquet 4*. Acoreus replies. First he refutes false theories about
the source of the Nile, then he gives his own views.

203 *by halting them*: 'the sun causes the planets, when they have reached
their fixed limits, to appear to remain stationary for a time and then
to return' (Haskins); see Vitruvius 9. 1. 11; Pliny, *Nat. Hist.* 2. 69–71.

205–9 Lucan's apportioning of planets' spheres of activity is paralleled
in Paulus Alexandrinus (pp. 42–3 Boer).

210–18 On Lucan's misunderstandings of astronomy, see Housman 334–7.

214 *the master of the waters*: Mercury: see above, 209. (The planet Neptune
was not discovered until the nineteenth century.)

221–2 *colour of the people burnt by sun*: cf. Seneca, *Nat. Qu.* 4A. 2. 18,
where too skin-colour is cited as proof that Ethiopia is very hot.

226 *Dog*: the Dog-Star, Sirius: its rising in July was associated with the
hottest weather (the 'dog-days').

250 *the middle region*: i.e. the equatorial zone.

254 *not a single stream*: a reference to the seven mouths of the Nile.

275 *they saw Nile steaming*: but did not reach its source.

276 *Sesostris*: an Egyptian king (Herodotus 2. 102–10).

278–9 *yet ... Rhône and Po ... Nile*: meaning he no more discovered
the source of the Nile than that of the Rhône or the Po: he is
not said to have visited Gaul and Italy.

279 *The mad Cambyses*: king of Persia in the sixth century BC; he conquered Egypt and took an expedition into the desert (Herodotus
3. 1–38).

280 *the people of long life*: the Macrobii, a people of Ethiopia (see Herodotus
3. 23).

287 *the middle region*: see 250 n.

306 *that line of the world*: a line drawn from Meroe to the sky; cf. 9. 528–30.

307 *the zones of Phoebus*: the torrid zone.

313 *Philae*: an island on the Nile near Syene (= Aswan).

324 *Abatos*: a rock in the Nile near Philae, Greek 'untrodden', because sacred.

325 *the river's veins*: the name given to two crags supposed to mark the point where the river begins to rise; cf. Seneca, *NQ* 4A. 2. 7.

332–98 Pothinus plots the death of Caesar and invites Achillas to commit the deed. This speech closely balances Pothinus' speech to the court of Ptolemy at 8. 484–535, where he urges Pompey's assassination, following which Achillas is sent to perform the murder.

337 *the avenging goddesses*: the Furies.

344 *the warning*: the warning to all tyrants represented by Brutus' dagger.

351 *the unwarlike boy*: Ptolemy XIII, aged 15 at this time. 'Unwarlike' was virtually a standard epithet of abuse.

356 *not just betrayed but given away*: betrayed by Cleopatra to Caesar then given by Caesar to Cleopatra.

371 *in vain*: because Caesar was not grateful.

378 *the shore*: where Pompey was killed.

384 *Those men*: who do control kingdoms and the wealth of nations.

395 *the Roman soldiers*: i.e. Romans fighting as mercenaries in the Egyptian army, such as Septimius at 8. 595–610.

398–433 Achillas moves into action and surrounds the palace with his troops. This passage includes Lucan's indignant apostrophe against the Roman mercenaries in Achillas' army.

421 *Both*: Pothinus and Achillas.

434–85 As Achillas' troops approach, Caesar barricades the palace and keeps Ptolemy with him as a hostage and bargaining-counter; he is under such pressure that he considers bargaining. Fighting oppresses him on all sides.

434 *the Casian rock*: see 8. 470 n.

464 *the barbarian of Colchis*: Medea of Colchis, who tore her brother Apsyrtus to pieces and threw his limbs in the way of her father Aeetes
who was pursuing her, wishing to punish her for betraying the kingdom and running away with Jason.

471 *universal law*: i.e. that ambassadors were inviolate.

472A This is a line inserted by Housman to fill a gap in the text where
something has fallen out.

476 *Pharnaces*: Pharnaces II (cf. 2. 637) led a revolt against his father,
Mithridates king of Pontus, joining Pompey in the civil war.

486–533 Caesar resists attack by ships too, so successfully that he is then
able to seize Pharos. He kills Pothinus; Arsinoe, the younger sister
of Ptolemy and Cleopatra, kills Achillas. The opposition to Caesar
continues, led by Ganymedes.

494 *wax*: the wax used on ships was a fire-hazard, cf. 3. 684.

510 *prophet Proteus*: see Virgil, *Georg.* 4. 387–95.

518 *what a crime!*: it outrages Lucan that the criminal Pothinus shared
the same death as his revered Pompey.

519 *Arsinoe*: the younger sister of Ptolemy and Cleopatra. For Caesar's
version of this plot see *Bell. Civ.* 3. 112.

520 *Ganymedes*: a eunuch, tutor of Arsinoe, whom she put in charge
of the army; see *The Alexandrian War* 4.

534–46 At the moment of extreme danger, Caesar is inspired by the
thought of Scaeva, whose *aristeia* was described at 6. 138–262. Here
the poem breaks off, incomplete or (probably) unfinished. It is curious
that it breaks off at the same point as Caesar's narrative of the civil
war.

GLOSSARY AND
INDEX OF NAMES

ABÝDOS 2. 674, 6. 55: a town on the Hellespont.

ACHÁEMENID 2. 49, 8. 224: Persian.

ACHÍLLAS 8. 538, 618, 10. 350, 398, 419, 523: a general of Ptolemy given the job of Pompey's assassination.

ACÓREUS 8. 475, 10. 174, 193: an aged member of Ptolemy's court, probably invented by Lucan.

ÁEGIS 7. 149, 570: the shield of Pallas (= Minerva, Athene).

AEGÓCEROS 9. 536, 10. 213: = Capricorn (lit. 'horned goat').

AEÓLIA, AEÓLIAN, ÁEOLUS 2. 456, 667, 5. 610, 9. 454: Aeolus was god of the winds, which he kept confined in a cave on Aeolia, a floating island, identified with the Liparian islands between Italy and Sicily.

AGÁVE 1. 575, 6. 357, 7. 780: mother of Pentheus, king of Thebes; after he forbade the worship of Bacchus, Agave and the other Bacchants tore him to pieces.

ALÁNI 8. 223, 10. 454: a Scythian race.

ÁLBA 1. 198, 3. 87, 5. 400, 7. 394, 9. 992: an ancient town in Latium, home of the house-gods brought by Aeneas.

ALCÍDES 1. 577, 4. 611 and often, 6. 391, 9. 365: = Hercules, a descendant of Alcaeus.

ÁMMON 3. 292, 4. 673, 9. 514 and often, 10. 38: a god worshipped in north Africa in the form of a ram and sometimes identified with Jupiter.

AMÝCLAS 5. 521, 539: a fisherman, probably invented by Lucan.

ANTONY 5. 478, 10. 71: Marcus Antonius (Mark Antony, the future triumvir) was commander of the troops left at Brundisium.

ÁQUILO, plural AQUILÓNES 4. 457 and often: the north wind.

ARÁXES 1. 19, 7. 188, 8. 431: a river in Armenia which joins the Cyrus then flows into the Caspian Sea.

ÁRCTOS 1, 252, 459, 3. 251, 6. 342, 10. 49, 220: the constellation of the Great Bear; hence 'Arctic', of the lands, peoples or climate of the north.

ÁRGO, ÁRGONAUTS 2. 717, 3. 193, cf. 6. 400–1: Jason and the Argonauts travelled in the first ship, the Argo, from Thessaly through the Clashing Rocks into the Black Sea and to the land of Colchis where Jason captured the Golden Fleece.

ÁRSACES, ÁRSACIDS 1. 108, 8. 218, 232, 306, 409, 10. 51: Arsaces was the first king of the Parthian dynasty; hence the 'sons of Arsaces' or 'Arsacids' = the Parthians; at 8. 218 = Orodes II, king of the Parthians; at 8. 409 = any Parthian king.

ÁTLAS 1. 555, 4. 672, 9. 654: a mountain-range in north-west Africa, created when the Titan Atlas was turned to stone.

AUSÓNIA, AUSÓNIAN 1. 216 and often: Ausonia was an old name for Italy, hence 'Ausonian' = Italian.

ÁUSTER, plural ÁUSTRI 1. 235 and often: the south wind.

BÁBYLON 1. 10, 6. 50, 450, 8. 225, 299, 426, 10. 46: a city in Parthia.

BÁCCHUS = wine 1. 610, 4. 198, 379, 10. 173; = vine 9. 434.

BÁCTRA 8. 299, 423: a city of the Medes.

BELLÓNA 1. 565, 7. 568: the Roman goddess of war: her priests made cuts in their arms and legs during sacrifice to her.

BISTÓNIAN(S) 3. 200, 4. 767, 7. 569, 826, i.e. Thracian, Thracians; the Bistonian tyrant is Diomedes, king of Thrace, 2. 163.

BOÓTES 2. 722, 3. 252, 10. 289, also called Arctophylax 8. 179: a constellation near the Great Bear, also called the Wain, hence the reference to a 'wagon' at 2. 722.

BÓREAS 1. 391 and often: the north wind.

BRÚTI, BRÚTUS 5. 207, 6. 792, 7. 39, 440: Lucius Junius Brutus, who expelled the kings (the Tarquins) and brought liberty to Rome, i.e. founded the Republic, cf. Tacitus, *Ann.* 1. 1. His first consulship was in 509 BC. At 6. 792 he is described as rejoicing because the tyrant Caesar will fall at the hands of his descendants. His death was mourned for a whole year by the matrons of Rome; cf. Livy 2. 7, Juvenal 8. 267.

BRÚTUS 3. 514, 535, 558, 563, 761: Decimus Junius Brutus Albinus, Caesar's admiral; he had served under Caesar in Gaul. His 'towered vessel' was the admiral's ship.

BRÚTUS 2. 234 and often, 5. 207, 7. 440 (plural), 587, 596, 8. 610, 9. 18, 10. 342, 398: Marcus Junius Brutus, one of Caesar's assassins in 44 BC. He was a follower of Cato and supported the Republican side in the civil war. After being defeated at Philippi in 42 BC by Antony and Augustus, he killed himself. See Introduction, ii. 9.

CÁLPE I. 555, 4. 71: Gibraltar.

CAMÍLLUS I. 169, 2. 545, 5. 28, 6. 786, 7. 359: Marcus Furius Camillus saved Rome from the Gallic invasion of 387/6 BC. The generic plural occurs at 2. 545 and 7. 359.

CÁMPUS I. 180, 580, 2. 222, 5. 392, 7. 306, 8. 685: the Campus Martius, Field of Mars, in Rome, where the elections were held.

CÁNNAE 2. 46, 7. 408, 800: the battle of Cannae in Apulia in 216 BC at which Hannibal defeated the Romans.

CANÓPUS 8. 543, 10. 64: a town on the westernmost mouth of the Nile, famed for its luxury.

CÁRTHAGE 2. 91, 4. 586, 788, 6. 789, 8. 284: a city on the north coast of Africa and Rome's chief rival in the Mediterranean in the third and second centuries BC, until after the Third Punic War Carthage was destroyed in 146 BC.

CÁTILINE 2. 541, 6. 793, 7. 64: Lucius Sergius Catilina, after failure in the consulship elections, resorted to violence in 63 BC, planning to stage an armed insurrection. Cicero as consul prevented him seizing Rome and he was defeated in battle. Hostile accounts of the 'Catilinarian conspiracy' are found in Sallust and Cicero.

CÁTO I. 128, 2. 238 and often, 3. 164, 6. 311, 9. 18 and often: Marcus Porcius Cato, the third major protagonist of the poem and the 'hero' of book 9. In Lucan and other authors, especially those of Stoic persuasion, Cato represents an ideal of stern and austere virtue: see Introduction, ii. 4 and 6. Lucan uses the generic plural at I. 313 and 10. 398.

CECRÓPIAN 2. 611, 3. 306, 10. 182: = Athenian, after Cecrops, the mythical first king of Athens.

CERÁUNIA 2. 626, 5. 457, 652: mountains on the coast of Epirus, mod. Khimera Mountains.

CÉRBERUS 6. 664, 9. 643, cf. 6. 703: the monstrous dog which guarded the entrance to the Underworld and had a mane of snakes. On his descent to the Underworld Orpheus soothed him with his singing, Virgil, *Georg.* 4. 483.

CÉRES 3. 347, 4. 381, 9. 857: the goddess of corn, identified with the Greek goddess Demeter; = corn.

CETHÉGI 2. 543, 6. 794: Gaius Cornelius Cethegus was a fellow conspirator with Catiline in 63 BC. It was apparently a family custom of the Cethegi to keep the arms bare, hence 'bare Cethegi', cf. Horace, *Ars* 50.

CHARÝBDIS I. 547, 4. 461: a whirlpool in the Straits of Sicily near the town of Tauromenium (mod. Taormina), hence 'Tauromenian' 4. 461.

CÍMBRI, CÍMBRIAN(S) I. 254, 2. 85: the Cimbri were a German tribe who in IOI BC entered Italy in the north-east and were defeated by Marius at the battle of Vercellae.

CÍNNA 2. 546, 4. 821: Lucius Cornelius Cinna held the consulship jointly with Marius in 86 BC.

CÍRRHA I. 65, 3. 173, 5. 95, 114, 137, 166, 6. 408: a town near Delphi, often used as a synonym for Delphi.

CORCÝRA 2. 623, 8. 37, 9. 32: Corfu, the large island in the Ionian Sea off the coast of Epirus.

CORNÉLIA 2. 349, 3. 22, 5. 726, 735, 8. 41 and often, 9. 51, 171: the daughter of Quintus Caecilius Metellus Scipio, she married Publius Crassus in 55 BC and Pompey in 52 BC. See Introduction, ii. 8.

CÓRUS, plural CÓRI I. 407 and often: the north-west wind.

CORÝCIAN 3. 226, 8. 26, 9. 808: in or from Mount Corycus or the city of Corycus in Cilicia.

CRÁSSUS, CRÁSSI I. II, 100, 103, 2. 552, 3. 127, 8. 90, 302, 327, 358, 394, 415, 422, 9. 65, IO. 52: Marcus Licinius Crassus was killed together with his son leading the Romans against the Parthians in 53 BC, a defeat which remained unavenged and was fresh in the memory at the time when book I begins (49 BC).

CÚRII I. 170, 6. 787, 7. 358, IO. 152: Manius Curius Dentatus, who as consul led the Romans to victory over the Samnites and defeated Pyrrhus in the third century BC. The Samnite ambassadors supposedly attempted to bribe him while he was working in the fields: hence he often appears as a type of rustic uprightness. The plural is a generic plural.

CÚRIO I. 269, 3. 59, 4. 583 and often, 5. 40: Gaius Scribonius Curio, an accomplished orator, was initially an enemy of Caesar but changed his allegiance on the understanding that Caesar would settle his massive debts. While tribune in 50 BC he acted in support of Caesar, and once his term of office was over fled to join him, afraid for his life. He was then defeated and killed by Juba in Africa. See Introduction, ii. 9. For Curio's actions cf. Caesar, *Bell. Civ.* 2. 23.

CYLLÉNIUS, THE CYLLÉNIAN I. 662, 9. 662, 676, IO. 209: Mercury, born on Mount Cyllene in Arcadia, Greece.

CYNOSÚRA 3. 219, 8. 180, 9. 540: the Little Bear.

CÝNTHIA I. 218, 2. 577, 4. 59, 8. 721: the moon.

CYRÉNE 9. 298, 874: the chief city of Cyrenaica, about 8 miles from the sea.

CÝRUS 3. 284, 8. 226: king of Persia in the sixth century BC.

DÁCIAN(S) 2. 54, 3. 95, 8. 425: a people of the lower Danube.

DÁHAE 2. 297, 7. 429: a Scythian tribe east of the Caspian Sea.

DARDÁNIAN 2. 393, 3. 187: = Trojan.

DÉCIUS, DÉCII 2. 308, 6. 785, 7. 359: father and son of the same name, Publius Decius Mus, who in the fourth and third centuries BC both 'devoted' themselves, i.e. gave their lives in battle to ensure Roman victory.

DICTÁEAN 2. 610, 4. 323, 6. 215, 9. 38: = Cretan, from Dicte, a mountain in Crete.

DIS 1. 456, 577, 6. 433, 514, 642, 798: the ruler of the Underworld in Roman religion.

DYRRÁCHIUM 6. 14: a city on the coast of Illyricum also called Epidamnus, as at 2. 624, 10. 545.

ELÝSIUM, ELÝSIAN ABODES, ELÝSIAN FIELDS 3. 13, 6. 600, 698, 782: Elysium or the Isles of the Blessed (at 3. 13 the Field of the Good) was the part of the Underworld said to be inhabited by the souls of good people.

EMÁTHIA 1. 1 and often: though actually in Macedonia, Emathia is used by Lucan for Thessaly, the location of the major battle.

ENÍPEUS 6. 373, 7. 116, 224: a river flowing past Pharsalus, in Thessaly.

EPIDÁMNUS 2. 624, 10. 545: = Dyrrachium.

EPÍRUS 3. 646, 5. 8, 496: north-western area of Greece, with a coastline along the Adriatic and bordering Thessaly on its eastern side.

ÉREBUS 1. 455, 2. 307, 6. 513, 635, 732, 738: the Underworld, hell.

ERÍNYS 1. 572, 4. 187, 6. 747, 8. 90, 10. 59: an avenging spirit, a Fury.

ETHIÓPIA, ETHIÓPIANS 3. 253, 8. 830, 9. 517, 651, 10. 219, 274, 293: the area to the south of Egypt and province of north Africa.

EUMÉNIDES, singular ÉUMENIS 1. 574, 3. 15, 6. 664, 695, 7. 168, 777: the Furies (Eumenides = lit. 'the kindly ones', by euphemism). They had snakes as hair, 9. 642.

EUPHRÁTES 2. 633, 3. 256, 259, 8. 214, 290, 358, 437, 10. 33: the great river rising in Armenia and running south into the Persian Gulf. It formed the boundary between the Roman and Parthian empires.

ÉURUS, plural ÉURI 1. 141 and often: the east wind(s).

FORUM 1. 320, 2. 161, 4. 799, 5. 31, 6. 324, 7. 66, 8. 734: the Forum in the centre of Rome was the location of the Senate-House and law courts.

GÁDES 3. 279, 4. 672, 7. 188, 9. 414, 10. 457: modern Cádiz in Spain; it was founded by Tyrians (hence 'Tyrian' 7. 188 and 10. 457).

GARAMÁNTES, GARAMÁNTIAN 4. 334, 680, 9. 369, 460, 512: a people of the eastern Sahara. At 9. 369 Lucan loosely indicates a port on the coast of Libya.

GÉTAE, GÉTAN 2. 54, 297, 3. 95: a Thracian tribe on the lower Danube.

GIANTS 1. 36, 3. 316, 4. 593, 6. 665, 7. 145, 9. 656: Jupiter and the other Olympian gods repulsed an attack by the Giants at the battle of Phlegra (the Gigantomachia). The story of the battle between the Gods and the Giants is presented with allegorical significance in many ancient authors, particularly from the Augustan age onwards.

GÓRGON(S) 6. 746, 7. 149, 9. 647 and often: Medusa and her two sisters; she had snakes as hair and her gaze could turn people into stone.

GRÁCCHI 1. 267, 6. 796: Tiberius Sempronius Gracchus and his brother Gaius, tribunes of the people, killed in 133 and 121 BC by their political opponents when their programmes seemed too threatening to the status quo. Under the Empire, a hostile view of them became standard, cf. Juvenal 2. 24, Tacitus, *Ann.* 3. 27. 2.

HAEMÓNIAN 3. 192, 6. 394 and often, 7. 825, 858, 8. 2: Thessalian.

HÁEMUS 1. 680, 3. 197, 5. 4, 6. 576, 7. 174, 480, 10. 449: a mountain-range in northern Thrace.

HÁNNIBAL 1. 305, 4. 789, 8. 286: the great Carthaginian general, 247–183 BC, who waged the Second Punic War against Rome, during which in 216 BC he inflicted on the Romans a terrible defeat at the battle of Cannae. See Introduction, ii. 10.

HENIÓCHI 2. 590, 3. 269: a people of the eastern shore of the Black Sea; the tribe was said to be descended from the Spartan charioteers (Heniochi means charioteers in Greek) of Castor and Pollux.

HÉRCULES 1. 405, 3. 178, 278, 4. 632, 6. 348, 354, 8. 800: the hero of Greek myth (Heracles in Greek) famed for his Twelve Labours. The Stoics interpreted his story as the advance towards wisdom. His cult was important at Rome. See Introduction, ii. 6 and 10.

HESPÉRIA 1. 28 and often: = Italy; literally 'the western land'; hence 'Hesperian' = Italian or western.

HIBÉRUS 4. 22, 335, 7. 15, 10. 476: the River Ebro in Spain.

HYDÁSPES 3. 236, 8. 227: a tributary of the River Indus and the limit of Alexander's advance (mod. Jhelum).

HÝDRA 4. 635, 9. 644: the second labour of Hercules was to kill the Hydra of Lerna, a water-snake with heads which redoubled as they were cut off: Ovid, *Met.* 9. 192, Horace, *Od.* 4. 4. 61–2.

HYRCÁNIAN FOREST 1. 327, 3. 268, 8. 343: near the Caucasus and the Caspian Sea (mod. Gorgan): for Hyrcanian tigers see Virgil, *Aen.* 4. 367.

IBÉRIAN(S) 2. 55, 549, 629, 4. 10, 5. 237, 6. 258, 7. 541, 755: a way of referring to the people of Spain; also *Iberia* 7. 232, *Iberian* = Spanish 3. 337, 5. 344.

IÓNIAN 1. 103, 2. 624, 3. 3, 5. 614, 6. 27, 362: the sea between Greece and southern Italy.

JÚBA 4. 670, 687, 715, 5. 57, 6. 309, 8. 443, 9. 212, 300, 868, 10. 146, 475: king of Numidia, an ally of Pompey.

JULIA 1. 111, 3. 9, 27, 8. 102, 10. 78: Pompey's former wife (m. 59), daughter of Julius Caesar, who died in 54 BC. See Introduction, ii. 8.

LÁGUS 1. 684, 5. 62, 8. 443, 692, 803, 10. 4, 86, 394, 413, 521, 527: the Ptolemies, the kings of Egypt, were descended from the Macedonian Lagus.

LÁTIAN 1. 9 and often: = Roman; Rome was in Latium.

LÉNTULUS 5. 16, 7. 218, 8 328: Lucius Lentulus Crus, consul in 49 BC, spokesman for the Senate.

LÉPTIS 9. 524, 948: Leptis Minor, on the African coast, south of Carthage.

LÉSBOS 5. 726, 743, 8. 41 and often: the largest of the islands in the Aegean Sea along the coast of Asia Minor. The inhabitants were loyal partisans of Pompey.

LÉTHE 3. 28, 6. 685, 769, = oblivion 5. 221: the river of forgetfulness in the underworld: when the shades drank from it they forgot their former lives.

LÉUCAS, LEUCÁDIAN 1. 43, 5. 479, 638, 7. 872, 8. 37, 10. 66: the island of Leucas off the coast of western Greece near which the battle of Actium was fought in 31 BC, in which Augustus defeated Antony and Cleopatra. The island had a promontory of the same name at its south-western point with a sheer drop of more than 500 metres (5. 638).

LIBÚRNIAN 4. 530, 8. 38: an Illyrian people.

LIBYA I. 205 and often: in antiquity Libya was the name for the continent of Africa, stretching from the Atlantic to the Red Sea.

LÚCIFER I. 232, 2. 724, 10. 434: literally 'the light-bringer', i.e. the Morning Star.

MAEÓTIS 2. 640, 3. 277, 5. 441, 8. 318: the sea of Azov at the north-eastern corner of the Black Sea.

MÁLEA 6. 58, 9. 36: Cape Malea is the promontory in Laconia at the south-east point of the Peloponnese, round which shipping passed between the Ionian and Aegean Seas; it was very dangerous. It is called Doric from the Dorian peoples who lived in the Peloponnese.

MAREÓTIS, MAREÓTIC 9. 153, 10. 161: a large lake in Egypt separated from the Mediterranean by a neck of land on which stood Alexandria.

MÁRIUS I. 582, 2. 69 and often, 4. 821, 8. 269, 9. 204; plural *Marii* 6. 794: Gaius Marius, 157–86 BC, rose through his military ability and won his first consulship in 107 BC. Defeating Jugurtha, the Teutones, and the Cimbri, he held the consulship in 104, 103, 102, 101, and 100 BC but waned in influence during the 90s. He attempted to win the consulship of 88 BC but when Sulla was elected fled to Africa. He returned to Italy, captured Rome, and became consul for the seventh time in 86 BC, punishing severely those who had betrayed him, but soon died.

MÁRMARI, MARMÁRICA 3. 293, 4. 679, 6. 309, 9. 893: a people/area of north Africa, between Cyrenaica and Egypt.

MASSÍLIA 3. 307, 360, 4. 257, 5. 53: mod. Marseilles, on the south coast of France.

MEDES, MÉDIA 2. 49, 4. 680, 7. 442, 514, 8. 216, 299, 308, 326, 368, 387: a people and land to the south-west of the Caspian Sea, which became part of the Persian Empire in the fifth century BC.

MEGÁERA I. 576, 6. 730: one of the Furies.

MÉMPHIS I. 640, 3. 222, 4. 136, 6. 450, 8. 477, 542, 10. 5, 272, 330: a town in Egypt.

MÉROË 4. 333, 10. 117, 162, 237, 251, 303: an island on the Nile in Ethiopia.

MOOR I. 210, 3. 294, 4. 678, 9. 301, 10. 455: a people of Africa; 8. 283 = Juba.

MÚLCIBER I. 545, 10. 448: a name of Vulcan, the god of fire whose forge lay beneath Etna. At I. 545 Lucan is describing a volcanic eruption.

MÚNDA I. 40, 6. 307, 7. 692: in Spain, site of a battle on 17 March 45 BC, the last in the civil war; here Caesar defeated the sons of Pompey with great loss of life.

MYTILÉNE 5. 786, 8. 109: Mytilene was the main city on the island of Lesbos.

NASAMÓNIANS 4. 679, 9. 439, 443, 458: a Libyan people to the south-west of Cyrenaica extending to the Great Syrtis.

NÉREUS 2. 713, 6. 348: the sea-god, hence = the sea.

NÓTUS, plural NÓTI 2. 460 and often: the south wind.

NÚMA 7. 396, 9. 478: the second king of Rome, especially associated with religious observance.

NUMÍDIANS 4. 677, 720, 746, 7. 229, 8. 287: a people of north Africa to the west of Carthage, ruled by King Juba.

NÝSA 1. 65, 8. 227, 801: a place associated with Bacchus, of unknown location.

OCEAN 1. 370 and often: Ocean was envisaged as a river or sea encircling the land mass of the known world; in particular, used with reference to the Atlantic.

ÓETA 3. 178, 6. 389, 7. 449, 483, 807, 8. 800: a mountain in Thessaly on which Hercules mounted his own funeral pyre and was cremated.

OLÝMPUS 2. 271, 6. 341, 348, 477, 7. 174, 478: a mountain in Thessaly; at 1. 540 and often the gods' abode and hence used to mean the sky.

ORÍON 1. 665, 9. 836: a constellation depicting the hunter, wearing a sword, who was killed by a scorpion sent by Artemis.

ORÓNTES 3. 214, 6. 51: a river of Syria (mod. Asi).

ÓSSA 1. 391, 6. 333, 347, 412, 7. 176: a mountain in Thessaly, northern Greece.

PÁLLAS 3. 206, 7. 149, 9. 350 and often: the goddess Pallas Athene, identified with Minerva, whose name Tritogeneia was said to come from her birth near Lake Triton.

PANGÁEA 1. 679, 7. 482: a mountain in Thrace, near Philippi.

PARAETÓNIAN 3. 295, 10. 9: = Egyptian; Paraetonium was a city of Egypt on one of the mouths of the Nile.

PÁRCAE 1. 112, 3. 19, 6. 778, 813: the Fates (Clotho, Lachesis, and Atropos).

PARNÁSSUS 3. 173, 5. 72, 77, 131: a mountain with twin peaks above the town of Delphi.

PÁRTHIA, PÁRTHIAN 1. 106, 230, 2. 475, 553, 3. 265, 6. 49, 7. 431, 8. 231 and often, 9. 267, 10. 51: Rome's greatest enemy at the time of the civil war; in 53 BC the Parthians inflicted a severe defeat on the Romans at the battle of Carrhae.

PÉLION 6. 336, 411: a mountain in Thessaly.

PÉLLA, PELLÁEAN 3. 233, 5. 60, 8. 237, 298, 475, 607, 9. 153, 1016, 1073, 10. 20, 52, 56, 511: Pella in Macedon was the birth-place of Alexander the Great; thus Pellaean = Macedonian, often used of the Ptolemaic kings of Egypt, whose power derived from Alexander.

PELÚSIUM, PELÚSIAN 8. 466, 543, 826, 9. 83, 10. 53: a marshy area on the easternmost mouth of the Nile along the Egyptian coast; Pelusian often = Egyptian.

PENÉÜS 3. 191, 6. 372, 377, 8. 33: a river in Thessaly.

PÉNTHEUS 6. 358, 7. 780: see Agave.

PÉRGAMUM 9. 968, 999: the citadel of Troy.

PHÁRIAN, PHÁROS 2. 636 and often: Pharos was the island at the mouth of the Nile opposite Alexandria on which stood a light-house; 'Pharian' generally = Egyptian.

PHARSÁLIA,. PHARSÁLIAN, PHARSÁLUS I. 38 and often: the chief battle in Thessaly (described in book 7) was fought in the district of Pharsalia, near the town of Pharsalus.

PHÁSIS 2. 586, 716, 3. 271, 4. 552: the River Phasis (modern Rioni) in Colchis (now Georgia, Transcaucasia).

PHILÍPPI I. 680, 694, 6. 581, 7. 591, 872, 9. 271: a town in eastern Macedonia, site of the defeat of Brutus and Cassius by Octavian and Antony in 42 BC; at I. 694, 6. 581, 7. 872, and 9. 271 Philippi is linked by Lucan with the battle of Pharsalus.

PHLÉGRA 4. 597, 7. 145, 9. 656: variously located in Thessaly, Macedonia or Campania, where the Giants, children of Earth, including Typhon, Tityos, and Briareus, fought against the gods.

PHÓEBE I. 77, 537, 6. 500, 8. 479, 9. 940: the moon, sister of Phoebus, the sun.

PHÓEBUS I. 48 and often: the god Phoebus Apollo, often identified with the sun.

PHÓLOË 3. 198, 6. 388, 7. 449, 826: a mountain in Thessaly, famed as the abode of the centaurs, whose upper half was human and lower part horse.

PHRÝGIAN I. 196, 3. 213, 9. 288 and often: = Trojan.

PÍNDUS I. 675, 6. 339, 7. 173, 482, 806: a mountain-range in northern Greece.

PO 4. 134, 6. 272, 278, 9. 751, 10. 252, 278: a river in northern Italy flowing into the Adriatic.

PÓNTUS, PÓNTIC I. 18, 2. 639, 3. 277, 8. 178, 10. 475: the Pontus was the Black Sea, also known as the Euxine in antiquity; also a region of northern Asia Minor including the south coast of the Black Sea, hence 'Pontic' I. 336, 7. 225, 636, 8. 27.

PTÓLEMY 8. 448 and often: the name of the Macedonian dynasty which ruled Egypt.

PÝTHON 5. 80, 6. 407, 7. 148: Apollo killed with his arrows the dragon Python sent by Juno to persecute Latona when pregnant with Apollo and Diana (Hyginus, *Fab.* 140).

RHÓDOPE 6. 618, 7. 450: a mountain in Thrace.

RIPHÁEUS 2. 640, 3. 273, 4. 118: a fabulous mountain-range in the extreme north, hence Riphaean = Scythian.

RODS (OF OFFICE) I. 178, 2. 19, 130, 3. 87, 5. 13, 385, 663, 7. 428, 8. 79, 270, 10. 11: the fasces, held by lictors, the officials who attended the chief magistrates, and thus symbols of high office.

ROSTRA, singular ROSTRUM I. 275, 4. 799, 7. 65, 305, 8. 685, 9. 216: the Rostrum was the speaker's platform at the *comitium*, the chief place of political assembly, to the north of the Forum.

SARMÁTIANS I. 431, 3. 94, 202, 270, 282, 7. 430, 8. 369: a people on the north-western coast of the Black Sea towards the Danube.

SÁSON 2. 627, 5. 650: an island off the west coast of Macedonia, south of Epidamnus/Dyrrachium, opposite Brundisium (hence 'Calabrian').

SCÍPIO 2. 472, 6. 310, 788, 7. 223, also 9. 277: Quintus Caecilius Metellus Pius Scipio, Pompey's father-in-law, in charge of Nuceria in Umbria. After Pompey's death he took charge of the war in Africa.

SCYLLA 2. 433, 6. 421: Scylla was the name of a dangerous whirlpool in the Straits of Messina between Italy and Sicily, and of a sea-monster who had a girdle of dogs' heads (1. 548).

SCÝTHIA, SCÝTHIAN I. 18 and often: an area located around the north coast of the Black Sea (mod. Ukraine).

SÉRES I. 19, 10. 142, 292: a nation envisaged in the south of Africa (see Heliodorus 9. 25), later identified with the Chinese.

SERTÓRIUS 2. 549, 7. 16, 8. 809: Quintus Sertorius, a leader under Marius. For a long time he occupied Spain and repelled the Roman forces sent to deal with him under Metellus Pius and Pompey. He was finally killed in 72 BC by his lieutenant Perpenna, although Lucan gives the credit for this to Pompey.

SISTERS 3. 18, 6. 703, 9. 838: the Parcae, the Fates.

STRÝMON 3. 199, 5. 712: a river in Thrace, home to cranes that in the winter migrated to Egypt.

STÝGIAN, STYX 3. 14, 5. 221, 666, 6. 91 and often, 7. 169, 612, 770, 785, 817: one of the rivers in the Underworld; hence Stygian = hellish.

SÚLLA 1. 326, 330, 335, 580, 2. 118 and often, 4. 821, 6. 302, 787, 7. 307, 8. 25, 9. 204: Lucius Cornelius Sulla Felix, 138–78 BC, was consul for 88 BC, but when he was deprived of the command of the war against Mithridates in favour of Marius he marched on Rome and captured it savagely. He was subsequently outlawed and returned from the east in 84 BC to invade Italy and defeat his opponents. He was then made Dictator and massacred his enemies in the proscriptions. In 79 BC he resigned the dictatorship to retire as a private citizen and died in 78 BC. Pompey as a young general enjoyed considerable success under Sulla and married Sulla's stepdaughter Aemilia.

SYÉNE 2. 587, 8. 851, 10. 234: a town in Egypt, modern Aswan, was thought to be on the equator.

SÝRTES, singular SÝRTIS 1. 367, 499, 687, 3. 295, 4. 673, 5. 485, 8. 184, 444, 541, 9. 302 and often, 10. 477: two rocky gulfs of shallow waters and sandbanks off the north coast of Africa between Cyrene and Carthage, notorious for their danger to shipping.

TÁENARUS 6. 649, 9. 36: a cave at the foot of the Malean promontory in the Peloponnese which emitted noxious vapours; thought to be a gateway to the Underworld.

TÁNAÏS 3. 272, 8. 319, 9. 414, 751: the River Don, which flows into the Sea of Azov, regarded as the boundary between Europe and Asia.

TARPÉIAN CITADEL/SEAT/SANCTUARY/ROCK 1. 196, 3. 154, 5. 27, 306, 7. 758, 8. 863: i.e. the Capitoline Hill in Rome, by the Tarpeian Rock, the location of the temple of Jupiter Capitolinus and Treasury.

TÁRTARUS 3. 17, 6. 650, 694, 748, 783, 7. 785, 9. 102: a dark region beneath the earth, in effect = the Underworld.

TÁURUS 2. 594, 3. 225, 8. 255: a mountain-range in the south of Asia Minor.

TÉTHYS 1. 413, 555, 2. 589, 3. 233, 4. 73, 5. 623, 6. 479, 10. 204: in mythology the wife of Oceanus, here representing the Ocean.

TÉUTON 1. 256, 2. 69, 6. 259: the Teutones were a German tribe who migrated together with the Cimbri. Marius defeated them at Aquae Sextiae in southern France (mod. Aix-en-Provence) in 102 BC.

THUNDERER 1. 35, 195, 2. 34, 3. 320, 5. 96, 6. 260, 7. 42, 8. 219, 872, 9. 4: Jupiter, who wielded the thunderbolt.

TÍGRIS 3. 256, 261, 6. 51, 7. 433, 8. 214, 369, 438: the great river rising in Armenia, running east of the Euphrates and flowing south-east into the Persian Gulf.

TÍTAN I. 15 and often: the sun.

TYPHÓËUS, TÝPHON 4. 595, 5. 100, 6. 92: a monster subdued by Jupiter and buried under Inarime (= Aenaria or Pithecusa, modern Ischia), a volcanic island off the coast of Campania, by the Bay of Naples.

TYRE, TÝRIAN 3. 217, 7. 188, 10. 124, 457: a city of the Phoenicians.

VÁRUS 2. 466, 4. 667, 713, 716, 8. 287: Publius Attius Varus, one of Pompey's most zealous generals. The town of Auximum in Picenum rose against him: Caesar, *Bell. Civ.* I. 12–13. He recurs in 4. 661–714, in Africa. He was the leader of the Pompeian forces in Africa.

VÉSTA I. 199, 549, 597: the goddess of the hearth, whose temple was in the Forum.

ZÉPHYR I. 407 and often: the west wind.

Bhagavad Gita

The Bible Authorized King James Version
   With Apocrypha

Dhammapada

Dharmasūtras

The Koran

The Pañcatantra

The Sauptikaparvan (from the
   Mahabharata)

The Tale of Sinuhe and Other Ancient
   Egyptian Poems

Upaniṣads

ANSELM OF CANTERBURY   The Major Works

THOMAS AQUINAS   Selected Philosophical Writings

AUGUSTINE   The Confessions
   On Christian Teaching

BEDE   The Ecclesiastical History

HEMACANDRA   The Lives of the Jain Elders

KĀLIDĀSA   The Recognition of Śakuntalā

MANJHAN   Madhumalati

ŚĀNTIDEVA   The Bodhicaryāvatāra

The Oxford World's Classics Website

www.worldsclassics.co.uk

- Information about new titles
- Explore the full range of Oxford World's Classics
- Links to other literary sites and the main OUP webpage
- Imaginative competitions, with bookish prizes
- Peruse the Oxford World's Classics Magazine
- Articles by editors
- Extracts from Introductions
- A forum for discussion and feedback on the series
- Special information for teachers and lecturers

www.worldsclassics.co.uk

American Literature

British and Irish Literature

Children's Literature

Classics and Ancient Literature

Colonial Literature

Eastern Literature

European Literature

History

Medieval Literature

Oxford English Drama

Poetry

Philosophy

Politics

Religion

The Oxford Shakespeare

A complete list of Oxford Paperbacks, including Oxford World's Classics, Oxford Shakespeare, Oxford Drama, and Oxford Paperback Reference, is available in the UK from the Academic Division Publicity Department, Oxford University Press, Great Clarendon Street, Oxford OX2 6DP.

In the USA, complete lists are available from the Paperbacks Marketing Manager, Oxford University Press, 198 Madison Avenue, New York, NY 10016.

Oxford Paperbacks are available from all good bookshops. In case of difficulty, customers in the UK can order direct from Oxford University Press Bookshop, Freepost, 116 High Street, Oxford OX1 4BR, enclosing full payment. Please add 10 per cent of published price for postage and packing.